£25.
R6D

The Preaching of the Friars

THE PREACHING OF THE FRIARS

Sermons diffused from Paris before 1300

BY

D. L. D'AVRAY

CLARENDON PRESS · OXFORD
1985

Oxford University Press, Walton Street, Oxford OX2 6DP
London New York Toronto
Delhi Bombay Calcutta Madras Karachi
Kuala Lumpur Singapore Hong Kong Tokyo
Nairobi Dar es Salaam Cape Town
Melbourne Auckland
and associated companies in
Beirut Berlin Ibadan Mexico City Nicosia

Oxford is a trade mark of Oxford University Press

Published in the United States
by Oxford University Press, New York

© D. L. d'Avray 1985

British Library Cataloguing in Publication Data
D'Avray, D.L.
The preaching of the friars: sermons diffused
from Paris before 1300.
1. Friars—Sermons
I. Title
252 BX2820
ISBN 0-19-822772-8

Set by Burgess & Son (Abingdon) Ltd.
Printed in Great Britain
at the University Press, Oxford
by David Stanford
Printer to the University

To my Father, Mother, and Sister

Acknowledgements

My greatest debt is to Père Louis-Jacques Bataillon, OP, who has given me many ideas and advised me on innumerable points of detail. It is his book as well as mine. Beryl Smalley has helped me much and in many ways, but perhaps above all through her own books, which have defined for me by example the kind of history I have been trying to write. The late Dr R. W. Hunt directed my early research; all the medievalists who came into contact with him will know the beneficent nature of his influence, and how much I miss him. I have repeatedly gained from exchanges of ideas with Nicole Bériou, whose fine research on 'live' sermons at Paris exactly complements my interest in model collections. Richard Rouse helped me with constructive comments and criticisms, especially on the *pecia* system. Nigel Palmer advised me on German sermons. Siegfried Wenzel gave up an afternoon in Bodley to discuss some of the arguments of the book. Professor C. H. Lawrence made a searching suggestion at my D.Phil. viva, the good sense and wide implications of which I have only gradually come to realize. Carlo Delcorno and Jean Longère gave me the chance to see their publications earlier than I could otherwise have done, as did Père Jacques Guy Bougerol, OFM, whose cheerful verve is a delight to his fellow workers in the field of thirteenth-century preaching. The late Professor Johannes Baptist Schneyer (without whose *Repertorium* the book could hardly have been written) put his own *Kartei* of incipits at my disposal. Gloria Cigman's *Medieval Sermon Studies Newsletter* (see the headnote to the Bibliography) and conferences have made research easier for me as for many others. When starting research on sermons I was helped and encouraged by the late W. A. Pantin. At an early stage in the book's genesis I gained from discussions with Malcolm Parkes, Randall Rogers, and Alan Fletcher. At the same stage Helen Spencer, then just beginning her brilliant researches on Middle English sermons, was an influence of a special kind, hard adequately to acknowledge. The British Academy and University College London granted money for microfilm and research journeys. I am grateful to my typists, but above all to Nazneen Razwi, whose accuracy lightened the load of checking. That kind of checking is best done by two pairs of eyes together. My father, mother, and sister had the generosity, and the requisite knowledge of languages, to help me with this task. Thanks to the Alexander von Humboldt Foundation I had ample leisure for final checking and the task of seeing the book through the press. I would finally like to thank my colleague David Morgan, many students at UCL, and Chantal Brotherton-Ratcliffe, for combatting—in utterly different ways—my tendency to become a *Fachidiot* in this oddly compulsive field.

D. L. d'A.

Munich,
2 December 1983

Contents

Note on Transcriptions

MY general rule has been to follow the spelling of the manuscripts. The rule does not help with abbreviations like *grā* (which could be extended as either *gratia* or *gracia*) and *quēdam* (which could be extended as either *quemdam* or *quendam*). I have normalized *c* and *t;* since there is no norm for *m* and *n* I have guessed the scribe's intention as best I can when the letter is swallowed up in an abbreviation. I do not use *j. u* and *v* are normalized—in transcriptions from early printed editions as well as from manuscripts. I have tried to adopt the scribe's abbreviations for books of the Bible, within the limits of typographical convenience. Occasionally I extend them a little, when it might otherwise be hard to tell which book is intended. Where such minutiae are concerned there is no agreed practice.

The Illustrative Text is a transcription, not an edition; its only purpose is to support the argument of those parts of the book where reference is made to it. I have not systematically identified the sources cited, as would be necessary for a critical edition, nor have I collated the manuscript I have used with others. I have, however, corrected the text (with an appropriate note) when it is evidently corrupt.

Substantial passages of Latin are as a rule quoted only from manuscript. When there is a modern edition I content myself with a page reference.

Introduction

MANY non-medievalists, even academic historians, are under the impression that sources for the Middle Ages are scarce. This is half-true of the twelfth century, fairly true of the period before, and fairly untrue of the period after. From the thirteenth century on the study of many topics suffers from the same embarrassment of riches as, say, the study of the First World War. The preaching of the friars is one of them. There is a *Repertorium* of Latin sermons, for the period 1150–1350.[1] This gives the beginnings and endings of sermons, and lists the manuscripts in which they are found. It runs to nine volumes,[2] more than 7,300 pages in all. A high proportion of the sermons listed are by friars.

Paradoxically, this may explain why not much is written about the content of the preaching of the friars. It is not because the friars are regarded as a historical backwater; on the contrary, they have a prominent place in the landscape of medieval history, both at the research and the undergraduate levels. It is acknowledged, furthermore, that preaching was central to their ideal and a principal reason for their enormous influence. Again, the theme of preaching in general has been given a special prominence in recent work on religious history; in this perspective the thirteenth century and the coming of the friars are taken to mark a decisive break in the development of European religion.[3] Perhaps if there had

---

[1] J. B. Schneyer, *Repertorium der lateinischen Sermones des Mittelalters für die Zeit von 1150-1350* (Münster, 1969–).

[2] Professor Schneyer died before completing the index volume. The task has been taken over by Professor Hödl.

[3] 'On ne s'étonnera pas de trouver, comme un leitmotiv au long des deux ouvrages, le thème de la prédication sous ses différentes formes . . . A mesure que la recherche historiographique progresse, elle réalise de plus en plus combien cette forme d'acculturation chrétienne a été importante jusqu'à une époque récente. De sorte qu'une véritable coupure dans la chronologie religieuse européenne peut être située au début du XIIIe siècle, moment de l'apparition des Ordres mendiants, dont la prédication devint un objectif essentiel (J. Delumeau (ed.), *Histoire vécue du peuple chrétien* (Toulouse, 1979), vol. i, p. 11 of his Introduction).

been less evidence scholars would have already found out more about what the friars preached. To isolate a body of evidence which is not absurdly large, some limitation by time and place is desirable.

This study is an attempt to put a rationally selected section of the mass of sermon evidence back into its various contexts. The section consists of 'model' sermon collections written by friars who were academics at the University of Paris, together with sermon collections diffused by the Paris University stationers. (Despite the university connection, these collections would have been mainly, though not exclusively, employed as aids for popular preaching; but of this more below). I have more or less confined myself to the period before 1300.

Paris has been chosen because of its strategic position in thirteenth-century culture. The thirteenth-century founder of the Sorbonne told this pious story:

Et nota quod quandoque plus proficiunt in parochia bonae mulieres quam etiam presbyteri, vel magistri in theologia regendo Parisius, per earum bona opera et exempla et bona verba. Exemplum de beguina quae venit Parisius emptum *Summam de vitiis et virtutibus*, quae, cum moraretur in quadam civitate ad quam saepe veniebant presbyteri subditi illi civitati, accommodabat eis per quaternos hujusmodi *Summam*, praequirendo si erant otiosi ante (quam) missam celebraverant, ita quod, per totam regionem illam, eam multiplicavit.[4]

Note that sometimes good women do more good in their parish than even priests, or Regent Masters in Theology at Paris, through their good works and examples and good words. An example about the béguine who came to Paris to buy the *Summa of Vices and Virtues*: when she was staying in a certain city, to which the priests who came under its jurisdiction often came, she used to lend them this *Summa* in quires (*per quaternos*), first asking if they had some free time before celebrating mass; in such a way that she multiplied it through the whole of that region.

---

[4] B. Hauréau, *Notices et extraits de quelques manuscrits latins de la Bibliothèque Nationale*, v (Paris, 1892), 158–9; cf. A. Dondaine, 'Guillaume Peyraut. Vie et œuvres', *Archivum Fratrum Praedicatorum*, 18 (1948), 162–236, at p. 188.

This *Summa* was almost certainly by the Lyons Dominican Guillaume Peyraut; it can be regarded as a preaching aid. Its author complained about the way all academics wanted to teach at Paris—*plus ça change . . .*[5]—but Paris was an obvious place to pick up a copy of his *Summa*. An anonymous commentary criticizes bishops who give benefices to men who have not studied theology, and imagines them saying: '. . . he will learn to preach well enough, he will get a sermon in a quire (*quaterno*) from Paris from some bookseller . . .'[6] That Paris was a centre for the diffusion of preaching aids is not the point of either story: it is taken for granted.

In the second passage the words 'some bookseller'—my free rendering of 'aliqua statione'—may be alluding to the university stationers (*stationarii*), who sold or hired works reproduced by the *pecia* system, which was in effect a system of rapid copying. The separate quires (*peciae*) of works could be rented individually from a stationer, 'a practice which permitted several copies at varying stages of completion to be made concurrently'.[7] The Paris *pecia* system played a large part in the diffusion of works written by friars (and not only Paris friars) to help preachers.

It is natural to study sermon collections by friars who were based at Paris in conjunction with collections diffused by the *pecia* system, and not only because the two categories overlap. Together they amount to something that can almost be called mass communication: the fanning out of ideas, aimed at and ultimately reaching a huge popular public, from a single

---

[5] See below p. 116.

[6] ' "Quidam eligunt garrulatores ut rustici in vineis faciunt regem magis garrulum, ut puri advocati, qui sunt ut ranae Aegypti, purum advocatum scientia divina minime imbutum. Hoc facit talis praelatus qui tales promovet et dicit: Satis per leges praedicabit, bene addiscet praedicare, habebit sermonem in quaterno de Parisius de aliqua statione . . . .". Extrait d'un commentaire anonyme sur le *Ps. II*, 6, Ms. B.N. lat. 14254, f. 18 D (XIIIᵉ s.)' (J. Leclercq, 'Le Magistère du prédicateur au XIIIᵉ siècle', *Archives d'histoire doctrinale et littéraire du Moyen Âge*, 21 (1946), 105–47, at p. 143 n. 5).

[7] R. H. and M. A. Rouse, *Preachers, Florilegia and Sermons: Studies on the Manipulus florum of Thomas of Ireland* (Toronto, 1979), 170.

centre.[8] There was not so much competition from rival mass media than in later centuries, and the impact of preaching must have been correspondingly greater. Through model sermon collections and other preaching aids much the same message would have been transmitted from Paris to audiences all over Europe. Preachers would have often made some changes when turning a model into living speech', even apart from translating Latin into the vernacular, so preaching was not a mass medium in the strict sense, but it was arguably the nearest thing to mass communication to be found in the thirteenth century. The most important center for the dissemination of ideas to a mass lay public happened also to be the intellectual capital of Europe in general and of the Franciscan and Dominican orders in particular, which adds to the interest of our twofold class of friars' sermons produced at or diffused from Paris.[9]

The social context to which I try to restore the content of this class of sermons is defined broadly. 'Society' sometimes tends to be equated with economic society, with the 'rise of the towns', when the central Middle Ages are in question. Society in this narrower sense cannot be left out of account, though it will be argued that the relation between the urban milieu and the content of preaching is much less close than it may seem at first. But the 'society' which demanded and supplied the model sermon collections was both a more

[8] Cf. R. Rusconi, 'Predicatori e predicazione (secoli IX–XVIII)', in the Einaudi *Storia d'Italia, Annali 4*, pp. 951–1035, at p. 984: 'Quanto detto fino ad ora intorno alla predicazione degli ordini mendicanti non sarebbe completo se non si tenesse conto della sua natura di mezzo di comunicazione di massa negli ultimi secoli del Medioevo', and further references ibid., n. 23; also J. Le Goff, 'Les Mentalités: une histoire ambiguë', in J. Le Goff and P. Nora (edd.), *Faire de l'histoire*, iii. *Nouveaux Objets* (Paris, 1974), 76–94, at pp. 87–8: 'Le palais, le monastère, le château, les écoles, les cours sont, au long du Moyen Âge, les centres où se forgent les mentalités ... Les *mass media* sont les véhicules et les matrices privilégiés des mentalités: le sermon, l'image peinte ou sculptée, sont, en deçà de la galaxie Gutenberg, les nébuleuses d'où cristallisent les mentalités.'

[9] In an ideal world this book would have also given full consideration to model sermon collections by non-mendicant Paris masters, and to the background of 'live' preaching to the people in the churches of Paris, but the task was too great for me. The second of these subjects is in the able hands of Mlle Nicole Bériou.

precise and a more complicated thing. The lay public (whose urban component can be overemphasized) is only one part of this society. The more immediate society of the sermon collections was one of small overlapping groups of men and systems: the élite orders of Franciscans and Dominicans, imbued with the apostolic ideals of which their books of sermons are a kind of archaeological survival; the men who copied the manuscripts or had them copied, thus determining the forms in which the sermons would circulate and in which they have come down to us; the university masters and students, whose studies were intimately linked with the preaching movement but not always in obvious ways. All these things make up the concrete reality in which the ideas of the sermons were embedded. The aim is to reconstruct this 'society' of the sermons, and to work out some of the relations between what they said and these different parts of their world.

Despite the danger of those 'clear-cut generalizations', those 'ghostly refinements of reflection', that 'stream-lined and neatly cupboarded history', which Sir Maurice Powicke rightly suspected,[10] it may be permissible to give a brief statement, in advance, of the main ideas which will be found in this book. The risk of over-simplification and dessication has seemed worth running for a reason which has also led me to keep the main text short, viz., that the students and scholars for whom the book is primarily intended will ration the time they give to it. 'And this suspicion, to be honest, arises, as is generally the case, from our own wicked heart; for we have ourselves been very often most horridly given to jumping as we have run through the pages of voluminous historians.'[11] The following, then, are the principal points which I shall try to make:

[10] Cf. F. M. Powicke, *The Christian Life in the Middle Ages and other essays* (Oxford, 1935), 49–50, and R. W. Southern, 'Sir Maurice Powicke', *Proceedings of the British Academy,* 50 (1964), 275–304, at p. 294.
[11] Henry Fielding, *Tom Jones,* Bk. XII, ch. 3.

1. The ideal of regular and popular preaching was already old in the thirteenth century; it was the closing of the gap between preaching aids and their users which was new (I. i).[12]

2. Paris is central in the history of the preaching of the friars; but also in the history of popular preaching before the friars, as far back as Maurice de Sully (ibid.).

3. Many of the lay people who listened to mendicant sermons were educated and sophisticated—especially but not only in Italy (I. ii).

4. There are reasons for thinking that the audience of mendicant preaching was not confined to the urban and commercial classes (ibid.).

5. Model sermon collections, and probably also a type of manuscript book in which they are frequently found, are a product of the ideal of the apostolic life (the meaning of which for the friars is well summarized in a sermon by Pierre de Reims); we cannot draw a clear line between a spontaneous, itinerant preaching, on the one hand, and a different, academic type of preaching, represented by the sermon collections that have come down to us. It is a false antithesis (I. iii).

6. Model sermon collections, though especially useful for the history of preaching, are one among a whole range of overlapping and interdependent genres. Moreover, we cannot exclude the possibility that this range of genres (including the model sermons) represents a second and supplementary level of preaching, which presupposed that the audience would have learned basic doctrines from a simpler and more catechetical sort of preaching. The two-tier structure of preaching found in seventeenth-century France may already have existed in a less developed form (II. i).

7. The established view that popular sermons were written down in Latin and preached in the vernacular—challenged in recent years, as it was in the nineteenth century—may be

---

[12] These references are to chapters and sections, as given in the headlines to each page.

reaffirmed as a broad generalization; it does indeed now seem possible that Latin and the vernacular were sometimes mixed together in 'live' sermons, but not that it was customary to preach the main substance of a sermon in a language which the principal part of the audience could not understand (II. ii).

8. A model sermon collection, transmitted to us by manuscript books, was both like and unlike a printed text, because it could be but did not have to be transmitted in a stable and standardized form (II. iii).

9. There is an affinity between a very common manner of abridging sermons in the course of transmission and the characteristic form—which was a form of thought, not just a rhetorical technique—of mendicant sermons (ibid.).

10. The audience and function of thirteenth-century model sermon collections was such that they tend to reflect the common factors in the religious culture of their age. Sermons originally preached to the clergy could be incorporated into model collections, and although popular preaching must have been the commonest way of using such collections, it is hard to show that they were specifically designed for that. The best hypothesis is that for most collections audience and function were relatively indeterminate. Thus, it is an over-simplification to categorize model sermons as a medium through which the clergy addressed the laity (II. iv).

11. In the thirteenth century Paris was the principal centre both of European scholasticism and for the diffusion of sermons. The problem is to decide whether the connection between these two functions of Paris University was accidental and extrinsic, or intrinsic and explained by an affinity between the forms of thought of preaching and scholasticism (III. i).

12. The majority (but not all) of the historians in this field have tended to think that there was such an affinity. In fact, however, the apparent similarities between the scholastic method and the form of mendicant preaching—distinctions, authorities, etc.—fade away on closer inspection. Moreover,

quaestiones even of a rudimentary kind are rare in thirteenth-century preaching, and the few exceptions merely prove the rule. In the light of this it is easier to understand why there is so little correlation, apart from Paris, between the centres of sermon production and the centres of scholastic thought (III. ii).

13. Nevertheless, the Paris schools were a favourable milieu for the diffusion of model sermons, for the academic and informal life of the university would have trained young friars in a number of ways to use the models more effectively. Even the part of the curriculum which can properly be called scholastic—the disputations and lectures on the Sentences —would have helped in certain indirect ways. The non-scholastic university exercises, however, were probably a more helpful background from this point of view. Lectures on the Bible told preachers (and future preachers) how important they were, and provided live examples of the type of thinking which the preaching aids embodied in an often rather dessicated form. So did university sermons, whose form and content cannot (as some imagine) be easily distinguished from the kind of thing one finds in model sermon collections. The fact that this kind of preaching had the high status of a major university exercise may be both a cause and effect of its success as a method of popular preaching. Finally, the oral culture of Paris University may have been a rich source of *exempla* which could be worked into the framework of model sermons (III. iii).

14. Model sermon collections enable us to test the valuable hypothesis that the language of the friars was 'heavily impregnated with a market-place vocabulary' and, by extension, the theory that their preaching is best interpreted as the product of an urban social context (IV. i).

15. But we tend to expect 'the rise of the towns' to explain too much. Feudal, aristocratic, and courtly society also leave their mark on thirteenth-century preaching. Gift exchange survived alongside the money economy, and sermons reflect both (IV. ii).

16. Furthermore, the reflections of urban and other social worlds do not imply a social conditioning of the content—a type of interpretation which many modern historians adopt a little too readily. The social imagery does not, paradoxically, have a primarily social explanation. It is only one manifestation of a mental habit: a passion for similitudes of all kinds, so pronounced as to bring thirteenth-century preaching nearer to the conventions of modern poetry than of modern prose (IV. iii).

17. Students of medieval preaching should attempt to identify more of these habits of mind, to which the theoretical treatises on the art of preaching are not on the whole an adequate key. We should, for instance, ask how the territory of thought is portioned out in mendicant sermons, what topoi were used, and how abstract and concrete types of thinking were combined. Specific hypotheses to test are: (i) that the overall structure of thought in a collection was liturgical, while the structure within individual sermons was that of a tiny artistic and symmetrical synthesis of the Christian scheme of things; (ii) that the commonest topoi take the form of clusters of concepts, like *intellectus-affectus-effectus* and *fides-proles-sacramentum;* and (iii) that divisions and authorities in sermons tend to represent abstract and concrete modes of thought respectively. These represent only a few of the possible questions and hypotheses, the number of which is only limited by the historian's powers of devising them. Here the comparative method—especially comparisons between different centuries—can be of assistance. It enables the historian to distinguish more accurately between the *longue durée* of preaching and the distinctive features of a particular century. It is, furthermore, the only way of bringing out the importance of what the sermons of a given period do *not* say. Thus, for instance, the emphasis on vocation and grace in marriage sermons of the late seventeenth and eighteenth centuries makes us aware of the silence of thirteenth-century marriage sermons on these topics (IV. iv).

The first of the four main chapters into which these ideas and findings are grouped deals with background developments: the preaching revival, the increasing sophistication of the lay public, and the *vita apostolica* movement. The remaining three chapters of the book deal respectively with the nuts and bolts of model sermons as a medium of communication, the university context, and the urban context. Certain themes cut across the different sections. The argument that the character of mendicant preaching cannot be accounted for in terms of an urban social context (IV. ii–iii) fits with the argument that the friars did not confine their apostolate to the towns and the bourgeoisie (I. ii). The various points made about distinctions and divisions should be connected: that they were not like scholastic divisions and distinctions (III. ii); that they were a vehicle for the mental habit of making individual sermons a small symmetrical synthesis (IV. iv); that they were (together with *auctoritates*) the part of a sermon that tended to survive the process of abbreviation (II. iii); that sermons transmitted or orginally composed in this skeletal form did not take up much space in the little pocket-books which are typical instruments of the mendicant preaching movement (I. iii)— all these observations should be held before the mind together. Or again, the fact that model sermons could be written apparently without any precise category of audience in mind (II. iv) makes more sense in the light of two of the other conclusions: namely, that lay congregations were by no means uniformly unsophisticated (I. ii), and that thirteenth-century sermons cannot,. on the whole, be assimilated to the much more intellectually demanding 'scholastic' method (III. ii).

The conclusions of an archaeological report or scientific paper are often the justification of the whole enterprise, whereas a statement of the 'results' or 'findings' of a historical work is usually a means rather that an end: a mere summary guide. At best they emphasize the contributions which the work claims to make to the progress of research at the expense of its character as the representation of a complex reality. The attempt to abstract a single overriding conclusion is therefore even more suspect that a list of a number of them. But if it were necessary to reduce the various arguments of this study to one formula, it might be something like this. Model sermon collections are not only a historical source but a historical fact in their own right; more specifically, they were one of the nearest things to a common factor in the experience of different sorts and conditions of men in the thirteenth century. Precisely because they cannot be classified as one of the outlying provinces of scholastic thought, or as an ideological emanation from urban society, and precisely because their audience and function are so hard to pin down, these collections cannot easily be reduced to an aspect of the history either of clerical culture or of popular religion. Forms of thought which we find in model sermons must have been the common property of quite different social groups. Furthermore, geographical as well as social boundaries were crossed, because of the Latin transmission and the international clerical network. We may never know the different ways in which people drew on this common stock, but the common stock is a phenomenon which is in itself worth studying.

There is still a certain tendency to present the history of the friars—to students especially—in terms of the law of spiritual gravity: the impetus of saintly founders, an upsurge of fervour and success, then controversies, abuses, and decline. The formula works well enough if we view the Franciscan and Dominican orders as movements whose function was to make their own members more perfect. It is not so helpful if we view the friars as a chapter in the history of the communication of ideas. From this angle, what we see is an international system, the infrastructure of preaching, which takes shape in the course of the thirteenth century and which lasted for centuries afterwards. If we do not take the trouble to understand the system, we are left with a schematic and one-sided notion of the impact of the friars on Europe.

I

The Background

i. The Preaching Revival

ONE of the friends whom the extrovert friar Salimbene met on his travels was a brother Maurice, who was lector (i.e. lecturer) in the Franciscan convent of Provins. Salimbene describes him as a noble and very learned man. Maurice had studied long at Paris and in the order.[1] He advised Salimbene to keep away from the Joachites (the apocalyptic theorists of history who helped keep the Franciscan order in a state of ideological ferment in the thirteenth century). Instead, he should assist Maurice himself in compiling a book of 'Distinctions', which would be most useful for preaching.[2]

Maurice wrote his book and it has survived. It is one of dozens of works compiled in the thirteenth century to help preachers, for in this period the production of preaching aids became a sort of industry. 'Distinctions' were one kind, and it will be necessary to return to them; there were others as well, of which books of stories, *exemplum* collections, are the best known, and cycles of model sermons the most important. They are the most important as evidence for the history of preaching because they were meant to provide the essential core around which a sermon would be built; other kinds of preaching aids were in a sense accessories. Model sermon collections are to be found in manuscript libraries throughout Europe, for this is one of those areas where the medievalist has an *embarras de richesses* rather than a shortage of evidence. Such sermon manuscripts are the principle source for this study.

---

[1] *Cronica Fratris Salimbene de Adam,* ed. O. Holder-Egger (Monumenta Germaniae Historica, Scriptores, vol. xxxii; 1905–13), 237.

[2] Ibid.

The proliferation of aids for preachers has rightly been regarded as the product of a new emphasis on preaching.[1] It is interesting to look at this preaching revival through the eyes of a historian who was himself a skilful and successful preacher.[2] Jacques de Vitry's *Historia occidentalis* will not give us an objective view of the revival, but it takes us inside the movement, for he was part of it.[3] He is the sort of guide who is too *engagé* to be relied upon without frequent reference to other sources, but to whom one finds oneself returning again and again.

The book begins with a chapter on 'The corruption of the West and the sins of Westerners',[4] and the first five chapters are a rhetorical presentation of the sins and evils of Europe in the period before the revival. Towards the end of this perhaps rather overstated indictment he tells a story which seems to imply that the *prelati*[5] were failing gravely in their duty to preach to their people:

But to the confusion and ignominy of the *prelati* and of those who ought to have instructed the people, the Lord preached the truth of the Gospel, or permitted it to be preached, through an evil spirit in a certain demoniac, who was then in Germany. When the latter was asked what his name was, and (*vel*) by whose authority he presumed to preach to and teach the people, he would reply: 'My name is pen in ink. For I am compelled by the Lord to preach the truth to shame

---

[1] See especially R. H. and M. A. Rouse, *Preachers, Florilegia and Sermons: Studies on the* Manipulus florum *of Thomas of Ireland* (Toronto, 1979) 42 and ch. 2 (pp. 43–64), *passim.* Cf. A. Forni, 'Kerygma e adattamento. Aspetti della predicazione cattolica nei secoli XII e XIV', *Bullettino dell'Istituto Storico Italiano per il Medio Evo e Archivio Muratoriano,* 89 (1980–81), 261–348.

[2] On his skill see D. L. d'Avray and M. Tausche, 'Marriage Sermons in *Ad Status* Collections of the Central Middle Ages', *Archives d'histoire doctrinale et littéraire du Moyen Âge,* année 55 t.47 (1980), 71–119, at p.86. Étienne de Bourbon paid tribute to his success: see A. Lecoy de la Marche, *La Chaire française au Moyen Âge . . .* (2nd edn., Paris, 1886), 53.

[3] There is a modern critical edition of the work: J. F. Hinnebusch, OP, *The* Historia Occidentalis *of Jacques de Vitry. A Critical Edition* (Spicilegium Friburgense, 17; Fribourg, 1972).

[4] Ibid. 73.

[5] I hesitate to render 'prelati' as 'prelate', for in this period the word does not always seem to mean the higher clergy only.

(*in contemptum*) the dumb dogs who are unable to bark, and because I am unable to say anything except what is true and deserves to be written down, Pen-in-ink is my name.[1]

This story illustrates the feeling of dissatisfaction with the way *prelati* were carrying out, or failing to carry out, their duty to preach.

There is, of course, other evidence for this feeling. Pierre le Chantre, one of the most attractive academic personalities of the later twelfth century,[2] filled a whole section of his best-known work with Scriptural texts 'Against the evil silence (*taciturnitatem*) especially of *prelati*',[3] and mentions as one sort of 'evil silence' their failure to preach.[4] A more important piece of evidence than the testimony of these moralists is the decree on preachers of the Fourth Lateran Council in 1215.[5] This decree is a sign of the shortage of preachers as well of the desire to put matters right. It recognizes that for a variety of reasons—and implies that ignorance cannot always be ruled out[6]—bishops may not be able adequately to minister in person to their people, especially in large dioceses. For this reason bishops are ordered to choose suitable men to perform the function of preaching, and to supply these helpers with necessities if need be.[7] The importance of this decree has been recognized by historians.[8] It would be hard to prove that the decree opened the door to an age of more frequent preaching; the hinge was certainly well oiled, for preaching was part of the ideal of the 'apostolic life' whose attraction was

[1] *Historia occidentalis,* ed. cit., pp. 86–7.

[2] J. W. Baldwin, *Masters, Princes and Merchants: The Social Views of Peter the Chanter and his Circle,* two vols. (Princeton, 1970), does Pierre justice.

[3] *Verbum Abbreviatum,* 62 *PL* 205, cols. 189–193.

[4] 'Tacetur etiam male ad praedicandum....' (*PL* 205, col. 191).

[5] 'X. De praedicatoribus instituendis' (Mansi, *Sacrorum conciliorum nova et amplissima collectio...,* t xxii (Venice, 1778), cols. 998–9).

[6] '... ne dicamus defectum scientiae, quod in eis est reprobandum omnino, nec de cetero tolerandum ...' (ibid., col. 998).

[7] Ibid.

[8] See especially Rouse and Rouse, *Preachers,* p. 57; also D. W. Robertson, 'Frequency of Preaching in Thirteenth Century England', *Speculum,* 24 (1949), 377 and n. 11.

so widely felt in the twelfth century and after,[1] and the Franciscan and Dominican orders, which dominate the preaching revival, were already beginning their work. Still, most scholars would agree that the decree marks, even if it did not cause, the beginning of a new age in the history of preaching, and that it calls attention to the gravity of the problem—too few popular sermons—which the friars in the event went far towards solving.

The orthodox establishment had, of course, been aware of the problem for centuries, and serious efforts, perhaps not entirely unsuccessful, had been made to ensure that the laity had a chance of hearing sermons reasonably often. In a sense the decree on preaching of the Fourth Lateran Council is one chapter in a history which goes back to Caesarius of Arles in the sixth century.[2] He presided over the Council of Vaison in 529, at which it was laid down that priests—'not only in cities but also in all parishes'—had the right to preach to the people.[3] The implication is that preaching by the bishop alone was not enough. The same solution and much the same wording were adopted at the reform synod at Arles in 813.[4] The other local reform synods of that year do not appear to go so far as Arles in extending the bishops' right and duty to preach to ordinary priests,[5] but Charlemagne and his advisers clearly believed that preaching was a responsibility of priests as well as bishops.[6] In declaring that the bishops

---

[1] Much has been written on the *vita apostolica* movement. H. Grundmann's *Religiöse Bewegungen im Mittelalter* (first edn., Berlin, 1935) was seminal. Note the 'Neue Beiträge ...' printed with the Darmstadt edition (1970), and especially pp. 503–13.

[2] On Caesarius see J. B. Schneyer, *Geschichte der katholischen Predigt* (Freiburg im Breisgau, 1969), 88–9.

[3] The decree is cited by R. McKitterick, *The Frankish Church and the Carolingian Reforms, 789–895* (London, 1977), 88 and n. 3.

[4] Ibid., esp. n. 2.

[5] This seems to be implied by M. McC. Gatch, *Preaching and Theology in Anglo-Saxon England: Ælfric and Wulfstan* (University of Toronto Press: Toronto and Buffalo, 1977), 34–5; see also next note.

[6] Ibid. 35 and 36, on the *Concordia Episcoporum*, canon x. Cf. McKitterick, *Frankish Church*, p. 82, on Charlemagne's *Admonitio Generalis* of 789, which includes the following provision: 'Sed et vestrum videndum est, dilectissimi et venerabiles pastores et rectores ecclesiarum Dei, ut presbyteros quos mittitis per

needed help with preaching the Fourth Lateran Council was thus restating an idea that had been around for a very long time.

The production of aids for preachers also goes back to long before the preaching revival of the central Middle Ages. A famous example is Gregory the Great's *Regula pastoralis,* the third part of which is in effect a handbook of preaching material.[1] It anticipates the twelfth- and thirteenth-century genre of sermons for different sorts and conditions of men. It is not the only work of Gregory's which has a place in the history of preaching aids. His forty homilies on the Gospel, for instance, were 'regarded as so essential that they were recommended by themselves as a handbook of homiletic material for the Frankish parish priest'.[2] Gregory's writings were an important source for Frankish homiliaries,[3] as were the sermons of Caesarius of Arles.[4]

The Carolingian period produced a large number of sermon collections (defining the phrase to include homiliaries).[5] There are implicit disagreements between modern scholars about which collections were preached to popular

---

parrochias vestras ad regendum, et ad praedicandum per ecclesias populum Deo servientem ut recte et honeste praedicent' (cited loc. cit.). McKitterick, p. 82 n. 4, also cites *Capitula a sacerdotis proposita, Cap.* 4 (*MGH Cap.* I, p. 106), which declares that all priests should preach on all Sundays and Feast-days: 'Ut omnibus festis et diebus dominicis unusquisque sacerdos evangelium Christi populo praedicet' (Episcopal Statutes are also discussed by McKitterick, p. 83). Her treatment of the Reform Councils of 813, especially pp. 83 and 88, should be compared with Gatch, *Preaching,* loc. cit. They appear to differ about the extent to which the priests' right to preach was generally accepted by the bishops, though Gatch's rather special terminology may make the difference seem greater than it is.

[1] See *PL* 77, cols. 49–126, for Part III.
[2] McKitterick, *Frankish Church,* p. 112.
[3] Ibid. 111–12.
[4] Ibid. 88.
[5] For an authoritative study of Carolingian homiliaries see H. Barré, *Les Homéliaires Carolingiens de l'école d'Auxerre* (Studi e Testi, 225; Vatican City, 1962). Though the Auxerre school is the main theme, the introduction (pp. 1–30) and the conclusion (pp. 139–42) to Part I include a survey of other homiliaries. For some comparisons with Bede's homiliary see now A. van der Walt, 'Bede's Homiliary and Early Medieval Preaching', unpublished Ph.D. thesis (London, 1980). There is a good general survey of the most recent work on Carolingian homiliaries and preaching in J. Longère, *La Prédication médiévale* (Études Augustiniennes; (Paris, 1983), 35 ff.

audiences.¹ Though only a few collections would be recognized as popular by a scholarly consensus, it appears that hitherto neglected or unkown popular sermons are at present being brought to light by research.²

There are links between the Carolingian revival of the ninth century and the monastic and pastoral movement in England which is called the 'tenth-century Reformation'. The vernacular homilies of Ælfric of Eynsham drew heavily on the homiliaries of Paul the Deacon and Haimon d'Auxerre,³ though the end product is Ælfric's own.⁴ The most remarkable thing about Ælfric's homilies, seen in their European context, is, of course, the very fact that they were written in Old English instead of Latin. In the tenth century, let alone before, there is very little in the way of vernacular sermon production on the Continent.⁵

There is a tenth-century continental work which would

¹ McKitterick, *Frankish Church,* p. 97, gives a short list of collections 'which, as far as can be judged, are reasonably certain to have reached a wider audience than a monastic community'. Gatch, *Preaching,* pp. 189–90 n. 28, seems to agree in part with this list, though pp. 28–30 may imply that he would exclude Paul the Deacon's homiliary. In general Gatch seems to be a 'minimalist' and McKitterick a 'maximalist' on the subject of popular preaching in the Carolingian period. Nevertheless, McKitterick leaves off her list the homiliary of Haimon d'Auxerre, of which M. Zink, *La Prédication en langue romane avant 1300* (Nouvelle Bibliothèque du Moyen Âge, 4; Paris, 1976), 184, writes: 'L'homéliaire carolingien d'Haimon est dès l'origine prévu pour servir à la prédication au peuple. Il est en latin, parce que l'on n'avait pas recours à la langue romane pour noter des textes de ce genre, ni pratiquement aucun texte, à l'époque où il a été composé, mais il s'adressait au peuple à travers les prédicateurs qui devaient l'utiliser.' There is clearly a problem here, which deserves further discussion.

² I owe this information to Mr Thomas Amos, who is doing important work on Carolingian popular preaching. A most interesting ninth-century collection of popular sermons by an anonymous author from north Italy is edited and translated by P. Mercier, *XIV Homélies du IXᵉ siècle* (Sources Chrétiennes, 161; Paris, 1970).

³ For his debt to Paul the Deacon see C. L. Smetana, 'Ælfric and the Early Medieval Homiliary', *Traditio,* 15 (1959), 163–204; and to Haimon d'Auxerre, Smetana, 'Ælfric and the Homiliary of Haymo of Halberstadt', ibid. 17 (1961), 457–69.

⁴ Cf. Gatch, *Preaching,* pp. 16–17.

⁵ '... les textes conservés sont pratiquement inexistants avant le XIIᵉ siècle, rares au XIIᵉ siècle, ...' (Zink, *La Prédication,* p. 13); for a list of early German vernacular collections, with further references, see Schneyer, *Geschichte,* pp. 104–6. I know of no Italian vernacular sermon collections before those of Giordano da Pisa in the thirteenth century (on whom see now C. Delcorno, *Giordano da Pisa e l'antica predicazione volgare* (Biblioteca delle 'Lettere Italiane', 14; Florence, 1975)).

have fulfilled much the same pastoral function as Ælfric's vernacular homilies. The *Florilegium* of Abbon de Saint-Germain is written in such deliberately simple Latin that it would have been relatively easy for a half-educated priest to preach from it.[1] Abbon and Ælfric have a special importance because their collections were adapted to the realities of clerical education in the early Middle Ages.[2]

Here we have a clue to a major difference between the central and the early medieval preaching movements, for Abbon and Ælfric are exceptions which prove a rule. It is arguable that in the early Middle Ages it was not so much preaching material as the Latinity of the parish clergy which was lacking, and Abbon and Ælfric were exceptional in taking account of this in their different ways. There is some reason to think that the average clergyman would find it hard to understand a homily, written in normal Latin, well enough to reproduce or paraphrase it in the vernacular for his parishioners.

The problem of how to educate the lower clergy was not solved until the Council of Trent and the establishment of the seminary system, though things seemed to have improved towards the end of the Middle Ages, when some parish priests had a university training. A recent study of religious practice and mentality in ninth-century Gaul concludes that more often than not priests were incapable of commenting on the liturgical texts, and that those bishops who wanted their clergy to preach regularly from a homiliary were not being very realistic.[3] This incapacity of the majority of parish priests to preach as they should is attributed to their inadequate

[1] J. Leclercq, 'Le Florilège d'Abbon de Saint-Germain', *Revue du Moyen Âge latin*, 3 (1947), 113–40, at p. 116.

[2] Ælfric's homilies at least seem to have met with considerable success, to judge from surviving manuscripts. According to N. R. Ker, *Catalogue of Manuscripts Containing Anglo-Saxon* (Oxford, 1957), 511, the *Sermones catholici* were copied as late as the early thirteenth century, and 'Homilies of the First Series occur in thirty-five manuscripts and homilies of the Second Series in twenty-nine manuscripts.'

[3] G. Devailly, 'La Pastorale en Gaule au IXe siècle', *Revue d'histoire de l'église de la France*, 59 (1973), 23–54, at p. 33.

training.[1] The candidate for the priesthood would seem to have been trained on what was in effect an apprenticeship system, and the parish priest who acted as mentor could not teach more than he knew himself.[2] One wonders whether the products of this kind of training would have possessed much facility in turning Latin homilies into the vernacular.

Although it seems unlikely to me that preaching by ordinary parish priests from Latin homily collections was normal in the Carolingian and post-Carolingian periods, I doubt if one could prove the matter either way, and historians of an optimistic turn of mind may rate the competence and conscientiousness of the lower clergy higher. There is perhaps a little more room for optimism about a different sort of preaching, namely, simple instruction based on the Creed and the Lord's Prayer.[3] This would not require so much Latin, though perhaps more intellectual initiative. It is a measure of how frustrating early medieval history can be that we cannot even be sure whether or not the overwhelming majority of the population could have known the basic doctrines of their religion. But however it may be with the Creed and the Lord's Prayer, the sketchy Latin culture of the lower clergy must be kept in mind when we are making guesses about the impact of Latin homiliaries.

There is some reason to think that even at the beginning of the thirteenth century the system of clerical education had not essentially changed. The decree of the Fourth Lateran Council which follows the one on preaching implies that not even every cathedral church had a proper school to train clerics of that church and other poor scholars.[4] The thirteenth

[1] G. Devailly, 'La Pastorale en Gaule au IXᵉ siècle', *Revue d'histoire de l'eglise de la France,* 59 (1973), 23–54, at p. 34.

[2] Cf. ibid 34–5. Devailly discusses the attempt of Théodulf d'Orleans to make each parish priest run a school, but implies that this was not the norm and that even at Orleans the ideal may not have been properly realized (Ibid. 34). In any case the teacher would still be the parish priest. It may be doubted whether a high proportion of aspiring priests attended an episcopal school.

[3] Cf. Gatch, *Preaching,* p. 37, and index entries s.v. 'Prone'.

[4] Mansi, *Sacrorum conciliorum nova et amplissima collectio . . .,* xxii (Venice, 1778), col. 999. Despite these good intentions, the lower clergy in the thirteenth

century marks a turning-point in the history of medieval preaching, not just because of the proliferation of preaching aids but because there were for the first time organizations—the mendicant orders—whose members were properly trained to make use of these tools.

With the mendicants the gulf between preaching aids and their users was bridged. It is probably true to say that most Carolingian homilies—adaptations of patristic originals— were written in a more 'difficult' Latin than the highly vernacularized prose of the preaching aids of the friars; it is certainly true that the average preaching friar was an infinitely better Latinist than the average parish priest of the Carolingian period, or long after, for that matter. This is one aspect of the more general truth that the mendicants were better educated in the employment of preaching materials which were easier to use and better adapted to their function. The gap between the books and the users was closed from both sides.

In parenthesis, it should be said that a semi-quantitative comparison between the production of preaching material in the early and in the central Middle Ages is desirable, though it would not be easy to do. Presumably, it would reveal that vastly more was produced in the central Middle Ages than before, but if one included homilies intended primarily for use in monasteries but potentially adaptable for popular preaching,[1] then the difference might not be so great as historians of the later period perhaps tend to assume. It would

century continued to leave much to be desired from an educational as from other points of view. Cf. L. Delisle, 'Le Clergé normand au XIIIᵉ siècle', *Bibliothèque de l'École des Chartes,* 2. Série, 3 (1846), 479–99, especially pp. 483–4, and 0. Dobiache-Rojdestvensky, *La Vie paroissiale en France au XIIIᵉ siècle d'après les actes épiscopaux* (Paris, 1911), especially pp. 171–5. Note the letter of Guillaume de Mâcon, bishop of Amiens, to the deans of his diocese, in 1305 (printed ibid., Appendix 3, pp. 185–6), which implies that there were schools in the diocese, but that they were no good.

[1] I am thinking in particular of the homiliaries of Paul the Deacon and Haimon d'Auxerre. There is some disagreement over whether they are relevant to the history of popular preaching (see above, p. 18 n. 1), but even if meant for monastic use only, they nevertheless provided a great part of the material for Ælfric's Catholic homilies. See above, p. 18 n. 3.

be necessary to take account not just of the number of collections, but also of the number and length of the sermons or homilies in them and the number of manuscripts in which they are transmitted. In the absence of such a quantitative study, one is still on sure ground in re-emphasizing the qualitative distinction between the thirteenth and earlier centuries: namely, that in the thirteenth century there was a large body of men equipped to make living sermons out of the Latin models which their confrères put into circulation. Just how they were trained to do this is a question to which we must return.

Another qualitative distinction between the sermon production of the thirteenth century and that of the preceding centuries is the degree of centralization. In the thirteenth century Paris far outstrips any other place as a centre of sermon production. It did not have a monopoly—important sermon collections were written elsewhere—but it is more important than other centres by an order of magnitude. From the ninth to about the mid-twelfth century there is nothing really comparable with this centralization. There is, of course, the school of Saint-Germain d'Auxerre, but this consists of three writers and their influence.[1] It is a notable school but it does not amount to 'centralization' in the same sense that Paris does in the thirteenth century.

The two novel features of thirteenth-century preaching which have been emphasized so far—centralization and the appearance of large numbers of men trained to preach—may both be traced back into the late twelfth century, and are both illustrated by the remarkable career of Foulques de Neuilly. For this we may turn again to Jacques de Vitry's *Historia occidentalis,* which describes with almost lyrical enthusiasm how this 'country priest, very simple and unlearned'[2] trained

[1] The three writers are Haimon (Haymon), Heiric (Héric), and Remigius (Rémi): see Barré, *Les Homéliaires,* pp. 29, 140–1, and *passim.* Barré seems to remain somewhat doubtful about his attribution of a homiliary (an abridgement of Héric), to Rémi; if Rémi is the author it is probable that he wrote it during his period of teaching at Paris (ibid. 131 and 141).

[2] *Historia occidentalis,* ed. Hinnebusch, p. 89.

himself to be one of the most successful preachers of the age by studying in Paris.

At first Foulques was not at all an exemplary priest, to judge from Jacques de Vitry's account.[1] Then he underwent a conversion, began a life of penance, and started to recall his congregation to the way of truth by word as well as example.[2] Ashamed of his ignorance, however, he set off for Paris, to learn in the theology schools.[3]

His teacher was Pierre le Chantre, and Foulques seems to have concentrated on moral doctrine.[4] He was lucky to be studying at a time when a school with so definite a pastoral orientation as Pierre's was flourishing. The earlier twelfth or the mid-thirteenth century were probably more fertile in original thought, and Pierre le Chantre was not of the same calibre as either Abelard or Aquinas, but his concern for practical moral problems was what Foulques needed. He could go to his church on Feast-days (I take this to mean or rather to include Sundays) and pass on to his flock what he had learned during the week.[5] Neighbouring priests invited him to preach, and he spoke simply and unpretentiously to ordinary laymen (presumably their parishioners).[6] Pierre noticed the fervour of this poor and ill-educated priest, and made him preach at the church of St-Severin in the presence of many learned men.[7] The story of Foulques's subsequent success is well known. The descriptions of his apostolate, and the many miracles attributed to him, testify to the impression he made on his contemporaries. He travelled 'through the whole kingdom of France and through a great part of the Empire'.[8] Itinerancy was perhaps the only way of reaching

---

[1] Ibid. 89.
[2] Ibid. 89–90.
[3] Ibid. 90.
[4] See ibid. 94, 90.
[5] Ibid. 94–5.
[6] Ibid. 95.
[7] Ibid.
[8] Ibid. 96. L.-J. Bataillon plausibly suggests that it was in the French-speaking parts of the empire that Foulques preached.

the masses who might not normally come into contact with a priest. Foulques's career is an early example of the European-wide influence of Paris on popular preaching.

It appears that Foulques's success was not confined to his lifetime, for, according to the *Historia occidentalis,* after his death many were fired by the fervour of charity and moved to follow his example.[1] Jacques says that they, too, were successful,[2] and he gives a list of the most important.[3] His list is an interesting one: it shows that some men of distinction and learning were becoming involved in the revival of popular preaching,[4] though we should not necessarily follow Jacques in seeing Foulques as the antecedent cause and inspiration of their preaching.[5]

It is interesting that the Cistercian abbot Adam de Perseigne is on the list:[6] the Cistercians could be regarded as reluctant forerunners of the friars. (It was the Cistercians who had been commissioned to preach against the heretics in southern France when Dominic arrived on the scene). The list also further highlights the role of Paris. Of the seven names that Jacques lists, at least four—Stephen Langton, Robert de

---

[1] Ibid. 102. On the aftermath of Foulques's preaching see now A. Forni, 'La "Nouvelle Prédication" des disciples de Foulques de Neuilly: intentions, techniques et réactions', in *Faire Croire. Modalités de la diffusion et de la réception des messages religieux du XIIᵉ au XVᵉ siècle* (Collection de l'École Française de Rome, 51; Rome, 1981), 19–37.

[2] *Historia occidentalis,* ed. Hinnebusch, loc. cit.

[3] Ibid. 102–3.

[4] By portraying these men as Foulques's successors, Jacques implies that they did not confine themselves to academic preaching.

[5] Stephen Langton came to Paris as a student *c.* 1170 and was a master in 1180; it is thus likely that many of his sermons go well back into the twelfth century. P. Barzillay-Roberts, *Stephanus de Lingua Tonante. Studies in the Sermons of Stephen Langton* (Toronto, 1968), seems to imply (pp. 52 and 73), that we have a great many sermons preached by Langton to predominantly lay audiences. It would seem quite possible that he was preaching regularly to the people before Foulques and that others were doing so too (L.-J. Bataillon drew my attention to this). Note, however, that P. Tibber, 'The Origins of the Scholastic Sermon, *c.* 1130–*c.* 1210', unpublished D.Phil. thesis (Oxford, 1983), 60, gives a quite different interpretation of Langton's audience. J. Longère, *Œuvres oratoires de maîtres Parisiens au XIIᵉ siècle* (Paris, 1975), 1 29, takes up a position which looks about right, somewhere between the two extremes.

[6] Bibliography on Adam in *Historia occidentalis,* ed. Hinnebusch, pp. 254–5.

Courçon, Alberic de Laon, and Jean de Nivelles—were associated with its schools.[1]

The *Historia occidentalis* thus shows us an orthodox revival of preaching well under way by the turn of the twelfth and thirteenth centuries. At Paris it goes back at least as far as Maurice de Sully, who wrote a model sermon collection in Latin to help priests of the diocese of Paris in their Sunday or Feast-day preaching.[2] Even if Jacques is misleading in treating Pierre le Chantre and Foulques, rather than say Maurice de Sully, as the fount and origin of the preaching revival, there is something very refreshing about the enthusiasm of his account of a movement to which he had himself been close. After his description of Foulques's successors, however, Jacques turns his attention to a shadow side of the movement, in a chapter entitled 'On pseudo- or false preachers'.[3] It contains violent denunciations of *pseudo-predicatores* who preach for evil motives, whether gain or vainglory.[4] Jacques might also have mentioned the competition from heretics, for both the Waldensians and the Cathars were zealous in their preaching.[5]

The success of both heretical preachers and Jacques de Vitry's 'pseudo-preachers' suggests that the period around 1200 was a critical point in the history of the relations between popular religion and the institutional Church. Almost any kind of wandering preacher, it would seem, had a chance of winning a following—one has the impression of a religious atmosphere unusually favourable to preaching of any kind, heretical or orthodox. In this atmosphere the medium was probably more powerful than the precise

[1] See ibid., notes to pp. 102–3; also biographical notices, ibid., Appendix C.

[2] Zink, *La Prédication*, pp. 144–5. The vernacular, which Zink believes to be an adaptation of the Latin original, was also primarily a preaching aid (ibid. 145–6). For the question of who made the vernacular adaptation, and when, see ibid. 32–5. On Maurice see too C. A. Robson, *Maurice of Sully and the Medieval Vernacular Homily . . .* (Oxford, 1952).

[3] *Historia occidentalis,* ed. Hinnebusch, p. 103.

[4] Ibid. 103 ff.

[5] Cf. P. Mandonnet *et al., S. Dominique. L'Idée, l'homme et l'œuvre,* ii (Paris, 1938), 22–4.

message. Jacques condemns evil preachers for taking in 'lay people ... and the simple, and over-credulous women';[1] it must have been easy to put a match to religious enthusiasm in the small crowded towns where they would have operated. Whether or not contemporaries were aware of it, there was a race between the institutional Church and its rivals to direct the unstable piety of the towns.

One contemporary who was aware of it was Innocent III. He had studied at Paris, and his sense of the importance of preaching may owe a lot to that.[2] There could be no picture of him more false than an image of a purely political pope; we have already noted how the Fourth Lateran Council, over which he presided, tried to raise the level of preaching and clerical education, and his treatment of the *Humiliati* shows his willingness to take risks in the hope of directing religious fervour into orthodox channels.[3] From rivals or enemies of the institutional Church he turned them into defenders of it. (He did much the same with some of the Waldensians.) It is characteristic that in 1199 he ordered that a group of laymen should be allowed to read the Scripture in the vernacular (in spite of a decision to the contrary by the bishop of Metz), and that he explained that he was doing so 'lest these simple people should be forced into heresy'.[4]

Jacques de Vitry gives a picture of the *Humiliati* which suggests that Innocent III's policy of tolerance had paid off, and which at the same time illustrates the unstable fervour of popular religious emotion. Jacques is very much interested in the preaching of the sect. We are told that not only the clerics but even educated (*litterati*) laymen among them had been given authority to preach by the pope. Moreover, they were not restricted to preaching within their own community. They

---

[1] 'laicis ... et ydiotis et nimis credulis mulieribus' (*Historia occidentalis,* ed. Hinnebusch, p. 105).

[2] Suggestion of L.-J. Bataillon. For Innocent at Paris see Baldwin, *Masters,* i, 343.

[3] Brenda Bolton, 'Innocent III's Treatment of the *Humiliati'*, in *Popular Belief and Practice* (Studies in Church History, 8, edd. G. J. Cuming and D. Baker; Cambridge University Press, 1972), 73–82.

[4] Ibid. 80.

might preach in public streets and in the cities, and in secular
churches, if they had the permission of the *prelati* who were in
charge of those places.[1] As a result, they converted many
noble and powerful citizens. Some of those they converted
renounced the world altogether, and joined their order
(*religionem*). Others, while remaining in the world in body,
and staying with their wives and children, lived an unworldly
life.[2] Priests and clerics also joined the *Humilati*.[3]

The *Historia occidentalis* gives a vivid picture of the way
the 'order' recruited new members. At the end of their
sermons, when the hearts of their listeners, set alight by the
power of the divine word (*virtute diuini sermonis feruentia*),
were more inclined to despise the world and serve their
creator, the *Humiliati* used to ask if there were any who
wished to join them. Intoxicated by the preaching and with
their spirits on fire (*in illa ebrietate et spiritus feruore*), there
were many who chose to do so, and thus the order spread with
great rapidity, and many convents of *Humiliati* sprang up in

---

[1] *Historia occidentalis,* ed. Hinnebusch, p. 145. Cf. R. Zerfass, *Der Streit um die
Laienpredigt. Eine pastoralgeschichtliche Untersuchung zum Verständnis des Predigtamtes und zu seiner Entwicklung im 12. und 13. Jahrhundert* (Freiburg im Breisgau,
Basle, and Vienna, 1974), 201–10, 259–61. Criticizing Grundmann, among others,
Zerfass argues that Innocent III 'hat 1201 nicht "zum erstenmal einer Laiengemeinschaft die päpstliche Vollmacht" erteilt, "ihre eigenen Prediger aufzustellen",
sondern er hat zum erstenmal verboten, einer Laiengemeinschaft das streitig zu
machen, was in ruhigeren Zeiten gläubigen Christen nie bestritten worden war,
nämlich sich als Brüder im Glauben zu stärken....' (ibid. 209–10). Again: '... von
einer Autorisation zur Verkündigung im öffentlichen Bereich, die zu der amtlichen
Verkündigung der Priester in Konkurrenz treten könnte und etwa aus diesem
Grunde auf die "Sittenpredigt" im Gegensatz zur "Glaubenspredigt" eingeengt
würde, keine Rede sein kann ...' (ibid. 205). At first sight, Zerfass's interpretation
would seem to be undermined by Jacques de Vitry's testimony. Conceivably, Jacques
is talking about the preaching of lay *Humiliati* living in convents, rather than
individually in the world. In these passages Zerfass seems to be talking about the
latter, and does not make his views on the former very clear. Cf. ibid 205 n. 36 (and
p. 259), on the one hand, with pp. 260–1 on the other; the latter passage seems to
imply that lay *Humiliati* in convents went beyond Innocent's concessions
of 1201: 'Zu den Regelwidrigkeiten, die der Papst hier rügt, könnte dann auch jene
seelsorgerliche Expansion des Dritten Ordens gehört haben, die ein Mann wie Jakob
von Vitry rühmen mochte, die aber dem Wortlaut des ursprünglichen Propositums
sicher nicht mehr entsprach.'

[2] *Historia occidentalis,* ed. Hinnebusch, p. 145.

[3] Ibid.

different cities.[1] Jacques goes on to say that the *Humiliati* were formidable enemies of the heretics,[2] many of whom they won back to the Church, so that 'those who had been teachers of error [he means the *paterini*] have become disciples of the truth.'[3] Thus, we see a sort of 'multiplier' at work: the *Humiliati,* won over by Innocent III to the side of the institutional Church, in turn won others over. It may be that, but for Innocent's policy of assimilating rather than excluding, these fiery and obviously effective methods would have been used against the Church rather than for it. In the early years of the thirteenth century it must have seemed hard to predict what direction popular piety would take.

Jacques de Vitry's account of the methods of the *Humiliati,* and the other passages from his *Historia occidentalis* which have been touched on here, all point to an almost feverish market for preaching. Demand was great: the problem for the Church was on the supply side. Preaching by the bishops could not begin to meet the demand. The general run of parish priests—like Foulques before conversion—still lacked the training to do so adequately. A beginning had been made: already there were some successful popular preachers who had studied at Paris. Yet one wonders how many of those who trained in the Paris schools went on to a life of regular preaching. University clerics would tend to gravitate towards the higher echelons of ecclesiastical and secular administration. Educated and orthodox men devoted to pastoral work, below the episcopal level, remained in short supply. The Paris-trained Foulques de Neuilly foreshadowed the work of the friars, but the real change took place in the course of the following century: in the twelfth century a sermon by an educated preacher must still have been an event, whereas by the end of the thirteenth such sermons were a normal part of the structure of ecclesiastical life in the towns.

---

[1] *Historia occidentalis,* ed. Hinnebusch, 145–6.
[2] He specifies the heretics 'quos paterinos appellant' (ibid. 146).
[3] Ibid.

ii. The Public

The appearance of a class of literate laymen made the need for educated preachers all the more acute. Jacques de Vitry's chapter on the *Humiliati* is thought-provoking in this respect also. 'The laity as well as the clerics do not omit to say all the canonical hours by day and by night', he tells us, and he goes on to remark that 'almost all are educated (*litterati*)'.[1] It seems possible that here he may be referring only to those lay *Humiliati* who lived in convents, rather than in their own homes,[2] but even so his words show how far the equation of lay with illiterate had broken down in practice. As we have seen, Jacques also speaks of *laici litterati* who had been authorized by the pope to preach. If there were educated laymen capable of preaching themselves, they would expect high standards of clerical preaching when they themselves were part of the audience. If congregations included such men it might be a mistake for preachers to ignore their needs.

Of course, it is difficult to know who went to sermons in the thirteenth century. The complaints of preachers are not necessarily a sure guide, for such evidence can be contradictory. 'It must be noted that the poor rarely go to church, and rarely to sermons; so that they know little of what pertains to their salvation'—so Humbert de Romans.[3] Guibert de Tournai, on the other hand, says that the poor follow preachers, while the great men of the towns, the *magni burgenses,* poisoned by usury and other sins, go off to the tavern instead.[4] Such inconsistencies need not surprise

---

[1] 'Omnes horas canonicas diebus et noctibus laici sicut et clerici non pretermittunt. Fere omnes litterati sunt. Qui autem horas canonicas discere nesciunt, sub certo numero dicentes orationem dominicam, debita recompensatione abluuntur' (Ibid. 144–5).

[2] Cf. above, p. 27 n. 1.

[3] Humbert de Romans, cited by A. Murray, 'Piety and Impiety in Thirteenth-Century Italy', in *Popular Belief and Practice* (Studies in Church History, 8, edd. C. J. Cuming and D. Baker; Cambridge University Press, 1972), 83–106, at 93. (For a general discussion of what Humbert can tell us about the religion of the poor, see A. Murray, 'Religion among the Poor in Thirteenth-Century France: The Testimony of Humbert de Romans', *Traditio,* 30 (1974), 285–324.

[4] '... predicatorem sequntur hodie pauperes propter salutem suam, sed magni

us—there would be nothing astonishing if they were found within the same man's sermons. A preacher might venture a generalization without thinking too much about it. No doubt some classes or subclasses of the population attended sermons more rarely than others,[1] but it is unsafe to assume that any large section of society went without preaching altogether.

Cities provided an environment in which the relatively new classes of merchants and lay lawyers could flourish; for the latter literacy was indispensable and for the former a decided advantage. There are fairly obvious connections between the expansion of popular preaching and the rise of the cities, and it is established that the friars concentrated their efforts on the urban population.[2] A Franciscan text admitted the policy and put forward a number of reasons in its defence. The gist of the argument is that there was only a limited number of friars, and that they should be deployed in places where the population was concentrated; congregations could be gathered more easily, food could be found for the friars, and so on; furthermore, the towns gave the most alms to the friars, and so more spiritual service was expected.[3] It is true that, if

---

(magis *ms?*) burgenses, presentientes odorem et toxicati veneno usure et aliorum peccatorum, descendunt in tabernam' (MS BN lat. 15943, fo. CXXIIII[vb]): from a sermon 'Ad cives rei publice vacantes', incipit 'Estote imitatores dei (*corr. from* dei imitatores) sicut filii karissimi. Eph. v. In deo est summa potestas, veritas et bonitas....' (not listed with Guibert's *ad status* sermons in Schneyer's *Repertorium*).

[1] Servants in large households, for example. Cf. Murray, 'Piety and Impiety in Thirteenth-Century Italy', p. 93.

[2] Cf. especially Jacques Le Goff, 'Ordres Mendiants et urbanisation dans la France médiévale. État de l'enquête', *Annales: Économies, sociétés civilisations,* 25/4 (1970), 924–46. See also D. Knowles and R. N. Hadcock, *Medieval Religious Houses: England and Wales* (London, 1971) 34, J. B. Freed, *The Friars and German Society in the Thirteenth Century* (Cambridge, Mass., 1977) and K. Elm (ed.), *Stellung und Wirksamkeit der Bettelorden in der städtischen Gesellschaft* (Berlin, 1981).

[3] *Determinationes quaestionum circa regulam fratrum minorum* Pars II, qu. XIX, in *S. Bonaventurae opera omnia* (Quaracchi ed.), t viii (1898), 370. There seems no strong reason for thinking that Bonaventura was the author. See I. Brady, 'The Writings of Saint Bonaventure regarding the Franciscan Order', *Miscellanea Francescana,* 75 (1975), 89–112, at p. 107. (Despite Le Goff, art. cit. 929 n. 1, Brady's data might suggest a late medieval date.) These arguments for an urban apostolate are also summarized by A. G. Little, *Studies in English Franciscan History,* (Publications of the University of Manchester, Historical Series, 29; Manchester University Press and London, 1917), 129–30.

read closely, the *Quaestio* does not imply quite such an exclusively urban ministry as it may seem to do at first sight,[1] but it certainly reflects a general preoccupation with cities. One of the most eminent thirteenth-century Dominicans, Humbert de Romans, also justifies a concentration of preaching in towns.[2] 'It should be noted that the Lord, when he sent prophets into the world, more often sent them to a city than to other smaller places. . . .'[3] These are the opening words of his address 'To the laity in cities', and he continues in the same vein, citing Jerusalem, Nineveh, and Babylon as examples of cities to which the prophets were sent. When the Lord came himself, says Humbert, he preached more often in cities than elsewhere, as is clear to anyone who examines the Gospel history. He cites an 'authority',[4] and moves on to the preaching of the apostles: 'Again, the apostles and disciples preached more often in cities than in other places, as is clear from history and the legends of the saints.'[5] After this, Humbert switches to the present tense, apparently applying his remarks to the preaching of his own day:

The reasons why this is to be done are these: In cities there are more people than in other places, and therefore it is better to preach there than elsewhere, just as it is better to give alms to more than to fewer people. Again, there are more sins there . . . Again, lesser places which lie around cities are more influenced by cities than vice versa, and therefore the good effects of preaching which takes place in the city are passed on to those places more than vice versa, therefore one should try to produce good effects by preaching in cities, in preference to other smaller places.[6]

It was probably in Italy that the proportion of educated laymen was greatest. It may not be chance that the movement

---

[1] See below, p. 40.

[2] Humbert de Romans, *De eruditione praedicatorum,* lib. II, Tractatus I, lxxii ('Ad laicos in civitatibus') in *Maxima Biblioteca Veterum Patrum,* xxv (Lyons, 1677), 491–2. Cf. Le Goff, art. cit. 929–30.

[3] Humbert de Romans, op. cit. 491.

[4] For the role of 'authorities' in sermons see p. 194 below.

[5] Humbert de Romans, loc. cit.

[6] Ibid.

of the *Humiliati,* with its literate and obviously articulate lay element, had a power base, as it were, in Lombardy.[1] Laymen with quite a high level of education had an important place in Italian city life even in the thirteenth century. The relative whom the Franciscan Salimbene describes as 'an educated (*litteratus*) man, a judge and assessor . . . who frequently acted as the lawyer of podestà' was probably not a very exceptional figure.[2]

The greatest university of Italy, Bologna, the European centre of academic law, was not an essentially clerical university like Paris. The atmosphere could hardly be more different: the jurist Accursius was able to claim that the sons of university doctors had a preferential right to succeed to vacant chairs, and from about the middle of the thirteenth century professors were commonly selected on the hereditary principle[3]—a method of filling professorial chairs which could hardly have been adopted at clerical and celibate Paris.

The Latin culture of lay lawyers could even find expression in forms like those which the preachers themselves used. A remarkable example is a speech which Francis Accursius— son of the glossator and himself a teacher of law at Bologna—delivered before Pope Nicholas III.[4] Francis Accursius served for a time under the King of England, and on this particular occasion he was acting on the latter's behalf, trying to persuade the pope to confirm the king's nomination of a new Archbishop of Canterbury. The speech seems to be incomplete, but we have enough to see that it is a carefully constructed piece of work, and reminiscent of a sermon. Perhaps the two most prominent features of thirteenth-

---

[1] *Historia occidentalis,* ed. Hinnebusch, p. 144.

[2] '. . . domnum Hugonem, qui fuit litteratus homo, iudex et assessor . . . qui semper ibat cum potestatibus, ut esset advocatus eorum' (Salimbene, *Cronica,* ed. Holder-Egger, p. 55).

[3] *Rashdall's Medieval Universities,* edd. F. M. Powicke and A. B. Emden (Oxford, 1936), i. 214.

[4] G. L. Haskins and E. H. Kantorowicz, 'A Diplomatic Mission of Francis Accursius and his Oration before Pope Nicholas III', *English Historical Review,* 58 (1943), 424–47.

century sermon form were 'divisions' and 'authorities'.[1] In Accursius' speech both are to be found.[2] Presumably these ways of thought—for the thought and the form can hardly be separated—seemed natural enough to him.

There was another layman, also a lawyer, who gave speeches which are sermons in a true sense. This was Albertano da Brescia,[3] who was born at the end of the twelfth or the beginning of the thirteenth century.[4] He was the author of a number of works, and his general culture is remarkable enough, but that he, a layman, should have been able to preach sermons of which a university cleric need not have been ashamed is from our point of view even more significant.

In 1250, in mid-Lent, Albertano gave a sermon to the lawyers (*causidicos*) of Brescia, at their 'customary meeting in the House of the Friars Minor'.[5] He preached on the fear of God. The structure of the sermon is possibly less rigid than that of the average contemporary clerical sermon, but the basic techniques are much the same. Many authorities are cited, and they are used with regularity to confirm the numbered points of the sermon. For example: 'Point eight: By means of the fear of the Lord we obtain his mercy. Wherefore the blessed Virgin Mary said: "And his mercy from generation to generation to those who fear him." Ninth point: By means of the fear of God we obtain his help and protection. For the prophet says . . .'[6] The sermon as a whole strikes one as the product of a learned and highly intelligent man.

---

[1] See below, pp. 172–4.

[2] For an example of a division, see Haskins and Kantorowicz, loc. cit. 445: 'Quatuor hec declarant, scilicet utilitas ecclesie atque necessitas, meritum persone, utilitas regni, affectio regis ... ' As for authorities, Accursius cites the Fathers (cf. ibid. 441) and the speech is thoroughly Scriptural, especially the part in which Nicholas III is compared to Samuel.

[3] With his customary generosity, Dr R. W. Hunt allowed me to use his dossier on Albertano and the context of his sermons. The account that follows largely retraces the ground he covered. The dossier is presumably still somewhere in his *Nachlass.*

[4] *Albertanus Brixiensis. Sermones Quatuor,* ed. M. Ferrari (Fondazione Ugo da Como; Lonato, n.d.), introduction p. i.

[5] Ibid. 55.

[6] Ibid. 59.

It is also significant that there were enough lawyers, well-educated men, presumably, even if not up to the level of Albertano, to make up an audience. The words 'at the customary meeting at the House of the Friars Minor' may imply a confraternity.[1] It would be interesting to know what these pious and literate laymen talked about among themselves and what they read in their leisure hours.

It has been argued that the listeners capable of making a *reportatio* of the Italian vernacular sermons of Giordano da Pisa were from among the members of the confraternities attached to the Dominican convent in Florence.[2] There is certainly evidence that Giordano assumed that some members of his audience would be literate: he advises his listeners to read 'good little books'.[3]

Even those confraternity members who were not educated or sophisticated (for it would be rash to go to the extreme of assuming that all were literate) would tend to become familiar with aspects of clerical culture if they attended regularly.[4] Research on congregations of the Virgin in Italy has shown how regular the exposure to sermons of some lay people would have been.[5] Anyone who attended the evening

---

[1] The 'congregatione solita' may be the same as or connected with a society whose ordinances have survived in a Brescia manuscript: see P. Guerrini, 'Gli statuti di un'antica Congregazione Francescana di Brescia', *Archivum Franciscanum Historicum,* 1 (1908), 544–68. In the heading they are described as the 'ordinances of the brothers of the society (*congregationis*) of the most blessed Virgin Mary and the most blessed confessor Francis at the house of the Friars Minor at Brescia' (ibid. 547). The ordinances mention some functions to which Albertano also refers, notably charity, lighting, and dining: cf. Guerrini, ibid. 553–6, with Albertano, *Sermones Quatuor*, pp. 1–15: 'Sermo factus super illuminatione et super spirituali et corporali refectione et que sint necessaria in refectione', and p. 19 ('refectionem pauperum').

[2] Delcorno, *Giordano*, p. 70ff.

[3] 'usando le dette cose e le prediche, e spezialmente di leggere buoni libricciuoli ...' (quoted by Delcorno, ibid. 67).

[4] Cf. G. Miccoli, in the Einaudi *Storia d'Italia* vol. 2, tom. I (Turin, 1974) 825: 'Si è già rilevato come uno dei principali strumenti messi in opera dagli ordini mendicanti per il disciplinamento e l'istruzione religiosa del laicato sia stato rappresentato, nel corso del XIII secolo, dalla fondazione di confraternite e associazioni pie. Francescani e domenicani furono in prima linea nel promuoverne l'istituzione con il duplice scopo di combattere sul loro stesso terreno le Chiese e i movimenti eretici e di conseguire nel contempo una più solida formazione religiosa del laicato ortodosso.'

[5] G. Meersseman, 'La Prédication dominicaine dans les congrégations Mariales

meetings of the congregation, as well as ordinary morning sermons, would be getting large and regular doses of religious instruction. It has even been calculated that if one adds together collations and ordinary morning sermons one gets a total of 240 to 250 sermons a year in each Dominican church.[1] Those who wrote model sermon collections would have to take into account this exposure to religious ideas of some of the public to which the sermons might be preached.

Preachers in Italy would thus be talking to many with a religious education, many with a secular education, and many with both. The existence of this sort of public was made possible, directly or indirectly, by the commercial expansion of the Italian economy, without which the cities, the confraternities which flourished within them, and the high demand for and production of academically trained lawyers would hardly be conceivable. The professional merchants who stimulated the expansion were not, perhaps, so highly educated as lawyers, but they would be a sophisticated element in the community. The commercial techniques they developed were a kind of revolution in practical thought, and the international networks they built up must have depended on written correspondence. An illustration both of the wide experience which they might acquire and of their articulate literacy is a sonnet written by a member of the Frescobaldi family giving advice to merchants going to England:

Wear no bright colours; be humble; appear stupid but be subtle in act. Spend freely and do not show yourself mean. Pay as you go; collect your debts courteously, pleading your need; do not be too inquisitive; buy as good occassion offers, but have no dealings with

---

en Italie au XIIIe siècle', *Archivum Fratrum Praedicatorum*, 18 (1948), 131–61. The great interest of this article is its account of *collationes* (relatively short evening sermons) preached to congregations of the Virgin at Imola and Milan, which have been preserved in MS Florence, Nazionale G. VII. 1464.

[1] 'Quand on ajoute au nombre des collations mariales celui des sermons ordinaires du matin, on obtient un total de 240 à 250 prédications par année dans chaque église dominicaine' (ibid. 149). These figures would not, of course, apply in places where there was not a congregation of the sort Meersseman describes, and the matter of their precision should perhaps in any case be treated with şome caution.

men of the court. Be obedient to the powerful, keep on good terms
with your fellow countrymen, and bolt your door early.[1]

An educated laity was by no means a purely Italian
phenomenon, even in the thirteenth century: it is much in
evidence also in at least some cities of the North. A
monograph on bourgeois society and literature at Arras in the
twelfth and thirteenth centuries gives evidence of laymen
whose cultural achievements were far from negligible.[2]
Though Arras is now in France, its cultural flowering should
be seen against the background of the great cities of what is
now Belgium, for there too we find bourgeois literacy and a
well-developed bourgeois taste for literature before the
fourteenth century.[3] We read that Beatrijs van Tienen (in
Brabant) could recite the Psalter at the age of five; she
was a precocious little girl, no doubt, but the interesting thing
is that she was given the opportunity to learn.[4] Later on
Beatrijs seems to have been sent to a school of the liberal arts.
This was quite probably coeducational: the biographer says
that she avoided any kind of contact with the schoolboys,
though he does not make it clear whether there were other
girls there.[5]

---

[1] F. M. Powicke, *The Thirteenth Century 1216-1307* (Oxford, 1962), 640. Powicke
adapts and shortens the translation of W. E. Rhodes, who also gives the text: see 'The
Italian Bankers in England and their Loans to Edward I and Edward II', in T. F.
Tout and J. Tait (edd.), *Historical Essays, first published in 1902 in commemoration of
the Jubilee of The Owens College, Manchester* (Publications of the University of
Manchester. Historical Series, 6; Manchester, 1907), 137–68, at pp. 151–2. S. L.
Peruzzi, *Storia del commercio e dei banchieri di Firenze in tutto il mondo conosciuto dal
1200 al 1345* (Florence, 1868) (Rhode's source for the poem), thought that it must
from its tone have been written after 1311 (p. 154).

[2] M. Ungureanu, *La Bourgeoisie naissante. Société et littérature bourgeoises d'Arras
au XIIe et XIIIe siècles* (Mémoires de la Commission des Monuments historiques du
Pas de Calais, 8; Arras 1955).

[3] Cf. H. Pirenne, *Histoire de Belgique* (5th edn., 1929), i, 351–7.

[4] *Vita Beatricis. De Autobiografie van de Z. Beatrijs van Tienen O.Cist. 1200-1268*,
ed. L. Reypens (Antwerp, 1964), 23–4. I owe this and the next reference to L.-J.
Bataillon.

[5] 'Per idem quoque tempus a patre magistris liberalium <artium> est commissa,
disciplinis scolaribus, quibus iam a matre, sicut prediximus, iniciata fuerat,
expeditius informanda. Ubi cum inter multitudinem scolarium cogeretur toto die
deuotissima christi discipula residere; horum tamen que ab hijs gerebantur vel

As one might expect, there seems to be a rough correlation between the degree of commercial development and the level of lay culture. In England, which was still a colonial economy in the thirteenth century, it seems harder to find evidence of specifically bourgeois literacy and culture than in Italy or Flanders.[1]

In the first issue of the journal *Annales* Pirenne wrote an article to show how merchants could have acquired an education.[2] He took the case of a monk named Abundus, of the abbey of Villers-en-Brabant, who died in 1228. He was sent to school with the monks by his father, a merchant of Huy, not to become a monk, but to acquire the skills which would be useful in business; clearly his father had seen the value of literacy for commerce.[3] In the event he decided to become a monk, but that was not the purpose of the exercise from his father's point of view. If his case was at all typical it is another warning against drawing a clear line between the culture of the clergy and the culture of the merchant class.

If a merchant did not find it convenient to send his son to a monastic school (or if he was afraid that the boy might become a monk himself, as Abundus did), there were other possibilities open. If he was rich, he could take on a cleric as a

---

dicebantur nichil penitus aduertebat. Sed et quantum potuit ab illis corpore pariter et animo sequestrata, facie quoque auersa, soli lectionis studio quam a magistro memorie commendandam acceperat intendebat.... (ibid. 25).

[1] Cf. M. Parkes, 'The Literacy of the Laity', in D. Daiches and A. Thorlby (edd.), *Literature and Western Civilization. The Medieval World* (London, 1973) 555-77, at p. 558: 'The evidence for pragmatic literacy in the commercial world is the most difficult to find'. His main evidence for book production for lay tastes is from the fourteenth century on, and when touching on thirteenth-century books (pp. 562-3) he does not say much specifically about the reading habits of merchants. M. T. Clanchy, *From Memory to Written Record. England 1066-1307* (London, 1979), points out (p. 188) that 'In England ... merchant dynasties like those of London took on the social colouring of the landed gentry and were not, in the thirteenth century anyway, a distinct "bourgeoisie". Knightly merchants were as educated as other knights. With lesser merchants, it is doubtful whether literacy in Latin was yet an essential skill, as they worked from memory and tally sticks.'

[2] H. Pirenne, 'L'Instruction des marchands au Moyen Âge', *Annales d'histoire économique et sociale*, 1 (1929), 13-28. My attention was drawn to this article by Stephen Ferruolo.

[3] Ibid. 20, especially n. 3.

private tutor: there is a text which mentions this as if it were quite a common thing to do.[1] Alternatively, there were town schools where members of the merchant class could get some education (one wonders whether some of the boys whom Beatrijs so carefully avoided at her school in Zoutleeuw[2] were sons of merchants). Much of Pirenne's article is about the precocious development of such schools in Flanders. He showed, for Flanders, that in the thirteenth century a basic education was widely available for members of the merchant class,[3] and made clear his view that literacy and advanced commercial development were intimately connected. In the thirteenth-century sermon collection of Thomas Lebreton we find it said, as something well known, that rich men are accustomed to hand over their boys to masters to learn their 'letters', as well as good morals.[4] He does not specify merchants, but the generalization presumably includes them.

One may assume that in the thirteenth century a successful merchant, whether or not he was literate, would have had to be able to do sums; for his occupation would itself have been an education in numeracy.[5] This may have a connection with the way preaching evolved—an indirect one, not susceptible to certain proof, but not to be discounted altogether. The thirteenth-century Dominican Giordano da Pisa said that the Florentine merchant 'did nothing day or night but think and calculate', and a perceptive modern synthesis, quoting him, adds: 'Such a man thought arithmetically, in and out of his countinghouse; and when he had children, whether they followed him into trade, or became friars or mathematicians, he would pass on to them a deep familiarity with number.'[6] A mental habit—amounting

[1] Ibid. 21–2.

[2] See above, p. 36 n. 5.

[3] Ibid. 26 and *passim.*

[4] 'Solent etiam isti divites pueros suos tradere magistris disciplinatis et bene morigeratis ut litteras instruant et bonis moribus informent....' MS BL Royal 3. A. XIII, fo. 30rb); from a sermon on the text 'Puer crescebat' (Luke 2:40) (Schneyer, *Repertorium,* v. 632, 'Thomas de Lisle', No. 10).

[5] Cf. A. Murray, *Reason and Society in the Middle Ages* (Oxford, 1978), 189–94.

[6] Ibid. 194.

almost to an obsession—of numbering parts and making them symmetrical becomes pronounced as the thirteenth century progresses. The 'deep familiarity with number' is not a sufficient explanation of this odd habit, but may possibly help us understand why preachers liked doing it, and their audiences accepted it and perhaps even enjoyed it.

In reaffirming the importance which modern scholars have attached to the urban and commercial context of the mendicant orders, it would be wrong to give the impression that either their preaching or the education of the laity was confined to the towns. This sketch of the educated element in the public for which sermon collections were written would be unbalanced if it ignored rural areas altogether. The two points—that the friars operated outside the towns and that there were literate laymen outside the towns—do in a sense cancel each other out, but if we ignore them we risk falsifying the picture.

The convents of the friars were founded in towns but it would be mistaken to suppose that they never worked away from base. On the contrary, the orders kept more of their itinerant character than the foundation of permanent convents might lead one to suppose. There is evidence that they periodically went on pastoral expeditions. A. G. Little recaptured the atmosphere of an early mission from the *Lanercost Chronicle.*

It happened that when Christmas was approaching the superior called the friars together and sent them out two and two to sow the wholesome seed of the Lord through the country. Two of them came to the neighbouring wood and took a rough path over frozen mud and snow, while blood marked their footsteps without their noticing it. The younger one said to the elder: 'Father, would you like me to sing to lighten your journey?' On his consenting, he struck up the *Salve Regina Misericordiae,* and after singing it through, he said to his companion as though asking for applause: 'Brother, was that anthem well sung?'[1]

---

[1] Quoted in Little, *Studies*, p. 125.

Successful preaching in rural parishes would normally have been dependent on the co-operation of the parish priest. In 1301 the parishioners of Colyton in the diocese of Exeter complained (in tactful terms) that their vicar, unlike his predecessor, did not invite the friars to instruct them on the salvation of their souls.[1] This example would seem to suggest that if some parish priests were not helpful, others were. The popular demand on the part of the parishioners is an indication of the pastoral success of the friars.

The Franciscan text dubiously attributed to Bonaventura, explaining why the Franciscans preach more frequently in towns, seems when read closely to be drawing a distinction not so much between town and country *tout court,* as between small and poor villages on the one hand, and towns and large villages on the other. The accusation is that the friars preach 'in good cities and towns *and villages*' (my italics).[2] One of the points which the Franciscan writer makes when answering the accusation is that 'In towns ... or villages (*villis*) where provisions are abundant more people can come together and they can be better supported, and among more people more fruit is expected ...'.[3] The writer does go on to say that preachers and confessors ought not to neglect 'poor little villages' (*villas pauperculas*),[4] but the tenor of the *quaestio* is that there was a tendency to do so. There is evidence, indeed, that there were peasants living out their lives 'in fields and woods', who rarely knew when it was a Feast-day, except when they did not see ploughs in the fields or hear trees being cut; and there was a story about an old man who managed to learn which days were Feast-days, and on those days put on red boots; seeing this his neighbours would say to their

---

[1] Ibid. 124.

[2] '... in bonis civitatibus et oppidis et villis frequenter praedicatis, in aliis autem locis raro vel nunquam' (*S. Bonaventurae opera omnia* (Quaracchi edn.), viii (1898), 370. The next sentence but one ('Vel quia in civitatibus multa habetis bona hospitia ...') mentions only cities, but the context seems to soften this.

[3] 'In oppidis autem seu villis, ubi abundant victualia, plures possunt confluere et melius sustentari, et inter plures maior fructus speratur ...' (ibid.).

[4] Ibid.

households: 'Today we ought to rest, because master Guncelinus is wearing red boots'.[1] For peasants living in large and prosperous villages with their own parish church it must have been very different, and in such villages substantial congregations could be gathered to hear a visiting friar. Furthermore, even villages which were not so large, but which were not far from towns with one or more convents of friars, are not likely to have missed the experience of the preaching of the friars, unless their parish priest made a point of keeping them out.[2]

Even in the country, however, there would have been educated laymen among those who heard their sermons. Recent research on the literacy of the laity in England has reached the conclusion that even outside the towns it was less unusual than one might be tempted to suppose. A minimal literacy—the ability 'to read a little Latin, sufficient to get the gist of a royal writ or to understand a line in the Bible or in a chronicle'—was fairly common among the gentry.[3] Furthermore, the knightly class had a 'learned' if primarily oral culture of its own. As a recent writer has argued, 'the slightest consideration of the languages an English knight needed to know, or any knowledge of the subtleties of heraldry or hawking, suggests that knightly education was equally

---

[1] '... quia quidam (quid' *ms*) sunt ita negligentes et agrestes, in agris et nemoribus conversantes, quod raro sciunt quando est festum nisi quando non vident carrucas in agris, vel non audiunt arbores scindi; sicut recitatur de quodam rustico sene qui usu (*corr. from* usum?) didicerat dies festos, et semper in illis diebus caligas rubeas calciabat, quod videntes vicini dicebant familiis suis: Hodie oportet nos feriare, quia dominus Guncelinus rubeas caligas portat ...' (BN MS lat. 15943, fo. cxxxv[va]). From a sermon from the *ad status* collection of Guibert de Tournai OM, incipit 'Labores manuum tuarum quia manducabis, et cetera [Ps. 127, 2]. Labor est penitentia iniuncta ...' (not listed by Schneyer, *Repertorium*). The sermon is not in the Lyons [1510?] or the Louvain [1473?] editions. As so often, Guibert is borrowing from Jacques de Vitry: cf. J. Th. Welter, *'L' 'Exemplum' dans la littérature religieuse et didactique du Moyen Âge* (Paris and Toulouse, 1927), 466. There are minor differences, including 'Gocelinus' instead of 'Guncelinus'. Welter prints the whole of the 'Sermo [LX] ad agricolas et vinitores et alios operarios' by Jacques, from which this comes. L.-J. Bataillon drew my attention to these passages. For the connection between the liturgical and the husbandman's yearly cycles see G. C. Homans, *English Villagers of the Thirteenth Century* (Cambridge, Mass., 1942), ch. 23.

[2] Cf. Little, *Studies*, p. 124.

[3] Clanchy, *From Memory*, pp. 197–8.

demanding intellectually though in a different way'.[1] The important question, for the student of thirteenth-century sermons, is not so much 'How literate was the lay public?' as 'How sophisticated was it?' Literacy is one criterion of the intellectual level of lay culture, but not the only one.

The advantage of literacy as a criterion is that it leaves evidence for the historian, who is thus on firmer ground than with oral culture, however sophisticated.[2] Interestingly enough, the surviving manuscripts give fairly clear evidence of literacy well below the level of the knightly class. There are treatises on estate management which were, it would seem, 'the reference books of experienced estate stewards who probably acted as teachers in their profession'.[3] There are, even from the early thirteenth century, treatises drawn up for the instruction of reeves.[4] 'There can have been no point in such treatises unless some degree of literacy was expected of such officers.'[5] Yet the reeve was 'almost always a servile tenant, fundamentally one of the local peasantry'.[6]

This evidence for literacy outside the towns comes from England because the English evidence has recently been well studied; but it is not likely that England was unique in this respect. It is desirable that more work should be done on continental evidence along the lines traced out by Parkes and Clanchy. In the mean time, it is reasonable to infer that even when they left the towns the friars would have to take account of a leavening of men with some education and presumably quite active minds. In the towns themselves, as we have seen, the same is true to a much greater degree.

[1] Clanchy, *From Memory*, 198.

[2] Clanchy, after remarking on the high intellectual demands of knightly culture, has to add: 'This suggestion cannot be incontrovertibly proved, however, because knightly culture before the fourteenth century has been largely lost to posterity, as it was primarily oral' (*From Memory* p. 198).

[3] D. Oschinsky, cited by Parkes, 'The Literacy of the Laity', in D. Daiches and A. Thorlby (edd.), *Literature and Western Civilisation. The Medieval World*, 561 and 574 n. 36.

[4] Ibid. 559.

[5] Ibid.

[6] Ibid.

By the end of the thirteenth century the cultural gap
between clergy and laity had been narrowed. The sermon
collections of the friars were an attempt to bridge the gap. Far
from all of their lay public were simple and ignorant people.
They may have felt that it would be easier for the preacher
who turned the model sermons into living sermons to water
them down intellectually, when the nature of the congregation demanded it, than the other way round.

iii. The Apostolic Life

Jacques de Vitry called the Franciscans not only a *religio* of
the poor of the crucified Christ (*crucifixi*), but also an 'order of
preachers'.[1] He says that the head of the order sends its
members 'through the different provinces of the world, for the
sake of preaching and the saving of souls'.[2] He then devotes
some lyrical lines [3] to their re-formation in themselves of the
way of life (*religionem*), poverty, and humility of the primitive
Church,[4] their effort to carry out evangelical counsels as well
as precepts in every way, and their imitation of the apostolic
life, after which he returns explicitly to their preaching. The
lord pope confirmed their rule, he says, and granted them the
authority to preach to whatever churches they came, though
the consent of the local *prelati* was required, for the sake of
reverence.[5] 'For they are sent two by two to preach as if before
the face of the Lord and before his second coming.'[6] Jacques
goes on to describe how they take nothing with them on the
road, and his words echo New Testament texts (Matt. 10:10,
Luke 10:4) that seem to have had a special resonance

---

[1] *Historia occidentalis*, ed. Hinnebusch, p. 158.
[2] 'Habent autem unum summum priorem cuius mandatis et regularibus institutis
reuerenter obediunt minores priores ceterique eiusdem ordinis fratres, quos per
diuersas mundi prouincias causa predicationis et salutis animarum ipse transmittit'
(ibid. 159).
[3] Ibid., lines 5–15.
[4] Ibid. 159.
[5] Ibid.
[6] Ibid.

in this age of movements to imitate the apostolic life. It was in the context of this ideal of the *vita apostolica* that Jacques put the preaching of the Friars Minor.

His chapter on the Friars Preachers—who appear as the 'canons of Bologna' in the *Historia occidentalis*[1]—does not use the language of the apostolic life to the same extent. He stresses their poverty—they 'run after the Lord and in nakedness follow him who is naked'[2]—and their preaching of what they had learnt in their studies.[3] He does not, however, refer explicitly to the apostolic life, and he does not say of them, as of the Franciscans, that they were sent two by two to preach. In fact, of course, the followers of Dominic, like those of Francis, were scattered throughout the world,[4] and the order combined poverty[5] and itinerant preaching in such a way that it may be regarded as one of the 'apostolic' movements.[6]

One could write the whole history of the medieval friars in terms of their interpretations of, fidelities to, and fallings away from the *vita apostolica* ideal. Even after the early years it was the mental framework in which their preaching activity was set. For this reason it is worth dwelling a little on two kinds of evidence which cast sidelights—illustrating rather than proving points—on the relation of preaching to the apostolic idea. The first is a sermon on the apostles by Pierre de Reims (d. 1247), who was prior of the Dominicans' Paris

[1] It has been suggested that these are not in fact the Dominicans but another group. Hinnebusch (following Mandonnet) is not convinced by this view (ibid. 18). For a general discussion of when and in what circumstances the *Historia occidentalis* was written see ibid. 16–20.

[2] Ibid. 143. The passage from which this comes implies a strict interpretation of poverty.

[3] 'Que autem diligenter audierint ... Christi fidelibus diebus festis in predicatione refundunt ...' (ibid.).

[4] In 1217. Cf. R. B. Brooke, *The Coming of the Friars* (London, 1975), 93–5 and 170 and W. A. Hinnebusch, *The History of the Dominican Order*, i (New York, 1966), 51.

[5] The general chapter of 1220 laid it down that 'Possessions and revenues are not to be accepted under any circumstances'. See ibid. 153 and ch. V, *passim*.

[6] Cf. ibid. 146 and R. B. Brooke, *The Coming of the Friars*, loc. cit., especially p. 95.

convent of St Jacques, twice prior provincial of France, and bishop of Agen.[1] The second kind of evidence is the testimony of small manuscript books which look like the kind the friars must have taken on their journeys.

The sermon on the apostles is one of a number which Pierre de Reims included in his series for the Common of the saints (i.e. the sermons are on categories of saints rather than individual ones).[2] The sermon is on the text 'I have appointed you to go out, and bear (*afferatis*) fruit...' (John 15:16).[3] Pierre says that Jacob could have said something like this to his sons, when he sent them out into Egypt to buy corn (cf. Gen. 42). Moses could have said the like to the spies (Pierre uses the word *exploratoribus*), sending them into the promised land to spy it out and bring fruit (cf. Num. 13). These Old Testament incidents are the basis of the sermon's structure: the first seems to be the cue for an analysis of preaching, the second for remarks on contemplation and the exercise of virtues. (That is to over-simplify the plan of the sermon somewhat, but broadly speaking it falls into those two parts.) To go through the whole sermon would serve no purpose here; it will be enough to select a small group of passages which serve as a commentary on the place of preaching in the apostolic life as interpreted by the friars:

[1] Schneyer, *Repertorium*, iv. 724, Kaeppeli, *Scriptores Ordinis Praedicatorum*, iii (Rome, 1980), 256.

[2] See Schneyer, *Repertorium*, iv. 752–7. The series was edited in the eighteenth century under the name of Anthony of Padua, in *Sancti Francisci ... nec non S. Antonii Paduani ... opera omnia*, ed. R. P. Joannis de la Haye, (Regensburg, 1739). It is not safe to trust this edition, at least until the transmission has been properly examined. I therefore quote from manuscripts, relying mainly on BL Arundel 206, partly for convenience but also because there is some evidence that it represents a 'Franciscan' edition of this originally Dominican series (see below, p. 112 n. 2), so that it has an appropriateness as a base for comments on both mendicant orders together. It also seems to me to be an early manuscript on palaeographical grounds. Since the text seems fluid, I have also consulted MSS Bodleian, Laud Misc. 506, and BN lat. 15960, without collating them systematically. As with most of the sermon collections which will be mentioned in the course of this study, a critical study of the whole manuscript tradition would be very desirable and very hard to do properly.

[3] This sermon on the text 'Posui vos' is No. 465 of the list for Pierre de Reims in Schneyer's *Repertorium*, iv. 753.

(1) In hac duplici missione tota vita apostolorum et apostolicorum virorum significatur, que fuit in duobus, scilicet predicatione et utilitate proximorum; item in contemplatione et exercitio virtutum.[1]

(1) In this double sending [presumably, the mission of Jacob's sons and the mission of Moses' spies] is signified the whole life of the apostles and apostolic men, which consisted in two things, that is, in preaching and usefulness to their neighbours; and again, in contemplation and the exercise of virtues . . . .

Vita apostolica could be interpreted in widely different ways: monks understood it one way, the Waldensian heretics another, and so on.[2] Here the emphasis is on preaching and contemplation.[3] Pierre de Reims's concept of the apostolic life allows for contemplatives who are not suitable for preaching.[4] Nevertheless, as long as a preacher is pastorally useful outside the cloister he ought not to return to it.[5] There seems in fact to be a suggestion that the preaching office takes priority, even that it is in some sense a more perfect way.[6]

[1] MS BL Arundel 206, fo. 46ʳᵇ.

[2] Cf. M.-D. Chenu, 'Monks, Canons and Laymen in search of the Apostolic Life', in his *Man, Nature and Society in the Twelfth Century. Essays on New Theological Perspectives in the Latin West*, selected, edited, and trans. by J. Taylor and L. K. Little (Chicago University Press, 1968; Phoenix edn., 1979), 202–38.

[3] They are given the same prominence in another *de apostolis* sermon in this collection, Schneyer, *Repertorium*, iv, p. 752, No. 462: 'Qui sunt isti qui ut nubes volant et quasi columbe ad fenestras suas. Ys. lx. Profectus apostolorum et volatui nubium et columbarum merito comparatur, quia tota vita eorum in duobus fuit, scilicet in predicatione et contemplatione, et quasi nubes per mundum volabant, ymbre predicationis corda populi fecundando et quasi columbe ad fenestras celestia contemplando' (MS BL Arundel 206, fo. 46ʳᵃ).

[4] 'Item nota quod non omnes filii missi sunt in Egyptum. Benyamin enim domi remansit: Ne forte, ait pater, in itinere quicquam patiatur mali. Per quod significantur novitii vel contemplativi, qui non sunt ydonei ad predicandum; qui remanentes pro exeuntibus orare tenentur' (ibid., fo. 46ʳᵇ); Sermon on the text 'Posui vos' (Schneyer, *Repertorium*, iv. 753, No. 465).

[5] '. . . quamdiu predicator extra fructum potest facere, vix aut numquam propter quietem corporalem vel spiritualem reverti debet. . . .' (ibid.); sermon on the text 'Qui sunt isti' (Schneyer, *Repertorium*, iv. 752, No. 462).

[6] '. . . Per has ergo iii columbas notatur [*sic*] tria genera predicatorum ab archa, id est a claustro emissorum. Quidam enim fructum facere non possunt propter defectum suum et auditorum. Hii statim reverti debent. Alii fructum facere possunt, sed quia imperfecti sunt ad se reverti debent ut sibi vacent. Tertii sunt perfecti: hii

A lofty conception of the preaching office is as characteristic of the Franciscans as of the Order of Preachers. Jacques
de Vitry, it will be remembered, called the Franciscans an
'order of preachers'.[1] John Pecham, a thirteenth-century Paris
theologian who became Archbishop of Canterbury, claimed
that the rule of the Friars Minor was unique among the rules
of religious orders in having two chapters devoted to
preaching.[2]

A Franciscan would certainly have included poverty in his
conception of the apostolic life, but so does Pierre de Reims.
In his *de apostolis* sermon on the text 'Who are these who fly
like clouds, and like doves to their windows *(fenestras)*' (Isa.
60: 8) he shows that his idea of the *vita apostolica* takes in both
poverty and the common life.[3] The preaching mission is thus
part, though possibly the most important part, of an ideal
which pulls together several of the conceptions of the
apostolic life which had been developed over the previous
hundred years or so.

(2) Fratres, scilicet predicatores, missi in Egyptum, id est
mundum, vadunt. Sed non sine pecunia, que significatur per v
talenta, Mt. 25, que dominus commisit servo, que sunt: reli|giosa

---

redire non debent' (ibid.). It would be rash to assume that Pierre thought
contemplation inferior to preaching. Cf. the passage beginning 'Sic enim non fallit
iudicium David qui dixit quod communis esset pars descendentium ad prelium et
remanentium ad sarcinas ...' (ibid.) (cf. 1 Sam 30:24); sermon on the text 'Posui vos'
(Schneyer, *Repertorium*, iv. 753, No. 465.).

[1] See above, p. 43.

[2] J. R. H. Moorman, *A History of the Franciscan Order from its Origins to the year
1517* (Oxford, 1968), 517.

[3] See the passage quoted above, p. 46 n. 3, after which Pierre continues: 'Merito
autem comparantur nubibus et columbis quorum utrumque congretatim volat: in
quo notatur unitas et concordia. Unitas scilicet: Rerum, Corporum, Animorum,
Doctrinarum. De tribus primis Act. 4: Multitudinis credentium erat cor unum et
anima una et cetera. De iiii° Mt. 23: Unus est enim magister vester et cetera. Ergo et
una doctrina. Ad hanc unitatem exprimendam in festo uniuscuiusque omnium fit
commemoratio, ut patet in officio eorum. Nubes ergo fuerunt quia alti et suspensi per
contemplationem. ... Item leves per paupertatem. ...' (MS BL Arundel 206, fo. 46ʳᵃ);
Schneyer *Repertorium*, iv, p. 752 No. 462. To reconstruct Pierre's notion of the *vita
apostolica* fully it would be necessary to study his sermons from that angle more
exhaustively than is possible here.

[*fo. 46va*] vita, sufficiens scientia, sermonis eloquentia, etas matura, et corporis fortitudo.[1]

(2) The brothers [Jacob's sons], that is, preachers, are sent into Egypt, that is, the world, and go. But not without money, which is signified by the five talents, Matt. 25, which the Lord entrusted to his servant. They are: religious way of life, adequate learning, eloquence of speech, a mature age, and bodily strength.

'Adequate learning' (*sufficiens scientia*) is perhaps the most significant phrase. Both the Franciscans—after the early years—and the Dominicans made an academic training a precondition for the office of preaching to the laity. Both orders had hierarchies of study centres, which must have been by far the most systematic and effective networks of higher education in thirteenth-century Europe.[2] The apex of the educational structure in both orders was, of course, Paris.

(3) Item, nota quod impediti sunt a frumento deferendo, insuper exploratores vocati. Item quando de patrie famositate, de patris auctoritate, de fratrum (f^u_m *ms*) multitudine (multip^ne *ms*) coram egyptiis se iactabant: fratres sumus filii unius, et cetera. In quo quorumdam fratrum superbia notatur, qui coram secularibus de ordinis dignitate, de fratrum (frumenti *ms*) multitudine, de perfectione scientie vel nobilitate se iactant, et sic a fructu spirituali retardantur et ex hoc exploratores dicuntur, id est vane glorie inquisitores, et proprie laudis venatores ...[3]

(3) Again, note that they were hindered from taking away corn,

---

[1] MS BL Arundel 206, fo. 46rb-va; sermon on the text 'Posui vos' (Schneyer, *Repertorium*, No. 465).

[2] For a lucid summary of the scholastic system of the Order of Preachers see D. Knowles, *The Religious Orders in England*, i (Cambridge, 1950) 152, and C. Douais, *Essai sur l'organisation des études dans l'ordre des Frères Prêcheurs au treizième et au quatorzième siècle (1216–1342)* (Paris and Toulouse, 1884). On the Franciscans see H. Felder, *Geschichte der wissenschaftlichen Studien im Franziskanerorden bis um die Mitte des 13. Jahrhunderts* (Freiburg im Breisgau, 1904), and Moorman, *History of the Franciscan Order*, pp. 123–4 and ch. 13, *passim*. On both orders, see now D. Berg, *Armut und Wissenschaft. Beiträge zur Geschichte des Studienwesens der Bettelorden im 13. Jahrhundert* (Geschichte und Gesellschaft, 15; (Düsseldorf, 1977), and *Le scuole degli Ordini Mendicanti (secoli xiii–xiv)* (Convegni del Centro di Studi sulla Spiritualità Medievale, 17 [1976]; Accademia Tudertina: Todi, 1978).

[3] MS BL Arundel 206, fo. 46va.

and indeed called spies. Again, when they were boasting to the Egyptians of the fame of their native land, the authority of their father, and the large number of brothers: 'We are brothers, sons of one man', etc. In this the pride of certain brothers is indicated, the ones who boast to the seculars about the dignity of the order, the large number of brothers, the perfection of learning, or nobility, and thus are held back from spiritual fruit, and for this reason are called spies, that is seekers of vain glory, and hunters of their own praise . . .

A recent attempt to account for the criticisms of the friars by the chronicler Matthew Paris has argued that it was their 'deliberate ejection of humility from the Mendicant amalgam' which most irritated the monk of St Albans.[1] Pierre de Reims's remarks certainly suggest that one reason for the quarrel between the secular clergy and the mendicants was the tendency of the latter to do full justice, if not more than justice, to their own merits.[2]

If the ordinary parish clergy were more modest, they had a good deal to be modest about. Except for a small minority, they would have been much less well trained than the friars, and if the laity preferred the latter as preachers and confessors it was probably because they knew their job better. On the question of whether parish priests preached regularly in the thirteenth century there is still room for disagreement.[3] Even

[1] W. R. Thomson, 'The Image of the Mendicants in the Chronicles of Matthew Paris', *Archivum Franciscanum Historicum*, 70 (1977), 3–34, at pp. 33–4.

[2] For a full-scale study of the storm-centre of the controversy, see M. M. Dufeil, *Guillaume de Saint-Amour et la polémique universitaire parisienne 1250–1259* (Paris, 1972); for reflections in university sermons, L.-J. Bataillon, 'Les Crises de l'Université de Paris d'après les sermons universitaires', in A. Zimmermann (ed.), *Die Auseinandersetzungen an der Pariser Universität im xiii. Jahrhundert* (Miscellanea Medievalia, Veröffentlichungen des Thomas-Instituts der Universität Köln, 10; Berlin and New York, 1976), 155–69, at pp. 157–65. For a clear statement of the wider conflict, see Knowles, *Religious Orders in England*, i. 182–8.

[3] D. W. Robertson, 'Frequency of Preaching in Thirteenth-Century England', *Speculum*, 24 (1949), 376–88, is optimistic though not categorical; on the other hand, see the passage from a sermon by Grosseteste cited by C. F. Bühler, 'A Lollard Tract: On Translating the Bible into English', *Medium Aevum*, 7 (1938), 167–83, at pp. 181–2. It is reminiscent of the canon cited by Devailly, 'La Pastorale en Gaule au ixe siècle', *Rev. d'histoire de l'église de la France*, 59 (1973), 33 n. 77. Cf. above, I. i, and below, II. i (on priests' manuals and catechetical preaching).

those parish priests who did preach would normally have less variety to offer, for in general they would have less academic and practical experience, and fewer collections of sermon materials at their disposal. Whether they composed their own sermons or used prefabricated ones, they would be less well equipped.

Conscious of their superior training, friars could also bask in the reflected glory of St Francis and St Dominic, and draw confidence from the *esprit de corps* of their centralized and dramatically expanding orders. It is perhaps not surprising if they sometimes felt that they were not as other men. The tendency to collective self-congratulation must surely have exacerbated their troubles with the seculars. Pierre de Reims showed a clear head in denouncing such attitudes, and in implying that they were a falling away from the ideal of apostolic preaching. Without humility, we are told, a preacher goes out unfruitfully.[1]

(4) Item: fructum afferatis (after. *or* aster. *ms?*). Fructum facit qui predicatione populi corda movet. Sed fructum affert qui confessiones audit, quia teste conscientia sua scit quod in confitente profecerit. Predicare enim seminare est, sed confessiones audire, fructum metere est.[2]

(4) Again, that you may bear fruit. [Here the sense of *fructum afferatis* seems to be 'bear *away* fruit'.] He who moves the hearts of the people by preaching causes fruit to grow (*Fructum facit*). But he who hears confessions bears fruit, because with his conscience as witness he knows what he has accomplished in the person who goes to confession. For to preach is to sow, but to hear confessions is to reap.

---

[1] 'Ideoque dicit eis verus Ioseph: adducite fratrem vestrum minimum (*ms adds* humilitas, *del. with red line*) ut possim vestros probare sermo|nes [*col. b*] et sciam quod non sitis exploratores; per fratrem vestrum minimum humilitas, sine qua infructuose egreditur predicator ...' (MS BN lat. 15960, fo. 111 va-b). MS BL Arundel 206, fo. 46va, gives a somewhat different version here, though the general argument is the same.

[2] MS BL Arundel 206, fo. 46va.

Preaching and hearing confessions were closely linked. Salimbene tells how a brother Humilis of Milan was 'zealously engaged in preaching and hearing confessions' (*instabat predicationibus et confessionibus audiendis*) at Fanano during Lent; and when the men and women 'de Alpibus' sent to ask him to come and hear their confessions, he went to them 'and preached and heard confessions for many days'.[1] There was a natural connection between the two things—sermons urged repentance, and confessions afterwards provided a vehicle for it. The friars were excellent confessors and well supplied with reference books. A very popular one was that of Raimundo de Peñafort, who was Master-General of the Dominicans from 1237 to 1245. This *Summa de casibus poenitentiae* often turns up in small portable manuscript books.[2] (As we shall see, sermon materials are often found in the same kind of book.) In an ideal world the doctrines of these books for confessors—so different in character from the early medieval penitentials—and of sermon handbooks would be studied together, for they were complementary parts of the friars' programme of religious education.[3]

(5) Item pecunia in saccis reponitur, quia scientiam in predicatione erogatam dominus magis multiplicat. Item de eadem pecunia sepius frumentum emitur, quia eundem sermonem omnino per quem fructus [*supply* factus] est repetere licet, quod est contra eos qui semper novi esse volunt et nova dicere.[4]

---

[1] Salimbene, *Cronica*, ed. Holder-Egger, p. 411.

[2] Cf. D. L. d'Avray, 'Portable *Vademecum* books containing Franciscan and Dominican Texts', in A. C. de la Mare and B. C. Barker-Benfield, *Manuscripts at Oxford. An Exhibition in Memory of Richard William Hunt . . . on Themes selected and described by some of his Friends* (Exhibition catalogue, Bodleian Library; Oxford, 1980), 60–4, at p. 63, No. xiv. 4. (The editors' improvements to 'Portable *Vademecum* books' amounted to collaboration.)

[3] J. G. Ziegler, *Die Ehelehre der Pönitentialsummen von 1200–1350* (Regensburg, 1956), shows how valuable the evidence of confessional handbooks can be. Cf. also P. Michaud-Quantin, *Sommes de casuistique et manuels de confession au Moyen Âge* (Analecta Mediaevalia Namurcensia, 13; Louvain, Lille, and Montreal 1962).

[4] MS BL Arundel 206, fo. 46ᵛᵃ. sepius] iterum *in MS BN lat. 15960, fo. 111 ᵛᵇ (with the whole context differently worded)*; quod est contra . . . dicere] quod est contra eos qui ad populum loquentes semper volunt uti novis sermonibus *in MS BN lat. 15960, fos. 111 ᵛᵇ-112ʳᵃ.*

(5) Again, the money is put back in the sacks, because the Lord multiplies more the knowledge which is paid out in preaching. Again, with the same money corn is bought again and again (*sepius*), because it is permitted to repeat the same sermon altogether when fruitful results have been achieved through it—which is against those who always want to be new and to say new things.

This passage illustrates the indifference of the friars to originality in popular preaching. It suggests indeed that there were some who strove for it, but Pierre de Reims is able to attack such an attitude as a rather disreputable one. It is not clear whether he is advocating the repetition by the preacher of sermons he had already preached or his use of model sermons written by another; perhaps the former, but his tone is such that one doubts whether he would have cavilled at second-hand sermons. It would be a mistake to be patronizing about this side of medieval popular preaching. For élite audiences some originality was indeed expected,[1] but when preaching to the people the thing that mattered was to be useful.

(6) Ut eatis, quod est contra eos qui tantum in locis propinquis predicare volunt, non procul. . . .[2]

(6) To go out (*Ut eatis*): which is against those who only want to preach in nearby places, not far away. . . .

Despite the proliferation of permanent convents, itinerancy remained part of the friars' ideal of the apostolic life. (Indeed, the permanent convents may have made their wanderings easier, rather as hostels do for the itinerant youth of today.)

Pierre de Reims's comment is reminiscent of the discussion of *discursus*—literally, 'runnings to and fro'[3]—by a more

---

[1] Cf. B. Smalley, *English Friars and Antiquity in the Early Fourteenth Century* (Oxford, 1960), 308.
[2] MS BL Arundel 206, fo. 46va. locis propinquis] *MSS BN lat. 15960, fo. 112ra*, and *Bodleian, Laud Misc. 506, fo. 76ra*, add et civitatibus ubi sunt.
[3] From *discurro*. 'Journeyings' or 'expeditions' would be fair translations.

famous thirteenth-century Dominican, Humbert de Romans.
'Journeyings through the world' are included in the list of
'things connected with preaching' (*annexa predicationi*) in his
Liber de eruditione praedicatorum. The section on these
journeyings is quite substantial. First he goes through a series
of Scriptural texts which include the word *discurro* or related
forms (it looks as though he had a concordance or similar tool
at his elbow).[1] After this preliminary he sets about inciting
those who, from laziness or for other even less creditable
reasons, are reluctant to go on preaching expeditions—and
this in spite of the fact that preachers are often called *pedes*
(feet) in the Scriptures, and called so because it is their task to
make preaching journeys (*discurrere causa praedicationis*).[2]

There are many things which should encourage them to
perform their duty. One of Humbert's arguments is that they
have excellent examples to follow. When Christ began to
preach, he had no house in which he might lay his head. He
travelled around preaching 'through villages (*castella*) and
cities, and through all Galilee' (here Humbert refers to Matt.
4 and Mark 6). The apostles too went throughout the whole
world and preached everywhere. What sort of preachers,
then, are those who always wish to stay quietly in their
houses, or in their cloisters?[3]

Another argument is the competition from heretical
preaching. Heretics, risking life and limb, continually travel
around from house to house and from town to town (*cum
periculo corporis non cessant per domos et villas discurrere*) in
order to pervert souls. What a disgrace that they should travel
to secure the damnation of souls while some preachers are
unwilling to stir a foot for the salvation of souls.[4]

Among the other incentives which Humbert lists is the
nature of the preacher's office. It is not a preacher's job to
stand still, but to keep on the move. Humbert then laconically

---

[1] *Liber de eruditione praedicatorum*, in *B. Humberti de Romanis ... Opera de vita
regulari*, ii, ed. J. J. Berthier (1956), 450–1.
[2] Ibid. 451–2.
[3] Ibid.   [4] Ibid. 452.

quotes John 15:16, 'Posui vos ut eatis'.[1] (This text, of course, was the starting-point of the *de apostolis* sermon of Pierre de Reims which was analyzed above.) He ends his lists of incentives (which need not all be rehearsed here), by saying that preachers ought to be provoked to emulate the merchants of this world. These men so long for gain that many of them spend all their life going through the world to increase their profits (*pro lucris augendis*); and the apostles did likewise, journeying through different provinces for the salvation of souls (*pro lucro animarum*).[2]

Humbert then proceeds to criticize preachers who go to the other extreme by being too ready to undertake journeys for the wrong reasons,[3] and to give a list of the ills which result from too much journeying.[4] His criticisms of the abuse of itinerancy suggest that, far from dying out as permanent convents became normal, it could be regarded as too common.[5] Another critic of useless journeys was Hugues de Saint-Cher (an eminent Dominican—he achieved the cardinal's hat). He gave his opinion on this matter, among others, in a letter to a general chapter of the Dominicans.[6] Later in the letter he mentions journeying (*discursum*) again, and connects it with the problem of an over-expansion in the number of Preachers General.[7]

Despite Hugues de Saint-Cher's and his own criticism of excessive journeying, Humbert de Romans regarded the right kind of *discursus* as both good and necessary for preachers,

---

[1] *Liber de eruditione praedicatorum*, in *B. Humberti de Romanis ... Opera de vita regulari*, ii, ed. J. J. Berthier (1956), 450–1.

[2] Ibid.

[3] Ibid. 453–4.

[4] Ibid. 454.

[5] Though one should not assume that all or even a majority of Dominicans were great travellers: cf. the *Expositio Magistri Humberti super constitutiones fratrum praedicatorum*, ed. Berthier, ii. 6: '... pauci sunt fratres qui transierunt per diversas provincias vel domos multas ...'

[6] Printed ed. cit., ii. 507–9 (in the notes), at p. 508: 'Amplius, diligentis et exquisiti studii sollicitudinis esse condecet fratres a superfluis discursibus submovere...'

[7] Ibid. 509. On preachers general see H. C. Scheeben, 'Prediger und Generalprediger im Dominikanerorden des 13. Jahrhunderts', *Archivum Fratrum Praedicatorum*, 31 (1961), 112–41.

and he gives a list of the seven things which are necessary for itinerant preaching to be praiseworthy. The first requisite, for instance, is an aptitude for this sort of work, 'for not just anyone is suitable for it'.[1]

The evidence for itinerancy is not confined to Dominican sources; it was part of the Franciscan life too, and we have a colourful narrative of the journeyings of a friar in the chronicle of Salimbene. One of Salimbene's friends, Giovanni da Parma, the Minister-General himself, commented on the wanderings of Salimbene and his *socius*.[2] 'You certainly get about, boys...',[3] he said, and according to Salimbene he was amused rather than annoyed. Salimbene and his friends do indeed seem to have hopped almost casually from region to region. The Minister-General himself had done something to encourage this tendency to wander, for, some time before the meeting at which he made the remark just quoted, he had offered to send Salimbene and his *socius* anywhere they liked (except Paris!) in the whole of the order. They were given a night to think it over. The next day, after the destination of Salimbene and his *socius* had been settled, Giovanni de Parma gave a further example of the informality of the itinerant spirit. He said to his friend, Hugues de Digne: 'What do you say, brother Hugues? Shall we go to Spain and do what the Apostle wanted to do?'[4] Brother Hugues decided not. Giovanni should go, but, for himself, he preferred to die in the land of his fathers.[5]

A good deal of Salimbene's travelling was done before he passed his preaching examination (though Innocent IV had given him some sort of permission to preach, some time before he got his licence from the order's authorities in the proper way). Even when dealing with the period after he got his preacher's licence he does not tell us as much as one would

---

[1] Ed. cit., ii. 454.
[2] i.e. his companion: friars normally travelled in twos.
[3] 'Multum discurritis, pueri ...' (Salimbene, *Cronica*, ed. Holder-Egger, p. 333). (My rendering is free: *pueri* probably had the technical meaning of 'young friars'.)
[4] Ibid. 313.   [5] Ibid.

like about itinerant preaching, as opposed to itinerancy *tout court.* He gives good coverage to the striking preaching successes of Berthold von Regensburg and of the 'Alleluia' movement, but examples of ordinary preaching journeys are the more precious in that they seldom attracted attention. The story about brother Humilis of Milan, to which reference was made earlier, gives us a glimpse of one: when invited by the men and women 'de Alpibus', who wanted to make their confessions to him, he took his *socius* and went to them and for many days preached and heard confessions.[1]

Salimbene is not the only evidence for the survival of Franciscan itinerancy even after permanent convents had become normal. Synodal constitutions in England from the last two decades of the thirteenth century try to smooth the way for the expeditions of Franciscans and Dominicans through the parishes during Lent or at other times to hear confessions (and presumably also to preach).[2] John Pecham (*c.*1220–92), in a polemical defence of the Franciscan order, seems to take itinerant preaching for granted.[3] Another piece of evidence is a Franciscan *exemplum* collection which appears to have been compiled between the years 1272 and 1297. It has been argued that the stories he tells show that the author must have been an itinerant preacher.[4]

There is evidence of an entirely different kind for the continued importance of itinerant preaching, for there are manuscripts in libraries all over Europe which are a visible and tangible illustration of the way itinerancy lasted into the later thirteenth and, indeed, fourteenth centuries. Such manuscripts, viewed as it were as physical objects, not only support the conclusion that this side of the *vita apostolica* was

---

[1] Above, p. 51.

[2] Little, *Studies*, pp. 124–5: he refers to the synodal constitutions of Exeter in 1287 and Winchester about 1295. Cf. above, pp. 39–41, where I discuss preaching by the friars outside the towns. On the whole this may also be taken as evidence for itinerancy, since their convents were usually in towns.

[3] John Pecham, *Tractatus Pauperis,* in *Fratris Johannis Pecham ... Tractatus Tres de Paupertate,* edd. C. L. Kingsford, A. G. Little, and F. Tocco (British Society of Franciscan Studies, 2; Aberdeen, 1910), 24.

[4] J. Th. Welter, *L' 'Exemplum',* p. 250

not abandoned, but give us a surer idea of how preachers prepared the sermons which they gave on their *discursus.* They suggest that itinerant preaching was not of a type sharply distinguishable from and more spontaneous than the kind which we can study through the surviving collections of model sermons. Itinerant preaching is in fact one of the contexts to which our surviving sources should be restored.

Small, portable 'vade-mecum books', often rather unprepossessing and utilitarian in appearance, were produced in great numbers to meet the needs of the friars.[1] In little manuscript books of this kind we find a variety of types of work which friars would need: not only sermons and preaching material[2] but also confessional handbooks,[3] bibles,[4] and breviaries.[5] The small format of these books, taken in conjunction with the nature of their contents, is most easily explained by the mobility that continued to be part of the way of life of the friars, and which they would have seen as an imitation of the *vita apostolica.*[6]

This genre of manuscript books easily escapes attention because small-format books and/or mendicant books are not concentrated together. Occasionally, such concentrations are found, and they deserve closer study than is possible here. One such is the medieval library of the Franciscan convent of Assisi. A large proportion of the books are now in the manuscript collection of the Biblioteca Comunale. Because the fourteenth-century convent library catalogue has survived, and because the manuscripts themselves as a rule have indications which make it possible to marry them up with the

---

[1] Cf. d'Avray, 'Portable *Vademecum* books', pp. 60–4 (on Oxford examples).

[2] Cf. ibid., Nos. xiv. 1–3.

[3] Cf. ibid., No. xiv. 4.

[4] Cf. ibid., No. xiv. 5.

[5] Cf. ibid., No. xiv. 6; also No., xiv. 7, described by Dr de la Mare.

[6] This is not to say that no pocket-books were made before the coming of the friars, nor that a small format must in itself imply that any individual book was designed to be carried on journeys; but such books are so common that their collective testimony converges with the other evidence for itinerancy, and makes it much more concrete.

entries in the catalogue, it is not difficult to pick out the books which belonged to the medieval library.[1]

The 'public' part of the library is not relevant for our purposes, because the books were to be read *in situ,* and could not be taken away, presumably not even on preaching journeys. Around 200 manuscripts survive from the private part, however, of which some are clearly for preachers and others not. A disproportionately large number of the former are in pocket format. The sample poses problems which makes it difficult to give exact figures. For instance, it is not always easy to decide from the medieval and modern catalogues whether or not a particular manuscript should be regarded as a preachers' book. (It is particularly hard with books described as 'postils'. The name usually refers to Bible commentaries, but some postils on the liturgical readings are, to all intents and purposes, sermon collections). I have seen many but by no means all of the manuscripts, and without a fuller analysis of the library it is likely that precise statistics would be inaccurate.[2] Nevertheless, the broad conclusion— that there is a proportion of preachers' pocket-books too high to be explained by chance—seems solid enough. The high proportion cannot be accounted for by accidents of survival, for such books would be more liable to wear and tear than most, and therefore less likely to survive.[3]

It is also worth glancing at another sort of sample. The section of the Bibliothèque Nationale which is composed of Latin manuscripts from the old royal library is organized

[1] The manuscripts of the medieval library were identified by L. Alessandri, in his *Inventario dell'antica biblioteca del S. Convento di S. Francesco in Assisi compilato nel 1381* (Assisi, 1906). See now C. Cenci, *Bibliotheca manuscripta ad Sacrum Conventum Assisiensem* (Il miracolo di Assisi. Collana storico-artistica della basilica e del sacro convento di S. Francesco-Assisi, 4; Casa editrice Francescana: Assisi, Regione dell'Umbria, Sacro Convento di Assisi, 1981).

[2] Cenci, op. cit., would provide the basis for a study relating the manuscripts of the convent of Assisi to our format.

[3] Cf. Alessandri, *Inventario*, p. xxxix (speaking of manuscripts of sermons): '...questi sono stati soggetti, più che le altre opere, ai guasti alle ingiurie del tempo; perchè, essendo fra i religiosi francescani assai comune il lavoro della evangelizzazione, i libri di quel genere, dovevano essere usati più che gli altri.'

according to format and the nature of the texts which the manuscripts contain. Thus there is a section devoted to preachers—'Oratores sacri'—in 'in-8°' format. We no longer know what the cataloguers meant by 'in-8°',[1] but to judge by the manuscripts themselves it was much smaller than the modern octavo, so that this may be regarded as a collection of pocket-books. Out of approximately twenty books, nine have Franciscan indications of one kind or another.[2] In some of the manuscripts the indications are fairly conclusive; with others there is only a fair probability and some doubt remains. When all the pros and cons have been weighed, the total is still remarkable.

In a sample of Franciscan books, then, there is a significantly high concentration of preachers' pocket-books, and in a sample of sermon manuscripts in pocket format there is a significantly high concentration of Franciscan books. These are illustrations rather than proof of a conclusion of which I am, nevertheless, fairly sure after years of work on sermon manuscripts, namely that Franciscans had a special liking for small portable books of sermons. The Dominicans may have used them as much, but for technical reasons Dominican sermon books are not so easy for modern scholars to recognize.[3]

---

[1] So I am informed by the specialists of the Cabinet des Manuscrits of the Bibliothèque Nationale.

[2] I discuss the Franciscan indications in these books in the appendix of 'The Transformation of the Medieval Sermon', unpublished D.Phil. thesis (Oxford, 1976), especially pp. 313–19. The in-8° *oratores sacri* manuscripts of the old royal library have been splendidly catalogued: Bibliothèque Nationale, *Catalogue général des manuscrits latins*, t vi (Paris, 1975), 616–734. For the organization of the manuscripts by nature of text and format which underlies this and the other catalogues of the old royal library, see H. A. Omont, *Concordances des numéros anciens et des numéros actuels des manuscrits latins de la Bibliothèque Nationale...* (Paris, 1903), pp. xl–xli.

[3] *De tempore* sermon collections follow the cycle of liturgical readings. The Franciscan cycle was that of the Roman *Curia*, a distinctive one in the thirteenth century, whereas no one to my knowledge has worked out in print a way of distinguishing between the Dominican cycle of readings and the cycle (cycles?) used by the secular clergy on the Continent, if indeed it can be done. Thus, if rubrics or marginal notes show that a series of sermons is following the Roman *Curia* calendar, it was most probably made for or used by a Franciscan; if it does not, it may be secular, or Dominican—or indeed Franciscan, since they preached in parish

One instance must suffice to give a more concrete idea of what these functional little books are like. An attractive example is MS NAL 270 of the Bibliothèque Nationale in Paris. This manuscript, which is dated to the second half of the thirteenth century, could have been tailor-made for a preacher who needed to make long journeys on foot. It is tiny but carefully produced; the pages vary somewhat in size, but it measures approximately 16.60 cm. × 11.10 cm. In many places the parchment is extremely thin. Throughout most of the manuscript the writing is minute but regular. The large spaces at the foot of most pages have sometimes been filled with writing in a script of the kind not infrequently used for rough notes. The greater part of the manuscript is taken up with series of sermons. The average length of the sermons is very short. For this reason, and because the script is so very compressed, individual sermons often fit into a remarkably small area of parchment. Thus, a sermon on fo. 29ra fits into a space of approximately 5 cm. × 4.3 cm. This sermon is a mere skeleton outline, a schematic summary which consists of little but headings (rhyming among themselves) and Scriptural texts to confirm them. There are many like it in the manuscript. Like the book itself, these sermons are extremely functional. The book is probably Franciscan.[1]

---

churches and might follow the seculars' calendar for that reason. For a seminal if highly compressed discussion, see L.-J. Bataillon, 'Sur quelques sermons de Saint Bonaventure', in *S. Bonaventura 1274-1974*, ii. *Studia de vita, mente, fontibus et operibus Sancti Bonaventurae* (Grottaferrata, 1973), 503 n. 38. See too M. O'Carrol, 'The Lectionary for the Proper of the Year in the Dominican and Franciscan rites of the thirteenth century', *Archivum Fratrum Praedicatorum*, 49 (1979), 79–103.

[1] The calendar evidence, though not quite straightforward, suggests this. On fo. 97^v there is a Gospel text for the second Sunday of Advent which fits the Dominican or secular calendar at one of the points where it differs from Franciscan usage, but this need not necessarily be evidence against a Franciscan origin: as we have seen, Franciscan writers did not always follow their own order's usage in their sermon series, though other writers would not follow the Franciscan usage. Thus, this is neutral evidence. The *de tempore* series in the earlier part of the manuscript are more helpful. Many sermons have a note beside them indicating which Sunday of the liturgical year they were intended for, and it seems likely that the person responsible for these calendar indications was a Franciscan. For example, there is a *de tempore* series which starts on fo. 28^r. On the verso of the same folio there is a sermon on the text 'Gaudete in domino semper' (Phil. 4: 4). A marginal note—badly written, but

Manuscripts like this, archaeological survivals of the preaching of the friars, give one a more vivid sense of the particular twist which the Franciscans and Dominicans gave to the *vita apostolica* ideal. On the one hand, the friars remained *Wanderprediger,* wandering preachers, highly mobile even though they worked from permanent bases. On the other hand, theirs was not on the whole a spontaneous or 'charismatic' preaching; or if it was, there was an infrastructure of prepared preaching material to serve as a springboard for spontaneity. Even when literary sources do tell us something about itinerant preaching, they do not give us a clear idea of the sermons which were delivered, or of how the friars prepared them. One is liable to get an over-dramatized picture, based on descriptions of exceptional preachers like Berthold von Regensburg. Salimbene says that when the latter preached about the Last Judgement (*de tremendo iuditio*) 'everybody trembled, just as a rush trembles in water. And they begged him for the love of God not to talk of such things, for they were weighed down with fear and horror when they heard him.'[1] It is easy to assume that such moving and powerful preaching was impromptu, or at least original. Berthold's, perhaps, was original, but the contents of preachers' vade-mecum books brings it home to us that the preaching offensive of the friars, which was undoubtedly successful, depended to a significant extent on ready-made sermons and other kinds of stereotyped material. Larger manuscripts point to the same conclusion, of course, but they smell of libraries rather than of the road; it must be the vade-mecum books—say manuscripts of 18 cm.

---

there is no doubt about the sense—assigns it to the third Sunday of Advent. (Though the marginal note is placed higher than the *G* of *Gaudete*, it is parallel with the higher part of the decoration and can hardly go with the sermon before, which starts on the previous page.) The Gospel beginning 'Gaudete in domino semper' falls on the third Sunday of Advent according to the Franciscan calendar, and this is one of the points where it is distinctive. There is further evidence of the same kind to suggest that a Franciscan had the book made, or used it.

[1] Salimbene, *Cronica*, ed. Holder-Egger, p. 560. The 'sicut iunccus tremit in aqua' is probably formulaic.

in height or less—that friars took in their satchels on their journeys.

Necessarily selective, this chapter has concentrated on three themes: the difference between the thirteenth-century preaching revival and early medieval attempts in that direction; the nature of the 'sermon-hearing public'; and the friars' interpretation and practice of apostolic preaching. The ideal of regular preaching to the laity goes far back into the early Middle Ages. The aim was clearly formulated in the Carolingian era and serious efforts were made to achieve it. If their success was not great, as to me seems likely, this was perhaps because the lower clergy were not equipped to use the kind of preaching aids produced for them. Only with the friars was the cultural gap between preaching aids and their users closed, both because preaching aids were better adapted to their function and because the Franciscans and Dominicans were intellectually equipped to use them successfully.

Paris played a special role in the Mendicant preaching system, both as a centre for the diffusion of preaching aids and as a corner-stone of the Franciscan and Dominican educational structures. But the significance of Paris for the history of popular preaching goes back before the friars. Jacques de Vitry describes with verve a preaching revival which fanned out from Paris in the late twelfth and early thirteenth centuries; but it goes back further still, at least as far as Maurice de Sully.

The audience to whom sermons were directed was becoming more sophisticated. In the towns, most of all in Italian towns, the higher end of lay culture overlapped to a considerable extent with the lower end of clerical culture. (It will be important to bear this in mind when we come to work out the relation of the friars' sermons to academic and popular culture.) Even in the countryside, the friars would not always have been talking to congregations composed solely of simple and uneducated men.

This leads to a further point, deserving of some emphasis as the historiography of the subject stands. The audience of the friars cannot be reduced to people in towns engaged in buying and selling. The friars were based in towns but took their apostolate into the countryside. Both in the countryside and in the towns, moreover, their audiences must often have included members of the knightly and noble class.

The preaching of the friars was, of course, one of the manifestations of the ideal of the apostolic life which was everywhere in the air in the central Middle Ages. A sermon by Pierre de Reims on John 15:16 indirectly casts many sidelights on the friars' version of the ideal: the respective importance attached to preaching and contemplation; the preconditions, including learning, for fruitful preaching; the harm done by the tendency to arrogance *vis-à-vis* the secular clergy; the close association of preaching and the hearing of confessions; the idea that a striving after originality for its own sake in popular preaching was wrong; and the feeling that a preacher must be prepared to travel.

The sermon comes from one of those model sermon collections which form the most important class of evidence for the preaching of the friars. The portable format of so many of the manuscript books in which model sermons (and other preaching aids) have come down to us warns us against drawing a distinction between a spontaneous itinerant preaching, and the preaching represented by the surviving model sermon collections.

II.

The Nature of the Medium

i Genres of Preaching Aids

THE various genres of preaching aids made up a system of communication: they are not only a source for thirteenth-century history but also a feature of it. When the sources are themselves survivals of the phenomenon which they record, the historian's normal duty to understand their technicalities becomes more pressing; and when the phenomenon is a mass medium, this technical knowledge is a *sine qua non* if we would work out the relation of medium to message. Some fairly dry and detailed discussion of preaching aids, both as sources and as a mass medium, is therefore inescapable for scholars studying the preaching of the friars. Those whose interest in the subject is not at the research level, on the other hand, might with good conscience move on to the conclusions at the end of this part of the book. Many of the findings are simply a recapitulation and critical assessment of the state of research, but two go somewhat further. One is that the audience and function of model sermon collections may have been much less specific than we have tended to assume. Though to preach them to the people was probably the most common way of using them, it is difficult to find evidence that this was their exclusive function or audience, while there is some evidence to the contrary that is hard to ignore. If the theory of the indeterminacy of audience and function is right, it follows that model sermons cannot be treated in a straightforward way as a medium of communication between clergy and laity. It may be better to think of them as a cultural phenomenon in which both clergy and laity participated in different ways and degrees. The other point is that model sermon collections, together with genres like *distinctio* and *exemplum* collections, may represent only the second tier in the structure of thirteenth-century preaching, the foundation of basic catechetical preaching being represented by genres which are not obviously preaching aids at all. Before developing this theory, however, it may be useful to give an idea of the range of overlapping genres which made up what one might call the supra-catechetical level of the thirteenth-century preaching movement.

Cum frater quidam ivisset Parisius, dimisit parentes ditissimos et potentes. In regresu [*sic*] vero invenit eos depauperatos (depauper-tos *ms*) propter guerram. Cui dixerunt: Hoc fecerunt nobis homines de Camerino. Ille vero contristatus oravit quadam die quod deus faceret vindictam de predictis, et statim audivit vocem propriis auribus dicentem: Deus in proximo faciet vindictam. Verum tamen quia indiscrete orasti, dolorem stomachi de cetero continue patieris, et in concha bibes. Et ipse scribens diem et horam statim timens ne in flumine quod Concha vocatur, quod iuxta Camerinum est, periclitaretur, transtulit se ad provintiam Marchie Trevisine. Illo igitur tempore homines de Camirino versi in seddittionem quam-dam, mutuo se trucidarunt. Quod cum au|disset [*fo. 84*] dictus frater, et senciens statim dolorem stomachi, tradidit socio cedulam sigilatam, in qua forma verborum continebatur, dicens: Istam cedulam reserva, et illam non aperies donec me migrasse audieris. Eumdo [*sic*] igitur ad dictam provintiam, devenit iuxta Montem Silicis, ubi fluvius qui vocabatur Concha de monte cum impetu descendens naviculam suffocavit, et fratrem. Quod audiens qui cedulam receperat, ipsam aperiens invenit omnia supra dicta.[1]

When a certain brother went to Paris, he left his parents very rich and powerful. On his return he found them impoverished through war. 'The men of Camerino did this to us,' they told him. Truly he was distressed, and prayed one day that the Lord would take vengeance upon these men (*de predictis*), and immediately he heard

---

[1] MS BL Add. 11872, fo. 84^{r-v}. (Here I do not normalize *c* and *t*, because the scribe's use of them almost amounts to a dialect form.) Cf. J. A. Herbert, *Catalogue of Romances in the Department of Manuscripts in the British Museum*, iii (London, 1910), 693–4, No. 15.

with his own ears a voice saying: 'God will shortly take revenge. However, because you have prayed recklessly, you will from then on (*de cetero*) suffer a pain in the stomach, and you will drink in the Concha. And he, writing down the day and the hour, and immediately fearing lest he be exposed to danger in the river which is called the Concha [Chienti], which is near Camerino, moved to the province of the march of Treviso. And so at the same time the men of Camerino became involved in some kind of civil war, and slew each other. When the aforesaid brother heard this, and since he immediately felt a pain in the stomach, he gave his *socius* a sealed document, in which a form of words was contained, and said: 'Keep this document, and do not open it until you hear that I have died.' And so, going to the aforementioned province, he came near Monselice, where a river which was called the Concha, pouring down from the mountain with great force, swamped the boat and the brother. When he who had the document heard this, he opened it and found all the aforementioned things.

This is a story from an *exemplum* collection, probably Franciscan and believed to date from the late fourteenth century.[1] It takes one straight into the real and imaginative worlds of a medieval friar.[2] *Exempla* were meant to hold the attention, and since scholars like human interest and anecdotes too, it is not surprising that the genre of *exemplum* collections has received a good deal of attention; and indeed the study of these collections has cast light on literature and folklore as well as on religious history.[3] The antecedents of the genre go far back into Christian history, but in the thirteenth century a new—and the most important—phase of its existence began.[4] Firstly, *exempla* seem to have been used more by preachers; that, however, was the development of an

---

[1] Cf. J.-Th. Welter, *L''exemplum' dans la littérature religieuse et didactique du Moyen Âge* (Paris and Toulouse, 1927), 287–9.

[2] The facts that the central figure is called *frater*, and that he has a *socius*, suggest (together with lesser indications) that this is a story abour a friar.

[3] The most comprehensive study of the genre is Welter, *L''Exemplum'*, but see now C. Bremond, J. Le Goff, and J.-C. Schmitt, *L'Exemplum'* (Typologie des Sources du Moyen Âge Occidentale, 40; Brepols, Turnhout, 1982).

[4] Cf. Welter, *L''Exemplum'*, p. 63.

existing trend. A major new departure was the compilation of handbooks of *exempla*, detached from the sermons themselves and arranged in some kind of order.[1]

In some ways Paris and France played a less important part in the history of this genre than did the British Isles.[2] (The diffusion of what one might call imaginative narratives seems to have been something of a British speciality, incidentally, for together with *exemplum* collections one thinks of the Merlin and Arthurian stories, the 'Miracles of the Virgin', and the inventively 'classicizing' friars of later thirteenth- and early fourteenth-century England.[3]) Still, Paris cannot be left out of the picture. We shall see that Paris was a sort of junction for the oral culture of intellectuals, where a friar could mix with students from all parts of Europe and pick up stories originating far from his birthplace.

The author of the earliest surviving 'purpose-built' *exemplum* collection had studied at Paris as a young man, and brings Paris into a number of his *exempla*.[4] This was Étienne de Bourbon, a Dominican, who was quite probably a student at Paris at the time when the order was just becoming established there.[5] It was very probably at Paris that he became attracted to the Dominican way of life, like many other intellectuals there; he may have actually taken the habit at Lyons, for we find him a member of the order's community there in 1223.[6] His 'Treatise on various materials for preaching' (which he never completed) was written not later

---

[1] For a list of these collections, see the table attached to the perceptive article of Jean-Claude Schmitt, 'Recueils franciscains d'"exempla" et perfectionnement des techniques intellectuelles du XIIIᵉ au XVᵉ siècle', *Bibliothèque de l'École des Chartes*, 135 (1977), 5–21.

[2] Ibid. 19–20.

[3] On the 'Miracles of the Virgin' see R. W. Southern, 'The English Origins of the "Miracles of the Virgin"', *Medieval and Renaissance Studies*, 4 (1958), 176–216; for the classicizing friars, B. Smalley, *English Friars and Antiquity in the Early Fourteenth Century* (Oxford, 1960). 'Miracles of the Virgin' and the classicizing movement are both important in the history of the *exemplum*.

[4] A. Lecoy de la Marche, *Anécdotes historiques, legendes et apologues tirés du recueil inédit d'Étienne de Bourbon, Dominicain du XIIIᵉ siècle* (Societé de l'histoire de France; Paris, 1877), pp. iv–vi, and s.v. 'Paris' in the 'Table alphabétique'.

[5] Ibid., pp. v–vi.

[6] Ibid., p. vi.

than 1260–1, the year of his death.[1] Although both 'reasons' (*rationes*) and 'authorities' (*auctoritates*) play an important part in the work,[2] the *exempla* have pride of place in the author's conception of it.[3] In his prologue he states that he had collected 'a variety of useful *exempla*, from a variety of books, and from a variety of materials, and under a variety of headings, and from a variety of good and learned men'— from whom he had heard many of them. He explained that his aim was to compress into a small space material which was scattered among many books; also to organize it and divide it up under headings.[4]

Clearly he was not trying to write a work of great originality; as he says in the same passage of his prologue, he left higher matters to those who were fitted for them, and wanted only to do something useful for the salvation of men, 'according to my littleness'.[5] Even when allowance has been made for the topos of the author's disclaimer, Étienne de Bourbon's statement of purpose probably gives a fair idea of the driving force behind his own and his contemporaries' efforts to put stereotyped material into circulation. Originality was not the point either for the composer or for the preachers who used the book. The point was to help other preachers—one remembers how brother Maurice asked Salimbene to help him compile a book which would be 'very useful for preaching'.[6]

The boundaries of the *exempla* genre, as of other kinds of

---

[1] Welter, *L'"Exemplum"*, p. 215. (According to Welter the *terminus post quem* is 1250.) On the *Tractatus* see, in addition to Lecoy's edition, the following: 'Le *Tractatus de diversis materiis predicabilibus* d'Étienne de Bourbon. Troisième partie: *De dono scientie*. Étude et édition par Jacques-M.-A. Berlioz', in École Nationale des Chartes, *Positions des thèses soutenues par les élèves de la promotion de 1977 pour obtenir le diplôme d'archiviste paléographe* (Paris, 1977), 25–33; also 'Le *Tractatus de diversis materiis predicabilibus* d'Étienne de Bourbon. Deuxième partie: *De dono pietatis*. Étude et édition par Denise Ogilvie-David', ibid. for 1978, pp. 133–6. J.-C. Schmitt, *Le Saint Lévrier. Guinefort, guérisseur d'enfants depuis le xiiiᵉ siècle* (Paris 1979) takes one of Étienne's *exempla* as its starting point, and adopts a novel approach to this kind of source.

[2] Étienne de Bourbon, ed. Lecoy de la Marche, p. 9.

[3] Ibid. 4–5.   [4] Ibid. 5.   [5] Ibid.

[6] Salimbene, *Cronica*, ed. Holder-Egger, p. 237.

preaching aid, are not always clearly marked. The author of the standard work on the *exemplum* includes a chapter on collections of what he calls 'moralized *exempla*'.[1] These collections—those of them, at least, which deal principally with the natural properties of things—might well be regarded as a separate genre both in character and origins, but there is probably little point in drawing categories too strictly. The purpose of such thirteenth-century collections overlaps with that of *exemplum* collections in the narrow sense and of preaching aids in general.

Étienne de Bourbon organized his *exemplum* collection around the seven gifts of the Holy Spirit (though he did not in fact finish all seven parts). Some kind of logical organization was usual in thirteenth-century *exemplum* collections, but there are a few which follow alphabetical order.[2] In the latter a preacher could look up the topic he wanted rather as we look up an article in an encyclopaedia. If, for example, he wanted material on marriage, he would see if his collection had an entry under *Matrimonium* or *Coniugium*.[3]

He might sometimes find more than one sort of preaching material under the heading. In the entry under *Matrimonium* in the collection called the *Tabula exemplorum secundum ordinem alphabeti* there is some variety. First comes a brief *exemplum* which fits most definitions of the word easily enough: 'Take note of the philosopher who, when two men, one rich and stupid, the other wise and poor, had been offered to his daughter, said "I prefer to give my daughter to a man in need of money rather than to money in need of a man." '[4]

[1] Welter, *L'"Exemplum"*, pp. 335–75.

[2] See ibid. 290, where Welter lists four collections from the second half of the fourteenth century, all by Franciscans. (Cf. Schmitt, 'Recueils', pp. 12–13.) On the progress of alphabetization see now Rouse and Rouse, *Preachers*, pp. 34–6. There is an apparent divergence with Welter: Rouse and Rouse might seem to imply that the *Alphabetum narrationum* (1297–1308) of Arnould de Liège was the first alphabetical collection.

[3] *La Tabula exemplorum secundum ordinem alphabeti*, ed. Welter (Paris and Toulouse, 1926), has an entry under *Matrimonium* (pp. 45–6) but not under *Coniugium*; the *Liber exemplorum ad usum praedicantium*, ed. A. G. Little (Aberdeen, 1908), has an entry for *De coniugio* (pp. 58–9) but not for *Matrimonium*.

[4] *La Tabula*, ed. Welter, p. 45.

The next part of the article begins like a story but turns into a list: a demon called Asmodeus killed seven men, that is, those who were joined in marriage in a way that was not permitted. This said, each of the seven men is made to stand for a class of sinners. The first are those who marry their relatives (*consanguineas*), the second those who marry one girl after promising to marry another, and so on. This *exemplum*, if it can be called that, is really an enumeration of forbidden actions.[1]

The article continues in a similar vein, listing the sins which an adulteress commits,[2] and then the good aspects of marriage.[3] Material like this is on the borderland of the *exempla* genre. However, the *Matrimonium* entry does conclude with what looks more like a proper *exemplum*, though the edition gives no more than the heading, 'On St Germanus and the dragon.'[4] (The modern editor (Welter) had the bad policy of abridging silently.)

Its title suggests that even this last *exemplum* may have bordered on another genre, that of 'Lives' of the saints. This was not a specifically homiletic genre, but preachers must have used 'Legends' of the saints, especially perhaps the famous *Golden Legend*. It does not seem likely that preachers omitted stories from saints' lives altogether, and the natural inference is that the cycles of *de sanctis* sermons were used in conjunction with saints' 'Lives'.[5]

The *Golden Legend* of Jacopo da Varazze, a Dominican who was bishop of Genoa near the end of the thirteenth

---

[1] *La Tabula*, ed. Welter, p. 45. (cf. Tob. 3:8)

[2] Ibid.

[3] Ibid. 45–6.

[4] 'De bº Germano et dracone' (ibid. 46).

[5] Cf. the *de sanctis* series of Aldobrandino Cavalcanti, MS Bamberg, Msc. Theol. 2, fo. 125ʳᵇ: 'Et post hoc dicere multa miracula eius potes (*corr. from* potes eius). Quere in legenda eius. . . .'; fo. 176ᵛᵃ: 'Item vite presentis sancta conversatio, unde Martinus obitum suum longe ante prescrivit. Ps. [4: 9], In pace in idipsum dorm(iam) et req(uiescam). Hec satis patent in legenda eius.' Cf. the advice of Guy d'Évreux that preachers using his 'themes' for the proper or the Common of the saints should give some biographical details about the person to be honoured: P. Michaud-Quantin, 'Guy d'Évreux O.P., technicien du sermonnaire médiéval', *Archivum Fratrum Praedicatorum*, 20 (1950), 213–33, at p. 228.

century, has a structure which could have been especially designed to meet the needs of the preacher.[1] It is true that the prologue says nothing directly about preaching; the likely hypothesis is that the work was meant to be used in more than one way. Nevertheless, the organization of the work is very much like that of a *de sanctis* sermon collection, and we may probably regard it as a handbook for preachers, among other things. The prologue explains the overall pattern of the liturgical year, and this pattern provides a framework for the legends of the saints. Furthermore, Jacopo does not confine himself to saints' legends. There are also chapters on great feasts—the Nativity, the Annunciation, the Resurrection, etc. We even find a chapter 'On the dedication of a church'.[2] Thus, the work has a markedly liturgical character and a strong family resemblence to sermons. It was in its way a vehicle for doctrinal instruction, of a kind.[3] Doctrinal instruction was available in dozens of sermon collections. They lack, however, the detailed hagiographical information about the saints which the *Golden Legend* provided. This is not a fixed rule, but generally speaking sermons on saints (as transmitted on parchment) keep surprisingly clear of their lives and legends, in the thirteenth century at least. One imagines, therefore, that a preacher preparing a sermon on a given saint might have both an ordinary *de sanctis* sermon series and the *Golden Legend* before him, and that the sermon he actually delivered would contain material from both. In the same way preachers would have combined material from *exemplum* collections with material from model sermon collections.

---

[1] For a recent study of Jacopo da Varazze and the *Legenda Aurea* see M. von Nagy and N. C. de Nagy, *Die Legenda Aurea und ihr Verfasser Jacobus de Voragine* (Berne and Munich, 1971); the structure of the *Legenda Aurea* is set out in its prologue: see *Jacobi a Voragine Legenda Aurea vulgo Historia Lombardica dicta*, ed. Th. Graesse (Dresden and Leipzig, 1846).

[2] Jacopo da Varazze, *Legenda*, pp. 845–57.

[3] Cf. e.g. cap. I, 'De adventu Domini', ibid. 3–12, cap. LIV (52), 'De resurrectione Domini', ibid. 235–45. For what might be regarded as an analysis of the 'language' and 'mentality' of the *Legenda Aurea*, see von Nagy and de Nagy, op. cit. 22 ff.

The article on marriage in the *Tabula exemplorum secundum ordinem alphabeti* shows that the *exempla* genre is somewhat blurred at the edges. The same may be said of Biblical *distinctiones*, which were another major class of preaching tool. Recent work has shown how much the genre altered in the course of a century until eventually it disappeared 'by the simple process of turning into something else'.[1] In the late twelfth century a *distinctio* was a list of different senses of a term contained in Scripture; often each of the 'four senses' of Scriptural interpretation was illustrated by a biblical text containing the word. However, the author or compiler did not have to confine himself to the 'four senses', and indeed the illustrations did not have to be from Scripture.[2] It was common to draw on moralized bestiaries and collections of *proprietates rerum*,[3] so here *distinctiones* begin to overlap with the *exempla* genre.

Alphabetized *distinctio* collections seem to have been from the beginning a biblical tool for preachers.[4] The mendicants, not surprisingly, found the genre congenial, and made a major contribution to it, modifying it as they did so. They tended to give more material for each word, and to concentrate more on virtues, vices, and related matters. The nature of the genre was changing, and it has been aptly said that 'At times, the entries seem not so much to be scriptural terms in want of definition, as to be topics in search of scriptural discussion'.[5]

Perhaps the best way to illustrate the character of the genre is to quote an entry. The section on *Oportunitas* in the *distinctio* collection of Maurice de Provins is untypical in its

---

[1] R. H. and M. A. Rouse, 'Biblical Distinctions in the Thirteenth Century', *Archives d'histoire doctrinale et littéraire du Moyen Âge*, année 49, t. 41 (1974), 27–37, at p. 37.

[2] Ibid. 28.

[3] Ibid.

[4] Rouse and Rouse, *Preachers*, p. 8. Cf. their earlier 'Biblical Distinctions', pp. 30–1, where there is some difference in emphasis. Conversations with Dr Gillian Evans have convinced me, however, that early collections of *distinctiones* may not have been exclusively oriented towards preaching.

[5] Rouse and Rouse, 'Biblical Distinctions', p. 34.

brevity, but in other respects it gives a fair idea of the genre around the mid-point of its development:

Est oportunitas loquendi. Prov. xv. sermo oportunus optimus est. Item operandi. Ecces. viii. Omni negotio tempus est et oportunitas. [*Omission in ms?*] Adiutor in oportunitatibus, in tribulatione. Item predicandi. ii ad Thi. iiii. predica verbum, insta oportune, importune.[1]

There is an opportuneness of speech. Prov. 15. An opportune word is the best. Again, of action. Eccles. 8. There is a time and an opportune moment for every business. * * * [Ps. 9: 10] A helper at the opportune moments, in time of trouble. Again, of preaching. 2 Tim. 4. Preach the word, dwelling on it continually, at opportune times and at inopportune times.

Maurice de Provins is presumably the same as the *frater Mauricius* who told Salimbene to keep away from the Joachites and help with a book of distinctions for preachers.[2] The passage just quoted illustrates the dry and impersonal character of his work; although dry, however, it was functional, for it was well adapted to the demands of the new sermon form which was reaching maturity about this time. Maurice's *distinctiones* appear on both the surviving lists of works available from Paris University stationers, so he was not the only one to think that the work would be 'useful for preaching'.[3]

The *distinctiones* genre overlaps with other types of homiletic aid. Model sermons could themselves be called 'distinctions'—at least, that name seems to have been applied to the summary sermons of Hugues de Saint-Cher.[4] This

---

[1] MS Bodleian, Rawlinson C. 711, fo. 138vb.

[2] Salimbene, *Cronica*, ed. Holder-Egger, p. 237.

[3] As he said to Salimbene (ibid.).

[4] J. B. Schneyer, *Beobachtungen zu lateinischen Sermoneshandschriften der Staatsbibliothek München* (Bayerische Akademie der Wissenschaft, philosophisch-historische Klasse, Sitzungsberichte, Jahrgang 1958, Heft 8; Munich, 1958), 39: 'Die Predigten des Kardinals Hugo v. S. Caro liegen im massgebenden Cod. Paris, Nat. lat. 15946 in drei Reihen vor ... Sie sind dort als "Distinctiones" (als ausführlichere Aufgliederungen von Predigten mit vielen Belegen aus der Hl. Schrift) gekennzeichnet ...'

need not be too surprising, for summary sermons often consisted of little more than divisions or distinctions with Scriptural authorities to conform each part or member; apart from the fact that they are not in alphabetical order, they bear a family resemblance to the *distinctiones* genre which has just been discussed.

It is worth dwelling a little on an astonishingly elaborate 'preaching machine' which could be regarded as a combination of the *distinctiones* and the model sermon genres, and which shows again how the boundaries between genres can become blurred. It is not easy to make its workings clear in a short space, but it is worth at least attempting to give some idea of its ingenuity and complexity.[1] The work falls into a number of distinct parts. There is a series of sixty-six Sunday sermons, all full-length, and also another block of long sermons 'on the blessed Virgin Mary and on the saints'. In each of these sermons there is a 'distinction' on a particular word, and one of the key sections of the whole *Summa* consists of an alphabetical list of these seventy-four words, abstracted from the full-length sermons in which they occur.

The rest of the work consists mainly of a large number of 'themes' for different categories of sermon series.[2] There are blocks of biblical texts by themselves, and blocks of biblical texts developed somewhat.[3] Both developed and undeveloped themes are followed by one of the words from the alphabetical list, through which they are linked to the full-length sermons. A preacher would choose a theme (perhaps picking a simple theme first, then turning to the corresponding block of developed themes to find the same text and some analysis of it). After each theme, whether developed or not, he would find a word, which he would look up in the *Index dictionum*, the alphabetical list of words. This in turn would

---

[1] Here I mainly follow Michaud-Quantin, 'Guy d'Évreux' which should be read together with Rouse and Rouse, *Preachers*, pp. 87–90. For the sake of brevity and clarity I oversimplify a little.

[2] For the different sorts of sermon cycle see below.

[3] 'Divisa et concordata'; Michaud-Quantin, 'Guy d'Évreux', p. 222.

direct him to a distinction in one of the full-length sermons. The author even intended the scribe to put beside each word on the alphabetical list the place in the manuscript where the relevant distinction could be found.[1] This was rather a tall order, since the folio number for each distinction would differ from one manuscript to another.

The point of the system was that a limited number of distinctions (in the full-length sermons) could provide material for a much larger number of themes, so that the preacher had a considerable range of choice in picking his theme. Suppose, for instance, that a preacher started from the following passage in the 'themes' section:

First Sunday in the Advent of the Lord. 'For now our salvation is closer to us'; let the sermon be from 'near' (*prope*) or from 'to save' (*salvare*). 'Let us put on the armour of light'; from 'to put on' (*induere*). Let us walk honestly, in the light of day; from 'to walk' (*ambulare*).[2]

If the preacher chose 'Let us put on the armour of light' as his theme, he would turn to the word *induere* in the alphabetical list of words (the *Index dictionum*). The *Index dictionum* would in turn direct him to the appropriate distinction.

The *distinctiones* genre is related to another kind of tool, which seems a less curious invention to us than Guy d'Évreux's elaborate machine, though it too could not have been devised without a good deal of ingenuity. This was the Bible concordance, for which modern scholars have the thirteenth century to thank. Some collections of distinctions could be used like a concordance, to find a number of different Scriptural passages in which a given word occurs. The distinction collections, however, did not attempt to be exhaustive.

A Bible concordance could be used for other purposes than preaching; nevertheless, a concordance was more important

---

[1] Cf. ibid. 221.
[2] Quoted ibid. 222, end of p. 221 n. 18 (my translation).

for preachers than might at first appear. The elaborate sermon form which most preachers had adopted by the second half of the century was easier to follow if some such tool was at hand. It was normal to confirm divisions and subdivisions with one or more Scriptural texts, and with a concordance (or indeed *distinctiones*) a large number of at least superficially appropriate texts could be collected quite easily. I suspect that sometimes preachers collected the texts first and then constructed the divisions around them. It would have been possible to look up one of the words from the theme text in a concordance, write out the other Scriptural passages listed, and then invent a structure to suit them.

During the course of the thirteenth century several concordances were written, for the tool was not perfected immediately.[1] The third concordance to be developed appears to have been much more successful that its predecessors.[2] It was multiplied by the *pecia* system and appears in the list of books made available by this system which has survived from the mid-1270s. The perfection of the concordance and its diffusion by the Paris *pecia* system were not the least important parts of the 'infrastructure' of the preaching of the friars.[3]

A typology of thirteenth-century preaching aids would have to include other genres still. Treatises on virtues and vices must have been another stand-by for preachers in need of material.[4] An important example is the *Liber de virtutibus et vitiis* of Servasanto da Faenza, who has been called 'the greatest moralist of the thirteenth century'.[5] This book is

[1] Its evolution is studied by R. H. and M. A. Rouse, 'The Verbal Concordance to the Scriptures', *Archivum Fratrum Praedicatorum*, 44 (1974), 5–30.

[2] Ibid. 21–2 and 25.

[3] Cf. Rouse and Rouse, *Preachers*, pp. 9–11.

[4] Cf. M. W. Bloomfield, B.-G. Guyot, D. R. Howard, and T. B. Kabealo, *Incipits of Latin Works on the Virtues and Vices, 1100–1500 A.D., including a section of incipits on the Pater Noster* (Medieval Academy of America, 88; Cambridge, Mass., 1979).

[5] 'Per il numero e la mole degli scritti, quasi tutti relativi alla cura pastorale, e per la bontà della dottrina, si può dire che Servasanto era il più grande Moralista del secolo xiii' (P. Livario Oliger, OFM, 'Servasanto da Faenza O.F.M. e il suo "Liber de Virtutibus et Vitiis"', in *Miscellanea Francesco Ehrle*, i. *Per la storia della teologia e della filosofia* (Studi e Testi, 37; Rome, 1924), 148–89, at p. 186).

essentially a preaching handbook,[1] and the epilogue says so explicitly.[2] The *Liber de virtutibus et vitiis* can be regarded as a combination of three different genres: alphabetical distinctions, *exempla* collections, and sermons proper.[3] One is again struck by the fluidity of the boundaries between genres. It has been suggested, however, that it is the very combination of elements from other genres that makes this *Summa* of virtues and vices a distinctive member of its own—different, for instance, from the famous *Summa de vitiis et virtutibus* of Guillaume Peyraut.

Anthologies from earlier writers—*florilegia*—provided yet another sort of help for preachers. One of these, the *Manipulus florum* of Thomas of Ireland (not a friar), has been the subject of a monograph which itself deserves to start a genre, showing as it does how successfully this codicologist's methods may be put to work to demonstrate the use and influence of individual homiletic works.[4] The *Manipulus florum* followed alphabetical order, which keeps turning up in the history of the thirteenth-century preaching movement. On the other hand, the *Liber pharetrae*, whose anonymous author seems to have been a Franciscan writing before 1261, is organized in four books, of which the first is on 'the variety of persons', the second on virtues and vices, etc.[5] The list of chapter-headings for the first book begins with 'On God' and ends with 'On demons', but most of the categories in between are human, so that this first book would have made a good source-book for sermons to different sorts and conditions of men.[6] The author makes it clear that the anthology could be used for several different purposes: meditation and disputation as well as preaching.[7]

---

[1] Ibid. 176. [2] Ibid. 174. [3] Ibid. 176.

[4] Rouse and Rouse, *Preachers.*

[5] '... Distinxi autem opusculum istud per quatuor libros, ut dicatur liber primus de personarum varietate, secundus de principalium vitiorum et virtutum multiplicitate, tertius de periculosis, quartus de gratiosis. In unoquoque libro posui quinquaginta capitula quia talis numerus est iubelei figurativus. ...' (MS BL Royal 8. C. XVI, fo. 169ra).

[6] e.g. 'De studentibus', 'De coniugatis', 'De militibus' (ibid., fo. 170rb).

[7] '... placuit michi ut ad ipsum fontem originalium recurrerem et ob maiorem

Artes praedicandi, treatises on the technique of preaching, are a type of preaching aid on which much has been written.[1] For all the attention that they have received, *artes praedicandi* do not seem to have been as popular as some kinds of preaching aid, if manuscript counts are anything to go by. Relatively small numbers of manuscripts of individual *artes* have been identified. For this genre ten manuscripts represents relative popularity, whereas for a collection of model sermons it would not be a lot; this in spite of the fact that sermon collections are generally rather long, whereas most *artes praedicandi* are short, so that the latter could have been multiplied more quickly. Of course, the manuscript count can be an unreliable guide. Precisely because they are small, *artes praedicandi* more easily remain hidden than sermon collections: it is therefore possible that the existing handlists of *artes praedicandi* may have missed more manuscripts than Schneyer's *Repertorium* of sermons.[2] Furthermore, it may be that time has taken a greater toll of *artes praedicandi*: one may speculate that they had a circulation in the form of booklets, which would have less chance than bound volumes of surviving. With all these reservations, it still seems to me that thirteenth-century manuscripts of *artes praedicandi* are less common than one might expect if they were really staple reading matter for preachers.

However it may be with the *artes praedicandi*, there can be no doubt about the influence of model sermon collections, which may probably be regarded as the most important single genre of preaching aid. The vast majority of thirteenth-century sermons are arranged around the liturgical year. The

---

certitudinem ipsemet aliqua exciperem que postmodum (*corr. from* postmodii?) ut scivi ordinavi, ut que ad meditationem predicationem disputationem ibidem essent utilia levius reperirentur. . . .' (ibid., fo. 169ʳᵃ).

[1] It may be noted here that although these *artes* have received a lot of scholarly attention there are few critical editions of them.

[2] H. Caplan, *Medieval Artes Praedicandi. A Hand-list* (Cornell Studies in Classical Philology, 24; Ithaca, NY, 1934), and *Medieval Artes Praedicandi. A Supplementary Hand-list* (Cornell Studies in Classical Philology, 25; Ithaca, NY, 1936). Cf. Schneyer's *Repertorium*.

great *Repertorium* of Latin sermons divides these into four types of sermon series: *de tempore, de sanctis, de communi sanctorum,* and *de quadragesima.*[1] The last two categories are fairly clear-cut. *De communi sanctorum* sermons are on general classes or types of saints, e.g. 'on one virgin', or 'on several virgins'.[2] *De quadragesima* sermons are sermons for each day of Lent.[3] The other two categories, *de tempore* and *de sanctis,* are not absolutely satisfactory, for some sermon collections are divided up according to a similar but not identical pair of categories, *de dominicis* and *de festis.*[4] There were, in fact, at least two ways of defining the boundary between two broad categories: one could draw the line between sermons for Sundays on the one hand and sermons for saints' days *and* great feasts like Christmas and Epiphany on the other;[5] or, alternatively, one could group the sermons for those great feasts—essentially different in character from feasts for saints—together with the sermons for Sundays, to make a *de tempore* collection complementing a *de sanctis* collection.[6] Whichever way one draws the line between the two categories, they must together account for an overwhelming proportion of thirteenth-century liturgical sermons, and probably of thirteenth-century sermons of any kind.[7]

---

[1] Schneyer, *Repertorium*, i. 4.

[2] For the range of sermons which Schneyer includes in the 'C' category see ibid. p. 21; he includes sermons 'in dedicatione ecclesiae' 'in consecratione altaris', etc.—i.e. sermons 'de occasionibus' as well as 'de communi sanctorum'.

[3] *Quadragesimalia* are far more common in the late Middle Ages. See J. B. Schneyer, 'Winke für die Sichtung und Zuordnung spätmittelalterlicher lateinischer Predigtreihen', *Scriptorium*, 32/2 (1978), 231–48, at p. 232.

[4] Cf. L.-J. Bataillon, 'Approaches to the Study of Medieval Sermons', *Leeds Studies in English*, NS 11 (1980), 19–35, at p. 20.

[5] In this case the categories would be *de dominicis* and *de festis*.

[6] This explains an apparent anomaly in Schneyer's *Repertorium*. He uses the symbol 'T' to indicate a *de tempore* sermon, and 'S' to indicate a *de sanctis* sermon, but sometimes one finds certain 'T' sermons in his list of incipits for cycles of 'S' sermons. See e.g. *Repertorium*, iv, s.v. Nicolaus de Gorran, pp. 283–4, Nos. 412–27, and pp. 286–7, Nos. 465–78 (sermons for the vigil of the Nativity, for the Nativity, for the Circumcision, and for Epiphany). For most practical purposes it does not matter greatly whether one speaks of a *de sanctis* series or a *festivale*, say, and Schneyer's usage will sometimes be a convenient shorthand.

[7] These are impressionistic estimates, but I doubt whether any specialist would disagree.

One genre of non-liturgical sermons, collections directed *ad status*, to a variety of sorts and conditions of men, have an interest for the historian out of proportion to their numbers. In these collections one may find sermons to members of different religious orders, sermons to crusaders, sermons to wives, sermons to merchants, etc. Of course, the selection of categories differs from collection to collection, though there are considerable overlaps. The way or ways in which society is divided up in these collections can itself be illuminating: it tells us much about the social categories of the time, which could be much more sophisticated than the traditional model of three orders (those who labour, those who fight, and those who pray). The individual sermons are full of rich material, which casts some light on social realities and more on mental attitudes.

Another genre which ought to cast much light on the mentality of the age is that of sermons on the dead. Of course, a high percentage of medieval sermons touch on death or the afterlife at some point. Moreover, sermons which bear directly on death or the dead could be integrated into a liturgical or an *ad status* sermon series;[1] but there are also distinct series devoted to the dead: that of Aldobrandino da Toscanella and 'Johannes de Opreno' in the thirteenth century,[2] as well as collections by later writers.[3]

At this point mention may be made of a collection of sermons, or rather of 'collations', which do not fit any one genre, while showing traces of the characteristics of several.

---

[1] Cf. Schneyer, *Repertorium*, i. 180; s.v. Aldobrandinus de Cavalcantibus, Nos. 428–33, and ibid. ii. 304; s.v. Guibertus de Tornaco, Nos. 261–5.

[2] Ibid. i. 246–7, Nos. 298–320 (cf. also p. 245, 'Tractatus pro defunctis'), and 645–56, Nos. 402–604.

[3] There are series of sermons relating to death by Bertrandus de Turre (see ibid. i. 577–83, Nos. 1051–1123); Johannes a S. Geminiano (ibid. iii. 758–65, Nos. 455–552); Jacobus Passavanti(?) (ibid. iii. 158–61, Prolog. and Nos. 1–28); 'Johannes de Neapel' (ibid. iii 605 ff., Nos. 16 ff.); Nicolaus de Asculo (ibid. iv. 215–19, Nos. 115–68); Fridericus de Franconibus (Kaeppeli, *Scriptores*, i. 403, No. 1149: see also Kaeppeli, *Scriptores*, iii. 145, correcting Schneyer's attribution to Nicolaus de Asculo); and Augustinus Triumphus de Ancona (Schneyer, *Repertorium*, i. 374). For the above I for the most part follow Schneyer.

The collection in MS Birmingham University 6/iii/19 looks like a draft of a collection of model sermons, for we find the author addressing himself to the potential user[1] but also referring to his own notebooks in a way that would hardly have been useful to anyone but himself.[2] Some of the collations would fit into a normal liturgical sermon cycle,[3] but there are also collations on less usual themes, such as 'the good woman',[4] 'the republic'[5] and 'war'.[6] The book is a little reminiscent of liturgical collections, a little of *ad status* collections, and a little of *distinctiones*; there is also a small *exemplum* collection attached (as well as many *exempla*, some personal, in the main body of the work). The net result is an individual sort of book, intriguing for historians. A table of its contents would read rather like a list of headings for a history of mentalities in the modern manner. It gives a less oblique reply than most sermon collections of the period do to the sort of questions that historians of attitudes like to ask.[7] By the same token it is untypical. The liturgical collections, much harder to read and more alien to our way of thinking, take us closer to normal middle-brow habits of thought of the period.

So far this section has attempted a rough typology or classification of the different kinds of preaching aid. It should have become clear that genres overlap, which is perhaps what one would expect. Of the various genres, it will be model sermon collections that have the central place in this study.

---

[1] 'Si vis autem huius vitii remedia predicare ut faciliter possis istud vitium vitare, invenies quod . . .' (MS Birmingham University 6/iii/19, fo. cxxxvii^rb).

[2] e.g. '. . . venit ad fratres minores. Require istud exemplum in quaternis vel in libro sermonum. . . .' (ibid., fo. xxxix^rb); '. . . Cum autem omnes pre timore fugissent, sola eius uxor remansit. Require istud exemplum in quaternis vel in alio libro. . . .' (ibid.).

[3] e.g. ibid., fo. cxli^rb, 'De epiphania . . .'.

[4] Ibid., fo. lii^rb.

[5] Ibid., fo. clvi^rb.

[6] Ibid., fo. clx^vb.

[7] I hope to devote a series of studies to this collection; to date see 'Another Friar and Antiquity', in K. Robbins (ed.), *Religion and Humanism* (Studies in Church History, 17; Oxford, 1981), 49–58 (this contains printing errors for which I am not responsible), and 'A Franciscan and History', *Archivum Franciscanum Historicum*, 74 (1981), 456–82.

They give us the best idea of what mendicant sermons were like as a whole. Other genres, generally speaking, provided accessory material which could be fitted into a sermon, so they give us a less balanced idea of the overall structure and pattern of thought.

Before turning to a more detailed examination of model sermons as source and as medium, however, it is worth considering a hypothesis which would put them and the other preaching aids we have discussed in a different perspective. It seems possible that there were two distinct types of preaching to the laity, one elementary and the other in a sense supplementary; and that the genres which have just been described were designed for the second and supplementary type of preaching. The latter is arguably more interesting, and more closely associated with the friars (at least so far as surviving texts go), but it is still important not to assume that there was nothing else. Our interpretation of it must change if it was a superstructure rather than a foundation. The relative infrequency of straightforward catechetical instruction in model sermons becomes more comprehensible if such instruction was given by a more elementary sort of preaching.

If there was a two-tier structure of communication between clergy and laity in the thirteenth century, one might regard it as an anticipation of a system which is clearly defined in seventeenth-century France. By this time we find an explicit distinction between *prônes* and less elementary preaching.[1] *Prônes* set out basic truths of faith and morals in a simple and straightforward manner. As a genre they are easily recognizable in this later period. For the thirteenth century I know of nothing which exactly corresponds to the seventeenth-century collections of *prônes*, but there are works which may have fulfilled a somewhat similar function, priests' manuals in particular.

Here the opening passages of Richard Wetheringsett's

[1] Cf. P. Bayley, *French Pulpit Oratory, 1598-1650. A Study in Themes and Styles, with a Descriptive Catalogue of Printed Texts* (Cambridge, 1980), Appendix 2, p. 300.

Summa 'Qui bene presunt'[1] are suggestive. The priest's duty to instruct is emphasized heavily,[2] and a little later Richard gives a list of what should be preached:

Maxime vero ad fidem et ad mores pertinentia et frequentius predicanda sunt: simbolum fidei, duodecim articulos fidei continens; oratio dominica, vii habens petitiones; dona dei generalia et specialia (*corr. from* spiritualia), specialiter (*corr. from* spiritualiter) vii dona spiritus que enumerat Ysas. xxx° ix° [*sic for Isa. 11*], que sunt sapientia, intellectus, consilium et fortitudo, scientia et pietas et timor; virtutes etiam (tamen *added and deleted in ms*) cardinales iiii°ʳ, que sunt iustitia, prudentia, fortitudo (fortudo *ms*), et temperantia; similiter gratuite et teologice, que sunt fides, spes, caritas. Et precipue predicanda sunt vii capitalia vitia, que sunt superbia, avaritia, tristitia, invidia, ira, gula, luxuria. Similiter innotescenda sunt vii sacramenta, que sunt baptismus, confirmatio, eucaristia, penitentia, ordo, coniugium, extrema unctio. Similiter et duo mandata caritatis, de diligendo deo et proximo. Predicanda sunt x moralia legis, que sunt de uno deo colendo, nomen domini in vanum non assumendo, de (*interlined*) sabbatis, id est festis, observandis, parentibus honorandis, non occidendo, non furtum faciendo, non mecando, non falsum testimonium peribendo, non concupiscendo uxorem proximi tui vel ancillam. Predicandum est etiam [*fo. 222ʳᵇ*] que sit iustorum merces in celo tam in corpore quam in anima, que sit malorum pena in inferno, tam in corpore quam in anima. Instruendi sunt subditi in quibus a multis erratur, quid vitare debeant, scilicet peccatum et consensum peccati et quod a superioribus proibitum est, quid agere debeant, scilicet quod

---

[1] For an introduction to this work and the problems of identifying the author see L. Boyle, 'A Study of the Works Attributed to William of Pagula, with special reference to the *Oculus Sacerdotis* and *Summa Summarum*', unpublished D.Phil. thesis (Oxford, 1956), i. 220 ff., especially n. 68. This thesis is seminal for the whole question of the role of *pastoralia* in the later Middle Ages.

[2] 'Et nota quod sequitur: "maxime qui laborant in verbo et doctrina." [1 Tim. 5: 17] In verbo, id est (id est *interlined*) in exortatione scientium; in doctrina, in (*om. ms*) instructione nescientium. In verbo quo ad mores, in doctrina quo ad fidem. Dicitur enim doctrina quasi trinitatis dogma, quod ad fidem pertinere dinoscitur. Et est "Summa" ut ipsi instructi (*corr. from* structi) populum instruant in fide et moribus. In fide etiam et moribus consistit summa christiane religionis. . . .' (MS BL Royal 4. B. VIII, fo. 222ʳᵃ). There are many manuscripts of the *Summa 'Qui bene presunt'* (see Boyle, 'Study' ii. 20–1) and signs of a complicated tradition. I have chosen this manuscript for convenience and because of its early date (perhaps mid-thirteenth-century).

pertinet ad officium uniuscuiusque vel statum, et maxime quod a
deo vel a superioribus preceptum est.[1]

The things which especially pertain to faith and morals and which
should more frequently be preached are: the symbol of faith [i.e. the
Creed], containing the twelve articles of faith; the Lord's Prayer,
with its seven petitions; the general and special gifts of God,
especially the seven gifts of the Spirit which Isaiah enumerates in
ch. 39 [*sic* for Isa. 11], which are wisdom, understanding, counsel
and fortitude, knowledge and piety and fear; also the four cardinal
virtues, which are justice, prudence, fortitude, and temperance;
similarly, the virtues conferred by grace, or theological virtues,
which are faith, hope, and charity. And one should especially
preach the seven capital vices, which are pride, avarice, sloth
(*tristitia*), envy, anger, gluttony, lust. Similarly, one should make
known the seven sacraments, which are baptism, confirmation, the
Eucharist, penance, holy orders, marriage, extreme unction. Similarly also the two commandments of charity, on loving God and
one's neighbour. One should preach the Ten Commandments,
which are about the worship of one God, not taking the name of the
Lord in vain, the observation of Sabbath days, that is Feast-days,
honouring one's parents, not killing, not stealing, not committing
adultery, not bearing false witness, not coveting one's neighbour's
wife or maidservant. One should also preach about what the reward
of the just is in heaven, with respect to both body and soul, and
what the penalty of the evil is in hell, with respect to both body and
soul. Members of one's flock (*subditi*) should be instructed about
things concerning which many people err; about what they should
avoid, that is, sin and consent to sin and that which is forbidden by
their superiors; about what they ought to do, that is, what pertains
to the function or state of life of each person, and especially that
which is commanded by God or by those with authority over them.

As one turns over the pages of Richard's *Summa* it becomes
clear that this list of things to be preached is a sketch of the
plan of the work as a whole.

The plan is a rational and systematic way of dividing up
the field of faith and morals as understood in the period.

---

[1] MS BL Royal 4 B. VIII, fo. 222[ra-b]. dona dei generalia] *a mark above* dona, *and in
marg., with corresponding marks*, creatio recreatio iustificatio.

Nothing surprising about that: it is just what a preacher would need, one might think. But model sermon collections, as opposed to priests' manuals, are not as a rule organized around this kind of plan in this period. At the level of *de tempore* collections as a whole, the cycle of liturgical readings constitutes the principle of organization. Though it is no longer normal in this period to give a running commentary on the Gospel or Epistle 'pericope' (at least on parchment), a text from these readings was nearly always the springboard for the sermon.[1] Furthermore, within the individual model sermon the treatment seems to be artistic rather than systematic. Ideas are arranged into symmetrical patterns, and the writer does not necessarily stick to a particular point of faith or morals, or try to give a thorough summary of the points he does treat.

By contrast, relevance and a comprehensive if elementary treatment of individual parts of belief are features of a treatise like Richard Wetheringsett's *Summa*. Take, for example, his section on the Eucharist.[2] Not all of it is directed towards preaching,[3] but the bulk of the section could have been used for catechetical preaching. For example, Richard suggests how Christ can be wholly present in each part of a consecrated host after it has been broken by the analogy of the pieces of a broken mirror, each of which reflects the same image that the whole mirror had reflected;[4] he describes how the sacrament strengthens against vices, increases virtues,

---

[1] I do not think that there was a fixed cycle of pericopes for *de sanctis* sermons, but the question has not been properly studied; in any case one would not expect to find a systematic coverage of doctrine in *de sanctis* collections.

[2] MS BL Royal 4. B. VIII, fos. 232rb–233va.

[3] When Richard warns priests about the type of bread and wine which should be used for mass, and the amount of water that should be added to the wine (ibid., fo. 232va), he is presumably writing for priests rather than the people.

[4] In context: 'Hoc sacramentum mirabile est et sigulare [*sic*]. Quia mirabile, non potest ratio de eo assignari plena; quia sigulare est, non potest perfectum exemplum assignari. Qualecumque tamen exemplum ponit Augustinus, scilicet de speculo. Cum forma oblate est integra, sub totali forma est totale corpus, et non sub partibus forme partes corporis. Si frangatur forma, sub singulis particulis erit totale corpus. Simile est videre in speculo. Cum integra est, una est forma. Si frangitur, sub qualibet (quelibet *ms*) particula forma est integra. Potest et qualiscumque ratio assignari. [*fo. 232va*] Quid enim mirum si idem corpus Christi totum integrum sit in multis altaribus,

etc.;[1] and he draws up a symmetrical series of oppositions between the properties of the wafers used for Mass and the 'seven mortal sins'.[2] Richard touches on many other aspects of the sacrament, perhaps most notably the prefiguring of it in the Old Testament, a theme to which he devotes a large proportion of the whole section.[3] It is difficult to say how much of all this was meant for the edification and education of priests, and how much for catechetical preaching, and how far the author bothered to distinguish the functions of one passage from another. Perhaps he felt that in aiming in a general way at the theological formation of his clerical readers, he was indirectly ensuring that they would be able to preach about the basics of faith and morals. Once they had the essentials in their mind,[4] they would know what was appropriate for the laity when preaching. We may note, however, that at one point near the beginning of the section he is explicit about what the laity should be told: 'Concerning this sacrament the laity are to be instructed in a simple way that they should firmly believe that the body and blood of Christ are transubstantiated from bread and wine, when a priest pronounces in the Church's form the transubstantiating words, that is: "This is my body", and "This is the chalice", etc.'[5]

---

cum eadem vox tota resultat in multorum auribus, eadem lux in multorum intuentium oculis, anima tota secundum philosophum in qualibet parte corporis' (ibid., fo. 232rb–va).

[1] '... et sic retine: Roborat, aumentat hoc sacramentum delet et unit. Roborat contra vitia. Aumentat virtutes. Delet venialia. Unit etiam amplius Christo. Sicut enim cibus materialis per os (*corr. from* hos *or* hec?) perceptus vivificat et vegetat omnia menbra in corpore aderentia, sic debita perceptio sacramenti, (*ms. adds and deletes* sicut) omnia membra capiti Christo aderentia. Unde et bene sanctorum communia dicitur. . . .' (ibid., fo. 232va).

[2] 'Signanter etiam conficitur corpus Christi de oblata. Illius enim proprietates inspecte, opponuntur vii peccatis mortalibus. Est enim alba contra luxuriam, que feda est; tenuis contra gulam, que multa appetit . . .' (ibid., fo. 232vb).

[3] Ibid., fo. 232vb–233va.

[4] To make doubly sure that they would, he frequently sums up a piece of exposition with a mnemonic.

[5] 'De hoc sacramento simpliciter instruendi sunt laici quod firmiter credant corpus Christi et sanguinem de pane et vino transsubstantiari, cum a sacerdote in forma ecclesie proferuntur verba transsubstantialia, scilicet: Hoc est corpus meum, et: Hic

The treatment of the Eucharist in the anonymous *Speculum iuniorum*[1] is another example of preaching material in a place where the historian of preaching might not think of looking. There is a good deal which would probably serve only for the enlightenment of the priest himself, but other parts could have been used for pastoral instruction. The author describes the excellence of the Eucharist, and compares it with other sacraments.[2] After this he explains the name 'Eucharist', giving its etymology (more or less correctly) and commenting on it.[3] The third part is on the institution of the sacrament. It mentions the foreshadowing of the sacrament in the Old Testament, the Last Supper, and the reasons for the institution of the Eucharist.[4] The fourth part of the analysis is important, for it includes a statement of the doctrine of transubstantiation.[5] The remaining two sections, 'On the reception of the Eucharist'[6] and 'On the cases which can come up concerning this sacrament',[7] complete what is a remarkably comprehensive summary of dogmatic and practical aspects of the Eucharist.

No doubt similar preaching material could be found in many other priests' manuals.[8] But explicitly pastoral manuals

---

est calix, et cetera. . . .' (MS cit., fo. 232[rb]). Richard goes on to say that the priest should not elevate the host before he has pronounced the words of consecration. He then says that the laity should be instructed: 'quod se prosternant et dominum suum adorant, et si non aliquam (aliquem *ms?*) orationem habeant specialem, simbolum decantant' (ibid.). The assumption that the laity would know the Creed should be noted. After telling clerics what they can say at the consecration, Richard adds that the laity—he seems to be speaking of them again—should be instructed on how they should show reverence when communion was carried to the sick through the streets. He does not make it clear how much of this instruction he thinks should be imparted from the pulpit.

[1] Also English, and written *c*.1250: see Boyle, 'Study', i. 237.
[2] Oxford, MS Bodleian, Bodley 655, fo. 81[v].
[3] Ibid., fos. 81[v]–82[r].
[4] Ibid., fos. 82[r]–83[r].
[5] This fourth section, 'De confectione', begins MS cit., fo. 83[r]. The section in which transubstantiation is discussed begins on fo. 84[r].
[6] 'De sumptione eucharistie' (begins ibid., fo. 87[r]).
[7] 'De casibus qui possunt contingere circa hoc sacramentum' (begins ibid., fo. 89[v]).
[8] At least for England. For the Continent we do not have a survey like Boyle's 'Study'.

of this genre are not the only sort of work in which material for catechetical preaching may lie concealed from the modern historian's view. Any short simple treatise dealing with faith or morals could be regarded as a potential aid for catechetical preaching.

An example would be the little work 'On the Articles of Faith and the Sacraments of the Church' which Aquinas wrote for the Archbishop of Palermo.[1] The first part of the section on the Eucharist, for instance, fits basic doctrine on the sacrament in a nutshell—well under 300 words—in such a way that a priest who had studied it could have passed it on from the pulpit.[2] The following passage gives the flavour:

> ... the effect of this sacrament is twofold. One of them consists in the actual consecration of the sacrament: for by virtue of the words quoted above the bread is changed into the body of Christ, and the wine into his blood; in such a way, however, that Christ in his entirety is contained under the appearances (*speciebus*) of bread, which remains without a subject, and Christ in his entirety is contained under the appearances of wine; and in each part, once separated, of the consecrated host, or the consecrated wine, there is Christ in his entirety. But another effect of this sacrament, which it produces in the soul of one who receives it worthily, is the uniting of man to Christ ...[3]

A priest who chose to borrow this passage for use in a catechetical sermon on the Eucharist might have to drop the phrase 'which remain without a subject', but otherwise it would serve him well.

It is instructive to compare these presentations of Eucharistic teaching with two sermons from a Franciscan model sermon collection, the one known as *Legifer* or the *Collationes fratrum*.[4] The titles written into a very early manuscript of the

---

[1] *Opera Omnia*, ed. Fretté, xxvii (Vives edn., Paris, 1875), 171–82.

[2] The second half of the section deals with errors concerning the Eucharist, and does not look so much like potential preaching material.

[3] Op. cit. 179–80.

[4] Cf. D. L. d'Avray, '"Collectiones Fratrum" and "Collationes Fratrum"', *Archivum Franciscanum Historicum*, 70 (1977), 152–6.

work[1] describe the subjects of the sermons as 'On the body of Christ and its effect/efficacy'[2] and 'On the paschal banquet [*or* banquets] to the faithful'.[3] They are structurally elegant, but eclectic. Direct and explicit exposition of the doctrine of transubstantiation is conspicuous by absence—not, I would suggest, because it was too difficult, but because it was taken for granted. Equally significant is what might appear to be a failure to stick to one subject. The first main section of the first sermon is brought to an end, after a few lines, with a cross-reference to an earlier sermon which is not about the Eucharist at all.[4] A good deal of the second sermon is not on the Eucharist either: the first and third sections of the first part deal respectively with the 'banquet of carnal persons' and the eternal banquet of the blessed.[5] It would probably be missing the point to see this as a sermon on communion with a low level of relevance. It might be nearer the mark to see the sermon as a pattern of ideas, designed to appeal aesthetically, in which the Eucharist figures prominently but in which other motifs are brought in to balance it. If we regard model

[1] Clm. 7932 (mid-thirteenth-century?). I do not know whether the compiler was responsible for the titles.

[2] Ibid., fo. 145[va]: 'De corpore domini et eius effectu', with 'efficacia' interlined. The sermon is Schneyer, *Repertorium*, vii. 5, No. 58.

[3] *MS* cit., fo. 146[ra]: 'De epulis paschalibus, ad fideles'. The sermon is Schneyer, *Repertorium*, vii. 5, No. 59.

[4] 'Primum est digna ad corpus dominicum recipiendum preparatio, et quantum ad hoc dicitur: Sanctificamini. . . . Circa primum attendendum est quod fidelis quilibet sanctificare et purificare se ipsum debet . . . De hac autem sanctificatione [*col. b*] require plenius supra in primo sermone dominice secunde in quadragesima' (MS cit., fo. 145[va-b]). The cross-reference must be to a sermon on the text 'Hec est voluntas dei', Schneyer, *Repertorium*, vii. 4, No. 44, fo. 139[va] in this manuscript, with the heading 'De sanctificatione fidelium . . .'.

[5] 'Primo invitat ad communicandum et idcirco dicitur: Epulemur. . . . Circa primum attendendum est quod triplex distinguitur epularum genus. Sunt enim epule scilicet: Carnalium. . . . Iustorum et iste sunt sacramentales epule que in corporis et sanguinis dei refectione consistunt. . . . Beatorum et iste fiunt [*sic*] eternales . . .' (MS cit., fo. 146[ra]). I would only tentatively interpret the second main part of the sermon as dealing with the Eucharist. In the initial division it is announced thus: 'Secundo assignat communicandi modum . . .' (fo. 146[ra]), but the actual treatment is so abstract that it might fit a variety of contexts: 'Circa secundum considerandum est quod . . . duplicem . . . distin|guit [*col. b*] apostolus epulandi modum. Primus consistit in remotione mali. Triplex autem malum debet quilibet removere a se ut epuletur digne, scilicet: Elationem (*corr. in ms?*) superbie . . . Cupiditatem avaritie . . . Voluptatem luxurie . . . Secundus consistit in positione boni. . . .' (MS cit., fo. 146[ra-b]).

sermons like these as quasi-artistic creations rather than as summaries of basic teaching, they make more sense; and the failure to bring home basic beliefs in a straightforward way seems less serious once we assume that the job was left to other genres.[1]

Model sermon collections are therefore one among a variety of genres designed to be or usable as preaching aids. Precisely because they are written as sermons, however, they probably give us a better idea than any other genre of the forms of thought which were embodied in mendicant preaching, and it is with model sermons that the rest of this study will be principally concerned. But these collections cannot be used as sources before we have faced the question of their language, transmission, and audience. It will be evident that these problems are bound up with the whole question of how sermons functioned as a quasi-mass medium during this period.

ii. The Problem of Language

Everyone knows that the friars were the most successful popular preachers of the thirteenth century, and it is at first sight surprising that so few of their sermons survive in the vernacular. For Italy, there is the corpus of sermons by Giordano da Pisa at the beginning of the fourteenth century,[2] but nothing of the kind before. The historian of French vernacular preaching before 1300 has noted the conspicuous absence of mendicant collections.[3]

---

[1] At least so far as England is concerned the 'crypto-preaching aids' which did the job—priest's manuals and any other types that can be identified—should be studied in conjunction with conciliar legislation. Cf. especially F. M. Powicke and C. R. Cheney, *Councils and Synods with other Documents relating to the English Church* (Oxford, 1964), ii, Part II, pp. 900–5. I have benefited from discussion of these ideas with Helen Spencer, Vincent Gillespie, and Nicole Bériou.

[2] 'In Italia occurre attendere l'alba del XIV secolo per trovare la prima ampia documentazione in volgare nel *corpus* delle prediche di fra Giordano da Pisa' (C. Delcorno, *La predicazione nell'età comunale* (Florence, 1974), p. 4.)

[3] Zink, *La Prédication*, p. 126: '... durant tout le XIIIᵉ siècle, presque aucun sermon conservé en langue romane ne porte l'empreinte des ordres mendiants'; again, ibid. 127: '... les ordres mendiants, jusqu'aux dernières années du XIIIᵉ siècle,

Thirteenth-century England seems to have produced relatively few sermon collections in any language, by comparison with France or to a lesser extent Italy or Germany.[1] For later medieval England it has been argued that 'writing-out of sermons . . . in Latin may well be an important mark of the friar's exclusiveness'.[2] Very few prose vernacular sermons definitely by friars have survived from the thirteenth century, and many or most of the mendicant or allegedly mendicant verse 'sermons' from the thirteenth century or after may not be sermons at all in the proper sense of the word: it is very hard to rule out the possibility that they were meant to be read by the literate rather than preached to the people.[3]

German vernacular sermons are a difficult case. There are a large number of them from the thirteenth century.[4] We

n'ont produit ni recueils de sermons types ni recueils de lectures édifiantes en français.'

[1] On English preaching in this period see J. Sweet, 'English Preaching 1221–1293' unpublished B.Litt. thesis (Oxford, n.d.), and also her 'Some Thirteenth-Century Sermons and their Authors', *Journal of Ecclesiastical History*, 4 (1953), 27–36. G. R. Owst's *Preaching in Medieval England* (Cambridge University Press, 1926) and *Literature and Pulpit in Medieval England* (2nd. edn., Oxford, 1961) deal mainly with a later period.

[2] Owst, *Preaching*, p. 227.

[3] Both on prose and verse sermons H. G. Pfander's *The Popular Sermon of the Medieval Friar in England* (New York, 1937) needs to be used with caution. There are some good things in it, but the title is misleading: the book has little to say about the Latin sermons which constitute the overwhelming bulk of the evidence for popular preaching. The only clear-cut example he gives of a thirteenth-century prose sermon written in English and associated with the friars (it is in MS Cambridge, Trinity 43, 'a Dominican manuscript of the thirteenth century') is the *Atte Wrastlinge:* see Pfander, ibid. 52. As for verse sermons, Pfander seems to me to assume too readily that they were actually to be preached. His arguments are not easy to follow (because of the vagueness of his cross-references). A principal one is that Alain de Lille condemned 'rhythmorum melodias et consonantias metrorum': cf. Pfander, ibid. 21 and 22 n. 14. This sort of condemnation, which was or became a topos, probably refers to *prose d'art*, perhaps especially rhyming *distinctiones*, which were common in prose sermons from the later twelfth century on. At any rate, one cannot assume that Alain had rhymed vernacular sermons in mind. The thirteeenth-century examples which Pfander gives (he ranges over a longer period in chapter II, which extends to only twenty four pages) need to be examined on their individual merits, to determine (1) whether the 'sermon' was definitely by a friar, and (2) whether it had been preached or was meant to be preached. Pfander's 'final proofs that a work is a sermon in finished form' (ibid. 28 n. 34) do not strike me as conclusive criteria.

[4] For a bibliography of those in print see K. Morvay and D. Gruber ['unter Leitung von Kurt Ruh'], *Bibliographie de deutschen Predigt des Mittelalters*.

should, however, be wary about assimilating these to the model sermons with which this study is concerned. It has been argued that the rise of the mendicant orders coincided with the appearance of a new sort of sermon collection, namely, books for pious reading, and especially for reading by women in religious communities.[1] The flowering of German vernacular sermons was first and foremost a feature of the close relationship between the mendicant orders and female religious communities which gives the history of German spirituality in the later Middle Ages a fervent and emotional flavour of its own—especially, of course, after Eckhart. At least some and possibly most German versions of Berthold von Regensburg's sermons seem to have been reading matter for women in religious communities, though there is no way of proving that it was for this purpose that the sermons were originally translated (not by Berthold himself) from the Latin.[2] Two manuscripts (both fifteenth-century) containing pieces by Berthold in German do indeed seem to be 'pastoral handbooks',[3] and, moreover, the thirteenth

---

Veröffentlichte Predigten (Münchener Texte und Untersuchungen zur deutschen Literatur des Mittelalters, 47; Munich, 1974), especially pp. 37–68. For an important discussion of how German vernacular sermons in general came to be written down see P.-G. Völker, 'Die Überlieferungsformen mittelalterlicher deutscher Predigten', *Zeitschrift für deutsches Altertum und deutsche Literatur*, 92 (1963), 212–27.

[1] '... Dennoch zeichnet sich mit der Entstehung der neuen Orden und dem Aufkommen der geistlichen Frauengemeinschaften ein Wandel im Gebrauch volkssprachlicher Predigtsammlungen ab....' (D. Richter, *Die deutsche Überlieferung der Predigten Bertholds von Regensburg* (Münchener, Texte und Untersuchungen zur deutschen Literatur des Mittelalters, 21; Munich, 1969), 213); '... die geschriebene Predigt erfüllt jetzt andere Funktionen. Sie ist zur bevorzugten Lektüre in den Kreisen frommer Laien, besonders geistlicher Frauen geworden' (ibid. 214).

[2] Richter argues that 'die Predigten der *Z-Gruppe schon in früher Zeit klösterliche Lesepredigten einer weiblichen Ordensgemeinschaft waren...' and that 'Für die Sammlungen X^{III}, X^{I}, und Y^{III} liess sich aufgrund des Inhalts und einzelner Wendungen ein Publikum geistlicher Frauen wahrscheinlich machen. Auch dort wird die Sammlung als Lesestoff gedient haben' (ibid. 217). He seems (ibid. 216–17) to imply that the X^{I} collection was also meant to be read rather than used for preaching, though his arguments here might possibly be open to question. According to Richter the majority of the 'einzelnen Handschriften' were also for reading, including three manuscripts which were made for members of the secular nobility: see ibid. 218–19. For the two manuscripts which he judges to be pastoral handbooks see ibid. 218.

[3] Ibid.

century does not mark a break in a continuous and old tradition of German vernacular sermons designed to be preached rather than read.[1] An important example is the so-called 'Schwarzwälder Prediger', who wrote about 1300 and who may have been a Franciscan.[2] Thus, I would not go so far as to assert that popular mendicant sermons are not transmitted in the vernacular, particularly since recent German research has taken the form of studies of the manuscript tradition of particular works rather than of synthesis, so that a general judgement would be premature. Yet it seems to me that the safer prima-facie assumption, when faced with a thirteenth-century mendicant sermon in German, would be that it was for nuns rather than ordinary lay people, and for reading rather than for preaching.

Where, then, are the popular sermons of the medieval friars? The consensus of reliable scholars who have worked in the field is that such sermons have survived in very large numbers, but in Latin. At first sight this seems paradoxical, and in the later nineteenth century there was a somewhat acrimonious controversy between two French scholars, Lecoy de la Marche and Hauréau, about the language in which such popular Latin sermons were delivered. Hauréau appears to have believed that it was quite normal to preach to lay people in Latin. He did not convince many scholars, but in recent years a sophisticated version of his interpretation has been revived by Lucia Lazzerini,[3] mainly with reference to late medieval Italy. Her main concern is with macaronic preaching, sermons in a mixture of Latin and the vernacular.

Research has not yet closed the question of whether macaronic sermons were preached 'live'.[4] It may be that

[1] Ibid. 213.
[2] Cf. ibid. 213. For a general study, G. Stamm, *Studien zum 'Schwarzwälder Prediger'* Medium Aevum, 18; (Munich, 1969). For the argument that he was Franciscan, W. Williams-Krapp, 'Das Gesamtwerk des sog. "Schwarzwälder Predigers"', *Zeitschrift für deutsches Altertum*, 107 (1978), 50–80, at pp. 64–5.
[3] '"Per Latinos Grossos..." Studio sui sermoni mescidati', *Studi di filologia italiana*, 29 (1971), 219–339. Note her approving comments, (p. 222 n. 2) about Hauréau's theory.
[4] Lazzerini does not draw a sharp enough distinction between evidence that

future investigations will show that some mixture of languages was not uncommon, at least when the congregation
included both lay people and clerics.[1] Comparisons between
northern Europe and Italy—where a substantial minority of
laymen had a training in Latin—would be one of the possible
lines of enquiry. The interest of the problem of macaronic
preaching should not, however, distract us from the central
issue of whether or not sermons were a normal method of
conveying ideas to ordinary laymen and women in the
thirteenth century. For if we leave aside special groups like
Italian lawyers and notaries, we may be sure that communication was not the function if Latin was the medium.

Fortunately, we are not driven to this conclusion. The
theory that sermons were regularly delivered entirely or
almost entirely in Latin to congregations consisting entirely
or almost entirely of lay people may be excluded. (Italy might
possibly turn out to be an exception which proves the rule,
since there many laymen knew Latin.) That the friars
achieved their undoubted successes by preaching in a
language which their audience could not understand is so
wildly implausible that the onus of proof is on those who
propose it.[2] Since we have explicit evidence that many
sermons were preached in the vernacular and written down in

---

written macaronic sermons were a conscious literary genre (a theory for which she
makes a good case) and evidence that they were delivered 'live' in this way. Here she
seems to be on much weaker ground. However, not all her evidence for 'live'
macaronic preaching can be dismissed out of hand: see especially ibid. 241 and
245–6.

[1] Even Lecoy de la Marche thought that there were circumstances in which 'des
fragments latins plus ou moins considérables, empruntés d'ordinaire à un livre saint'
might have been said in Latin and then translated or explained in the vernacular (*La
Chaire française au Moyen Âge* . . . (2nd. edn., Paris, 1886), 253–4), and he seems to
have admitted that exceptions to his rule that macaronic sermons were not preached
'live' might yet be found (ibid. 257). There are passages from Berthold von
Regensburg which could be taken to imply macaronic preaching: see A. Schönbach,
'Studien zur Geschichte der altdeutschen Predigt. Fünftes Stück: die Überlieferung
der Werke Bertholds von Regensburg, II', *Sitzungsberichte der philosophisch-
historischen Klasse der kaiserlichen Akademie der Wissenschaften* [Vienna], 152/7,
(1906), 1–112 at pp. 66–7, 71, 94.

[2] Lecoy de la Marche, *La Chaire*, pp. 259–66, is still worth reading.

Latin,[1] common sense compels one to think, in the absence of evidence to the contrary, that it was the same with other popular sermons which have been transmitted to us in Latin;[2] and the sermon collections with which this study is concerned are all transmitted in Latin. Small pieces of French—proverbs or translations of the Latin divisions—are embedded in the text of some sermons. These islets in a sea of Latin were probably designed to help the user with the job of translating.[3]

The overwhelming advantage of Latin as the language of model sermon collections was that it could be translated into any vernacular. Their usefulness was not restricted to one language or dialect area. The collections produced at or diffused from Paris could be used by a friar or any priest with reasonable Latin in Denmark or Spain or Poland. The veil between the historian and the sermons as actually preached to the laity is thicker because the language of transmission is Latin. This does not reduce their value as evidence: it simply means that they are evidence for a system of communication rather than for the direct religious experience of the laity. The Latin with which the historian works should constantly remind him that the system was international, and that the sermons of the friars are not best studied within the framework of histories of preaching in one or another country. Latin transmission made mendicant preaching one of the common factors shared by the cultures of different regions.

---

[1] See now Bataillon, 'Approaches', pp. 22–4.

[2] Sermons to clerics could naturally be preached in Latin, though this was not always the case: cf. ibid. 25. Sermons to nuns would probably be in the vernacular.

[3] It will be argued below that model sermon collections other than *ad status* series may not always have been intended for a specific category of audience, though they would in practice have most often been used for popular preaching. It follows that they could have been preached in Latin to a clerical audience, or 'macaronically' to a mixed congregation of lay people and clerics, but that they would most often have been preached to ordinary lay congregations entirely in the vernacular, apart perhaps from the *auctoritates*.

iii. The Problem of Transmission

These Latin sermons were transmitted throughout Europe in manuscript books, a type of manuscript different in kind from archival documents. The model sermon collections studied here would presumably have been printed in the thirteenth century if printing had been invented. Though copied by hand, they were put into general circulation, and we can legitimately speak of their being 'published'. The problem of transmission is to identify the stages a text could go through before it reached its public. This problem has evident connections with that of the audience and function of model sermons, and it would have been equally logical to treat the two questions in the reverse order.

It should immediately be said that these are problems which will probably not be cleared up finally without monographs on or, ideally, critical editions of individual collections. The conclusions of the present more general study must have a provisional character. I have tried to take in all the thirteenth-century friars who wrote model sermon collections when based at Paris, or whose sermon collections were diffused by the Paris University 'stationers',[1] but I have worked on only one or two manuscripts for each preacher (except in a few cases), and read a sample of his sermons only. It is fair that the reader should be aware of this, for one cannot be confident about the transmission of a given sermon collection without studying all or at least a large selection of the manuscripts; and again, unless one studies every sermon in a given collection one can miss clues to the nature of the original audience of individual sermons or the intended audience of the collection as a whole. Nevertheless, the subjects of transmission and audience are too important to be ignored, and it is possible to make generalizations with a high degree of probability.

---

[1] It would be rash to claim that I have missed nobody who comes into those categories, and of course, on the other hand, I have worked a good deal on sermon collections which fall outside them, but which provide a wider context.

The recent critical edition of the *Sermones dominicales* of St Bonaventura provides a more secure base for generalizations about transmission than had been available hitherto.[1] A summary of the history of this particular collection may be a clearer way into the problem than an abstract analysis would be. The various stages that these sermons went through illustrate the differences between sermons preserved by the notes of a listener (*reportatio*), sermons put into general circulation as a 'model' collection, and the subsequent use of material from the collection by scribes who did not choose to reproduce it in its entirety.

Bonaventura's collection of 'Sunday sermons' are ultimately derived from sermons preached 'live' in various places, including Paris.[2] According to the reconstruction by the most recent editor, these sermons were taken down as *reportationes* by Marco da Montefeltro, together with many others. The original *reportationes* of Marco have not been found, but a Paris and a Milan manuscript contain sermons copied from them in an abbreviated form.[3] Bonaventura selected a sermon for each Sunday from the *reportationes* and reworked them, drawing on his exegetical and theological works, to form a collection designed to help preachers.[4] Hence the 'Sunday sermons', now edited separately. The work of revising the 'reported' version may have been done by Bonaventura himself; alternatively, he may have entrusted the task to Marco. In any case, the 'Sunday sermons' were, so to speak, published—put into general circulation. In a later age this would have been a printed edition. They were meant

---

[1] *Sancti Bonaventurae Sermones dominicales*, ed. J. G. Bougerol (Bibliotheca Franciscana Scholastica Medii Aevi, cura PP. Collegii S. Bonaventurae, 27; Grottaferrata, 1977). Another valuable tool for the study of transmission is vol. vi of the *Catalogue général des manuscrits latins* (Paris, 1975) of the Bibliothèque Nationale. This volume covers a large number of sermon collections, and the detailed descriptions of them set a standard for future cataloguers of sermons to emulate.

[2] Only in a few cases do we know the date and place at which sermons in the 'definitive edition' were originally preached. See Bougerol's edition, pp. 27–9.

[3] Ibid. 20–3.

[4] Ibid. 17–30, especially p. 17 and 23; also p. 127.

to be copied in a standardized form and often were so copied. However, there was nothing to stop people departing from the standardized form by taking one or more sermons from the collection and putting them together with sermons by other authors; when doing so there was nothing to stop them altering the text as well.[1] Sermons borrowed from the 'published' text are often mere schemas or résumés.[2]

There is thus an essential difference between sermons put into general circulation as a collection by their author and sermons transmitted by *reportatio*.[3] Such collections intended for general circulation may derive from *reportationes*, or indeed from the preacher's own notes, but they acquire a different literary identity when 'published'.

A successful 'published' collection will be found as a coherent corpus, with a more or less standardized text, in a large number of manuscripts. To judge by the number of surviving manuscripts containing the definitive corpus of Bonaventura's 'Sunday sermons', it was only a moderately successful collection.[4] Nor does it appear to have been diffused by the Paris University *pecia* system.

The *pecia* system at Paris was an efficient way of rapidly producing standardized copies of sermon collections, as well as of other types of preaching aid, and of more obviously academic works. The general working of the system has been well summarized in a model study of the transmission of a preaching aid:

A Parisian university stationer produced an exemplar of a work in demand. The exemplar in theory, but evidently not often in

---

[1] '... ou est-il au contraire, un texte rédigé après coup, d'après la "reportatio" de Marc de Montefeltro, un texte tellement remanié sous la direction de saint Bonaventure qu'il ne fut jamais prêché comme tel, mais qu'il représente une œuvre dédiée par l'auteur aux prédicateurs; ceux-ci ne sont pas faits faute de recopier, de raccourcir ou d'allonger selon leurs besoins, ce qu'ils lisaient' (ibid. 23). Bougerol makes it clear that he considers this hypothesis to be the true one.

[2] Cf. ibid. p. 25–6, 53.

[3] On *reportatio* of sermons see Bataillon, 'Approaches', pp. 21–2, and N. Bériou, 'La Prédication au béguinage de Paris pendant l'année liturgique 1272–1273', *Recherches Augustiniennes*, 13 (1978), 105–229, at pp. 111–16.

[4] For the manuscripts containing the corpus see Bougerol's edition, pp. 31–42.

practice, was an authoritative text, representing a carefully written and scrupulously corrected copy of the author's autograph or his fair copy. This exemplar was written in quires of four or eight folios, called *peciae*, which were numbered in sequence and were left separated, instead of being bound as a codex. Any scholar who wanted a copy of the work, rented, or had a scribe rent, the exemplar from the stationer, one or more *peciae* at a time—a practice which permitted several copies at varying stages of completion to be made concurrently.[1]

Here we have a type of transmission not so very different—in effect if not in method—from publication by printing.

On the other hand, collections published with or without the help of the *pecia* system were fair game for anyone who wished to depart from the standardized version, as we have already seen in the case of Bonaventura's corpus of Sunday sermons. There were various ways in which this could happen, so that only the main variables can be given here. One way of departing from the standardized version was to break up the corpus, to fragment the collection. One could simply omit many or most sermons from a collection or collections.[2] Again, one could mingle sermons from different collections to make a compilation (without necessarily altering the text of the individual sermons, though there was nothing to stop one doing this too). MS BN lat. 3737 combines sermons from collections by a number of preachers whose names will crop up again in the course of this study: Jean de la Rochelle, Nicolas de Biard, Guibert de Tournai, Luca da Bitonto, Thomas Lebreton, and Pierre de Saint-Benoît.[3] MS BN lat. 3731 has a similar mixture of sermons

---

[1] Rouse and Rouse, *Preachers*, p. 170.

[2] For example, in MS BN lat. 3574, fos. 25^r–41^r, there is a 'série très incomplète de sermons extraits des recueils *Abjiciamus* pour les dimanches et *Suspendium* pour les saints...' of Guillaume de Mailly (*Catalogue*, p. 256). For the rest of the manuscript see ibid. 256–9.

[3] MS BN lat. 3737 is described ibid. 678–84. Note the sermon by 'Guillelmus de Lexi' (see ibid. 679), who was at Paris c. 1267–78, and who achieved the position of Regent Master in Theology (see Kaeppeli, *Scriptores Ordinis Praedicatorum Medii Aevi*, II (Rome, 1975) 109). There are many unidentified sermons in the manuscript. MS BN lat. 3737 is a characteristic example of the genre of small portable preacher's

by different authors: Gauthier d'Aquitaine, Guibert de Tournai, Guillaume de Mailly, Thomas Lebreton, Pierre de Saint-Benoît, Jean de la Rochelle, and (very strongly represented) Konrad Holtnicker,[1] as well as anonymous sermons.[2] In MS BN lat. 3740[3] one sermon from the collection of Nicolas de Byard is found among otherwise anonymous sermons.[4] It seems quite likely that MS Reims 585 is a compilation, containing not only the collection of Pierre de Saint-Benoît but also a certain number of pieces from other writers of sermons, among them Nicolas de Biard.[5] In the *de tempore* collection which goes under the name of 'Graeculus' we find Konrad Holtnicker, Jacopo da Varazze and the so-called 'Peregrinus' represented.[6] This is interesting because the 'Graeculus' *de tempore* collection was itself in general circulation. (The other composite collections—in the Reims and Bibliothèque Nationale manuscripts—which have just been discussed were more probably made for the personal use

books discussed above (I. iii). It measures 150 × 100 mm. There is calendar evidence to connect the manuscript with the Franciscan order. For example, a sermon on the text 'Homo quidam erat dives' (Luke 16: 19) is assigned to the eighth Sunday after Pentecost (see MS cit., fo. 60[r]), which fits the calendar of the Franciscans and the Roman *Curia* but not the calendar of the Paris seculars and Dominicans. (The latter two shared either the same or nearly the same cycle of Gospel and Epistle readings). There are other calendar indications of the same kind which suggest that the manuscript was written by or for the use of a Franciscan.

[1] *Catalogue*, pp. 630–8.

[2] MS BN lat. 3731 is another pocket-book (140 × 100 mm.), and it too is probably Franciscan: in a table of contents (fo. c[v]) a sermon on a text from Matt. 11 is implicitly assigned to the second Sunday of Advent. It was on this Sunday that the Franciscans read the pericope in which the text occurs, but according to the Paris secular/Dominican calendar it was read a week later. Similarly, a text from Phil. 4 is assigned to the third Sunday, in accordance with the calendar of the Franciscans and Roman *Curia* but not the Paris secular/Dominican one. This evidence amounts to a high probability that the table was composed by a Franciscan.

[3] See *Catalogue*, pp. 693–7; this is a fourteenth-century manuscript.

[4] Ibid. 694 (MS BN lat. 3740, fos. 46[r]–49[v]). There is also a sermon attributed (by Schneyer) to Jacques de Lausanne (MS cit., fos. 145[r]–149[r]), though the editors of the *Catalogue* (p. 696) are cautious about this attribution.

[5] L.-J. Bataillon, 'Sur quelques sermons de Saint Bonaventure', in *S. Bonaventura 1274–1974*, ii. *Studia de vita, mente, fontibus et operibus Sancti Bonaventurae* (Grottaferrata, 1974), 495–515, at p. 498. Bataillon does not firmly commit himself to this view.

[6] Schneyer, *Beobachtungen*, p. 44 (on Clm. 4791). Cf. Schneyer, *Repertorium*, ii. 206–20, Nos. 1, 2, 6, 7, 9, 16, 20, 35, 43, 59, 71, etc.

of one individual. Admittedly, it would not be easy to prove this decisively.) It should be said, however, that the equations between sermons by 'Graeculus' and by Konrad Holtnicker and others which are indicated in Schneyer's *Repertorium* do not necessarily apply to the entire sermon. Strictly speaking, they tell us only that the incipits (the opening sentence or two) of the sermons in question are identical. In fact, the author of the 'Graeculus' sermons seems to have used other collections with discretion: sometimes he borrows the plan or part of it, sometimes the development as well.[1] He took what was useful from his source, shortening or lengthening it as he thought fit.[2]

This leads us to the other main way in which copies of a sermon collection could depart from the standardization, namely alterations of the text itself within individual sermons. Manuscripts containing sermons of Jean de la Rochelle, a Franciscan Paris master of the first half of the thirteenth century, are a good illustration of this, since a selection of them have been edited and studied in a scholarly manner.[3] It is clear that there was a standardized text. The editor was able to say of a number of the manuscripts, 'Many times we may go through almost a column of transcription and collating without any variant occurring. Such variants as do occur, are in the main omissions or minor changes of text.'[4] Two of the manuscripts he uses, on the other hand, behave very differently. In MS Ragusi 190[5] the variants 'oftentimes

---

[1] For the relation between 'Graeculus' and other collections see A. Franz, *Drei deutsche Minoritenprediger aus dem xiii. und xiv. Jahrhundert* (Freiburg im Breisgau, 1907), 147–9, with a preliminary note of caution sounded on p. 146.

[2] Ibid. 149.

[3] K. F. Lynch, (ed.) *John de la Rochelle, O.F.M. Eleven Marian Sermons* (Franciscan Institute Publications, Text Series, No. 12; The Franciscan Institute, St Bonaventure; New York, Louvain, and Paderborn, 1961).

[4] Ibid., p. xvii.

[5] Otherwise Dubrovnik, Knjižnica Male Braće 190. Cf. L. Duval-Arnould, 'Trois Sermons synodaux de la collection attribuée à Jean de la Rochelle', *Archivum Franciscanum Historicum*, 69 (1976), 336–400, at p. 391 n. 1. I have not seen this manuscript, but it is clearly interesting. As well as Rupellian sermons it contains sermons from the Franciscan collection called *Legifer*. I have verified this from the *fichier* of incipits in the Section Latine of the Institut de Recherche et d'Histoire des Textes at Paris.

come down to a remaking of the text, nothing added, but the word-order consistently changed, Scripture texts expanded or contracted, and the like'.[1] Furthermore, in MS Paris, Arsenal 547, the text is altered throughout. Words are replaced by synonyms and 'Sometimes whole sentences are changed around.' The alterations of the text in the Ragusi and especially in the Arsenal manuscripts are clearly different in kind from straightforward scribal errors.[2]

A particularly common way of altering the text is abridgement. In MS BN lat. 3731 a number of sermons by Guibert de Tournai are abridged, in several cases by including only the first part of the sermon.[3] The manuscript also includes many abridged sermons by Konrad Holtnicker.[4] The critical edition of Bonaventura's 'Sunday sermons' also casts light on the way in which sermons tended to get shortened in the course of written transmission. We have already seen that sermons which have been detached from the main body of the 'published' collection of Sunday sermons (and which are transmitted in the company of sermons not from the collection) are often mere schemas or résumés.[5] Once in circulation, sermons from a 'model' collection could be borrowed and abridged at the convenience of the user.[6]

Thus, it will be apparent that there were several ways of altering the text of individual sermons as well as several ways

---

[1] Lynch's edition, p. xvii.

[2] The editor was of the opinion that these two manuscripts each represent a different edition, though he does not spell out fully what he means by this. See his edition, p. xvii, '*Ragusi* 190 would appear to be another and different manuscript edition . . .', and p. xviii, 'in our opinion it is a re-edited manuscript'.

[3] See *Catalogue*, pp. 630–9, e.g. (p. 631): 'F. 22ᵛ–38. [Guibertus Tornacensis, Sermones de sanctis.] . . . [In Purificatione b. Mariae], 1ᵉʳᵉ partie du sermon . . . Schneyer, *ibid.* nᵒ 105 (26ᵛ–27) . . . "De angelis" (titre en marge), abrégé . . . Schneyer, *ibid.* nᵒ 149 (36) . . .'

[4] Ibid. 630, 633–8. Note, by contrast, ibid. 635: '[In festo b. Johannis evangelistae] plus long que l'éd. (*éd. cit.*, 1597, 24–26); cf. Schneyer, *op. cit.*, I, 750 nᵒ 32 (104ᵛ–105) . . .' Nevertheless, the vast majority of modified versions of Konrad's sermons in this manuscript seem to be short forms. My impression is that this is generally true: i.e., that it was more common for a text to be abridged than for it to be expanded in the course of its written transmission.

[5] Bougerol's edition, p. 31; and p. 53, with the preceding descriptions.

[6] Ibid. 23.

of breaking up the corpus of whole sermon collections. When these two variables are both taken into account together, the number of possible ways of copying thirteenth-century sermons, other than simply reproducing a standardized text, will be seen to be large. There is no point here in venturing further into that maze of possible combinations. Although it is important to be aware of the variety of different types of written transmission, our concern is first and foremost with the standardized texts diffused from Paris.

In the context of the question of transmission it is again necessary to point out that one is always at least one degree removed from the sermon that a congregation would have heard. A reportation could not be complete and perfectly accurate. On the other hand, even when an author has left an autograph version of a sermon he preached, the written text may give an inadequate impression of the living sermon. Thus, 'If we compare the same sermon written by [Matthaeus ab] Aquasparta in his own hand, and as reported by a hearer, we see that in the autograph an example is merely indicated as *exemplum de puero mutinensi*, the story of the young man of Modena, but that in the reported version there is a very lively description of a scene, witnessed by Aquasparta himself, between a cautious provincial and a generous young candidate for the Franciscan order.'[1]

With the model sermon collections, with which we are more particularly concerned here, the gap between the written and the spoken word is in a sense even harder to gauge, because each preacher who borrowed and preached a model sermon may have adapted it in a different way. Probably the most common way was to expand the written text. It has already been suggested that there was a tendency for sermons to get boiled down to mere schemas in the course of transmission. There were also sermon collections which seem originally to have been written in that form. Two

---

[1] Bataillon, 'Approaches', p. 22.

important Dominican Paris masters, Hugues de Saint-Cher and Nicolas Gorran, wrote collections of this kind. The Franciscan collection called *Legifer* almost comes into this category, for there is not so very much in it apart from divisions, subdivisions, and 'authorities'. Any preacher who used sermons from these collections or abbreviated written versions of originally fuller sermons would have been bound to add flesh to the bones. More rarely, preachers must have been forced to shorten a long model sermon for the purpose of oral delivery. Thus, the full sermons in the preaching handbook of Guy d'Évreux were probably meant to be shortened or used selectively, as were the Sunday sermons of the secular Jacques de Vitry.[1] Again, model sermons would be combined with material from the other genres of preaching aids, and we have already seen that there were plenty to choose from. The model sermon, perhaps, would have been the main ingredient, but the others would have spiced it and filled it out, and we can hardly tell what recipes each individual preacher followed. For all that, there is no need to be too pessimistic about the value of these sermons as evidence. They tell us what experienced preachers thought would be useful to other preachers, and they almost certainly give a true picture of the underlying structure of thought in preaching.

iv. The Problem of Audience and Function

The phrase 'model sermons' has so far been used without much explanation. It is now time to look more closely at what

---

[1] Michaud-Quantin, 'Guy d'Évreux', p. 225; Jacques de Vitry, *Sermones in Epistolas et Evangelia dominicalia* (Antwerp, 1575 for which I use BL 1474. d. 11): '... Attendat igitur prudens Lector, et cautus Praedicator, ne forte quaecunque invenerit scripta in uno sermone, velit uno die maxime laicis praedicare. Melius est enim quod in appetitu audiendi adhuc dimittantur, quam prolixitate graventur. Totum enim spiritum suum profert stultus: sapiens autem differt, et reservat in posterum. Ob hoc enim plerunque in uno sermone plura collegimus, ut copiosum, et non superfluum redderemus praedicatorem. Qui secundum qualitatem temporis, et circumstantias personarum, quae necessaria sunt, debet eligere, et alia quae relinquit, alteri tempori reservare ...' (from the 'Proëmium', not foliated or paginated).

it implies, as a preliminary to another major critical problem, that of audience. In fact, the question of what model sermon collections were for, merges into the question of whom they were preached to. In the abstract, the problem of function might be separated from that of audience, but in reality they amount to more or less the same thing.

How then should a 'model sermon collection' be defined? I think that the phrase would be understood by most scholars nowadays to mean sermons written for a proximate public of users and an ultimate public of listeners. (It is further assumed that this ultimate public would generally be lay, on which point more must be said shortly.) There are various ways of detecting that a collection of sermons comes into this category. If a collection was in general circulation in a standardized text, there is a fair likelihood that it was a handbook of model sermons, though it is not a certain proof. It has already been noted that the sermon collection by the Franciscans Bonaventura and Jean de la Rochelle were in general circulation in standardized texts, and the same is true, almost by definition, of all sermon collections available from the Paris University stationers. Cross-references, or more general references to material to be found elsewhere, are another sort of indication—one which marks off model sermon collections from straightforward *reportationes* (I say straightforward *reportationes* because it is possible to imagine *reportationes* being adapted to make them a collection of model sermons). References of this kind are not uncommon in the sermon collections which the Paris University stationers made available.[1]

[1] e.g., in the collection called *Legifer*, after a brief exhortation on holiness in a sermon on the text 'Sanctificamini, cras comedetis carnes' (Num. 11: 18), we find the following direction, which is not a marginal note but a part of the text: 'De hac autem sanctificatione require plenius supra in primo sermone dominice secunde in quadragesima' (see above, p. 89 n. 4)—*Legifer* is full of cross-references; from Guillaume Peyraut: 'Si vis loqui de confessione require de ea in illo sermone ultime dominice: In diebus illis salvabitur Iuda, et in tractatu de accidia in capitulo de dilatatione confessionis' (MS BN lat. 16472, fo. 24ra), from a sermon on the text 'Dominus prope est' (Phil. 4: 5), Schneyer, *Repertorium*, ii. 544, No. 142); From Nicolas de Biard: '. . . De primis duobus dictum est alibi . . .' (MS BN lat. 13579, fo.

Cross-references are not always an entirely satisfactory sign that one is dealing with a 'model' sermon collection, for they would also be possible in sermons which were intended only for private reading. If the cross-reference takes the form of some such phrase as 'If you wish to *speak* of the epistle, see above...' (my italics), then one is on fairly safe ground in assuming that the sermons were not merely for reading. Again, a sermon collection with cross-references is unlikely to have been for private reading if it consists of mere schemas— divisions and authorities with little or no development. In general, however, the surest signs that a collection consists of 'models' would seem to be instructions to the preacher in the sermons, or a prologue which explicitly states that the collection is meant to help other preachers.

Instructions to preachers are of various kinds (indeed, some cross-references could be included in this category), and it is worth giving some examples, if only because they give a clearer idea of the relationship between the written text and the living sermon. In one of Guillaume de Mailly's sermon cycles the user is told '...here you may go into the commandments of the Church...'.[1] This suggests (what is in

---

30[vb], from a sermon on the text 'Gaudete in domino semper' (Phil. 4: 4), Schneyer, *Repertorium*, iv. 230, No. 15); [this may be a cross-reference to Biard's own *distinctio* collection beginning 'Absconditur malum a dyabolo sub delectatione sicut pedica sub folio': here the entry for *Gaudium* distinguishes (like the sermon) between three kinds of joy ('culpe', 'gratie', and 'glorie'), but treats only the first two (at least in MS BN lat. 16488, fo. 66[ra-vb]); at any rate the *alibi* seems not to refer to another passage from the same sermon]; from Thomas Lebreton: 'Hoc habes expositum dominica in ramis palmarum' (MS BL Royal 3. A. XIII, fo. 17[va]), or again: 'De adventu huius regis nota in ultima dominica ante adventum et in ramis palmarum....' (ibid., fo. 17[vb])—both quotes are from a sermon on the text 'Ecce rex tuus venit' (Matt. 21: 5), Schneyer, *Repertorium*, v. 632, s.v. 'Thomas de Lisle', No. 2; from Aldobrandino Cavalcanti: 'Si vis loqui de ewangelio quere supra in festo apostolorum' (MS Bamberg, Msc. Theol. 2, fo. 156vb), from a sermon on the text 'Dirupisti vincula mea' (Ps. 115: 17), Schneyer, *Repertorium*, i. 174, No. 346; from Pierre de Saint-Benoît: 'De hiis tribus require supra in sermone Veniet desideratus....' (Clm. 2672, fo. 10[r]) (cf. MS Venice, Marc. Fondo antico lat. 92 (collocazione 1897, Valentinelli, vi. 36), fo. 11vb), from a sermon on the text 'Qui post me venturus est' (John 1: 27), Schneyer, *Repertorium*, iv. 783, No. 11.
  [1] '...potes hic descendere ad mandata ecclesie....' (MS BN lat. 16475, fo. 9[va]); from a sermon on the text 'Unanimes uno ore' (Rom. 15: 6), Schneyer, *Repertorium*, ii. 483, No. 3, where Schneyer gives the text as 'Unanimes honorificemus' (Rom. 15: 6).

any case inherently plausible) that authors of model sermon collections did not always bother to include material that would be so well known to the preacher that he could talk about it off the top of his head. In this case the preacher is simply given his cue. In a similar way Guillaume Peyraut says 'Here you can go into individual vices and virtues.'[1] (Peyraut may have thought that if the preacher should be short of material on virtues and vices he could turn to Peyraut's own *Summa de vitiis et virtutibus*. Earlier in the same sermon he says 'If you wish to expand this material look in the treatise on vices in the chapter on idleness (*otio*)'; he probably means his own book.[2]) Thomas Lebreton, after quoting the words of the prodigal son, 'I will rise up and go to my father and say to him, "Father, I have sinned" etc.', simply adds: 'Note what follows in (*de*) the parable....'[3] This sounds like an instruction to the preacher to finish the parable, though a remark of this kind might just conceivably be found in a book of sermons for private reading. An instruction to tell a biblical story in a sermon by Aldobrandino Cavalcanti, on the other hand, makes no sense at all if the sermon was not ultimately intended for oral delivery: 'David said of his dead son, "Since he is dead, why fast? Will I be able to bring him back from the grave? I will rather go to him. But he will not return to me." Tell that story briefly.'[4] Other preachers use the imperative

---

[1] '... Hic potes descendere ad singula vitia et virtutes....' (MS BN lat. 16472, fo. 12va), from a sermon on the text 'Sic nos existimet homo' (1 Cor. 4: 1), Schneyer, *Repertorium*, ii. 544, No. 135.

[2] 'Si vis dilatare materiam istam respice in tractatu de vitiis in capitulo de otio' (MS BN 16472, fo. 11va). The chapter in question may be 'De vit. Tract. v. De accidia Pars II Ca. iiii. De otiositate...' (fos. 62rb–63va of the 'vices' half of the Basle edn. (1497)).

[3] 'Luc. 15 dicitur de filio prodigo: Surgam et ibo ad patrem meum et dicam ei: Pater peccavi et cetera. Nota quod sequitur, de parabola....' (MS BL Royal 3 A. XIII, fo. 155ra); from a sermon on the text 'Adolescens libi dico' (Luke 7: 14), Schneyer, *Repertorium*, v. 638, s.v. 'Thomas de Lisle', No. 98.

[4] 'Reg. xii: dixit David de filio suo mortuo: Quia mortuus est, quare ieiuno? Numquid potero revocare eum amplius? Ego magis vadam ad eum. Ipse autem non revertetur ad me. Dic breviter hystoriam illam' (MS Bamberg, Msc. Theol. 2, fo. 175va); from a sermon on the text 'Nolumus vos ignorare' (1 Thess. 4: 12), Schneyer, *Repertorium*, i. 178, No. 394. For 'that story' see 2 Sam. 12, especially verse 23.

in a similar way: '. . . make the seven properties correspond to the seven deadly sins' (Pierre de Reims).[1] Or again: 'Note that although a gambler sometimes apparently makes a profit, it can never last, but in the end he is thrown naked out of the bar: so it is with the world. Compare and expound.'[2] Or again, Jacques de Lausanne (whose floruit really falls outside our period), after starting an analogue to a proposition he is making, simply says 'Applica', 'Apply it'.[3]

Up to a point the evidence of these short passages—cross-references and instructions to the preachers—is complemented by that of prologues. Many sermon collections (including most of those with which this study is especially concerned) are not known to have a prologue in the proper sense of the word, but when we do find what we would recognize as a prologue or preface it can cast light on the function of model sermon collections in general. The prologue beginning 'Narraverunt iniqui . . .' (Ps. 118: 85) of a widely copied sermon collection by Luca da Bitonto, OM, is worth looking at (even though I know of no connection between this Franciscan and Paris).[4] The language of the prologue suggests that the work may have been designed first and foremost for preachers within the order. The prologue is

---

[1] '. . . nota quomodo per has proprietates quilibet debet esse nubes, et fac vii proprietates respondere vii mortalibus peccatis' (MS BL Arundel 206, fo. 46ra) (cf. MS Bodleian, Laud Misc. 506, fo. 74rb: 'Nota quomodo per has proprietates debet spiritualiter quilibet esse iustus nubes. Vel fac vii proprietates nubis circa vii peccata mortalia et cetera'); from a sermon on the text 'Qui sunt isti qui ut nubes volant' (Isa. 60: 8), Schneyer, *Repertorium*, iv. 752, No. 462.

[2] '. . . nota quamvis aleator quandoque lucretur ut videtur, numquam tamen potest ei durare, sed demum nudus eicitur de taberna: ita de mundo est. Compara et expone' (Clm. 2672, fo. 8r) (cf. MS Venice, Marc. Fondo antico lat. 92 (collocazione 1897, Valentinelli, vi. 36), fo. 9vb–10ra); from a sermon on the text 'Quecumque scripta sunt' (Rom. 15: 4), Schneyer, *Repertorium*, iv. 783, No. 7).

[3] MS BN lat. 18181, fo. 1va, from a sermon on the text 'Sicut in die honeste ambulemus' (Rom. 13: 13), Schneyer, *Repertorium*, iii. 54, No. 2. Jacques de Lausanne was a Dominican Paris master: in 1317 John XXII ordered the Chancellor of Paris to give him the Licence in Theology. He became prior provincial of France (1318–21) and died in 1321 (for these details see Kaeppeli, *Scriptores*, ii. 323–4). His sermons were diffused by the *pecia* system, for Destrez found manuscripts bearing *pecia* indications. See the blue folder on Jacques de Lausanne in the Destrez notes, now kept at Le Saulchoir, Couvent St-Jacques, in Paris.

[4] For Luca da Bitonto see Schneyer, *Repertorium*, iv. 49 ff—'claruit c. 1233'.

addressed to the Minister-General of the Franciscans.[1] He explains that he had composed his work under obedience (*mandato superioris urgente*) and because some of the brothers desired him to do so.[2] All this perhaps belongs to the realm of introductory commonplaces, but they are the sort of commonplace which may have a basis in fact.

'... I wished to be of service to brothers who are unskilled and as yet inexperienced...':[3] so Luca explains his purpose. The natural interpretation of his words is that he wanted to help Franciscan preachers who lacked skill or experience by providing them with ready-made sermons. It appears prima facie unlikely that he meant them to use his sermons on other clerics; would 'unskilled and inexperienced' brothers be asked to preach *coram clero*? Often enough to justify a model sermon collection designed to help them do so?

The same a priori presumption—that sermons for less-educated priests were most probably to help them preach to the laity—is raised by the remarks which introduce the Sunday sermons of Guy d'Évreux. (The *Sunday sermons* are the first part of the *Summa Guiotina*, the elaborate preaching machine discussed above.) 'It should be said at the beginning of this work, that there is no need to be afraid if the sermons seem lengthy, because they are composed, and the authorities compiled, in such a way that they can be easily abridged at the will of each preacher, even one who is not very strong in sacred theology...'[4] Strictly speaking, of course, this does not imply that the work was *only* meant for use by preachers who were 'not very strong in sacred theology'. Guy's remarks nevertheless leave the same impression as the prologue to Luca da Bitonto's sermons, and the best modern analysis of the *Summa Guiotina* does indeed assume that lay congregations were, generally speaking, the ultimate audience for which the bulk of the material in it was intended.[5]

---

[1] 'pater totius ordinis minorum minister' (MS BN NAL 410, fo. 3va).
[2] Ibid.
[3] '... rudibus et nondum exercitatis fratribus prodesse volui...' (ibid. fo. 3va).
[4] Michaud-Quantin, 'Guy d'Évreux', p. 225 n. 25.   [5] Ibid. 232.

Moving forward slightly outside our period, to Bertrand de la Tour, a Franciscan who belongs more to fourteenth- than to thirteenth-century history,[1] we again find prologues which leave one with an impression, something short of a certainty, that an ultimate audience of lay people is envisaged. In the manuscript I have used of his *Postil on the Gospels for Sundays and ferial days* there appear to be two prologues.[2] In the first he speaks of 'unsophisticated homilies for the use of simple people'.[3] It is not absolutely clear whether the 'simple people' (*simplicium*) are the first public of the work (the preachers), or the ultimate public (their congregations); but either way the natural inference is that the ultimate public would be lay. The second introductory section also seems to imply this: 'The preacher of the Gospel, who, like the Apostle, [St Paul], ought not to be ashamed of the gospel . . . ought every Sunday to set before the faithful peoples specified sections of the Gospel . . . like specified measures of wheat . . .'[4] The phrase 'faithful peoples' (*fidelibus populis*) suggests that Bertrandus envisages lay congregations.

---

[1] On Bertrand and his sermons and *collationes* for the liturgical year see B. Smalley, *English Friars and Antiquity in the Early Fourteenth Century* (Oxford, 1960), 242–4.

[2] The incipits are 'Quis putas est fidelis . . . Sicud per ordeum' (MS BL Royal 4. D. IV, fo. 1ra) and 'Vidi alterum angelum . . . Predicator evangelicus' (ibid., fo. 1rb). These fit the two incipits given for Bertrand de la Tour's *Postilla super Evangelia dominicalia et ferialia totius anni* given in P. Glorieux, *Répertoire des maîtres en théologie de Paris au XIIIᵉ siècle*, ii (1933), 239–40, s.v. 'Bertrand de la Tour', No. 349.

[3] 'Nos igitur qui, opitulante domino, non sermone falerato sed rudibus omeliis ad utilitatem simplicium exposituri sumus evangelia singulis dominicis et temporibus secundum ordinationem Gregorii et sacrosancte romane ecclesie ordinariam convenientiam, ab adventu domini sumamus exordium . . .' (MS BL Royal 4. D. IV, fo. 1rb). falerato] famulato *ms* (*falerato* is the reading in MS Toulouse 326, fo. 1va, as quoted by Smalley, *English Friars*, p. 243 n. 2).

[4] 'Predicator evangelicus, qui more apostoli non debet erubescere evangelium, ut enim ait Apostolus ad Ro. i: Non (*om. ms.*) erubesco evangelium—est enim in illo virtus divina ad salutem omni credenti—debet singulis dominicis determinatas particulas evangelii secundum approbatam ecclesie ordinationem, et maxime secundum romanam, quam ordinavit fidelis dispensator dei beatus papa Gregorius, ut iam dictum est, fidelibus populis tanquam determinatas mensuras tritici apponere, ut egentes et famelici recreentur, et quoniam ut sua predicatio fructum afferat oportet ipsum esse sinceriter viventem, subtiliter scandentem, equaliter prebentem, fideliter credentem, salubriter docentem, idcirco . . .' (MS BL Royal 4 D. IV, fo. 1rb).

One would certainly expect a priori that the ultimate audience of model sermon collections should be lay. There is some reason to think that at least in theory university congregations expected originality,[1] which would, one might have thought, have been a deterrent to using material from a model sermon collection when preaching to an academic congregation. One might also have thought that it would have been difficult to take sermons from a collection of models when preaching to a congregation of monks and friars: there would be a danger that at least someone in the audience would know where the sermon had come from. Nuns and béguines? They are a serious possibility; but I find it difficult to believe that the primary function of the vast corpus of model sermons was to provide material for preaching to religious women, and I know of no positive evidence that this was the case. It is true that much of the German vernacular homiletic literature of the later Middle Ages probably derives from the special pastoral relationship between the friars and religious women,[2] but these mystical sermons are strikingly different in general character from the Latin model sermons of the thirteenth century and after. Again, it seems unlikely that collections of model sermons were intended for congregations of the lower clergy. The latter were, indeed, poorly educated, and they would probably not have minded about originality, but how often would they have been gathered together on Sundays and Feast-days? They would come together for synods, but there survive special sermons for those; a *de tempore* or a *de sanctis* cycle intended for their ears would have been useful only occasionally. The laity are the only major class of thirteenth-century society left.

When this convoluted passage is read as a whole it seems clear that Bertrand is talking about preaching on the Gospel readings, rather than simply reading them or translating them to the people.

[1] Smalley, *English Friars*, pp. 37–8 and 308 (*Quodlibet* of Gervase of Mont Saint-Éloi).

[2] This special relationship is one of the principal themes of Grundmann's *Religiöse Bewegungen.* Cf. above, II. ii. p. 92 n. 1.

Thus, it is not without reason that scholars have assumed that model sermons are, as it were, purpose-built and ready-made popular sermons. Nevertheless, it has begun to seem to me that, while not wrong, this assumption is not quite right either.[1] Not wrong, because we must surely assume (if only for the a priori reasons given above) that the model sermons were used for popular preaching more often than for anything else. Not quite right, because there are passages in model sermon collections which were probably not written for ordinary lay congregations, though the degree of probability differs from case to case.

In some manuscripts of *de communi* sermons by Pierre de Reims, we meet in the middle of a sermon the words 'In another way to our brothers', or 'Again, to our brothers', which seem to mark off the remainder of the sermon as intended for an audience of friars.[2] This part of the sermon, which may really be a separate sermon, would seem either to have been originally delivered to a Dominican audience, or to have been intended for one, or both.

In a sermon of Guillaume Peyraut we find the words 'But if the sermon is to clerics, for them you should touch on the love

---

[1] The first doubts were sown in my mind in a conversation with Dr Michael Richter.

[2] '...et fortitudo deitatis. Aliter ad fratres nostros. Simile est regnum celorum. Regnum celorum est religio vel anima sancta....' (MS BN lat. 15960, fo. 163vb); 'Ferrum quod omnia devincit est potentia. Item ad fratres nostros. Simile est regnum celorum, id est religio vel [*fo. 59va*] anima sancta....' (MS BL Arundel 206, fo. 59^{rb-va} [new foliation]); '... est fortitudo et potentia deitatis. Item ad fratres nostros. Simile est regnum celorum, id est religio vel anima sancta....' (MS Bodleian, Laud Misc. 506, fo. 106va). The passage comes at the break-point between two sermons listed under the name of Petrus de Remis by Schneyer, *Repertorium*, iv. 755, Nos. 504–5, though they appear to be merged into one sermon in the three manuscripts quoted. An interesting variant suggests that MS BL Arundel 206 represents a Franciscan edition. On fo. 59va this manuscript says that 'Thesaurus in agro est ordo fratrum minorum et aliorum predicatorum in mundo'; MSS BN lat. 15960, fo. 163vb, and Bodleian Laud Misc. 506, fo. 106va, have instead 'ordo predicatorum in mundo', which is more likely to be the original version since Pierre was Dominican. My attention was drawn by L.-J. Bataillon to the sermon of Pierre on the text 'Animal primum simile leoni' (Rev. 4: 7), Schneyer, *Repertorium*, iv. 753, No. 473, which must also have been intended for and/or originally delivered to an audience of Dominican friars.

of Sacred Scripture. . . .'[1] He is probably still addressing himself to a potential clerical audience when, a little further on, he speaks of the benefits of study 'even of the liberal arts' at Paris.[2] The whole question of the audience of model sermons needs to be rethought in the light of remarks like these.

Furthermore, there are certain images and analogies in other collections which strengthen these doubts about the nature of the audience. Individually, they might be explained away, but when taken together with the passages just quoted they are not so easy to disregard. The use of the second person in the following passage from a sermon by Nicolas de Biard is surely significant:

Exemplum si essent in una ecclesia prebende vacantes, in alia ecclesia alie prebende vacantes, et scires quod de hiis venirentur [*sic*] ad episcopatum, de aliis (*supply* ad) patibulum, quam istarum acciperes? Karissimi fratres, mundus vocat nos (*or* vos) et dominus vocat nos (*or* vos), sed dominus ad penitentiam, mundus ad gaudium et letitiam. Sed de penitentia venitur sepe ad eternam gloriam, de gaudio mundi venitur ad tristitiam inferni . . .[3]

For example, if there were vacant prebends in one church, and other vacant prebends in another church, and you knew that one set (*de hiis*) led to a bishopric, and the other (*de aliis*) to the gallows, which of these would you take? Dearest brothers, the world calls us and the Lord calls us, but the Lord to penance, the world to delight and gladness. But penance often leads to eternal glory, and the world's delight leads to the misery of hell . . .

The passage reads as though it were meant for the ears of

---

[1] 'Si vero fiat sermo clericis, tangendum est illis de amore sacre scripture. . . .' (MS BN lat. 16472, fo. 202va); from a sermon on the text 'In diebus illis salvabitur Iuda' (Jer. 23: 6), Schneyer *Repertorium*, ii. 550, No. 232.

[2] 'Item tangendum est eis quantam munditiam faciat studium etiam liberalium artium in scolaribus Par. . . .' (ibid.).

[3] MS BN lat. 13579, fo. 19rb, from a sermon on the text 'Benedictus qui venit' (Matt. 21: 9), Schneyer, *Repertorium*, iv. 229, No. 9. A passage shortly before the one I translate, from the same sermon, is also relevant: 'Exemplum si episcopus [*col. b*] Parisiensis vocaret aliquem clericum ad aliquam prebendam, quot sunt qui surgerent. Rex celorum vocat . . .' (MS cit., fo. 19ra-b).

ambitious young secular clerics, possibly in an academic milieu.

The academic milieu (which in a northern European context means a clerical mileu) comes through explicitly in imagery employed in a sermon by the Franciscan Pierre de Saint-Benoît. There is a long passage in which a knowledge of how the schools worked is required to make the allegory effective. A couple of extracts will serve to illustrate this. In the first, it will be evident that a quite technical knowledge of academic teaching arrangements is presupposed:

Dedit enim nobis doctorem primum: filium suum. Mt. xxii. Magister scimus quia ve(rax) es, et cetera. Dedit doctorem secundum: spiritum sanctum. De quo dicebat primus doctor, id est filius, qui habet primam sedem in scolis: ille vos do(cebit) o(mnia), et sug(geret) vobis o(mnia), et cetera. Iste est qui habet secundam [*correction in ms?*] sedem, quasi submagister, quia: de meo, inquit, accipiet et an(nuntiabit) vobis. Dedit enim bacalarios quasi repetitores (repetitiores *or* repetittores *ms*), apostolos videlicet et doctores, quibus dictum est: euntes docete omnes gentes, docentes eos servare quecumque mandavi vobis. Mt. ult. . . .[1]

For he gave to us a first doctor, his Son. Matt. 22 [16] 'Master, we know that you tell the truth', etc. He gave a second doctor, the Holy Spirit. About the latter the first doctor, that is, the Son, who has the first chair in the schools, used to speak: [John 14: 26] 'He will teach you everything and will recall to your minds everything', etc. He it is who has the second chair, like an assistant professor,[2] because, he says: [John 16: 14] 'He shall receive of mine and show it to you.' He even gave bachelors, *repetitores* as it were, that is, the apostles

---

[1] Clm. 2672, fo. 8ʳ (cf. MS Venice, Marc. Fondo antico lat. 92 (collocazione 1897, Valentinelli, vi. 36), fo. 9ᵛᵇ); from a sermon on the text 'Quecumque scripta sunt' (Rom. 15: 4), Schneyer, *Repertorium*, iv. 783, No. 7).

[2] 'Submagister'; Du Cange's *Glossarium mediae et infimae latinitatis* (Graz, 1954 reprint of Favre edn., 1883–7), vii, has the following entry for this word (p. 361): 'Secundus magister. Gall. *Sous-maître*. Stat. colleg. Navar. ann. 1315. In libro rub. Cam. Comput. Paris fol. 515. rᵒ: *In dicta domo ponatur quidam ydoneus gramaticus bonae vitae, qui submagister vocabitur, ad instruendum juniores in primitivis scientiae gramaticae.*' Thus *submagister*, attested by Clm. 2672, looks more plausible than *sub magistro*, attested by MS Venice, Marc. Fondo antico lat. 92 (collocazione 1897, Valentinelli, vi. 36), fo. 9ᵛᵇ, though the latter reading also makes sense.

and doctors, to whom it is said: 'Go and teach all nations, teaching them to observe whatever I have commanded you.' Matt. (28) [19–20] . . .

If the foregoing words had been found in a sermon to a university congregation one would think it the most natural thing in the world, and one cannot help but suspect that they were originally spoken in some such context. One cannot rule out an ordinary parish or cathedral congregation in a town dominated by a *studium*, but it seems to me less likely. The same may be said of the following extract, though it lacks the semi-technical allusions to specific academic arrangements:

Item ipse est qui proficientes promovet ad maiora, unde non oportet scolas eius relinquere propter servitium divitum, ut promoveantur discipuli eius, quia ipse dicit, Io. xv.: Si manseritis in me, et verba mea in vo(bis) man(serint), quodcumque (quod *ms*) vo(lueritis) pe(tetis), et fi(et) vobis (nobis *ms*?). Sic ergo providet in libris, in magistris, et in expensis. Sed multi omnium istorum ingrati nihil proficiunt, sed eius expensas libenter accipiunt, sed nec scolas intrant, nec libros eius inspiciunt, similes pravis scolaribus, qui cum deberent mane ire ad scolas artium, vadunt ad scolas talorum, ubi quod habent amittunt.[1]

Again, it is he who promotes those who make good progress to higher things—for which reason one should not leave his schools for the service of rich men—so that his disciples may be promoted, for he himself says, John 15 [7]: 'If you abide in me, and my words abide in you, you will ask whatever you wish, and it shall be done to you.' Thus, therefore, he provides for books, masters, and expenses. But many people, ungrateful for all those things, make no progress, but willingly accept the expenses he pays, but neither enter the

---

[1] Clm. 2672, fo. 8ʳ (cf. MS Venice, Marc. Fondo antico lat. 92 (collocazione 1897, Valentinelli vi. 36), fo. 9ᵛᵇ). My translation of the first part of this passage—making 'unde . . . divitum' a parenthesis—is not the only possible construction with Latin as unclassical as this is; but the general sense is not in doubt. On 'ut promoveantur discipuli eius . . .' cf. the following remark in a sermon by Thomas Lebreton: 'Et propterea illi qui proficiunt in scientia dei eius scolares sunt. Et scimus quod bonus magister scolares suos diligit et promovet . . .' (MS BL Royal 3. A. xiii, fo. 31ʳᵃ), from a sermon on the text 'Puer crescebat' (Luke 2: 40), Schneyer, *Repertorium*, v. 632, s.v. 'Thomas de Lisle', No. 10.

schools, nor look at his books; they are like vicious students who, when in the morning they ought to go to the schools of arts, go to the gambling schools, where they lose what they have.

Twentieth-century French academics resemble their thirteenth-century counterparts: the *turbo-profs* who make weekly *voyages pénitentiaires* to the provincial universities where they teach are waiting for a Paris chair, and in the thirteenth century the pull of the greatest university city was even more powerful. 'The third infidelity is in those who sell the wares of the Lord where they are less saleable, as is the case with those who teach at Paris, where their teaching is scarcely listened to, and do not want to teach elsewhere, where their teaching would be held dear....'[1] So Guillaume Peyraut, OP, whose known connections are with Lyons rather than with Paris.[2] However true then and now, his remark would perhaps be more naturally addressed to an academic than to an ordinary lay audience.

A fascinating sermon on the text 'Erunt signa' (Luke 21: 25) by Jean de la Rochelle raises the same problem. This sermon is interesting from many angles and deserves close study, but here we must confine ourselves to a brief glance from the point of view of the problem of audience. Jean brings the clergy of Paris into his sermon in such a way that one is led to think that he is addressing them. The world of the Church, we read, has a heaven above, that is the clergy, and a heaven below, that is the laity, 'like the earth'. He proceeds to the *lumina*, the sources of light, in the heaven of the clergy, and explains that 'The light of the clergy at Paris is threefold: the light of theology, like the sun; the light of secular knowledge, like the moon; the light of philosophy, which has many parts,

---

[1] 'Tertia infidelitas est in eis qui merces domini vendunt ubi minus vendibiles sunt, sicut accidit in eis qui Parisius docent ubi doctrina eorum vix auditur, et alibi nolunt docere ubi doctrina cara [*col. b*] haberetur' (MS BN lat. 16472, fo. 18ra-b); from a sermon beginning, in this manuscript, 'Item sermo de eadem epistola. "Queritur inter dispensatores"...' (1 Cor. 4: 2), Schneyer, *Repertorium*, ii. 544, No. 138.

[2] Cf. Kaeppeli, *Scriptores*, ii. 133, and Dondaine, 'Guillaume Peyraut. Vie et œuvres', *Archivum Fratrum Praedicatorum*, 18 (1948), 162–236.

like the stars. . . .'[1] His classification and the way he subsequently develops it raises some problems—in particular the precise meaning of 'secular knowledge' (*secularis scientie*) and 'philosophy', and the borderline between these concepts as he understands them. This problem can only be noted here. But the reference to the clerics of Paris is explicit, and in this context there can be no doubt that he means university clerics. It is worth quoting a few more extracts, to convey the tone of the passage. Thus, for instance, in the section on theology: 'If, therefore, you see a man most evil and wretched in his way of life elegantly preaching, teaching, or disputing or lecturing, you should not wonder, because it is said of the most evil Antichrist: [Job 41: 2] "Beneath him will be the rays of the sun" etc. . . .'[2] Again, in the section on *secularis scientia*, towards which his tone seems somewhat hostile: 'The moon of secular knowledge is to disputation about earthly things as the sun of theology is to day, that is to contemplation of divine things. . . . This moon waxes extraordinarily in the consummation of the age, while (*cum*) we now see that there are almost as many doctors of law as there are cities. . . .'[3] On the other hand Jean begins the section on *philosophia* in an approving vein:

[1] '. . . Habet autem mundus ecclesie (*supply* celum) sursum, scilicet statum clericorum, sicut celum deorsum, scilicet statum laicorum, sicut terram. Et in celo clericorum est accipere lumina, de quibus dicitur: Erunt signa in sole et luna et stellis. Triplex est lumen clericorum Parisiensium (Parisieñ. *ms*): theologie, sicut sol; secularis scientie, sicut luna; philosophie multiplicis, sicut stelle. . . . (MS BN lat. 16477, fo. 12ʳᵇ); from a sermon on the text 'Erunt signa in sole' (Luke 21: 25), Schneyer, *Repertorium*, iii. 704, No. 6.

[2] 'Si ergo videas pessimum et miserum in vita eleganter [*fo. 12ᵛᵃ*] predicantem, docentem, vel disputantem aut legentem, non mireris, quia de antichristo pessimo dicitur: sub ipso erunt radii solis et cetera. . . .' (MS BN lat. 16477, fo. 12ʳᵇ⁻ᵛᵃ).

[3] '. . . Luna secularis scientie est disputationi terrenorum sicut sol theologie diei, id est contemplationi divinorum. Mensis: tempus incarnationis filii dei, de quo Exo. xii. [2] Mensis iste vobis (nobis *ms?*) principium mensium erit in mensibus anni (aū. m. *ms?*). Consumatio huius mensis fuit in hora passionis, cum dixit dominus: Consummatum est. Tunc valde diminuta est luna, id est secularis scientia. Unde exclamat Paulus, i. (ii. *ms*) Cor. i [23 *and* 20]: Nos predicamus Christum crucifixum, iudeis quidem scandalum, gentibus autem stultitiam. Ubi ergo sapiens vir, scriba? (vir scriba? *sic in ms*) Ubi conquisitor huius seculi? Nonne stultam (*corr. from* stultitiam) fecit, et cetera. Hec luna crescet mirabiliter in consummatione seculi, cum iam videmus quod fere quot sunt civitates, tot sunt legum doctores. . . .' (ibid., fo.

De stellis philosophie dicitur, Iud. v., Stelle manentes in ordine suo pugnaverunt contra Sysaram. Sysara, exclusio, significat heresim. Stelle sunt doctores phisicis rationibus instructi, ut †dicit† Dionysus et Hylarius, qui circuierunt omnes scolas Grecie, et Augustinus et alii qui pugnaverunt contra Sysaram, quoniam non tantum scripturarum auctoritatibus sed etiam phisicis rationibus hereses confutaverunt. . . .[1]

Of the stars of philosophy it is said, Judg. 5 [20], 'The stars remaining in their order fought against Sisara.' Sisara—'exclusion'—signifies heresy. The stars are doctors versed in the arguments of natural philosophy (*phisicis rationibus*), as . . . Dionysus and Hilarius, who went around all the schools of Greece, and Augustine and others who fought against Sisara, since they confuted heresies not only with Scriptural authorities but also with arguments from natural philosophy. . . .

He goes on to say, however, that 'philosophies' are not to be studied for their own sake, but as auxiliaries to theology, and that this sort of study should be regarded as a stage in a career, on the way to theology, rather than as the end of the line.[2]

Most will agree that Jean was probably addressing university clerics. Perhaps not them alone, for a little further on he explicitly states that there were lay people present: ' "And on the earth distress of nations" [Luke 21: 5], that is among the

---

12ᵛᵃ). The last quoted sentence suggests that by *secularis scientia* Jean means civil law. A problem with this is that the general context is an analysis of the situation at Paris ('Triplex est lumen clericorum Parisiensium'), while the study of civil law was forbidden at Paris in 1219 by Honorius III (*Rashdall's Medieval Universities*, edd. F. M. Powicke and A. B. Emden, i (Oxford 1936), 322): I do not know how far the prohibition was observed. The remark with which Jean concludes his section on the heaven of the Church further complicates the problem of his scheme of classification: 'Hec autem sunt signa in celo ecclesie ut clero: sole, luna, et stellis: id est, theologis, legistis, phisicis sive decretistis' (MS cit., fo. 12ᵛᵇ). I suspect that Jean may have used a confused *reportatio* of a sermon he actually delivered, and that he failed to revise it properly.

[1] MS BN lat. 16477, fo. 12ᵛᵃ. ut dicit Dionysus *the* dicit *may have been supplied by the scribe in error: he may have read the text to mean* '. . . *as Dionysus says* . . .'

[2] 'Sed notabile est quod dicit: in cursu et ordine. In ordine: notatur quod philosophie non sunt addiscende propter se, sed propter sacram scripturam. In cursu: notatur quod non semper in studio illo sedendum est, sed quasi transeundum (*corr. from* transeundo) est ad theologiam. . . .' (ibid., fo. 12ᵛᵃ).

laity a distress (*pressura*) of injury, a disorder of knowledge, a drying up of mercy. This is the earth, through which the condition (*status*) of the laity is signified; since they are present, I pass over [this]. . . .'[1] It is possible that a *non* has dropped out of the text, and that what Jean really said was 'since they are *not* present', meaning that there was no point in rebuking the absent. But even if this emendation is not adopted, the phrase would not imply that there were *only* lay people present—rather the contrary, if anything. If we leave the text of this sentence as it is and take it in conjunction with the other passages quoted from this sermon, the picture that emerges is of a mixed congregation, including both academics and laity. One retains the impression that it was first and foremost to the academics that Jean was speaking.

The remark about the laity 'being present' has a further implication: that this was a sermon which had actually been delivered. Should we therefore infer that the sermon cycle to which it belongs is not a 'model' collection? That does not follow, as should become clear. True, the sermon is so unusual that one wonders whether Jean de la Rochelle's collection might have a different function from that of the other collections to which reference has been made, yet the grounds for so supposing are really rather slight, since Jean de la Rochelle's collection seems from surviving manuscripts to have been circulated in much the same sort of way as they were, and since it is not the only collection with passages apparently directed towards academics.

What all this amounts to is that there is a considerable problem about the function and audience of sermon collections. On the one hand, we have seen that there are forcible arguments to back up the assumption that model sermons were tools for popular preachers. On the other hand, there are the passages apparently directed to audiences utterly different from the normal lay congregation.

---

[1] 'In terris vero pressura gentium, id est in laicis pressura iniurie, confusio scientie, ariditas misericordie. Hec sunt in deorsum. Hec est terra, per quam status laicorum significatur, qui quoniam sunt presentes dimitto' (ibid., fo. 12ᵛᵇ).

The elements of a solution to this paradox may be found in the prologue to the liturgical (as opposed to the *ad status*) sermon collection of Guibert de Tournai. This tells the story of how he came to 'publish' the collection, and amidst the commonplaces of prologues there are some revealing passages. This is not the place to translate the prologue as a whole, but the parts of it which bear directly on our problem deserve to be quoted.[1]

He begins with what one might call the 'they urged me to publish' topos, but in the course of it he mentions that the sermons in question had originally been delivered to the clergy of Paris in Latin: 'Having been frequently asked to gather together and unite in one volume—like different twigs in one little bundle—certain sermons which I had preached in Latin to the clergy of Paris...'[2] The implications for our problem are obvious.

Guibert could not decide what to do. He wanted to satisfy the people who asked him to publish, but he feared to loose tongues to the detriment of his reputation. Anyway, he had not finished it. (There is an endearing reference to the difficulty of finishing the work when preoccupied with lecturing duties.)[3] Then—for Guibert seems to have been highly thought of in his day—he received letters from the pope on the subject, and this left him little choice but to produce something. (Two letters from 'Pope Alexander [IV]', presumably genuine, are indeed appended to the introduction, together with a reply from Guibert.)

'Therefore, when I found a period of time a little more free from pressure of work, I collected certain sermons or

---

[1] It was at the suggestion of L.-J. Bataillon that I read the prologue properly, and with the problem of audience and function in mind.

[2] 'Rogatus pluries ut sermones quosdam quos ad clerum Parisiensem latina (*ms adds and expunges* verba) predicarem lingua in volumen unum conpingens quasi diversos surculos in unum fasciculum congregarem...' (MS BN lat. 15942, fo. 2ra). predicarem] predicaveram *MS Brussels, Bibl. Roy. II. 1125 (cat. No. 1891), fo. ccclxxxvii^{va}. (Minor variants also).*

[3] '... nec non officio lectionis animo plurimum occupatus partem longe maiorem totius operis (*corr. from* opere) que deficiebat opusculo propter occupationes anxias perficere non poteram bono modo' (MS BN lat. 15942, fo. 2ra).

collationes—especially sermons for saints' days (*de sanctis*)
—in the form in which I had delivered (*contuleram*) or
preached them, and did not alter them, but wrote some new
ones and added them, and sent it off to the supreme pontiff.'[1]
This shows the different ways in which sermons could find
their way into a compilation: some Guibert took out of the
drawer, as it were, where he had left them after delivering
them on some definite occasion in the past (in Latin to the
clergy of Paris?), while he seems to have written others
specially to send to Alexander.

The passage which follows is not entirely clear, though
certainly relevant to the problem: 'However, since the
venerable father of pious memory passed away and the little
work was not yet perfected, I did not think it presumptious or
harmful if the same pen were to revise the unfinished
material, and bring the revised version to perfection, and
administer it to meet the needs of the more simple sort of
persons in the way that a tube of lead administers a little drop
of liquid.'[2] If the work was unfinished, what had he sent to the
pope?[3] I assume that Guibert had cobbled together a book of
sermons to send to Pope Alexander, but that he was not
happy with it and wanted to rewrite it. The most significant
point for our purpose is that he was revising it to fit the needs
of the more simple sort of person ('simpliciorum usibus').
Whether he means the more simple sort of preacher, in need
of models, or the more simple sort of congregation, is not
entirely obvious. Either way, popular preaching seems the
likely function.

---

[1] 'Cum igitur tempus paulo vacantius reperissem, sermones quosdem de sanctis
maxime sive collationes sicut ea contuleram vel predicaveram recolligens non
mutavi, quosdam superaddendo de novo conficiens, summo pontifici destinavi'
(ibid., fo. 2[ra]).

[2] 'Verum quia venerabilis pater pie memorie transiit (transito *ms*) ex hoc mundo
nec dum opusculo consummato, presumptuosum vel iniuriosum non credidi si
materiam inchoatam stilus ipse repeteret, repetitam perficeret, et simpliciorum
usibus [*col. b*] talem qualem humoris stillulam plumbi fistula ministraret' (ibid., fo.
2[ra-rb]).

[3] I have understood 'summo pontifici destinavi' (see n. 1) to mean 'I sent [it] to the
pope', rather than, say, 'I intended it for the pope'.

'. . . But since I have spoken on the same theme frequently both to clergy and to laity, those who read these things should not be filled with scorn if I have pursued the theme I have chosen through several sermons. It seemed indeed ridiculous to me to promise something in the division of the theme, which was not rendered in speech when he who had made the promise carried it out, with the help of the grace of God.'[1] The high-flown language thought necessary in prologues, and which (in my opinion) does not suit Guibert at all, not only makes the Latin difficult to express in reasonable English, but also fails to convey the thought without ambiguity. The basic point, that Guibert has sometimes announced a plan which is carried out in the course of several successive sermons, is clear enough, but what exactly does he mean by 'both to the clergy and to the laity (*populo*)'? Does he mean that the congregations were mixed? Or does he mean that he had given some sermons to clerics and others to lay people? The latter seems more likely, but how does it fit with what he says about divisions announced in advance? Surely he does not mean that he had sometimes announced a plan at the beginning of a sermon to one type of audience, and continued the execution of it for the benefit of a different category of congregation? Perhaps he is saying that he had preached blocks of sermons united by a plan to clerics, and other such blocks to lay people, though if this is what he means he might have said so more clearly. Guibert's lack of verbal or mental clarity is irritating at times. Fortunately, it is not essential for us to know exactly what he was driving at here; what matters for our purpose is the clear implication that the sermon collection has a mixed origin: it is not composed exclusively of sermons originally delivered to the clergy, nor of sermons originally delivered to the laity.

---

[1] 'Verum quoniam super eodem themate pluries tam clero quam populo sum locutus non afficiantur fastidio qui hec legerint, si thema propositum diversis fuero sermonibus [*fo. 2*ʳᵃ] prosecutus. Ridiculum mihi siquidem videbatur aliquid in thematis divisione promittere quod in prosecutione promittentis (*ms adds and expunges* verbis) verbum non redderet divina gratia commitante' (MS BN lat. 15942, fo. 2ʳᵇ⁻ᵛᵃ).

To summarize the conclusions (or rather, those relevant here) which may be drawn from Guibert's prologue:

1. The starting-point of the collection's history was a set of sermons delivered in Latin to the clergy. Later Guibert included sermons originally delivered to congregations either wholly or partly lay.

2. The collection was intended to meet the needs of 'the more simple', so that the ultimate audience envisaged was more probably lay.

3. Some modifications were made to suit the sermons for this function. Yet, when worried whether it was acceptable to include successions of sermons on the same text, he would not appear (from his own words) to have envisaged changing the plan that bound them together, or boiling them down into a single sermon. Moreover, we know that in the version which he sent to the pope he included some sermons unchanged, just as he had delivered them. Other preachers may also have included unrevised sermons in 'published' collections.

Drawing these threads together, one is led towards the conclusion that the line between clerical and popular preaching was a faint one, easy to cross when a model sermon collection was being put together. Guibert de Tournai's sermons to the Paris clergy could be adapted—or perhaps not much adapted—for the use of the simple. Sermons 'to both clergy and laity', *tam clero quam populo*—whatever the precise meaning of the phrase—could be represented in the collection. Guibert does not seem to find this lack of homogeneity surprising. Were his sermons to the people very different from his sermons to the clergy, except for the language? We shall have to return to the question of how far preachers varied the form and content of their sermons according to audience.

Meanwhile, the bearing of Guibert's prologue on the problem of audience and function hardly needs to be spelled out. Individual sermons which formed part of a 'published' collection might, when originally delivered, have had a function and audience different from those of the collection of which they had come to form a part; no wonder, then, if model sermon collections sometimes contain passages intended for academic clerics. If the collections were put together in a way anything like the process that Guibertus describes, it would be amazing if no sermons betrayed traces of their earlier existence. A tension between the predominantly popular function and audience of the collection as a whole and the academic and/or clerical function and audience of some parts of it would be quite natural.

Yet the very fact that it was possible to incorporate sermons delivered to academic clerics into 'published' model sermon series should give pause for thought about the function of these collections. That they were mainly for popular preaching I would be very loath to deny, for I doubt whether anything else could explain the large number and wide diffusion of model sermons. That they were *exclusively* for popular preaching, on the other hand, must now seem doubtful.

Peyraut's remark that 'if the sermon is to clerics, for them you should touch on the love of sacred Scripture'[1] becomes comprehensible on the assumption that the collection was aimed at an ultimate public *either* of lay people *or* of clerics, according to demand. Preachers would need to give sermons to the laity much more often than to clerics, but in principle sermons from the same collection could be adapted to either sort of audience. It was pointed out in the first part of this book that one cannot draw a sharp line between learned culture and lay culture, and in the next part it will be argued that even university sermons were more like popular sermons than like scholastic exercises. Once these antitheses begin to fade away, it seems unnecessary to assume that they had a specific function and audience. The commonest way of using them need not have been the only way of using them.

There seems no reason why they should not have been used

---

[1] See above, p. 113, n. 1.

on occasion to provide material for sermons to nuns, or for clerics if it was an occasion in which no great originality was required. To preach a ready-made model as an official university sermon would no doubt have been bad form. However, it may be that future research will show that models were used, selectively and with adaptations, even for academic preaching.[1] Some sermon collections may even have been used for private reading.[2] Who is to say that the model sermons of St Bonaventura were not sometimes copied and read for the same reasons as his treatises? Again, it has been argued for the later Middle Ages that one reason for publishing Latin sermon collections was literary self-consciousness.[3] Perhaps such motives played a part in the thirteenth century, as Guibert de Tournai's denial of them suggests.[4] However, this particular line of interpretation should not be pursued too far. Literary self-consciousness might explain why a preacher would want to put a book of sermons into circulation, but that in itself would not make people copy the work, unless the author were famous. It is worth noting than many of the authors of model sermon collections are very obscure, and

---

[1] This may be the implication of unpublished research by L.-J. Bataillon and Nicole Bériou.

[2] I do not know how much weight to put on Jacopo da Varazze's use of the word 'readers' at the end of the prologue to his *de tempore* sermons: '... ut presens opusculum ad laudem suam dirigat, et ad legentium utilitatem convertat...' (ed. Conrad Winters: Cologne, [1478?]; I use BL IB. 4101).

[3] 'Nur in einem Punkt hat man bisher authentische Predigtüberlieferung angenommen: die lateinischen Predigtsammlungen des späteren Mittelalters seien vom Verfasser selbst aufgezeichnet worden als homiletisches Hilfsmittel für den Klerus. Aber die Betrachtung der lateinischen Predigten als nur homiletisches Hilfsmittels trifft nicht ganz ihre wirkliche Bedeutung, denn die Aufzeichnung lateinischer Predigten geschieht auf einer sehr bewussten literarischen Ebene, nicht um der reinen Zweckhaftigkeit willen. Das Selbstbewusstsein des Autors und der Stolz auf sein Werk treten vor oder neben den Gesichtspunkt homiletischer Verwendung....' (P.-G. Völker, 'Die Überlieferungsformen mittelalterlicher deutscher Predigten', *Zeitschrift für deutsches Altertum und deutsche Literatur*, 92, (1963), 212–27, at p. 226.

[4] 'Nec indignentur obsecro michi qui meliora scripserunt quia scientia me precellunt et facundia. Non enim in eorum nominis vel operis derogationem hec scripsi (*ms adds and expunges* et ad), non ad favorem hominum, deus novit (*corr. from* novis), sed ex caritatis imperio accedente et antecedente, quasi necessitate precepti....' (MS BN lat. 15942, fo. 2ʳᵇ).

that there are a vast number of anonymous manuscripts. A collection as important as the Franciscan *Legifer* (the '*collationes fratrum*') can remain completely anonymous. Moreover, theories of this kind do not account for collections of sermons too drastically abbreviated for normal reading, nor instructions to preachers like those discussed above. I would suggest no more than that some collections may have been used like treatises, and that some writers of model sermons may have had this kind of use in mind, as a subsidiary function of the work.[1]

If model sermon collections were a multi-purpose genre, which could provide reading matter for clerics and sermons to be preached to them as well as sermons for lay congregations, then the place of these collections in the religious culture of the thirteenth century will have to be partially redefined. Clerics not only drew the water from the bottomless well of homiletic material, but drank from it together with the laity. Or, to change the analogy, clerics were on the demand as well as on the supply side. The ideas and structures of thought in sermon collections would seem to be a common element in clerical and lay culture.

---

[1] In this connection it is worth noting a passage from the *Sermones in Epistolas et Evangelia dominicalia* of Jacques de Vitry, although he was not a friar. It begins: 'Et quoniam identitas generat fastidium, et aliqua placent uni, et alia alii, in officio cuiuslibet Dominicae tria themata ponentes, et tertium plerunque prolixius exponentes, diversis hominum generibus satisfacere curavimus, parvos, mediocres, et maiores contexando sermones . . .' (from the unpaginated 'Proemium' of the 1575 Antwerp edn., for which I use BL 1474 d. 11). The gist of the remarks which follow would seem to be that Jacques was providing three kinds of sermons: short ones for people who did not have much time free for 'study or reading' (*studio aut lectioni*), middle-length ones for those with somewhat more leisure for study but no taste for prolix sermons, and finally longer sermons for those given over to a life of contemplation. Here I am left with the impression that Jacques may be thinking of the use of the collection for reading rather than preaching. On the other hand, in the same passage he speaks of the 'capacitatem auditorum'. Moreover, the following passage suggests that this is a model sermon collection to be preached to the laity: 'Quando vero in conventu et congregatione sapientum Latino idiomate loquimur, tunc plura dicere possumus, eo quod ad singularia non oportet descendere: laicis autem oportet quasi ad oculum, et sensibiliter omnia demonstrare, ut sit verbum praedicatoris apertum, et lucidum, velut gemmula carbunculi in ornamento auri. . . .' (ibid.). The 'Proemium' needs to be studied together with the sermons. In the mean time my guess is that this is a multi-purpose collection.

The task of adjusting, expanding, or contracting the material to suit the needs of specific congregations was probably left to the individual user of the models. Early in his *de epistolis* collection Guillaume Peyraut instructs the preacher as follows: 'For the different kinds of sins from which one should rise up, see in the *Treatise on Vices,* according to the diversity of those to whom you will preach.'[1] It is true that Peyraut is not speaking explicitly about clerical and lay congregations. A remark in a sermon of Pierre de Reims is clearer on this point, though brief. 'Note concerning the ten commandments to the laity'[2] would seem to mean that the sermon could be, but did not have to be, preached to the laity. The words are in effect a cue for a preacher who wished to use the model for a sermon to the laity to insert further remarks, on the principle that some things might need to be spelled out to them which could be taken for granted in a clerical congregation.[3] The inference to be drawn is that this model sermon was meant to be preached either to a clerical congregation or to a lay one, or presumably even to a mixture of the two. In the light of the other passages which we have examined it seems likely that this ambivalence was normal. The exceptions would be the *ad status* sermon collections, in which sermons are tailor-made for particular walks of life. But major *ad status* collections are few in number—there are only three or four from the thirteenth century[4]—so that they

---

[1] 'De diversis vero modis peccatorum a quibus surgendum est require in tractatu de vitiis (iudiciis *ms*) secundum diversitatem illorum quibus predicabis' (MS BN lat. 16472, fo. 4ʳᵇ); from a sermon on the text 'Hora est' (Rom. 13: 11), Schneyer, *Repertorium,* ii. 543, No. 130. This should probably be taken to mean that the sermon could be used for different sorts of audiences, and that the preacher should add material on vices appropriate for any given audience. An alternative interpretation, understanding Peyraut to mean the diversity of people within a given audience, does not seem so likely.

[2] 'Nota de decem preceptis ad laicos' (MSS Bodleian, Laud Misc. 506, fo. 77ᵛᵇ, BN lat. 15960, fo. 115ᵛᵇ). de] *Paris ms om.* The sermon is Schneyer, *Repertorium,* iv. 753, No. 468. I have failed to find this sermon in MS BL Arundel 206, though I have only searched thoroughly in the part of the manuscript where it ought to be.

[3] Cf. the passage from Jacques de Vitry quoted above, p. 126, n. 1 (end).

[4] Those of Guibert de Tournai, Jacques de Vitry, and Humbert de Romans; the genre of John of Wales' *Communiloquium* is more ambiguous.

are exceptions which prove the rule. Perhaps they provided all the specific sermons that were needed, so that the other collections, the overwhelming majority, could concentrate on the common ground which clergy and laity shared.

To understand the language and mentality of mendicant sermons we must reconstruct the contexts to which they belonged. The Apostolic movement, towns and their hinterland, changes in lay culture—these are the aspects of the setting which first meet the eye. But the more precise and immediate context was a system of communication, of which the surviving manuscript books are archaeological survivals. Model sermon collections are a part of the second tier of this system. They would have been used together with *exemplum* collections and other preaching aids; the first tier—a hypothesis, but one for which evidence is accumulating—would seem to be represented by different types of preaching aid, which may not be explicitly designated as such.

Mendicant model sermons (and other preaching aids) of this period were normally transmitted in Latin, which gave them what might be called a spaceless character: they were not tied to local or national contexts. Paradoxically, Latin transmission left more room for the preacher's initiative. When preaching to the laity he would normally turn the Latin into the vernacular, and this would probably lead him to give a freer rendering than if his written model had been in the same language as the living sermon he was going to preach. (For some sorts of clerical audience, on the other hand, he might feel he had to adapt his model in order not to seem too derivative.) The fact that model sermon collections were used in conjuction with other preaching aids would also tend to make the living sermon freer, for it was left to the preacher to do the combining. The differentiation between model sermon collections and other genres of preaching aid imposed a work of synthesis on the preacher: he would often have to decide where to introduce an *exemplum*, for instance, if his model sermon did not include any.

The substantial degree of initiative which the nature of the medium left to the preacher limits our knowledge of living sermons. That side of the historical reality we will seldom be able to recover. But the model sermon collections themselves represent a historical reality: a sort of distilled essence of what was thought worth preaching.

One sermon collection could be a point of departure for innumerable preachers and sermons. The fact that sermons were reproduced in a semi-standardized way to supply this market has its significance for cultural history. Although every manuscript is unique, its individuality does not leave a mark on the thought if the copy is more or less standardized. If near-identical copies were widely available and used, the mentality which lies behind a sermon collection must be seen as a sort of common possession, something linking many minds whose individual identity is now lost.

A model sermon collection, whose concrete historical existence took the form of many manuscript books, is like a printed text and not like a printed text: like a printed text because it could be reproduced in a standardized way, unlike one because it did not have to be. For there would also be manuscript copies which underwent changes far more drastic than scribal errors. Sermons from different collections could be mingled, which is a different way in which model sermons represent a communally owned cultural property. Then again, there are modifications of the text of individual sermons, frequently taking the form of abridgement to schemas of divisions and Scriptural authorities. The habit of abbreviating in this way also has its relation to the language and mentality of the sermons. Divisions and authorities are precisely the distinctive features of the new sermon form which crystallized in the thirteenth century and which is itself a way of thinking rather than a simple matter of literary presentation. There is thus a congeniality between this form—a form of thought—and a very common manner of abridging sermons in the course of transmission.

A reconstruction of the audience and function of sermon

collections is possibly even more indispensable for an understanding of their forms of thought. One's appreciation of any text is necessarily limited if one does not know for what and for whom it was intended. A model sermon collection can represent different chronological layers of intention. We have seen that when putting together a collection for publication a preacher might incorporate sermons he had previously delivered. He could take a sermon originally preached to academic clerics, and put it into the sort of collection which historians—more rightly than wrongly—have assumed to be popular. We may thus have to deal with at least two levels of intention, both embodied in the surviving collection: an initial intention to persuade an audience of clerical intellectuals, say, and a subsequent intention to make stereotyped material available to an anonymous double public of preachers and their listeners. The subsequent intention might even be that of a different man, a compiler. Such a manner of compilation—this prehistory which lies behind at least some collections—must have fostered (and perhaps also presupposes) an assimilation by different social orders of a common language of thought. It is the same with our other more tentative conclusion about audience, that the models were not intended to serve popular preaching to the laity only. This too implies that the forms of thought in the sermons were a kind of lingua franca, comprehensible to both clerics and laymen. 'In the pulpit, the speaker has no choice but to take his audience as he finds them. He can but draw them on to the conclusions already involved in their premisses.'[1] If the audience of model sermons is as multiple as I have suggested, then it is the common factors in thirteenth-century religious culture that the collections will tend to reflect. They were not simply a language which the clergy spoke to the laity (any more than they were just a language which the clergy spoke to the

---

[1] M. Pattison, 'Tendencies of Religious Thought in England, 1688–1750', in *Essays and Reviews* (2nd edn., London, 1860), 254–329, at p. 277.

clergy). This will have to be borne in mind when we come to ask whether the sermon collections can be explained as a product of an urban environment, or, alternatively, as a spin-off of scholasticism.

III.

Mendicant Preaching and the World of Learning

i. The Geography and Prosopography of Preaching

... quia tales infatuantur et in necessitate deficit ei [*sic*] sensus et scientia et cetera, sicut fabulose dicitur quod vulpes obviavit gatto: Bone compater, vos videmini michi animal bone industrie et elegantis forme, si astutia apparentie respondeat. Dicatis ergo in amore dei que est ars vestra? Respondit gattus: Ego scio capere mures, et nichil aliud scio facere. Cumque hoc dixisset, quesivit a vulpe: Et vobis, bone compater, que est ars vestra? Respondit vulpes: Ego longo tempore studui Parisius, et scio capere galinas et capones optimos; et si vis venire mecum, docebo te artem meam. Respondit gattus: Et quomodo potestis effugere manus hominum? Respondit vulpes: Ego optime evado, propter meam astutiam. Cumque pariter loquerentur, veniunt venatores et statim gattus ascendit arborem.—Modo probabitur sapientia vestra. Veniunt canes ad vulpem, capiunt fugientem. Cumque eam canes enormiter depilarent, ait gattus: Bone compater, ubi est modo tanta sapientia quam Parisius didicisti? ...[1]

... for such people make idiots of themselves, and in time of need they are left without sense and knowledge etc., as it is told in the fable that a fox met a cat [and said], 'My good fellow, you seem to me to be a very industrious and an elegantly formed animal, if cleverness (*astutia*) corresponds to appearance. In the love of God, then, say what your art is.' The cat replied, 'I know how to catch mice, and I do not know how to do anything else.' And when he had said this, he asked the fox, 'And you, my good fellow, what is your art?' The fox replied, 'I studied for a long time at Paris, and I know how to catch hens and excellent capons: and if you want to come with me, I will teach you my art.' The cat replied, 'And how are you

---

[1] MS Birmingham University 6/iii/19, fo. cxviii[vb].

able to escape the hands of men?' The fox replied, 'I get away from them very successfully, because of my cleverness.' And while they were talking together, up come some hunters, and the cat immediately climbs a tree. 'Now your wisdom will be put to the test,' [he said]. Up come the dogs to the fox, and they catch it as it flees. While the dogs tear at it horribly the cats says, 'My good fellow, where now is all that wisdom which you learned at Paris? . . .'

The anonymous Italian Franciscan[1] who brings this story into a *collatio* on 'Hope' is himself a little inclined to dwell on his time at Paris: 'The same point is made by what a certain Master of Theology at Paris preached . . .',[2] he says in a *collatio* on the Devil; 'The same point is made by what I found written at Paris in a work (*scripto*) which was old and pretty well thought of',[3] in a *collatio* on 'correptio' (reproof or chastisement). There are other examples of this kind of thing in the collection—it is rather an endearing feature. It would seem likely that this Italian friar had been sent by his province to Paris to study. Both the Franciscan and Dominican orders had systems for selecting academically gifted friars from all parts of Europe for a period of study at the intellectual capital of Europe, and if the anonymous Franciscan had been a member of this élite it would not be surprising if he was a little conscious of it.[4] Occasional references in

---

[1] Cf. above, p. 81.

[2] 'Ad idem facit quod quidam magister in theologia Parisius predicavit . . .' (MS Birmingham University 6/iii/19, fo. clxxxxi^va).

[3] 'Ad idem facit quod inveni scriptum Parisius in quodam antiquo scripto et satis approbato' (ibid., fo. clxx^va).

[4] For estimates of numbers and sidelights on the system, especially that of the Dominicans, see A. Dondaine, 'Documents pour servir à l'histoire de la province de France. L'Appel au Concil (1303)', *Archivum Fratrum Praedicatorum*, 22 (1952), 381–439, at pp. 384–9. For the Franciscans, cf. L. Beaumont-Maillet, *Le Grand Couvent des Cordeliers de Paris. Étude historique et archéologique de XIIIᵉ siècle à nos jours* (Bibliothèque de l'École des Hautes Études, IVᵉ Section, 325, Paris, 1975), 24–6, H. Felder, *Geschichte der wissenschaftlichen Studien im Franziskanerorden bis um die Mitte des 13. Jahrhunderts* (Freiburg im Breisgau, 1904), 234–7, and D. Berg, *Armut und Wissenschaft. Beiträge zur Geschichte des Studienwesens der Bettelorden im 13. Jahrhundert* (Geschichte und Gesellschaft, 15; Düsseldorf, 1977), 75–6 and 121–4. On the Dominicans, see also Berg, ibid. 60–4 and 119–21, C. Douais, *Essais sur l'organisation des études dans l'ordre des Frères Prêcheurs au treizième et au quatorzième siècle (1216–1342)* (Paris and Toulouse, 1884), especially p. 130, and

Salimbene's chronicle give us a picture, from his personalized angle, of Paris as the Mecca for the most talented men of his order.[1] There is, for instance, the case of the two friars who arrived at Arles at about the time that Salimbene took his preaching examination, on their way to study at Toulouse.[2] Salimbene says that they had studied together with him for several years in the Pisan convent, and that they were good (*boni scolares*).[3] He reports the aggrieved words of a brother Mark, who had unsuccessfully asked a favour on their behalf: 'It is the truth, that they come from their minister, who knows them, and because he knows that they are good, therefore he sends them to the Toulouse *studium*, so that afterwards they may go to Paris.'[4]

Though an élite, such friars were numerous enough to have made a big impact on their orders. There were certainly far more of them than we know about. If we were to base an estimate on the number of known Franciscan and Dominican Paris masters[5] it would fall short of the mark by a very long way (even if a large allowance were made for masters whose names have not come down to us), for the simple reason that only a small proportion of friars sent to Paris to study were expected to try for a degree. No friars took the Paris arts degrees and the vast majority never proceeded to the theology degrees.[6] They did not stay long enough to do so. The normal

---

W. A. Hinnebusch, *The History of the Dominican Order*, ii (New York, 1973) 39. For both orders see Giulia Barone, 'La Legislazione sugli "Studia" dei Predicatori e dei Minori', in *Le scuole degli Ordini Mendicanti (secoli xiii–xiv)*, (Convegni del Centro di Studi sulla Spiritualità Medievale, 17 [1976]; Accademia Tudertina: Todi, 1978), 207–47, especially pp. 212–15, 224–5, 231–2, 235, 236–7, 240, 242.

  [1] See the passages put together by Felder, *Geschichte*, 235–7.
  [2] Salimbene, *Cronica*, ed Holder-Egger, p. 311.
  [3] Ibid.
  [4] Ibid. 312.
  [5] Cf. P. Glorieux, *Répertoire des maîtres en théologie de Paris au xiiie siècle*, two vols. (Études de Philosophie Médiévale, 17, 18; Paris, 1933).
  [6] The contrary assumption dies hard even among good scholars: G. Barone, 'La legislazione sugli "Studia" dei predicatori', in *Le scuole degli Ordini Mendicanti*, p. 237: '. . . a S. Jacques viene inviato solo chi si dimostra effettivamente capace di raggiungere il grado di maestro'; J. Moorman, *A History of the Franciscan Order from its Origins to the Year 1517* (Oxford, 1968), 123: 'Finally, there were the schools at the

period of study for friars selected to study at Paris seems to have been three years for a Dominican, and four years for a Franciscan.[1] The *crème de la crème* selected to take the theology degrees stayed on a good deal longer.[2] Thus, the *c.*120 Franciscans and Dominicans listed in Glorieux's *Répertoire* of thirteenth-century Paris masters[3] are only the tip of an iceberg. What we know of the quotas sent per province by the two orders, together with some figures from the beginning of the fourteenth century, make it clear that the leavening of former Paris students must have been numerically substantial.[4]

---

universities to which the most apt students could be sent in order that they might take the full academic course, graduate as masters of theology, and so become themselves lectors in other convents.'

[1] Dondaine, 'Documents', p. 384. See Beaumont-Maillet, *Le Grand Couvent des Cordeliers de Paris*, p. 25 and especially p. 27.

[2] According to Beaumont-Maillet, a Franciscan singled out for longer period of study would follow the theology courses not for four but for five years. Then in his sixth year he would lecture on the Bible *cursorie* (one year of this in the thirteenth century, two in the fourteenth). After that he could be nominated Bachelor of the Sentences by the Minister General, and ultimately be licensed as a Master of Theology. Presumably the pattern was not very different for the Dominican *crème de la crème*. According to J. A. Weisheipl, *Friar Thomas d'Aquino. His Life, Thought, and Work* (New York, 1974), 50, Dominicans did not lecture cursorily on the Bible at Paris. I do not know whether Beaumont-Maillet is mistaken in supposing that Franciscans did. Bartholomaeus Anglicus 'totam Bibliam cursorie Parisius legit', according to Salimbene, *Cronica*, ed Holder-Egger, p. 94, but Salimbene did not say whether Bartholomew had already joined the Franciscan Order when he did so.

[3] Cited above, p. 134 n. 5.

[4] The Dominican and Franciscan arrangements were similar but not identical. The Dominicans laid down the number of students to be sent *each year* (three per province). (When some provinces were broken up in the last years of the thirteenth and at the beginning of the fourteenth century this was reduced to two students for some of the new provinces: see Dondaine, 'Documents', p. 384 n. 12.) As we have seen, they would normally stay three years. In 1260 the Franciscans laid down the number of students from each province for whom the Paris convent was bound to provide (books apart) at any one time: two students per province (there being thirty-two provinces at this time). It seems to have been a total, not an annual, quota. These were called 'de debito' students. In addition to them, provinces could send 'de gratia' students, for whose support the Paris house was not responsible. A. Dondaine calculates that at the time of the appeal to the Council (1303) there were at least 170 members, without taking account of novices, *conversi*, etc. (ibid. 386–7). Figures for the Dominicans are more approximate: *c.*250 or even more, though novices, *conversi* etc. might have to be included to make up this high total (ibid.). I imagine that both convents would include a number of friars—even apart from novices, *conversi*, etc.—who were not specially selected students.

It is therefore with justice that Paris has been regarded as the keystone of the Franciscan and Dominican educational systems. Of course, there was in each order a whole network of lesser theological schools—the Dominican system being especially well organized—so that a friar who did not make it to Paris might still receive a thorough theological training.[1] There was, furthermore, a definite trend towards decentralization in the course of the thirteenth century and after.[2] None of this alters the fact of Paris's supremacy. It may well be (as one historian argued) that Salimbene failed to become a lector because he had missed or neglected his chance to study at Paris for his province.[3]

Academically speaking, the friars were as important for Paris as Paris was for the friars. 'The mobility and the centralization of the new religious orders responded adequately to the evolution of society and the Church. . . . The Englishman Alexander of Hales, the German Albert the Great, the Italians Bonaventura and Thomas Aquinas, made Paris the intellectual capital of Christendom. . . .'[4] The history of philosophy and theology in the last three-quarters of the thirteenth century is dominated by Paris friars. It was

[1] Cf. 'Panorama geografico, cronologico e statistico sulla distribuzione degli Studia degli ordini mendicanti' (the contributions by Paul Amargier, Mariano d'Alatri, Colette Ribaucourt, Joanna Cannon, and Jerzy Kłoczowski) in *Le scuole*, pp. 35–149, Berg, *Armut und Wissenschaft*, chs. IV and V *passim*, especially pp. 94–100, 102–3, 108–15, 127–36, 139–40, 142, Hinnebusch, *The History of The Dominican Order*, ii. 29–32, 39–43, Moorman, *History of the Franciscan Order*, 123–4, 133–9.

[2] See the references in the preceding note, and also G. Barone, 'La legislazione sugli "Studia" dei Predicatori e dei Minori' in *Le scuole*, pp. 215, 218, 226, 231–2, 235–8, 242, 244–6.

[3] Felder, *Geschichte*, p. 236. Cf. Salimbene, *Cronica,* ed Holder-Egger, p. 322: 'Et dixit michi frater Rufinus minister: "Ego te misi in Franciam, ut studeres pro provincia mea, et tu ivisti ad conventum Ianuensem, ut habitares ibi? Noveris, quod valde habeo pro malo, quia pro honore mee provincie studentes de aliis provinciis facio venire Bononiam."' It will be noted that Paris is not explicitly mentioned here, but Felder's assumption that it was there that Salimbene had been sent to study seems reasonable. For an ordered chronology of this part of Salimbene's career see B. Schmeidler, in his Preface to Salimbene, *Cronica,* ed Holder-Egger, pp. xi–xiii.

[4] M.-D. Chenu, *Introduction à l'étude de Saint Thomas d'Aquin* (Université de Montréal Publications de l'Institut d'Études Médiévales, 11; (Montreal and Paris, 1950), 18 (my translation).

not that nothing went on anywhere else. Robert Grossesteste (to name one striking example) belongs to the history of Oxford, where a distinctive tradition becomes discernible. Paris had no monopoly, but so far as scholasticism is concerned it did make everywhere else look a little provincial.

The story is not so different when we return to the history of preaching, and our problem is to find out what connections (if any) there may have been between these two parallel phenomena. First, however, the second of them has to be established. Not that it is especially controversial. The reaction of most scholars, if told that Paris was the main centre for the production and diffusion of sermon material in the thirteenth century, would be to say that they had assumed as much. As a matter of fact, however, no one has ever properly compared Paris with other centres in Europe, probably because most monographs on medieval sermons have studied preaching in one country. Here one is in the vexing position of having to prove a point which everyone has tacitly accepted without sufficient reason, and this as a preliminary to the main problem. Still, it is worth while to see where Paris stands in relation to the sermon production of Europe as a whole—to take an overall view of the geography of preaching and try to bring it into focus. So that the comparative importance of Paris may be weighed as well as counted, I include some (much too summary) assessments of preachers listed.

One may begin by trying to establish how many Paris friars wrote model sermon collections. It is not easy to fix an exact number. Should one include a friar like Remigio de' Girolami, who did lecture on the Sentences at Paris but whose career was chiefly set in Florence? On the whole it seems best not to count them as Paris friars, and for this purpose to include in that category only those friars who were at Paris for a substantial period of time, more than just a few years. Nor does it seem helpful to include friars whose sermons never went into general circulation (another reason for excluding Remigio). On these criteria one gets a minimum estimate, but this is preferable to a shaky maximum. It should be said immediately that the categories are not clear-cut, and that what follows is only an attempt to get a better sense of the order of magnitude.

The minimum total is about six, or perhaps eight if one counts a couple of Franciscans who are on the margin of our categories. There are three Dominicans; only one is known to have been a Master of Theology, but the other two are so closely associated with the Paris Dominican house of St-Jacques that it would be artificial to exclude them. Thus, Pierre de Reims was prior of St-Jacques from 1227–30, and served at least twice as provincial of France; his links with the Dominican community at Paris were presumably close, then, even though I know of no evidence that he taught in the theology faculty.[1] We have already had occasion to look at one of the sermons on the Apostles of Pierre de Reims (for the ideas about the *vita apostolica* that it draws together).[2] In addition to his series for the Common of the saints, from which this sermon comes, Pierre composed a *de tempore* series and a *de sanctis* series on particular saints.[3]

Like Pierre de Reims, Hugues de Saint-Cher was both prior of St-Jacques and provincial of the French province (twice), but he was also a university master of great influence.[4] Three series of model Sunday sermons have been attributed to him: one based on the Gospel readings, one on the Epistle readings, and one on both together.[5] The attributions seem

---

[1] For a brief *Lebenslauf* see Schneyer, *Repertorium*, iv. 724, and Kaeppeli, *Scriptores*, iii. 256.

[2] See above, pp. 44–52.

[3] Schneyer, *Geschichte*, p. 155. From Schneyer's data there would seem to be further sets of sermons in MS Brussels, Bibl. Roy. II. 1132. See ibid. and *Repertorium*, iv. 740–52.

[4] For a *Lebenslauf*, together with a bibliography and a list of Hugues' works and manuscripts, see Kaeppeli, *Scriptores*, ii. 269–81.

[5] Cf. Kaeppeli, ibid. ii. 280, Schneyer, *Geschichte*, pp. 141–2, and *Repertorium*, ii. 758–78. Schneyer also gives incipits for 'Sermones excerpti et variati: Clm. 12660; cf. Innsbruck, *UB 312*', ibid. 778 ff.

secure enough.[1] These model sermons tend to consist principally of schematic divisions or distinctions and authorities, but there are a good many manuscripts, so they were presumably in demand.[2]

The model sermons of our third Dominican, Nicolas de Gorran,[3] also seem dry and telegraphic. As with those of Hugues de Saint-Cher, their success makes more sense on the assumption that they were not meant to be read as religious literature, but to be used. Some of the introductory passages are not too telescoped and unreadable; there is a thoughtful attempt to settle the problem of evil at the start of a sermon, for instance.[4] Though brief, it is less arid than the remainder of the sermon would seem to most modern readers. (As a 'live' preacher, on the other hand, Nicolas de Gorran must have been rather effective. Pierre de Limoges, connoisseur and collector of sermons, includes no fewer than twenty-eight sermons or extracts in the manuscripts which are now BN lat. 16481 and 16482.[5] The sermon which Nicolas preached to the Paris Béguinage on Monday, 1 May 1273, recently edited by Nicole Bériou, shows how enjoyable he can be when we have a full sermon rather than a compressed model.[6]) Though never a Master of Theology, he deserves to be called a Paris theologian. He belongs to the history of St-Jacques, of which

---

[1] Lecoy de la Marche, *La Chaire*, pp. 124–5, cautiously suggested Hugues Aycelin de Billom (d. 1297) as an alternative candidate, but L.-J. Bataillon points out to me that one of the manuscripts, MS BN lat. 16473, is among the books left to the Sorbonne by Robert de Sorbon, who died in 1274. Cf. L. Delisle, *Le Cabinet des Manuscrits de la Bibliothèque Nationale*, ii (Paris, 1874), 173.

[2] Cf. Schneyer, *Geschichte*, p. 142. My own judgement of the content is merely an impression, based on random forays into MS BN lat. 15946.

[3] On Nicolas see Lecoy de la Marche, *La Chaire*, pp. 135–6, and Schneyer, *Geschichte*, p. 156.

[4] Sermon on the text 'Scitis, quoniam cum gentes essetis' (1 Cor. 12: 2), Schneyer, *Repertorium*, iv. 268, No. 203: 'Antiqua quaestio fuit unde malum habuit ortum. Non ita unde bonum: quia planum est quod omne bonum est a summo bono. Vidit enim Deus cuncta quae fecerat et erant valde bona: unde ergo malum? Dicendum quod malum hominis fuit a voluntate deficiente: daemone suggerente: et homine consentiente. Et haec tria notantur in verbo proposito' *(Fundamentum aureum* (Antwerp, 1620), 53; cf. MS BL Royal 9 B. IV, fo. 21vb).

[5] N. Bériou, 'La Prédication au béguinage de Paris pendant l'année liturgique 1272–1273', *Recherches Augustiniennes*, 13 (1978), 105–229, at p. 174.

[6] Printed ibid. 222–9.

he became prior *c*.1276,[1] and he wrote a number of Bible commentaries,[2] so he was in some sense in the same league as the Masters of the Sacred Page. His output for preachers, it should be added, includes not only sermons but also a collection of *distinctiones*. These belong to a late phase in the history of their genre. 'The words which are distinguished are more likely to be restricted to virtues, vices, actions good and bad, and other moral topics, rather than to include the birds, beasts, and curious persons and places which had captured the attention of the earlier collectors.'[3]

If this inevitably rather dry catalogue of Paris Dominicans were to be extended into the early fourteenth century, the sermons of Jacques de Lausanne[4] would deserve a place in the foreground. His free use of the technique of comparisons—a lengthy comparison between salvation history and the foundation of a new university by the pope, for instance[5]—makes his sermons seem colourful and lively after the model collections of Hugues de Saint-Cher and Nicolas de Gorran. A line has to be drawn somewhere, however, so we must leaves Jacques and move on to thirteenth-century Franciscans.

The natural starting-point is Jean de la Rochelle. He belongs to the early days of his order's involvement with learning and the higher reaches of academic life. According to the most probable hypothesis, he became master in the private *scola* of the Franciscan house at Paris in 1238, and in

---

[1] Ibid. 174; according to the *Histoire littéraire de la France*, xx (Paris, 1895 edn.), 327, Nicolas became prior of St-Jacques 'après y avoir rempli les fonctions de lecteur'.

[2] Cf. Bériou, 'La Prédication', p. 174; C. Spicq, *Esquisse d'une histoire de l'exégèse latine au Moyen Âge* (Bibliothèque Thomiste, 26; Paris, 1944), 326–7, Kaeppeli, *Scriptores*, iii (1980), pp. 165–6.

[3] R. H. and M. A. Rouse, 'Biblical Distinctions' p. 34.

[4] On whose life and works see Kaeppeli, *Scriptores*, ii. 323–9.

[5] 'Quantum ad primum sciendum quod sedes apostolica, quando instituit universitatem, solet ei dare privilegia et gratias, et quia privilegia nichil valent sine protectore et defensore, ideo, datis privilegiis, dat defensorem contra iniurias et conservatorem privilegiorum. Deus in primis instituit universitatem humani generis . . .' (and so forth) (MS Toulouse 337, fo. xi^vb); from a sermon on the text 'Mitto angelum meum' (Matt. 11: 10), Schneyer, *Repertorium*, iii. 56, No. 23.

1241 succeeded Alexander of Hales as a public regent Master of Theology: that is to say, he moved from being a professor of theology for the Franciscans only to being a professor in the eyes of the university as a whole.[1] Alexander and Jean seem to have been closely associated, with Jean playing second string;[2] but for the history of Franciscan preaching Jean is much more important, for it was he who left full sermon cycles,[3] and the passage from an Advent sermon which was briefly examined in the previous chapter shows how interesting a preacher he can be.[4] (It was argued that this passage shows that the sermon was probably preached 'live' in a Paris University milieu, before being incorporated into the model collection.) Another unexpected and interesting passage, which I cannot forbear from quoting, is his defence of philosophy in a sermon on St Anthony of Padua:

Unde, fratres karissimi, non est arguendum aliarum scientiarum studium, dummodo fiat bona intentione. Immo multum timendum est, ne istud accidat quod figuratur in 1 Reg. XIII: *Porro faber ferrarius non erat in Israel. Cavebant enim Philistei ne forte Hebrei facerent gladium aut lanceam.* Fabri ferrarii sunt doctores philosophie, qui inflexibiles et indomabiles dubitationes extendunt et in modum gladiorum ingenia acuunt et, quasi lanceis splendentibus, rationibus de longe feriunt. Cautela ergo demonum est dissipare studium philosophie, quia nollent quod christiani haberent acutum ingenium.[5]

Wherefore, dearest brothers, the study of other sciences is not to be censured, so long as it is done with good intention. Indeed it is much

---

[1] Here I follow M. M. Dufeil, *Guillaume de Saint-Amour et la polémique universitaire Parisienne 1250-1259*, (Paris, 1972), 6. The question of the Franciscan chairs at Paris is a tangled one, however: see ibid. 6–9. My use of the word 'professor' is of course somewhat anachronistic.

[2] Cf. P. Michaud-Quantin (ed.), Jean de La Rochelle, *Tractatus de divisione multiplici potentiarum animae* (Paris, 1964), 7–8.

[3] Relatively few sermons by Alexander are known: see Schneyer, *Repertorium*, i. 269–70.

[4] See above, pp. 116–19.

[5] Balduinus ab Amsterdam, 'Tres sermones inediti Joannis de Rupella in honorem S. Antonii Patavini', in *Collectanea Franciscana*, 28 (1958), 33–58, at p. 38 and 50–1. I am indebted to L.-J. Bataillon for directing me to this passage.

to be feared that what is prefigured in 1 Kigs. 13 [= 1 Sam. 13] may happen: 'But there was not a single smith in Israel. For the Philistines feared that the Hebrews might perchance make sword or lance.' Smiths are doctors of philosophy, who put forward inflexible and indomitable questions (*dubitationes*) and sharpen intelligences like swords and, as if with gleaming lances, strike with arguments from afar. Therefore, a device of demons is to destroy the study of philosophy, because they do not want Christians to have a sharp intelligence.

(But Jean is not always so interesting).[1]

One of the series of sermons attributed to Jean de la Rochelle may not be by him at all, for there is reason to think that the *de communi* sermons are the work of Eudes Rigaud. Eudes was also Franciscan, and it seems to have been he who succeeded Jean de la Rochelle in the Franciscan's public chair at Paris;[2] he went on to become Archbishop of Rouen. The *de communi* series in question includes not only sermons for general categories of saints, but also other kinds, including synodal sermons.[3] According to a recent study, it is 'highly probable' that one of these had been delivered by Eudes Rigaud, as Archbishop of Rouen, to a diocesan synod in 1250, and 'very possible' that the whole *de communi* collection was Eudes's work.[4] If so, Eudes Rigaud should perhaps be added to the list of Paris friars who wrote sermon collections. But he is one of the marginal cases, for even if he did write the collection it was presumably put together after he had left Paris for Rouen.

The next Franciscan regent master but one after Eudes at

[1] It is highly desirable that more of Jean de la Rochelle's sermons should be edited, especially since the ground has partly been cleared, notably by K. Lynch (ed.), *Jean de la Rochelle, O.F.M. Eleven Marian Sermons* (Franciscan Institute Publications, Text Series, No. 12; The Franciscan Institute, St Bonaventure; New York, Louvain, and Paderborn, 1961), and by L. Duval-Arnould, 'Trois Sermons synodaux de la collection attribuée à Jean de la Rochelle', *Archivum Franciscanum Historicum*, 69 (1976), 336–400, ibid. 70 (1977), 35–71.

[2] Dufeil, *Guillaume de Saint-Amour*, p. 9.

[3] Cf. Duval-Arnould, 'Trois Sermons synodaux' (1976), 342.

[4] Ibid. 400.

Paris was Bonaventura.[1] He is one of the most studied of medieval friars[2] and one of the easiest to study, because of the editorial work of the Franciscan research college of Quaracchi (now at Grottaferrata). The recent edition of his *Sermones dominicales* shows this to have been a 'published' collection for general circulation, compiled from sermons that Bonaventura had preached on various occasions.[3] Interestingly enough, this 'published' collection is not known to have been sold by the university 'stationers' at Paris, even though it may have been put together there.[4] Most of the remainder of Bonaventura's homiletic *œuvre* falls into two categories. Firstly, there are the *reportationes* of 'live' sermons made by his secretary Marco da Montefeltro; these are not directly relevant to our survey of 'published' model sermon collections.[5] Then, secondly, there are Bonaventura's three sets of *collationes*. A number of different things can be implied by the term *collationes*;[6] here it means a long series of (?evening)

---

[1] Cf. Dufeil, *Guillaume de Saint-Amour*, pp. 9, 87, 157–8, 200.

[2] For recent work on him see L.-J. Bataillon, 'Bulletin d'histoire des doctrines médiévales. Le treizième siècle (suite)', *Revue des sciences philosophiques et théologiques*, 64 (1980), 101–31, at pp. 103–7, 122–31.

[3] Cf. Bataillon, ibid. 128, and see above, II. iii.

[4] Cf. *Sermones dominicales*, ed. Bougerol, pp. 29–30. Bougerol implies that he thinks that the collection was finally put together at Paris, or rather at Mantes nearby, but takes the precaution of saying that the question of when this definitive redaction took place 'demeure dans le domaine de l'hypothèse' (ibid. 29).

[5] They are nevertheless very interesting, and indirectly relevant. Two manuscripts descended from Marco's own manuscript are known: MSS Milan, Bibl. Ambrosiana A. 11 sup., and Paris, BN lat. 14595. The Milan manuscript gives us something rather rare—detail about where and to whom sermons were preached. (It includes some other preachers as well as Bonaventura. See Bougerol, ed. cit., 20, and Fidelis a Fanna, *Ratio novae collectionis operum omnium sive editorum sive anecdotorum... S. Bonaventurae* (Turin, 1874), 122. This offers one a chance to break out of the vicious circle that bedevils attempts to determine the audience of 'live' sermons from the content. For it is often foolish to rush in and guess the audience of a sermon from internal criteria, when we do not know the audience of a sufficient number of sermons to establish the criteria in the first place. The abridged and schematic form in which the sermons in the Milan manuscript are transmitted reduces its value for some purposes, but not necessarily for ours, since model sermon collections are also often just schematic summaries; so when one compares them with the schemes in the Milan manuscript one is comparing like with like. This is useful if one wishes to know how far model sermons differed from summaries of 'live' sermons to various sorts of audience.

[6] On the meaning of *collatio* cf. Th.-M. Charland, *Artes praedicandi. Contribution*

talks on a special theme. (The series of sermons by Thomas Aquinas on the Creed, the Lord's Prayer, the Hail Mary, and the Ten Commandments, all given in Italy, are *collationes* of a similar kind.[1]) Bonaventura's series were all preached at Paris,[2] so they were originally 'live' sermons, but since they were subsequently put into general circulation they are directly relevant. A leading preoccupation of Bonaventura in these rather special sermons was Averroism (a type of Aristotelianism which might possibly, at one point, have had the same sort of effect on the theology of the thirteenth century as Darwinism and the Higher Criticism did on the theology of the nineteenth). But there is much else in these *collationes*,[3] including an important theology of history.

The last Franciscan Paris academic who directly concerns us is Guibert de Tournai, who was active in the Paris schools both before and after his conversion to the order. He is one of those intellectuals who must have seemed more impressive to his contemporaries than he does to us. By comparison with Bonaventura or Aquinas he looks third-rate, but his external

---

à l'histoire de la rhétorique au Moyen Âge (Publications de l'Institut d'Études Médiévales d'Ottawa, 7; Paris and Ottawa, 1936), 224 n. 1, D. L. d'Avray, '"Collectiones Fratrum" and "Collationes Fratrum"', *Archivum Franciscanum Historicum*, 70 (1977), 152–6, at p. 155, and J. G. Bougerol, *Introduction a l'étude de Saint Bonaventure* (Tournai, 1961), 178. For a fourteenth-century attempt to define differences between a *sermo* and a *collatio* see F. Delorme, 'L'"Ars faciendi sermones" de Géraud du Pescher', *Antonianum*, 19 (1944), 169–98, at pp. 180–1 and 183: but usage of the word does not fit neatly into Géraud's categories. For instance, the fascinating sermons on various subjects in MS Birmingham University 6/iii/19 are called *collationes*, but can hardly be confined within Géraud's definition.

[1] Cf. Weisheipl, *Friar Thomas d'Aquino* (2nd edn., Oxford 1975), 401–3. They were all preached at Naples, except perhaps the 'Collationes super Ave Maria', which may have been preached in Rome (ibid.).

[2] '...6 Mart.–17 Apr. 1267 Parisiis. *Collationes de decem praeceptis*...25th Febr.–7 Apr. 1268 Parisiis. *Collationes de septem donis Spiritus sancti*...9 Apr.–28 Maii 1273 Parisiis. *Collationes in Hexaëmeron*...' (from the chronology published in *S. Bonaventura 1274–1974* (Collegio S. Bonaventura; Grottoferrata, Rome), ii (1973), 13).

[3] For summaries see Bougerol, *Introduction a l'étude de Saint Bonaventure*, pp. 178–88, and E. Longpré, 'Bonaventure (Saint)', in *Dictionnaire d'histoire et de géographie ecclésiastique*, ix (Paris, 1937), cols. 741–88, at cols. 770, 772–3, 777–9.

academic career was not much less successful.[1] He achieved
the office of regent master in the theology faculty, and later
reminisced about it ('... I remember when I was ruling [i.e.
Regent Master] in theology at Paris...'[2]). There is some
dispute about his regency: it is not agreed whether or not he
had a spell as Regent Master of Theology before he became a
Franciscan as well as afterwards. The most likely solution
would seem to be that he held a chair in the arts faculty
before his conversion,[3] and in the theology faculty, as Regent
Master, when he was a Franciscan, perhaps in the years
1259–61.[4] Guibert seems to have attracted attention in high
quarters. His *Eruditio regum et principum* was written at the
request of Louis IX himself, and we have already seen that his
collection of sermons for the liturgical year was put together
after prompting from Pope Alexander IV. Yet, at least in his
sermons, Guibert can leave us with the feeling that he was not
a very clever man. It is not so much because he borrows from
the earlier Jacques de Vitry on a grand scale: he did try to
reorder it, and his age was more concerned with usefulness
and less with literary property than ours is.[5] A more serious
criticism is that (at least in the sermons I have studied closely)
Guibert is not always good at digesting and marshalling his
material, despite his liking for superficially neat divisions. I

[1] For a brief summary of Guibert de Tournai's career, with further references, see
d'Avray and Tausche, 'Marriage Sermons', pp. 74–5 and n. 23. On his life and works
(especially the latter) see B. de Troeyer, *Bio-Bibliographia Franciscana Neerlandica
ante Saeculum XVI, I. Pars Biographica: Auctores editionum qui scripserunt ante
saeculum XVI* (Nieuwkoop, 1974), 15–43.

[2] E. Bonifacio (ed.), Guibert de Tournai, *De modo addiscendi* (Turin, 1953), 13.

[3] His conversion was *c.*1235 or perhaps a few years later (E. Longpré (ed.),
Tractatus de pace auctore fr. Gilberto de Tornaco (Quaracchi, 1925), p. ix).

[4] See d'Avray and Tausche, 'Marriage Sermons', p. 75 n. 3; also the 'Tableau
hypothétique des chaires à la Faculté de Théologie' in Dufeil, *Guillaume de Saint-
Amour* (no page number). De Troeyer, *Bio-Bibliographia*, vol. cit. above (n. 1), p. 38,
discusses the problem. Unless I have misunderstood him, he seems to make an
unnecessary attempt to hold on to the theory of a first Paris regency in theology. A
possible hypothesis is that Guibert was doing some theological teaching at a lower
level—say lecturing cursorily on the Bible—while holding a chair in the Arts faculty.

[5] The dependence of Guibert on Jacques has long been established. See e.g.
Longpré (ed.), *Tractatus de pace*, Preface, p. xxiii n. 1. For an extended confrontation
of their respective treatments of marriage in their *ad status* sermons see d'Avray and
Tausche, 'Marriage Sermons', pp. 85–117.

suspect that he sometimes worked too quickly, or, alternatively, that he did not have a very clear mind. Yet one should resist the temptation to be patronizing: Guibert certainly had something. One takes away an impression of a likeable and far from harsh personality.[1]

Jean de la Rochelle, Bonaventura, and Guibert de Tournai are all in their way major preachers and together they constitute what may almost be called a Paris Franciscan tradition of aids for preachers. Then there are the more marginal candidates who should perhaps be added to the list. The case of Eudes Rigaud has already been discussed. If Gauthier d'Aquitaine, OM, may really be identified with Gauthier de Bruges, we have yet another distinguished Paris academic who wrote sermon collections. But this would seem to be uncertain.[2] Again, it is a serious but unproved possibility that the anonymous Franciscan collection called *Legifer* was based on *collationes* given in the houses of the Paris friars.[3] Yet another marginal case is John of Wales, a sort of humanist who helps to bridge the gap between John of Salisbury and the 'classicizing' friars of the early fourteenth century. John became a Master of Theology at Paris and he wrote both sermons and treatises which were intended at least in part to help preachers.[4] The problem is that a great part of his academic career was set in Oxford, and it is possible that his works for preachers do not belong to his Paris period at all.[5] Finally, there is a Franciscan Paris master who falls just

---

[1] Note certain differences between the way he and his source Jacques de Vitry treat marriage. (ibid. 109–17).

[2] Compare Schneyer, *Repertorium*, ii. 102–3, with his *Geschichte*, pp. 148 and 158.

[3] See d'Avray, ' "Collectiones Fratrum" and "Collationes Fratrum" ', pp. 152–6.

[4] See W. A. Pantin, 'John of Wales and Medieval Humanism', in J. A. Watt *et al.* (edd.), *Medieval Studies Presented to Aubrey Gwynn, S.J.*, (Dublin, 1961), 297–319, and Smalley, *English Friars*, pp. 51–4; for the sermons: Schneyer, *Repertorium*, iii. 480–510.

[5] The chronology of the treatises is being established by Jenny Swanson, who has in hand what should be an intellectual portrait worthy of a fascinating man. [Mrs Swanson now tells me that John's *Communiloquium* must have been completed after he moved to Paris. I should therefore have devoted more space to him; but Mrs Swanson's 1983 Oxford D.Phil. thesis will fill this lacuna.]

beyond our period. Bertrand de la Tour (d. 1332) was a copious author of sermons, but he belongs more to four-teenth- that to thirteenth-century history.[1]

Thus, on a low count, and leaving out the more marginal cases, we have six friars whose careers belong more to Paris than to any other place, and who wrote important model sermon collections: in the first half of the century (roughly speaking), the Franciscan Jean de la Rochelle and the Dominicans Pierre de Reims and Hugues de Saint-Cher, and in the second half the Franciscans Bonaventura and Guibert de Tournai and the Dominican Nicolas de Gorran.[2] This may not seem a very large collection. It is, nevertheless, decisively larger than can be produced for any other centre in France, and indeed for any other centre in Europe except perhaps one.

In France the centre which comes next in importance to Paris is Lyons. Several interesting writers of sermon material were based at the Dominican convent there. Étienne de Bourbon, OP, whose treatise on the seven gifts of the Holy Spirit has one of the richest *exemplum* collections—a gold-mine for historians—seems to have been based at Lyons for most of his adult life. It is at least the only Dominican house to which he is known to have been attached, though he was an itinerant preacher and travelled widely.[3] Humbert de Romans, OP, was lector (*c.*1226) and prior (1237) of the Lyons convent, before going on to higher things (prior of the Roman province, provincial of France, and Master-General

---

[1] On Bertrand see Schneyer, *Repertorium*, i. 505–91; Glorieux, *Répertoire*, ii. 238–42, and Smalley, *English Friars*, pp. 242–4.

[2] Franciscans and Dominicans are the only orders of friars important in intellectual life and as producers of preaching materials before the fourteenth century, but one Augustinian Hermit, Alberto da Padova, just deserves a mention. He is 'marginal' because rather late for our period, but he was a friar, there is some evidence that he taught at Paris at least for a short while, and he wrote model sermons which seem to have been copied widely. See *Dizionario biografico degli Italiani*, i (Rome, 1960), 747, A. Zumkeller, *Manuskripte von Werken der Autoren des Augustiner-Eremitenordens in mitteleuropäischen Bibliotheken* (Cassiciacum, 20; Würzburg, 1966), 50–2 and 565, Schneyer, *Repertorium*, i. 124–50, and id., *Geschichte*, p. 163.

[3] See e.g. Schmitt's *Le Saint Lévrier*, pp. 23–4. Étienne died in 1261.

of the order).¹ Many of his writings survive,² perhaps most notably, for our purposes, his *De eruditione praedicatorum*, the second (practical) book of which includes sermons 'to all conditions of men' (*ad omne genus hominum*) and for every variety of circumstances (*in omni diversitate negotiorum*).³ One may also note his *exemplum* collection, the *Treatise on the Gift of Fear,*⁴ and his *On the Preaching of the Cross against the Saracens.*⁵ (It is true that all three works seem to have been written after Humbert ceased to be prior of the Lyons house.⁶)

It is probable that before Humbert had left the Lyons convent Guillaume Peyraut had become a member of it.⁷ Peyraut was eventually to become prior himself.⁸ He wrote a number of works,⁹ of which the most important for our purposes are his sermon cycles¹⁰ and his *Summa* on virtues and vices, which would seem to have been primarily for preachers. The sermon series were widely used, to judge by the number of manuscripts of them which have been found, but the *Summa de vitiis et virtutibus* is a special case: it has been said that few works in the whole of literary history have known such success.¹¹ It survives in an astonishing number of manuscripts¹², and of course each manuscript that survives must represent many others that have been lost.

¹ Kaeppeli, *Scriptores*, ii. 283.
² See ibid. 284–95.
³ Ibid. 287–8; also, e.g., A. Murray, 'Religion among the Poor in Thirteenth-Century France: The Testimony of Humbert de Romans', *Traditio*, 30 (1974), 285–324, and d'Avray and Tausche, 'Marriage Sermons', pp. 74, 81–5.
⁴ See Kaeppeli, *Scriptores*, ii. 285–7.
⁵ Ibid. 288–9.
⁶ According to Kaeppeli he became prior of the Roman province in 1240 (ibid. 283), while the *De eruditione* should be dated to *c*.1266–77 (ibid. 287), the *Tractatus de dono timoris* to *c*.1240–77 (ibid. 285), and the *De praedicatione crucis contra Saracenos* to '1266–8 c.' (ibid. 288).
⁷ A. Dondaine, 'Guillaume Peyraut. Vie et œuvres', *Archivum Fratrum Praedicatorum*, 18 (1948), 162–236, at p. 172.
⁸ Kaeppeli, *Scriptores*, ii. 133.
⁹ Ibid. 133–52.
¹⁰ Ibid. 143–7.
¹¹ 'Peu d'ouvrages, dans toute l'histoire littéraire, connurent un aussi brillant succès...' (Dondaine, 'Guillaume Peyraut', p. 162).
¹² See the list in Kaeppeli, *Scriptores*, ii. 134–42.

Peyraut had already made a reputation by the middle of the thirteenth century, for Salimbene (writing several decades later, it must be admitted) tells the following story of a meeting with him in 1248:

And once, when I was at Vienne, brother Guillielmus, of the Order of Preachers, who did the *Summa of Vices and Virtues*, came from Lyons to Vienne for the purpose of preaching and hearing confessions. And because the Friars Preachers did not have a place in that city, he came to stay with the Friars Minor; and it was the guardian's wish that I should bear him company, and I got on very well with him (*familiariter fui cum eo*), and he with me, because he was a humble and courteous man, although he was short in stature. [!] And when I asked him why the Friars Preachers did not have a place in Vienne, he told me that they preferred to have one good convent at Lyons, rather than to have such a multitude of places. And I asked him to preach to the brothers (*fratribus*) on the Feast of the Annunciation of the Blessed Virgin, which was approaching, because I very much wanted to hear him. For he had made a sermon collection (*tractatum de sermonibus*) as well as the *Summa. . . .*[1]

The combination of these three men makes Lyons an important centre for the history of preaching.[2] Lyons also had a respectable *studium*,[3] but it was not among the cluster of *studia* which came immediately after Paris in the pecking order of Dominican intellectual centres. Its significance for preaching history is much greater than its importance for intellectual history.

When we turn to England and Oxford it is the other way

---

[1] Salimbene, *Cronica*, ed Holder-Egger, p. 233. Cf. Dondaine, 'Guillaume Peyraut', p. 165 and 182.

[2] It is worth adding that Pierre de Tarentaise, the future Pope Innocent V, probably had Humbert as superior and Étienne and Peyraut as confrères at Lyons (Dondaine, 'Guillaume Peyraut', p. 172), though it was at Paris that he was to make his name as a theologian. On his career see Glorieux, *Répertoire*, i. 107, No. 17. The surviving works of Innocent V include some sermons (see ibid. 110–11 and Schneyer, *Repertorium*, iv. 803–5), but no complete series.

[3] C. Ribaucourt, 'Panorama . . . degli Studia . . . (Francia centro settentrionale)' in *Le scuole*, at p. 75.

round: remarkable intellectual achievements but few model sermons or preaching aids. Both Franciscans and Dominicans had an efficiently functioning network of schools in England, and it was perhaps the friars, together with Grosseteste, who did most to make Oxford a 'centre of excellence' in theology, arguably second only to Paris, in the thirteenth century.[1] Until the fourteenth century, however, friars based in England do not appear to have played a major part in the production of material to help preachers.[2] It is not that no interesting material was written to help preachers by thirteenth-century Englishmen. One might single out the exceptionally original and readable *Summa on the Art of Preaching* by Thomas of Salisbury,[3] and the sermons of Odo of Cheriton.[4] Neither Thomas nor Odo were friars,[5] however, and John of Wales is the only obvious example of an Oxford friar who produced material for preachers. Nor is it even certain as yet that his sermons and the relevant treatises were written and 'published' while he was still based at Oxford. It is true that this may not be quite the whole story. There are

[1] See e.g. D. Knowles, *The Religious Orders in England*, i (Cambridge, 1950), 135, 166, 205–37, with further references (especially p. 207 n. 1, the references to studies by A. G. Little). On the Dominican school see too B. Smalley, 'Robert Bacon and the early Dominican School at Oxford', *Transactions of the Royal Historical Society*, 30 (1948), 1–19, and W. A. Hinnesbusch, *The Early English Friars Preachers* (Rome, 1951), 332–419. On Dominican educational organization see now M. O'Carroll, 'The Educational Organisation of the Dominicans in England and Wales 1221–1348: a Multidisciplinary Approach', *Archivum Fratrum Praedicatorum*, 50 (1980), 23–62.

[2] For a conspectus see Schneyer, *Geschichte*, pp. 165–6. For works on thirteenth-century English preaching in general see above, II. ii p. 91 n. 1.

[3] J. J. Murphy, *Rhetoric in the Middle Ages. A History of Rhetorical Theory from Saint Augustine to the Renaissance* (Berkeley, Los Angeles, and London, 1974), 317–326. Murphy showed that this early *ars praedicandi* is one of the most interesting of the whole genre; a critical edition is much to be desired. [I believe that Franco Morenzoni, of the University of Geneva, plans to study and perhaps edit this *ars*.] See also F. Broomfield (ed.), *Thomae de Chobham Summa confessorum*, (Analecta Medievalia Namurcensia, 25, Louvain and Paris, 1968), 597.

[4] A. C. Friend, 'Master Odo of Cheriton', *Speculum*, 23 (1948), 641–58, and id., 'Life and Works of Odo of Cheriton' in University of Oxford Committee for Advanced Studies, *Abstracts of Dissertations for the Degree of Doctor of Philosophy*, ix [dissertations accepted during 1936] (Oxford, 1937), 43–8.

[5] Schneyer describes Odo as 'OCist' (*Repertorium*, iv. 483) and 'OP' (*Geschichte*, p. 166), but I know of no evidence that he was a religious: cf. Friend, 'Master Odo of Cheriton', p. 649.

collationes by John Pecham, OM, which may have been given in England.[1] One wonders whether the shadowy 'Nicolaus de Aquaevilla' may have been English, for many of the manuscripts of his *de tempore* collection (as listed in Schneyer's *Repertorium*) are in English libraries (but was he really Franciscan?). Again, even if the Franciscan and Dominican houses at Oxford do not appear to have been centres for the production of model sermon collections, their members are prominent in university preaching.[2] Or again, the British Isles are important in the history of *exemplum* collections.[3] In the end, however, one has to come back to the contrast between England's great importance in the intellectual life of the mendicant orders at this time, and the rather slight contribution of English friars to the production of model sermons.

In neither Germany nor Italy was there a theological centre equal to Oxford in status, but both countries bulk larger than England in the history of thirteenth-century friars' sermon collections. Germany cannot compare with Italy in quantity, but its contribution to thirteenth-century preaching literature is significant, above all, though not exclusively, because of Berthold von Regensburg (Bertholdus de Ratisbona), with whom no other preacher of the period can be compared.[4] 'And note, that brother Berthold had a special gift of preaching from God. And everyone who heard him says that from the Apostles to our own times no one could be

---

[1] This is thought likely by D. L. Douie, *Archbishop Pecham* (Oxford, 1952), 11, and 'Archbishop Pecham's Sermons and Collations', in R. W. Hunt, W. A. Pantin, and R. W. Southern (edd.), *Studies in Medieval History Presented to F. M. Powicke*, (Oxford, 1948), 269–82, at p. 277.

[2] See A. G. Little and F. Pelster, *Oxford Theology and Theologians* c.*A.D. 1282–1302* (Oxford Historical Society, 96; Oxford, 1934), 149–215.

[3] See above, p. 67.

[4] For a general survey of thirteenth-century German preaching see A. Linsenmayer, *Geschichte der Predigt in Deutschland von Karl dem Grossen bis zum Ausgange des vierzehnten Jahrhunderts* (Munich, 1886), 317–90; this old though not valueless survey should be used in conjunction with the more up-to-date summary in Schneyer, *Geschichte*, pp. 167–71. The important group of Cistercian preachers should be noted (ibid. 168).

compared with him in the German language....¹:' so Salimbene; and there is plenty of other evidence for Berthold's phenomenal success.² Unlike Foulques de Neuilly, who had the same kind of dramatic success as an itinerant preacher, Berthold not only preached 'live' but also made written sermon collections, in Latin.³ Although the scholar who probably knew Berthold's Latin versions better than anyone before or since thought that much of the magic had been lost in the process of revision for 'publication' in Latin,⁴ even through this medium something of Berthold's genius as a popular preacher comes through.⁵ Berthold is the most

---

¹ Salimbene *Cronica*, ed. Holder-Egger, p. 559. Salimbene goes on to say a lot more about Berthold.

² Cf. Berthold von Regensburg, *Vollständige Ausgabe seiner Predigten*, edd. F. Pfeiffer and J. Strobl (Vienna, 1862 and 1880), i [by Pfeiffer], pp. xx ff. (note the 1965 reprint, with 'Vorwort' and 'Anhang' by Kurt Ruh.).

³ It seems to be common ground that the vernacular sermons (the standard edition of which is still that of Pfeiffer and Strobl—see preceding note) were not written down by Berthold himself, whatever their relation to his 'live' sermons. On the whole problem of the relation between the Latin and vernacular sermons see Richter, *Die deutsche Überlieferung*, pp. 224–41. For a good general bibliography of Berthold see ibid. 286–91, wherein note especially the different 'Studien zur Geschichte der altdeutschen Predigt' by Anton Schönbach. F. G. Banta gives a good short survey in *Die deutsche Literatur des Mittelalters. Verfasserlexikon*, 2nd revised version, ed. K. Ruh, i (Berlin and New York, 1978), cols. 817–23.

⁴ Schönbach, 'Studien zur Geschichte der altdeutschen Predigt', p. 14–15.

⁵ Though I have only read a few of Berthold's (unpublished) Latin sermons, they strike me as more powerful than Latin sermons in other contemporary collections. (I have mainly used MS BL Harley 3215; I have not investigated its place in the transmission, though I imagine that it belongs to the family of Berthold's official 'published' sermons.) Richter, *Die deutsche Überlieferung*, p. 233, judged that 'In vielen Punkten könnten die lateinischen Sermones, richtig interpretiert, noch manches von der Faszination, die Berthold auf seine Hörer ausübte, verständlich machen.' If Berthold failed to capture some of his own liveliness and colour in his official 'published' Latin version, there are, according to Schönbach, some Latin manuscripts, *not* of the main 'published' family (i.e. the three 'Rusticani: de dominicis, de sanctis,* and *de communi*), which may help supply the loss. Schönbach gives a summary of his conclusions about the Latin transmission in 'Studien zur Geschichte der altdeutschen Predigt', pp. 98–102. L. Casutt's *Die Handschriften mit lateinischen Predigten Bertholds von Regensburg, O. Min ca. 1210-1272* (Fribourg, 1961) will provide another springboard for the critical edition of the Latin sermons which is one of the great lacunae in medieval scholarship. Richter rehabilitates the German sermons—the X¹ collection at least—as evidence for the way Berthold really preached. He says of this collection that 'Es darf als sicher gelten, dass der Verfasser dieser Predigten unter dem unmittelbaren, lebendigen Eindruck der Reden Bertholds stand. Er hat dann lateinische Predigten als Hilfsmittel und als Grundlagen für seine Arbeit benutzt, sich bei der Gestaltung und Ausformung der

important preacher of a small but interesting group of thirteenth-century German Franciscans. He had a formative influence on another German Franciscan preacher, known as 'Frater Ludovicus', whose sermons are thought to belong to the end of the thirteenth century.[1] To be derivative was no disgrace in this genre, and Ludovicus seems to have used Berthold intelligently.[2]

Two other German preachers, Konrad Holtnicker, OM, and the so-called 'Schwarzwälder Prediger', present a still more interesting example of dependence.[3] It is a rather unusual case: vernacular sermons, arguably by a Franciscan,[4] intended not for pious reading, but to serve as models for real preaching, drawing heavily on a successful Latin Franciscan *de tempore* collection.[5] All these things mark it out from the general run of mendicant sermons of this period in German, for in the later thirteenth and in the fourteenth

---

Texte aber wahrscheinlich immer wieder am Redestil Bertholds orientiert' (*Die deutsche Überlieferung*, p. 240). Richter earlier shows the weakness of the arguments for two opposite theories: on the one hand, that the sermons transmitted in German are only connected to Berthold's actual preaching via the written Latin sermons, and on the other hand, that they give a direct and fairly faithful picture of how he preached (see especially pp. 234, 236, and 224–41 *passim*). In his view a German sermon of Berthold may represent three elements: what the author of the German version derived from hearing Berthold preach 'live'; what he derived from the written Latin sermons; and finally the element introduced by the vernacular writer himself (cf. ibid. 240). It may never be possible to separate out these three elements. The matter is further complicated by the fact that different German collections are by different authors (cf. ibid.).

[1] On Ludovicus see A. Franz, *Drei deutsche Minoritenprediger aus dem xiii. und xiv. Jahrhundert* (Freiburg im Breisgau, 1907), 49–103. On his dates, ibid. 53–5. An early fourteenth-century date also seems possible to me.

[2] 'Berthold hat auch kaum einen zweiten Schüler gehabt, der, dem Frater Ludovicus gleich, seine reiche Gedankenwelt in so klarer und durchsichtiger Darstellung wiederzugeben verstand' (ibid. 97).

[3] On Konrad see Franz, *Drei deutsche Minoritenprediger*, pp. 9–46, S. Girotto, *Corrado di Saxonia, predicatore e mariologo del sec. xiii* (Biblioteca di Studi Francescani, 3; Florence, 1952), and Schneyer, *Repertorium*, i. 748 ff. (as 'Conradus Holtnicker de Saxonia OM'). On the Schwarzwälder Prediger see references above, p. 93.

[4] Cf. above, II. ii, p. 93 n. 2.

[5] For a confrontation of a selection of the Schwarzwälder Predigers sermons with Konrad Holtnicker's Latin see the edition by G. Stamm, *Predigten des 'Schwarzwälder Predigers'* (Kleine deutsche Prosadenkmäler des Mittelalters, 12, Munich, 1973).

centuries communities of religious women and pious educated lay readers are, in Germany, the more characteristic
publics of such sermons. As for communities of religious
women, a new pattern of Dominican preaching would be set
by Eckhart, but that is another story, and one which belongs
more to fourteenth-century history. German Dominicans
hardly bulk large in the history of thirteenth-century model
sermon collections.[1] Nevertheless, Berthold and the other
Franciscans are enough to put Germany on the map of
the thirteenth-century preaching movement. Certainly, Germany imported preaching materials, but it produced its own
as well.

Even though the number of sermon collections by German
friars is respectable—even impressive in comparison with,
say, Spain or Scandinavia[2]—there is no single centre remotely
comparable with Paris; indeed it is probably safe to say that
Paris produced more preaching aids than the whole of
Germany put together. It is only when we turn to Italy that
we find production of model sermon collections quantitatively comparable with that of Paris and France.

To discuss even all the principal Italian writers of sermon
collections and preaching aids from the thirteenth century
would be outside the scope of this study, and good summary

---

[1] There is 'Peregrinus de Oppeln', whose sermons have generally been dated to
before 1305, but still he really belongs as much to the fourteenth as to the thirteenth
century and as much to Poland as to Germany, if the distinction is valid. See the
Lebenslauf in G. Meersseman, 'Notice bio-bibliographique sur deux frères prêcheurs
silésiens du xiv s. nommés Peregrinus', *Archivum Fratrum Praedicatorum*, 19 (1949),
266–74, at p. 268. See too Schneyer, *Repertorium*, iv. 548 ff. Martin von Troppau is
one of the thirteenth-century preachers included in the section on 'Volksprediger in
Deutschland' (in the thirteenth and fourteenth centuries) in Schneyer's *Geschichte*,
pp. 167–71, at pp. 170–1; Martin was a member of the Polish province, but an
important part of his career was set in Italy. See the article by B. Stasiewski in
Lexikon für Theologie und Kirche, vii (Freiburg im Breisgau, 1962), col. 119. I do not
know when his sermons were composed.

[2] The contribution of Spain and Scandinavia to mendicant preaching literature of
this period was negligible, or remains unknown, to judge by the silence on these two
countries in the section on 'Die Volkspredigt des 13. und 14. Jahrhunderts' in
Schneyer's *Geschichte*, pp. 154–71. (Schneyer's overall knowledge of the general field
of central medieval preaching was such that it is not absurd to argue from his
silence.)

surveys already exist.[1] There are too many of them to be dismissed in a paragraph or two: among the Dominicans, Tommaso Agni da Lentini, Bartolomeo di Vicenza (Bartholomeus Vicentinus), Jacopo da Benevento, Jacopo da Varazze, 'Johannes de Opreno', Ambrogio Sansedoni, Remigio de' Girolami, Aldobrandino Cavalcanti, Aldobrandino da Toscanella, Reginaldo da Piperno, and, on the far edge of our period, Giordano da Pisa and Antonio Azaro parmense; among the Franciscans, Anthony of Padua, Luca da Bitonto, Bonaventura d'Iseo, and Servasanto da Faenza.[2] One or two of these are well known, in particular Anthony of Padua,

---

[1] The best is C. Delcorno, *La predicazione nell'età comunale* (Florence, 1974); chs. 9–12 (pp. 22–35), dealing with Italian Dominican and Franciscan preachers of the thirteenth century, are the most relevant. See too Schneyer, *Geschichte*, pp. 161–4, L.-J. Bataillon, 'La predicazione dei religiosi mendicanti del secolo xiii nell'Italia Centrale', *Mélanges de l'École Française de Rome. Moyen Âge—Temps Modernes*, 89/2 (1977), 691–4, and A. Murray, 'Piety and Impiety in Thirteenth-Century Italy', in C. J. Cuming and D. Baker (edd.), *Popular Belief and Practice* (Studies in Church History, 8; Cambridge, 1972), 83–106.

[2] This list does not claim to be exhaustive. It is somewhat miscellaneous, since it includes authors of sermon collections which survive in only one known manuscript, as well as preachers whose 'published' collections were widely diffused. For further bibliography on the preachers listed, see the works of Schneyer and Delcorno cited in the preceding note; also Schneyer, *Repertorium*, s.vv., and, for Dominicans, Kaeppeli, *Scriptores*. On Tommaso Agni da Lentini, see Bataillon, 'La predicazione', p. 691; on Jacopo da Varazze, id., 'Iacopo da Varazze e Tommaso d'Aquino', *Sapienza*, 32/1 (1979), 22–9 (Bataillon shows that Jacopo used the *Catena aurea* of Aquinas); on Servasanto da Faenza, note the brief but important remarks by Bataillon in 'Approaches', p. 21 (suggesting that the models which Servasanto wrote for his younger colleagues were sermons he had actually preached when younger), and in 'L'Emploi du langage philosophique dans les sermons du treizième siècle', in A. Zimmermann (ed.), *Sprache und Erkenntnis im Mittelalter* (Miscellanea Mediaevalia, Veröffentlichungen des Thomas-Instituts der Universität zu Köln, 13/2, Berlin and New York, 1981), 983–91, at pp. 989–91 (on his citations of Aristotle); on Jacopo da Benevento, Schneyer, *Geschichte*, p. 165, and *Repertorium*, iii. 6, who makes him a fourteenth-century figure, but according to Kaeppeli, *Scriptores*, ii. 304, he is known to have been active in the third quarter of the thirteenth; on Bartolomeo di Vicenza (Bartholomaeus Vicentinus) (who is also called Bartholomaeus de Bregantiis, apparently without much foundation), T. Kaeppeli, 'Der literarische Nachlass des sel. Bartholomaeus von Vicenza O.P. (†1270)', in *Mélanges Auguste Pelzer* (Université de Louvain, Recueil de Travaux d'Histoire et de Philologie, 3ᵐᵉ Série, 26ᵐᵉ Fascicule; Louvain, 1947), 275–301, at pp. 275–6. I omit 'Supramons de Varisio' from the list because his floruit seems uncertain. Aquinas might well have been included on the list, since his *collationes* on the Lord's Prayer, the Creed, and the Ten Commandments belong to the history of Italian, not of Parisian, preaching; we also have some (highly abridged) *reportationes* of sermons by St Bonaventura given in Italy—cf. Bataillon, 'La predicazione', p. 692.

enormously popular as a Franciscan saint, and a forerunner of the 'intellectual' friars who came to dominate the order.[1] Nevertheless, some preachers almost forgotten now were important and influential in the Middle Ages; it seems likely that the sermons of the obscure Luca da Bitonto were more used and read than those of Antony of Padua.[2] A careless allusion in Salimbene's chronicle shows how familiar the sermons of Luca were to him: 'Note the example of that shoemaker or artisan who in the land of the Saracens moved the mountain and freed the Christians. See in the sermon "Salvatorem expectamus" of brother Luke.'[3] There is indeed a sermon with the incipit 'Salvatorem expectamus' in Luca da Bitonto's collection; I cannot find the story in this sermon, but in the sermon which immediately follows it in the manuscript I have used there is a story which must be the one that Salimbene means.[4]

Preachers so influential as Luca deserve to be studied, however dry their sermons may seem. The field of Latin sermons by Italian friars remains wide open for research. But for our purpose, which is to find yardsticks by which to measure the influence of Paris, the place that matters most is Florence. It is the only town in Italy, or indeed in Europe, which rivals the importance of the northern university town in the history of thirteenth-century preaching—even though Florence did not have a university at all in this period.

---

[1] Anthony is one of the few thirteenth-century preachers whose sermons may be read in a modern critical edition. That of Locatelli (Padua 1895–1913) has now been replaced by B. Costa *et al.*, *S. Antonii Patavini . . . Sermones dominicales et festivi*, three vols. (Padua, 1979). For a good presentation of Anthony's sermons see B. Smalley, 'L'Uso della Scrittura nei "Sermones" di Sant 'Antonio', *Il Santo*, 21, ser. II, fasc. 1 (1981), 3–16.

[2] The number of surviving manuscripts of each gives a (very approximate) indication: for Anthony, see Costa *et al.*, (edd.) *S. Antonii . . . Sermones*, i, pp. lxxiii ff., and Schneyer, *Repertorium*, i. 325; for Lucas, ibid. iv. 70–1.

[3] Salimbene, *Cronica*, ed. Holder-Egger, p. 215.

[4] The story occurs on fo. 294ra of P MS BN NAL 410, in a sermon on the text 'Loquente Iesu ad turbas ecce princeps . . .' (Matt. 9: 18) (Schneyer, *Repertorium*, iv. 63, No. 180), inc. fo. 293ra. The sermon on the text 'Salvatorem expectamus' (Phil. 3: 20) (Schneyer, *Repertorium*, iv. 63, No. 179) begins MS cit., fo. 291rb, and ends ibid., fo. 293ra.

In the thirteenth and into the fourteenth centuries the Dominican and Franciscan convents at Florence must have been the major centres for the diffusion of ideas in the city.[1] So far as the history of preaching is concerned, one Franciscan and three Dominican names stand out. One of the Dominicans, Giordano da Pisa, is the first Italian preacher whose sermons have come down to us in the vernacular. Some 700 of them, preached in the early years of the fourteenth century in various piazzas and churches of Florence, above all in the Dominican convent of Santa Maria Novella, have been preserved.[2] The manner in which they have been transmitted gives them a special value for the history of 'live' popular preaching.[3] Remigio de' Girolami was a somewhat older[4] and senior[5] colleague of Giordano da Pisa.[6] His writings have been described as 'the nearest thing to a serious attempt by a university-trained scholastic to adapt the learning of the schools to the specific problems of Florentine city politics',[7] though it would of course be quite

[1] Cf. G. Holmes, 'The Emergence of an Urban Ideology at Florence *c.*1250–1450', *Transactions of the Royal Historical Society*, 5th ser., 23 (1973), 111–34, at p. 114; cf. C. T. Davis, 'Education in Dante's Florence', *Speculum*, 40 (1965), 415–35, at pp. 421–35.

[2] Delcorno, *La predicazione*, p. 38.

[3] The standard work is Delcorno, *Giordano da Pisa*; see too D. R. Lesnick, 'Popular Dominican Preaching in Early Fourteenth Century Florence', unpublished Ph.D. thesis (Rochester, 1976), especially chs. IV and V; Lesnick attempts, *inter alia*, to interpret Giordano's sermons in social terms.

[4] Delcorno, *La predicazione*, gives the dates *c.*1245–1319 for Remigio de' Girolami (p. 28) and 1260–1311 for Giordano (p. 38).

[5] Cf. Lesnick, 'Popular Dominican Preaching', p. 124–5.

[6] For bibliography on Remigio see C. Delcorno, 'Il racconto agiografico nella predicazione dei secoli xiii–xv', in *Atti dei convegni lincei*, 48. *Convegno Internazionale, Agiografia nell'occidente cristiano secoli xiii–xv* (Accademia Nazionale dei Lincei; Rome, 1980), 89 n. 36. Note especially S. Orlandi, *'Necrologio' di S. Maria Novella*, i (Florence, 1955), 276–307. But the bibliography on Remigio is rapidly lengthening: see e.g. C. T. Davis, 'Remigio de' Girolami O.P. (d. 1319), Lector of S. Maria Novella in Florence', in *Le scuole*, pp. 281–304 (excellent), and F. Tamburini (ed.), Fra Remigio dei Girolami, OP, *Contra falsos ecclesie professores* ('Utrumque Ius', Collectio Pontificiae Universitatis Lateranensis, 6; Rome, 1981) [with a preface by C. T. Davis].

[7] Holmes, 'Urban Ideology', p. 121. Cf. C. T. Davis, 'An Early Florentine Political Theorist: Fra Remigio de' Girolami', *Proceedings of the American Philosophical Society* 104/6 (1960), 662–76, and M. C. De Matteis, *La 'teologia politica comunale' di Remigio de' Girolami* (Bologna, 1977).

wrong to suppose that he was concerned only with political problems. It is possible, though not certain, that Dante heard the lectures of Remigio; there are at any rate some striking correspondences between their ideas.[1] It was Remigio who preached the funeral oration on Aldobrandino Cavalcanti,[2] who died in 1279.[3] The latter's sermons (unlike those of Remigio, which seem not to have been put into general circulation[4]) were widely copied.[5] They are an instance of a paradox which quite often confronts students of medieval sermons, namely, the international diffusion of collections which may seem to us dry and abstract. In the case of Aldobrandino, as of others, the explanation may be that it was precisely the detachment of the content from any immediate social context that enabled them to 'travel'. As for the Franciscans at Florence, the one who stands out is Servasanto da Faenza, an important part of whose life was spent there, at the convent of Santa Croce.[6] He wrote a number of helps for preachers, including sermons, but perhaps most notably his *Summa* of virtues and vices, an example of the genre quite different from the famous work on the same subject by Guillaume Peyraut.

This somewhat breathless survey of the geography of preaching has shown that two centres, Florence and Lyons, can bear comparison with Paris as centres for the production of sermons and preaching aids. Nevertheless, these findings

---

[1] See Davis, 'Education in Dante's Florence', pp. 433–5.

[2] Delcorno, *La predicazione*, p. 28.

[3] On Aldobrandino see the article by A. Paravicini Bagliani in *Dizionario biografico degli Italiani*, xxii (Rome, 1979), 601–3, and Kaeppeli, *Scriptores*, i. 35–8.

[4] With the exception of a few folios in a Paris manuscript, no manuscripts of Remigio's sermons have been found outside the Biblioteca Nazionale in Florence. See Schneyer, *Repertorium*, v. 134, and cf. Davis, 'Remigio . . .', in *Le scuole*, pp. 286–7.

[5] For lists of manuscripts of Aldobrandino's sermons see Kaeppeli, *Scriptores*, i. 35–8.

[6] '. . . il periodo più importante della sua vita si svolge nel convento di Santa Croce a Firenze . . .' (Delcorno, *La predicazione*, p. 34). For further bibliographical references see Delcorno, 'Il racconto agiografico', p. 83 n. 17. Note especially L. Oliger, 'Servasanto da Faenza O.F.M. e il suo "Liber de Virtutibus et Vitiis"' in *Miscellanea Francesco Ehrle*, i. Per la storia della teologia e della filosofia (Studi e Testi, 37; Rome, 1924), 148–89.

do not seriously affect the supremacy of Paris, for a number of reasons. To begin with, the concentration at these two places is decidedly smaller, even if not by an order of magnitude: three at Lyons and three or four at Florence,[1] against about six (on a conservative estimate) at Paris.

Again, some of the preachers at Florence and Lyons also had links, though more tenuous ones, with the University of Paris. Two of the three Lyons Dominicans discussed above, Étienne de Bourbon and Humbert de Romans, had studied at Paris as young men. It is true that, granted their age, they may have mainly or exclusively studied the arts course there.[2] On the other hand, Humbert was already a Master of Arts when he joined the Dominicans at Paris,[3] and in both cases it could have been the presence and character of the community of St Jacques that won them to the order in the first place.[4] (It may be that arts students seemed excellent recruits, and this not only because of the intellectual formation they would have received, but also because certain aspects of their student life 'in the world' would tend to form a mentality receptive to mendicant ideals; for students would be accustomed to urban forms of social life, many of them would have already uprooted themselves from their original geographical and social contexts, and some would be accustomed to extreme poverty.[5]) The Florentine group also had Paris connections. We are told in the obituary of Remigio de' Girolami in the *Necrologio* of Santa Maria Novella that he

[1] Four if one counts Remigio, but his sermons were apparently never in general circulation.

[2] For Étienne's age see J.-C. Schmitt, *Le Saint Lèvrier*, p. 23; for Humbert's, Kaeppeli, *Scriptores*, ii. 283.

[3] 'Parisiis vero, magisterio in artibus iam decoratus, Ord. Praed. nomen dedit (30 XI 1224)' (Kaeppeli, ibid.).

[4] Étienne de Bourbon's editor speculated that 'c'est sans doute le spectacle édifiant de leur ferveur primitive qui lui inspira la pensée d'entrer dans cet ordre naissant . . .' (Lecoy de la Marche, *Anecdotes*, p. v). Cf. J. Verger, 'Studia et universités', in *Le scuole*, p. 182: 'Une seconde raison qu'ont pu avoir les Mendiants de rattacher certains de leur *studia* aux universités ressort elle aussi clairement de l'histoire des débuts de ces ordres. Ce fut le désir de recruter de nouveaux frères parmi les maîtres et les étudiants.'

[5] Here I am more or less following the remarks of Verger, ibid. 182–3.

was already *licentiatus in artibus* at the University of Paris
when he joined the Dominican order 'in the first flower of his
youth', and that later he was sent back to Paris to read the
Sentences, 'so that he could reach the highest level of
theological science'.[1] His confrère Giordano da Pisa also
studied at Paris,[2] and there is evidence that when he died he
was on his way to Paris to lecture on the Sentences and
become a Master of Theology.[3] As for the Franciscan at
Florence whom we have singled out, Servasanto da Faenza,
we do not know for certain that he had studied at Paris, but it
is at least a serious possibility.[4]

What puts Paris in a different category from any other
centre, however, is that it was a centre for the diffusion as well
as for the production of preaching aids. The *pecia* system of
the Paris University stationers must have enormously increased the circulation of a substantial number of model
sermon collections and preaching aids, not necessarily composed by Paris scholars. It is arguable that preaching aids are
more important as mass communication than as original
creation. In this perspective the place where a work was made
widely accessible matters as much as the place in which it was
first written. Thus, even the sermons of Guillaume Peyraut of
Lyons were in a real sense part of the empire of Paris.[5]

The number of preaching aids made available through the
Paris *pecia* system is large enough to eclipse any of the other
centres we have discussed. The identification of the preaching
aids on the two known *pecia* lists, and also of preaching aids
not on these lists but found in *pecia* manuscripts, involves
laborious detail which it has seemed best to concentrate in an
appendix.[6] It will be apparent to those who have the patience
to read it that our knowledge of the *pecia* transmission

---

[1] I follow C. T. Davis, 'Remigio de' Girolami O.P.', in *Le scuole*, p. 283.
[2] Delcorno, *Giordano da Pisa*, p. 9.   [3] See ibid. 20.
[4] Oliger, 'Servasanto', pp. 180–1.
[5] The Sunday Epistle and the *de sanctis* sermons of Peyraut are listed on the first
pecia list. According to the Destrez notes his sermons on the Sunday Gospels and his
Summa of virtues and vices were also made available by the *pecia* system. See
Appendix.
[6] Below, pp. 275–81.

of sermon materials is in an untidy state, though the preliminary work of clearing the ground has been done[1] and a fruitful method has been demonstrated by the Rouses' pioneering work on the *Manipulus florum*.[2]

It should be emphasized that the importance of the *pecia* transmission of sermons is not a function of the importance of the authors whose collections are transmitted. Since these collections belong more to the history of mass communication than of creative thought, they are worth studying even if their authors are third- or fourth-rank figures. As a matter of fact, some of the collections are by men who are very obscure indeed. Thus, all we know of the sermon collection called *Legifer* is that it is Franciscan and that the *sermones festivales* section at least was put together 'from collations at the houses of the friars' (at Paris?). Or again, there are the Dominican *Sermones Alleabatenses* or *attrebatenses*, whose author or compiler is also unknown. We are not much better off with some of the preachers who are named. Pierre de Saint-Benoît was Franciscan, but we can say little else about him, except that he knew both Orleans and Paris[3] and that he was familiar with academic arrangements.[4] Thomas Lebreton (= Brito), Guillaume de Mailly, and Nicolas de Biard are still more obscure. We know that they were 'religious' rather than secular clergy, and—as authors of sermon collections in the mid- to late thirteenth century—there is an a priori likelihood

---

[1] See Appendix, nn. 1 and 2.

[2] *Preachers, passim.*

[3] Orleans: 'Veniet desideratus et cetera. Aurilianus [*sic*] agnoscitur esse festum cum audiunt pulsari desideratum, signum scilicet sic vocatum . . .' (MS Venice, Marc. Fondo antico lat. 92 (collocazione 1897, Valentinelli, vi. 36), fo. 7ᵛᵃ); Schneyer, *Repertorium*, iv. 782, No. 2. Paris: '. . . Pone exemplum de ludentibus ad barras in garennia (*or* garemna, *etc.*) sancti Germani Par(isius), quomodo discalciabant se una tantum induti (induci *ms?*) tunica, ut currant expedite; quod si nimis videtur aspera (apera *ms*) via, conceditur infirmo currere in calceis, hoc tamen constante quod non precurrit ad bravium cuius cor conprimitur vel constringitur amore temporalium, sed cuius cor dilatatur desiderio supernorum. . . .' (MS cit., fo. 29ᵛᵇ). discalciabant se] *followed in ms by* et-sign, *or line-filler, or scribal error*; bravium] *some words have probably dropped out of the text before or after this word.* From a sermon on the text 'Sic currite' (1 Cor. 9: 24), Schneyer, *Repertorium*, iv. 785, No. 33. It would be possible to cite other passages which imply that he knew the academic world of Paris.

[4] See above, pp. 114–16.

that they were friars, but none of them has been securely identified as belonging to a particular order.[1] Conversely, the sermon collections of at least two distinguished Paris masters appear not to have been transmitted by the *pecia* system at all. No one to my knowledge has yet found any *pecia* manuscripts of sermons of Hugues de Saint-Cher or of Bonaventura's *de tempore* sermon cycle. There is no obvious explanation for these omissions. It is conceivable, though perhaps not likely, that the high casualty rate of *pecia* manuscripts is responsible.

The casualty rate of *pecia* manuscripts is in any case something to be stressed in its own right, as a warning not to underestimate the influence of *pecia* texts. It seems fairly clear that the role of the system in diffusing at least two texts was much larger than the number of surviving manuscripts with *pecia* indications would lead one to suppose. The Rouses have shown for the *Manipulus florum* that 'of the many manu-scripts . . . copied from Parisian [*pecia*] exemplars, only a few still contain *pecia* notes or other evidence of having come from a university exemplar'.[2] The *Legifer* collection seems to have survived in even fewer *pecia* manuscripts (two), yet there are technical reasons for thinking that the work was in some demand at the university stationers.[3] This is not to deny that stationers may sometimes have backed a loser. The *Sapientia sanctorum* collection of Aldobrandino Cavalcanti may be one

---

[1] L.-J. Bataillon first pointed out to me how shaky the assumptions about the orders of these three preachers are. A passage from Nicolas de Biard—if he is the author of the sermon as well as compiler of the collection to which it belongs—sug-gests some connection with Paris: 'Exemplum si episcopus Parisiensis vocaret aliquem clericum ad aliquam prebendam . . .' (MS BN lat. 13579, fo. 19[ra-b]); from a sermon on the text 'Benedictus qui venit' (Matt. 21: 9), Schneyer, *Repertorium*, iv. 229, No. 9.

[2] *Preachers*, p. 170. Taking account of indirect descendants, they argue that 'In the period of time during which the *Manipulus florum* was available in pieces, enough copies were produced to father at least three-quarters of the some 200 surviving manuscripts' (p. 181). If I understand them correctly, they imply that only eight manuscripts with *pecia* indications, or nine including the *pecia* exemplar, are know to survive from the second university edition (pp. 176 and 180), and that only one manuscript with *pecia* indications is known to survive from the first and apparently unsuccessful edition (p. 171–2).

[3] See Appendix.

such. Though it is on the first Paris *pecia* list, no *pecia* manuscripts of it are known and hardly any copies of the work have been found in French libraries.[1] As a general rule, however, it is unsafe to assume that a *pecia* transmission of any work is unimportant, and there can be no doubt whatever about the collective impact of the *pecia* system on European preaching.

To conclude: the map of preaching in the thirteenth century hardly extends beyond the boundaries of England, Germany, Italy, and France, and it is dominated by the latter two countries. The most important centres for the diffusion of preaching material are Florence, Lyons, and Paris, but Paris outstrips either of the other two several times over if we count preaching aids diffused by the *pecia* system together with preaching aids by Paris friars. These orders of magnitude are of interest in their own right, but they also bring us back to the more general problem of the relation between the two roles of Paris: as a centre of mass communication and as intellectual capital of Europe.

ii. Preaching and Scholasticism

It would be wrong to rule out a priori the possibility that pure chance is the explanation. It is conceivable that there was no connection between these two functions of the greatest university town, and that they may be understood, as it were, in watertight compartments. Perhaps the university was the context of the sermons written or mass-produced there in a physical sense only. On the other hand, it would be wrong as well as dull to adopt this explanation, or non-explanation, without first exploring more positive hypotheses.

An attractive one might run something like this. The age of

---

[1] Cf. Kaeppeli, *Scriptores*, i. 35–6: he lists one manuscript in a French library. One should, however, note the number of manuscripts in libraries from the German *Sprachraum*: it is not impossible that the work travelled from Italy to Germany via the Paris University stationers.

mendicant preaching is also the age of scholastic preaching: their sermons are a popularized scholasticism, in method and perhaps also in content. Paris was the fountain-head of scholasticism in the thirteenth century. Therefore it is natural that Paris should be the place where most sermon collections should be composed. The diffusion of sermon collections by the university stationers would be an indirect spin-off, rather as Oxford's role in academic bookselling and publishing is a spin-off of the university's presence. Most sermon collections (but not all) would be by friars, just as with more purely academic works of scholastic theology.

The hypothesis might also be formulated in weaker terms. Setting aside the question of why Paris was the centre of mass communication by preaching, it could be argued that the character of the medium and message was deeply coloured by the fact that the city was also the principal foyer of scholastic thought. The scholasticism of the university would affect both the type of sermon collection which was composed and the type which was in demand from the university. A still more watered down version would leave aside the question of influence altogether, and simply present scholasticism as a form of thought shared by sermons and academic theology, a part of the general intellectual climate at Paris.

Since the purpose of this book is to put mendicant preaching in its different contexts, it is clearly essential to work out where it stood in relation to the scholastic method in general. The discussion which follows—like the attempt to clarify the map of preaching—will be fuller than if it were only a means to solve a problem about Paris, though it is that too.

The characterization of thirteenth-century preaching as scholastic needs to be taken seriously if only because there is a distinguished historiographical tradition behind it, above all, though not exclusively, in what one might call the German school. It is interesting to trace the idea's history. Cruel's *Geschichte der deutschen Predigt im Mittelalter* (Detmold, 1879) makes a natural starting-point, for together with Lecoy

de la Marche's *La Chaire française au Moyen Âge* (1st edn.,
1868) it marks the beginning of modern scholarly work on
medieval preaching. Cruel rightly saw the advent of the 'new
sermon form' as marking a new period, and he explained the
new form as the product of scholastic influence. The
preaching of the first period (600–1200) had, he argued, an
'unorganic structure', by contrast with the sermons of the
second period, whose parts are carefully co-ordinated according to a central plan.[1] The essential feature would seem to be
systematic division of one form or another.[2] He admits that
the 'new form' can be found in his first period, but only in
exceptional cases, when it was the obvious procedure
anyway.[3] According to Cruel the new form had its origins in
the transformation of the whole of theology in France, where
a formal philosophical school of thought—scholasticism
—had developed since the eleventh century on the basis of
Aristotle's works.[4]

Two major German studies followed a few years after
Cruel's, and both explained the new form in terms of
scholasticism. A. Linsenmayer believed that the academic

---

[1] 'Man suchte nämlich jetzt aus einer zu Grunde gelegten Einheit eine
regelmässige Gliederung des Redestoffes hervorgehen zu lassen' (Cruel, *Geschichte*,
p. 279).

[2] Cruel makes the point that the skeletal 'organic' framework did not invariably
need to take the form of division in the strictest sense of the word. It could also
depend on the 'Anwendung der logischen Kategorien'. However, the examples he
gives imply that such cases are really divisions under a rather different form: see p.
281. He then mentions another type of sermon which he also groups under the
general heading of 'the new preaching form'—the sermon based on a metaphor or a
picture, in which the points of comparison between the imaginary object and the
subject of the sermon make up its various parts. Once again, the method is combined
and fused with division in the examples he gives, e.g. 'Luc. 6. Ascendens Jesus in
unam naviculam. etc. Circa quod est notandum, quod quadruplex est navis:
poenitentiae, ecclesiae, crucis, mentis' (p. 282).

[3] Ibid.

[4] 'Die neue Form der Predigt ging mit der Umwandlung der ganzen Theologie
von Frankreich aus, wo sich seit dem elften Jahrhundert auf Grund des Studiums
aristotelischer Werke eine formal-philosophische Richtung ausbildete, die bald unter
dem Namen der Scholastik in allen Schulen die Oberhand gewann' (ibid. 290). Cruel
believed that the influence of scholasticism made itself felt in the person of Bernard
of Clairvaux, arch-enemy of the scholastic movement itself. He justifies this paradox
with the argument that 'kann auch er die genossene philosophische Schulbildung
nicht verleugnen' (ibid. 292).

tendencies of the time, and more specifically scholasticism, were a powerful influence on the internal development of preaching.[1] The influence of scholasticism on the form of preaching could be called 'epoch-making'.[2] Scholasticism also left its mark on the content—on the explanation and justification of the truths of faith, on the choice of themes, and on the explanation of Scriptures.[3] A few years later it was stated in D. Keppler's scholarly survey of the development of preaching form[4] that from the thirteenth century on the influence of scholasticism on German preaching was 'unmistakable'.[5]

In more recent times the scholastic interpretation has been adopted by Johannes Baptist Schneyer, the scholar who has done more than any other for the study of medieval sermons. Schneyer also attaches great importance to the influence of the universities,[6] and attributes to this the scholastic character of preaching. University teachers took a leading part in the production of 'scholastische Predigtliteratur', including whole *summas* of model sermons to help the secular and regular clergy.[7] The universities were in fact a driving force

---

[1] '. . . hier vor Allem die wissenschaftliche Bildung und Richtung der Zeit nicht ausser Ansatz gelassen werden kann, zumal wenn sie eine die gesammte geistige Thätigkeit so ganz und gar beherrschende und durchdringende ist, wie diess die Scholastik war' (*Geschichte der Predigt in Deutschland von Karl dem Grossen bis zum Ausgange des vierzehnten Jahrhunderts* (Munich, 1886), 71).

[2] 'In formeller Beziehung kann man den Einfluss der Scholastik auf die Predigt geradezu einen Epoche machenden nennen' (ibid).

[3] Ibid. 72.

[4] 'Beiträge zur Entwicklungsgeschichte der Predigtanlage', *Theologische Quartalschrift* (Tübingen), 74 (1892), 52–120, 179–212.

[5] 'Vom 13. Jahrhundert an ist der Einfluss der Scholastik auf die deutsche Predigt unverkennbar. . .' (ibid. 62–3). Like Cruel, Keppler proposes the paradox that Bernard of Clairvaux was responsible: '. . . doch in einer Reihe von Predigten mit wohlgefügter Disposition, mit hervortretender Partition und festgesetztem Einheitspunkt zuerst den homiletischen Einfluss einer neuen Geistesbildung zur Wirkung kommen lässt, einer Geistesbildung, deren Lebensnerv scharfe, Geist und Seele, Mark und Gefüge der Gedanken scheidende Logik ist. Er hat der Scholastik den Zugang zur Kanzel vermittelt. . .' (p. 63).

[6] '. . . sandten gerade die Bettelorden ihre begabtesten Mitglieder an die Universitäten und erkämpften sich dort eigene Lehrstühle. Von den *Universitäten* gingen die begabtesten und fruchtbarsten Prediger der Kirche aus. . . .' (Schneyer, *Geschichte*, p. 130).

[7] Ibid. 131.

in the preaching movement of the period.[1] The influence which scholasticism exercised over preaching was not an unmixed blessing.[2] The penetration of the scholastic method of teaching and disputation—that is, defining, dividing, arguing, giving examples, raising contradictions (*Kontrahieren*)—could at most appeal to masters and students.[3] However, we should not judge scholastic preaching from the abbreviated sermon models in which only a more or less developed schema is transmitted.[4] The sermons which were actually preached and which have survived are a different matter: while keeping to the basic principles of scholastic sermon composition, they can nevertheless be full of life, whether preached to the clergy or the laity.[5] Schneyer adds that around the middle of the thirteenth century we see the arrival of what he calls 'scholastic popular preaching', which retained the framework (*Kompositionsgerüst*) of the preaching which derived from the lecture theatre but left plenty of room for less austere material.[6]

Against these authorities we may (in the manner of scholastic *quaestiones*) set another which takes a quite different view. In Étienne Gilson's essay on Michel Menot and the technique of medieval preaching[7] we are told that the rhetoric of the *artes praedicandi* was derived neither from

---

[1] 'So gingen damals von den Universitäten die treibenden, vorwärts drängenden Kräfte in der Predigt aus' (ibid.).

[2] 'Wir übersehen hier nicht, dass das von den Universitäten ausgehenden scholastische Überwicht der Predigt auch empfindliche Nachteile brachte' (ibid.).

[3] Ibid. Cf. his 'Die Erforschung der scholastischen Sermones und ihre Bedeutung für die Homiletik', *Scholastik*, 39 (1964), 1–26, at pp. 18–19.

[4] 'Wir dürfen hier jedoch nicht übersehen, dass von vielen nicht ausgeführten scholastischen Predigtvorlagen nur dieser mehr oder weniger ausgeführte Dispositionsbau überliefert ist' (ibid. 19), speaking of divisions, subdivisions, subsubdivisions . . .

[5] Ibid. and *Geschichte*, pp. 131–2.

[6] Ibid. 132. It is not fully clear whether or not Schneyer means to distinguish this *scholastische Volkspredigt* from the popular preaching which he discusses later in the book. A more important criticism is that the principle according to which preachers and sermon collections of the thirteenth century have been divided between ch. II. 2 ('Die Überlegenheit der Universitätspredigt in der Hochscholastik . . .') and ch. II. 3 ('Die Volkspredigt des 13. und 14. Jahrhunderts') seems open to question.

[7] 'Michel Menot et la technique du sermon médiéval', repr. in his *Les Idées et les lettres* (Paris, 1932), 93–154.

the dialectic of Aristotle nor the rhetorical techniques of Cicero. The function of preaching was not to silence an opponent or to win a legal case, but to save souls, and to achieve this end a new method had to be invented.[1] The technique that was invented was originally quite distinct from scholastic argument.[2] It is true that when we move from the period of St Bonaventura to Michel Menot himself we find that scholasticism had indeed begun to play a large part in preaching; sermons are divided into two sections, one of which is devoted to a veritable *quaestio disputata*.[3] This, however, was a later development. In the time of St Bonaventura disputations were for the schools, and sermons for church.[4] Furthermore, Gilson makes it clear that the essential parts of the technique he is describing were used for sermons to the people as well as for educated clerical congregations.[5]

Here, then, are two apparently contrasting interpretations of the relation of preaching to scholasticism in the age of Bonaventura. The problem is partly one of how we understand scholasticism. This does not mean that it is an imaginary problem: a substantial proportion of major historical problems are in part problems of semantics. Not only concepts like 'Feudalism' and 'Humanism', but also apparently innocuous words like 'the manor', 'slavery', 'war', 'a victory', involve implicit or explicit choices by the historian between differently moulded concepts. Now clearly there is no absolute right or wrong about such choices. Nevertheless, different sets of terms vary enormously in their degree of usefulness, and criteria may be formulated for choosing one rather than another. A *sine qua non* is that the usage chosen

[1] 'Michel Menot et la technique du sermon médiéval', repr. in his *Les Idées et les lettres* (Paris, 1932), 100.
[2] Ibid. 134.   [3] Ibid. 134–5.   [4] Ibid. 134.
[5] Ibid. 93–6. Gilson's points do not seem to have been taken by M.-D. Chenu, introduction to Th.-M. Charland, *Artes praedicandi. Contribution à l'histoire de la rhétorique au Moyen Âge* (Publications de l'Institut d'Études Médiévales d'Ottawa, 7; Paris and Ottawa, 1936), at pp. 9–10, and H. Caplan, 'Classical Rhetoric and the Medieval Theory of Preaching', *Classical Philology*, 28 (1933), 73–96, at p. 88.

must not be a private language—so different from previous usage that no other historian will accept it—but the main criterion is that a usage is bad, or rather less helpful, if it blurs the distinction between different phenomena.

It is by this second criterion that Gilson's interpretation seems superior to what I have called the 'scholastic' interpretation. The use of the word 'scholastic' to describe thirteenth-century preaching blurs some fundamental differences between it and the disputations, *summas*, and Sentence commentaries of thirteenth-century masters, and, indeed, the treatises of Abelard or Anselm. If thirteenth-century preaching is to be called scholastic, then we would need to find another word for the intellectual phenomenon which everyone has hitherto called by that name. Those historians who did describe preaching as scholastic were indeed making a valid point, and what follows is in no sense an attack on these fine syntheses; but their point (to which we will return) must be formulated differently, or else other truths become obscured.

Gilson's argument about *quaestiones* is important. Of course, any universal generalization about thirteenth-century preaching would be rash when there are tens of thousands of surviving sermons,[1] but unless the sample I have seen is quite untypical it may be said that *quaestiones* are abnormal in this period. I have come across a few examples of something approaching the *quaestio* method—apparently contrasting authorities brought together in a sermon by Aldobrandino Cavalcanti,[2] difficult problems raised by Jean de la Rochelle and Guibert de Tournai[3]—but they are hard to find and rudimentary by comparison with contemporary *quaestiones* in genres which may properly be called scholastic.

---

[1] Cf. L.-J. Bataillon, 'L'Emploi du langage philosophique', p. 991: 'les sermons...se comptent par dizaines milliers.'

[2] On the text 'Beati mortui' (Rev. 14: 13), Schneyer, *Repertorium*, i. 180, No. 430, inc. fo. 189[vb] in MS Bamberg, Msc. Theol. 2.

[3] Jean: 'Si queratur de illo qui preventus est morte...' (MS BN lat. 16477, fo. 8[va]); from a sermon on the text 'Erunt signa' (Luke 21: 25), Schneyer, *Repertorium*, iii. 704, No. 5. Guibert: see d'Avray and Tausche, 'Marriage Sermons', p. 91.

The absence of fully fledged *quaestiones* (i.e. formally posed question–conflicting authorities and arguments–solution–answers to/explanation of arguments and authorities) would not in itself be decisive.[1] It is, however, symptomatic of two more fundamental 'negative facts' about thirteenth-century preaching. One is that sermons did not normally proceed by raising problems, the other is that formal logical argument (when we meet it at all) is in a manner of speaking the icing on the cake, and not mixed into the batter as it is in Sentence commentaries, *summa*s and disputed questions. Of course, these two negative facts are related.

Sermons present doctrine, arrange it in patterns, orchestrate the Scriptural and patristic authorities for it, but they do not normally formulate problems such as 'How can one prove God's existence by reason?', 'Why did he become man?', 'Would he have done so if man had not sinned?', 'Did original sin weaken man's intellect as well as his will?', and so on.[2] The technique used to solve such problems in Sentence commentaries etc. was formal logic and (by the later thirteenth century) the constructions of human reason, represented above all by the corpus of Aristotle's works. No reason, no scholastic method: the connection between *ratio* and *auctoritas* (Scripture, patristic tradition) was structural and essential. In thirteenth-century preaching their relation is quite different. The sermon collection of Reginaldo da Piperno, which is heavily influenced by the scholastic theology of Aquinas, is exceptional and seems to survive in only one manuscript.

It is true that one can find philosophical language in thirteenth-century sermons,[3] but its function is more cosmetic than essential. The scholar who has studied the phenomenon describes the use of such language in two sermons preached before a university public as 'parodique,

---

[1] Cf. M. Grabmann, *Die Geschichte der scholastischen Methode*, i (Freiburg im Breisgau, 1909), 31–2.

[2] Cf. M.-D. Chenu, *La Théologie comme science au XIIIᵉ siècle* (Paris, 1957), 23–4.

[3] L.-J. Bataillon, 'L'Emploi du langage philosophique', *passim*.

sinon caricatural', and not so different from the use of proverbs or *exempla*.[1] The example cited in the same study from the model sermon collection of Pierre de Saint-Benoît, OM, while it carries the interesting implication that the sermon may have originally been preached live before a congregation of students,[2] cannot usefully be described as scholastic reasoning. It is a kind of play on the logical and religious senses of the word 'conversion'. If the original audience had consisted of students, or if they had somehow acquired a tincture of logical terminology, this may possibly have seemed an effective rhetorical device. The logical language is dressing up a simple proposition: conversion should be entire. Moreover, to judge by the sample of Pierre's sermons I have read,[3] reason and philosophy do not play anything like the crucial role assigned to them in the careful definition of the scholastic method by Grabmann.[4] It is difficult to see in these sermons the 'application of reason and philosophy to the truths of faith', and their presentation of their truth is artistic, Scriptural, and liturgical rather than 'systematic and organically comprehensive'.

Reasoning did have a role in thirteenth-century sermons. It was one of the ways of developing the framework of divisions and authorities. But it had to take its place with the other 'ways of dilating' (*modi dilatandi*) a sermon,[5] and was not

---

[1] Ibid. 987.

[2] Ibid. 988 (see also above, II. iv, pp. 114–16). Bataillon also points out (pp. 989–90) the frequent citations of Aristotle in the sermons of the Italian Franciscan Servasanto da Faenza. This would seem to fit the argument advanced, above, I. ii, about the relatively high cultural level of the audience of preaching, especially in Italy.

[3] Chiefly his advent sermons.

[4] 'Die scholastische Methode will durch Anwendung der Vernunft, der Philosophie auf die Offenbarungswahrheiten möglichste Einsicht in den Glaubensinhalt gewinnen, um so die übernaturliche Wahrheit dem denkenden Menschengeiste inhaltlich näher zu bringen, eine systematische, organisch zusammenfassende Gesamtdarstellung der Heilswahrheit zu ermöglichen und die gegen den Offenbarungsinhalt vom Vernunftstandpunkte aus erhobenen Einwände lösen zu können. In allmählicher Entwicklung hat die scholastische Methode sich eine bestimmte äussere Technik, eine äussere Form geschaffen, sich gleichsam versinnlicht und verleiblicht' (*Geschichte der scholastischen Methode*, i. 36–7).

[5] Cf. Gilson, 'Michel Menot', pp. 127–48.

necessarily any more important than *exempla* or similitudes. Furthermore, the reasoning tended to be much less formal; it lacks the philosophical self-consciousness of the arguments in a Sentence commentary.[1]

The really essential features of thirteenth-century mendicant sermons transmitted in Latin would seem to have been divisions and authorities, rather than *rationes*. We have already seen (II. iii) that model sermons were commonly transmitted in the form of divisions and authorities and little else. These dry schemata, so apparently unpromising to the historian, can show us what was thought to be the hard core of a sermon.

We can learn the same lesson from fuller sermons. The sermon 'To citizens living in communes' by Guibert de Tournai (printed on pp. 260–71 as an Illustrative Text) is dominated by Scriptural *auctoritates* and by divisions or distinctions. (On the whole, it is not helpful to distinguish between divisions and distinctions in our terminology.[2]) In the manuscript I have used there are 136 words in the short section at the end on *divitie supercelestes*. The framework is clearly marked:

Sunt etiam divitie supercelestes...

> Iste vero sunt in magnificentia potentie, in sapientia providentie, in affluentia misericordie, et magnificentia glorie.

[1] Cf. the passage from the pseudo-Bonaventuran *Ars concionandi* quoted by Gilson, ibid. 134 n. 1: 'Ne praedicatio videatur esse disputatio, oportet, quod sic fiat, quasi non esset argumentatio, ut scilicet non praemittantur propositiones, et postea inferatur conclusio; sed magis dicatur sic: nam ita est, et hoc multiplici ratione.'

[2] Cf. Gilson, 'Michel Menot', p. 127: 'Les distinctions ne sont en effet que les subdivisions introduites successivement par l'orateur au cours de ses développements... ces deux problèmes... dans la pratique, ne sauraient être légitimement isolés.' Furthermore, the initial divisions of sermons can be exactly what one would find in a distinction collection. Thus, the sermon under discussion is based around what is in effect a *distinctio* on the word *divitie*: 'Sunt autem temporales. Sunt spirituales. Sunt celestes. Sunt et supercelestes.'

> De primo . . .
>
> De secundo . . .
>
> De tertio . . .
>
> De quarto . . .

This occupies twenty-seven words. Of the remaining 109, no fewer than 100 belong to Scriptural quotations.[1] Some exegesis of the Scriptural texts cited would be normal in Latin sermons which were not drastically abridged, but there might not be much else. *Exempla* could be inserted when the sermon was actually preached, but it would not be so easy to work in *rationes* if they were not already on parchment. This predominance of divisions/distinctions and authorities aroused criticism.[2]

At this point it may be objected that distinctions and authorities are the two features most generally associated with scholasticism. A 'scholastic distinction' in this sense, however, means something different and its relation to authorities is quite different from that of the kind of distinctions we have been discussing. This is best explained by examples. The distinction with which Guibert de Tournai's sermon 'To citizens living in communes' begins is implicitly on the word 'riches'. (The text of the sermon is Eccles. 5: 9, 'He who loves riches will take no fruit from them.' We are told that 'There are temporal ones. There are spiritual ones. There are

---

[1] I include the references. It should be noted that of the seven *auctoritates* quoted, all include either the word *dives* or a form of the word *divitie*. There is doubtless a *distinctio* collection or concordance somewhere behind this.

[2] Passages from Roger Bacon in Felder, *Geschichte*, pp. 353–4. Note that the strange phrase 'vocal concordances' almost certainly refers to Scriptural *auctoritates* (of a particular kind): cf. Thomas Waleys, *De modo componendi sermones*, ed Charland in his *Artes praedicandi*, p. 385. Another critic is Humbert de Romans (though he may be speaking of excesses rather than the practices *per se*): 'Sunt alii qui student ad dicendum multa: multiplicantes modo membra sermonum, modo distinctiones, modo auctoritates . . . [he lists other practices]: quae valde vitiosa sunt in sermonibus' (*De eruditione praedicatorum* Prima Pars, VII, in *B. Humberti de Romanis opera de vita regulari*, ed. J. J. Berthier, ii (1956?), 395. Cf. also the remarks by Pierre de Baume on new preaching techniques, discussed by Smalley, *English Friars*, p. 43.

celestial ones. There are supercelestial ones.'[1]) Each of these then becomes the beginning of a main section of the sermon, and each is confirmed by at least one authority and followed by subsections and more authorities. The role of authorities is to confirm the members of a distinction/division or subdistinction/-division.

The relation of 'scholastic distinctions' to authorities is almost inverse. Here the authorities are confronted and meanings of a word are distinguished to show that the authorities are not really contradictory. The first article of the *Summa theologica* of Aquinas provides an example. The question is: 'Is another teaching required apart from philosophical studies?'[2] Aquinas starts by citing a Scriptural authority in support of a negative answer to the question: '(1) Any other teaching beyond that of science and philosophy seems needless. For man ought not to venture into realms beyond his reason; according to Ecclesiasticus, "Be not curious about things far above thee." Now the things lying within range of reason yield well enough to scientific and philosophical treatment. Additional teaching, therefore, seems superfluous.'[3] He gives a second argument for a negative conclusion, with an authority from Aristotle, and then proceeds to set against these two arguments an authority which apparently contradicts them: 'On the other hand the second Epistle to Timothy says, "All Scripture inspired of God is profitable to teach, to reprove, to correct, to instruct in righteousness." Divinely inspired Scripture, however, is no part of the branches of philosophy traced by reasoning. Accordingly it is expedient to have another body of sure knowledge inspired by God.'[4] Aquinas then gives his reasoned *responsio* to the question—which need not concern us here—and ends the article by 'defusing' the two arguments

---

[1] Cf. above, p. 172, n. 2, and below, p. 260.

[2] St Thomas Aquinas, *Summa theologiae*, Blackfriars ed. and trans., vol. i, ed. T. Gilby (London and New York, 1964), 5.

[3] Ibid.

[4] Ibid. 7.

and authorities advanced at the beginning, to show that they do not really contradict the argument set out in the *responsio* or the authority from the second Epistle to Timothy. To do this he employs distinctions. Thus, he defuses the argument advanced at the start of the article by drawing a distinction between two ways of investigating the things which are— echoing Ecclesiasticus—'too high for human knowledge'. They are not to be investigated by the reason (*per rationem inquirenda*), but when revealed by God they should be received by faith (*suscipienda per fidem*).[1] Clearly this is not at all the same sort of distinction as the distinction between temporal, spiritual, celestial, and supercelestial riches in Guibert de Tournai's sermons.

'Scholastic distinctions' in the useful sense are not, of course, used only to defuse apparent contradictions between Scriptural authorities. In the article of the *Summa* which we have been examining Aquinas also uses distinctions to defuse the argument in which the authority of Aristotle is cited.[2] Furthermore, distinctions can be used without reference to a particular authority.[3] A characteristic function which these different sorts of scholastic distinction share, however, would be that they are used to solve problems, and it is just this

---

[1] Ibid. 8.

[2] The argument is that '. . . the philosophical sciences deal with all parts of reality, even with God; hence Aristotle refers to one department of philosophy as theology or the divine science. That being the case, no need arises for another kind of education to be admitted or entertained' (ibid. 7). At the end of the article Aquinas meets the point by distinguishing between different ways of knowing things: '. . . there is nothing to stop the same things from being treated by the philosophical sciences when they can be looked at in the light of natural reason and by another science when they are looked at in the light of divine revelation. Consequently the theology of holy teaching differs in kind from that theology which is ranked as a part of philosophy' (ibid. 9).

[3] e.g in I. a. 1, 7 of the *Summa theologiae*: '2. Besides, all matters about which a science reaches settled conclusions enter into its subject. Now sacred Scripture goes as far about many things other than God, for instance about creatures and human conduct. Therefore its subject is not purely God.' (ibid. 25). This objection is disposed of by a distinction between two ways in which God may be the subject: '2. All other things that are settled in Holy Scripture are embraced in God, not that they are parts of him—such as essential components or accidents—but because they are somehow related to him' (ibid. 27).

problem-solving mentality which seems to be absent from thirteenth-century preaching.

Salimbene mentions a Magister Guillelmus, who 'had a great gift for disputation. For when he disputed at Paris, no one disputed better than he. For he was a great logician and a great theologian; however, when he took on the task of preaching, he did not know what to say...'[1] Whatever the reasons in William's case, we should not be surprised that such different skills did not always go together.

One feature which thirteenth-century mendicant sermons do share with the academic genres to which I would restrict the word 'scholastic' is the passion for dividing and subdividing. Here one must be precise. It is true that the structure of a sermon collection as a whole is most often liturgical and thus has little in common with the carefully articulated structure of a Sentence commentary or *summa*. It is also true, as we have already hinted, that the structure of a *quaestio*[2] does not really resemble the structure of the individual sermon, whose parts start from a single point and fan out artistically, without confrontation of arguments or authorities, like a symmetrical family tree of notions, each supported by a text. But the structure of individual sermons does bear a resemblance to the overall structure of individual Sentence commentaries and *summa*s, the common factor being the structure of numbered sections and subsections.

This is the truth which lies behind the designation of thirteenth-century preaching as scholastic by the German school and some other historians.[3] We should, however,

---

[1] Salimbene, *Cronica*, ed. Holder-Egger, p. 214. The last words might also be translated: 'He did not know what he was talking about.'

[2] It should be noted that in the *Summa theologiae* the *quaestio*- structure is to be found in the individual *articuli* that go to make up the divisions of the text which are entitled *quaestiones*. The structure of the *articuli* has been usefully analysed into five stages: '*a.* the title, *b.* the opening arguments for a position opposed to the one he will take up, *c.* a brief countering statement, *d.* the exposition and settlement of the issue, *e.* the replies to the opening arguments' (*Summa theologiae*, i, ed. Gilby, Appendix I ('Structure of the Summa'), p. 45.

[3] Notably by Ch.-V. Langlois, 'L'Éloquence sacrée au Moyen Âge', *Revue des deux mondes*, 115 (1893), 170–201, especially p. 186: scholastic sermons are

retain their insight without their language, which makes one concept try to do the work of two. For there are two phenomena that need to be held before the mind, a more general one and a more specific one. To put it as the scholastics themselves would have done, the academic genres in which reason and philosophy were married to the Bible and patristic tradition are a species of the genus of works characterized by division and subdivision of the text. It seems more useful to keep the word 'scholastic' for this species and to find another word for the genus: perhaps 'the subdividing mentality'.[1] Sermons are a different species of this genus, and Bible commentaries a third species of it.[2]

It has not yet been established whether or not the subdividing mentality came to permeate preaching under the influence of the logic of the schools. To find the origins of the new sermon form which crystallized around or just after the middle of the thirteenth century is important in itself, but it is not so important for our understanding of the relation between preaching and scholasticism once their respective methods had crystallized. In the same way it would not follow that humanism should be called an Aristotelian movement, even if it could be shown that thirteenth-century Aristotelianism was one origin of Renaissance humanism.[3]

If it should prove to be true that the germ of the subdividing mentality was caught from scholastic logic, then

---

characterized by 'un appareil rebutant de divisions, de subdivisions, de définitions, de distinctions, emprunté à la méthode des logiciens; et par l'emploi exclusif de cette langue barbare, forgée à Seville et à Tolède par les philosophes arabisans, qu'Abailard n'aurait pas comprise'. Langlois complicates matters by drawing what seems to me an artificial distinction between academic and popular preaching (see below, p. 193 ff.) and implying that popular preaching is not 'scholastic' in this sense.

[1] Of course, one need not insist on this particular terminology; the important thing is that we should not use the same word for the more general *and* for the more specific phenomenon.

[2] On divisions and subdivisions in Bible commentaries see B. Smalley, *The Study of the Bible in the Middle Ages* (2nd edn., Oxford, 1952), 296 and n. 2; also in *The Cambridge History of the Bible*, ii. *The West from the Fathers to the Reformation*, ed. G. W. H. Lampe (Cambridge, 1969), 210.

[3] Cf. W. Ullmann, *Mediaeval Foundations of Renaissance Humanism* (London, 1977), 88 ff.

preaching's relative immunity to the scholastic technique of problem-solving by systematic logical argument is the more striking. In fact, however, it is not yet clear that the habit of systematically dividing sermons should be traced back to scholastic influence. The history of sermon form in the twelfth and thirteenth centuries is still being worked out.[1] Cruel's theory that the new form goes back to St Bernard's sermons—especially the brief schematic ones—remains attractive, while his further theory that Bernard himself was influenced by scholasticism seems highly speculative.[2] The full-length sermons of the later thirteenth century, with their hierarchy of divisions and subdivisions, are clearly a very different matter from these skeletal summaries, but the transition from one to the other might be accounted for by internal evolution plus the influence of distinction collections.

Any hypothesis about the way the subdividing mentality penetrated preaching must be proved or falsified from the sermons themselves, for it is dangerous to jump to conclusions from remarks in *artes praedicandi*. Logic provided a ready-made terminology for *describing* the practice of division,[3] but that does not in itself prove that logic influenced its evolution. However, the question of origins will not be settled before more is known about preaching techniques

---

[1] For the thirteenth century the best study to date is Rouse and Rouse, *Preachers*, pp. 65 ff. There is a provisional reconstruction in my unpublished D.Phil. thesis on 'The Transformation of the Medieval Sermon' (Oxford, 1976), 92–110. For theory see Murphy, *Rhetoric in the Middle Ages*. Twelfth-century developments have now been brought into focus by P. Tibber's excellent unpublished D.Phil. thesis on 'The Origins of the Scholastic Sermon, *c.*1130–*c.*1210' (Oxford, 1983). He uses the word 'scholastic' in a looser sense than I have done: he means that the sermons he studies were a form of academic expression, rather than that we find in them the 'scholastic method' as defined by Grabmann. Except in our choice of concepts and terms I do not think we differ much.

[2] See Cruel, *Geschichte*, pp. 291 ff. Cf. also J. Leclercq, *Recueil des études sur St Bernard et ses écrits*, iii (Rome, 1969), 161, and Tibber, 'The Origins of the Scholastic Sermon', pp. 89–90 and 142–8 (where he puts Gebouin, a secretary of Bernard, on this particular map).

[3] Richard of Thetford uses it in his discussion of division: '... Utendum est in predicatione maxime autem hiis duabus, scilicet generis in species, sive superioris in inferiora vel (ut *ms*) totius in partes; quoniam iste due divisiones sunt (*om. ms*) magis proprie et magis faciunt rem cognosci. Oppositio autem membrorum sive diversitas est observanda in divisione' (MS Bodleian, Bodley 848, fo. 6rb).

before the coming of the friars, and in any case it is somewhat peripheral to the present argument.

Once we recognize that mendicant preaching and scholastic theology, though they shared a 'subdividing mentality', were essentially different in the thirteenth century, then some features of the geography of preaching and learning become clearer. Leaving aside Paris, the greatest centres for scholastic theology in the thirteenth century were Oxford and Cologne. Although the sermons preached 'live' in these centres are interesting,[1] neither place is especially important for the production and diffusion of model sermon collections and preaching aids. For this the principal centres outside Paris would seem to be Lyons and Florence, neither of which bulk large in the history of scholastic theology.[2] This lack of correlation should now be unsurprising.

We must also conclude that there is no direct connection between Paris's achievements in scholastic theology and its role as a centre of mass communication. It would nevertheless be wrong to draw the further conclusion that the academic context of Paris is irrelevant to the history of the mendicant

[1] For Cologne, cf. J. B. Schneyer, 'Predigten Alberts des Grossen in der Hs. Leipzig, Univ. Bibl. 683', *Archivum Fratrum Praedicatorum*, 34 (1964), 45–106. On Oxford, Little and Pelster, *Oxford Theology and Theologians*, and B. Smalley, 'Oxford University Sermons 1290–1293', in J. J. G. Alexander and M. T. Gibson (edd.), *Medieval Learning and Literature. Essays presented to Richard William Hunt* (Oxford, 1976), 307–27.

[2] 'In both the clerical and the lay traditions of thought the Florentine participation . . . was provincial and peripheral. In comparison with a number of other cities Florence was poorly equipped to be a centre of creative thought. . . .' (so Holmes, 'Urban Ideology' p. 124, writing of the fourteenth century); on the whole this holds good for the thirteenth century. From an academic point of view the three most important friars to teach in thirteenth century-Florence were the Franciscans Olivi and Ubertino da Casale and the Dominican Remigio. In the field of scholastic theology they do not stand out against the background of the brilliant mendicant schools at Paris (with which all three had some connection) or Oxford, though the Franciscans were prominent in controversy. It is significant that neither Florence nor Lyons was among the first four *studia generalia* which the Dominicans set up alongside Paris. Cf. Hinnebusch, *The History of the Dominican Order*, ii. 39. Florence became a *studium generale* later, around the time when a 'generale studium et solempne' for most provinces became the Dominican ideal. Cf. d'Alatri, on 'Italia', in *Le scuole*, p. 57, and Barone, on 'La Legislazione sugli "Studia" dei Predicatori', ibid. 238. I am not sure how precise and consistent a meaning the phrase *studium generale* had.

preaching movement. We must now examine some of the connections.

iii. Paris and Preaching

There were a number of ways in which the academic environment of Paris would have indirectly equipped friars (and other students) to use model sermon collections more effectively. When set in this context—of men specially fitted to use the collections so readily available at Paris—model sermons look a more effective medium of mass communication. It is also not surprising that a relatively large number of model sermon collections were produced in this encouraging environment.

Before exploring these connections a caveat is necessary. It is the rather obvious point that a friar could become a preacher without being specially selected for advanced training, at Paris or elsewhere. Friars selected to study at Paris, even at the lower level, might well be practised preachers already. An important part in the training of preachers seems to have been played by practical experience early on in a friar's career.[1]

---

[1] Cf. S. Bonaventura, *Opera omnia*, viii (Quaracchi, 1898), 360: '... in plerisque tamen etiam propter hoc aliquoties ad haec officia promovemus iuniores, ut interim discant per exercitium, quia, cum vident se ad haec officia assumtos, diligentius student, qui alias forte segniores essent in studendo et minus proficerent. Minus etiam obest, si minus adhuc perfecti sunt promoti, dum vivunt adhuc seniores, qui eos possunt informare et corrigere et defectus illorum in consiliis supplere, quam si illi deficerent penitus, et nemo eos tunc sciret instruere, si tunc primo exercitari deberent. ...' (from 'Opusculum xiii. Determinationes Quaestionum. Pars II'; this work seems not to be by Bonaventura: see above, p. 30 n. 3). The author goes on to argue that in any case the services of the younger friars were needed to help meet the heavy demands made on the order for *praedicationes et confessiones et consilia*. It is interesting that Salimbene seems to have been licensed to preach before he became a priest: see Schmeidler's Preface to Salimbene *Cronica*, ed. Holder-Egger, p. xiii. (He was licensed to preach in September 1248 and consecrated priest in December. On 9 October of that year he would have been 27: cf. ibid. p. vii.) In the Dominican order too a friar could become a preacher before he became a priest: cf. J.-P. Renard, *La Formation et la désignation des prédicateurs au début de l'Ordre des Prêcheurs (1215-1237)* (Fribourg, 1977), 109–112. Renard argues that non-priests could be fully fledged preachers (ibid. 111), but he also shows that practical exercises played an important part in the preliminary training of a Dominican preacher. In the second

Roger Bacon went so far as to express scepticism about the value of theology—the kind taught by his contemporaries—as a preparation for preaching. Even little old ladies know many things about virtues and vices, heaven, purgatory, and hell.[1] Every man has in his heart one great book of vices which he has committed from his youth, and which he observes in other people; the virtues, being the opposite of the vices, may be inferred; thus, peasants (*rustici*) and little old ladies—not only among the Christians, but even among the Saracens and other infidels—are able to persuade on the subjects of virtues and vices, purgatory, hell, and heaven.[2] Furthemore,

because of the custom of the Church's teaching (*consuetudinem ecclesiasticae doctrinae*) all Christians have a considerable know- ledge of the things which pertain to salvation. And it is not a great thing for these intellectual (*studentibus*) orders to speak to the people concerning virtues and vices, purgatory, hell, and heaven (*poena et gloria*); especially since there are many things in the Bible which are very plain to any man who has any education (*qui literas novit*), and who studies in the books of the Fathers (*sanctorum*); from which it is very easy even for the ignorant to adduce[3] authorities against vices and purgatory and hell and in favour of virtue and heaven, and other things necessary for salvation. Besides, these things belong to the Church's office (*ecclesiastico officio*); for it is the job of the *praelati* to explain the articles of faith and morals to the people; and the Church knows these things without the study of theology, and did so from the beginning through the teaching of the Apostles. Nor do the theologians have the authorities to preach[4]

---

half of the thirteenth century, he argues, exercises in preaching were held in the presence of the brothers, before a preacher was let loose on the general public (ibid. 121, 125, and 240 n. 26), but earlier on there seems to have been a system of exercises in itinerant preaching outside the convent, under the guidance of an experienced *socius* (ibid. 123–4)—'exercises au cours desquels le candidat apprend à prêcher dans les conditions mêmes qui seront celles de son futur ministère' (ibid. 124).

[1] Roger Bacon, *Compendium studii philosophiae*, in *Fr. Rogeri Bacon opera quaedam hactenus inedita* ed. J. S. Brewer (Rolls Series, London, 1859), 427.

[2] Ibid. 427; 'poena' probably means both purgatory and hell.

[3] 'even . . . adduce': or just conceivably: 'for the uneducated even to adduce'.

[4] 'auctoritates praedicandi' this probably means permission to preach, but might be taken to mean authoritative texts used to prove points in sermons.

unless they are granted them by the *praelati*; and therefore the task of preaching is an office not of theologians, but of the *praelati*, who entrust that office to whom they like. Indeed we know for certain and see everywhere that one simple brother, who never heard a hundred theology lectures, [or] if he heard them still did not care, preaches incomparably better than the greatest masters of theology.[1] And therefore it is obvious that preaching does not depend on the study of theology . . . preaching precedes the study of theology . . .[2]

After what has been said about the relation between preaching and scholasticism, it will be apparent that Bacon's remarks cannot be dismissed out of hand. But Bacon seems to have had a genius for seeing things from a new and revealing angle—through a distorting lens. Although the forms of thought of scholastic theology were quite different from those of thirteenth-century preaching, the two did after all have the same basic subject-matter: Scripture and patristic tradition, faith and morals. Furthermore, Paris theology cannot simply be equated with scholastic theology. Other academic exercises were just as much a part of the life of the theology faculty, even though they may seem less interesting to historians attracted only by the most creative intellectual achievements. To get a balanced view of the thought of teachers and students of theology, we need to set Bible lectures and university sermons besides Sentence commentaries and disputations. The scholastic as well as the non-scholastic exercises might have helped a friar to use model sermon collections more effectively. In retreating from too simple a

[1] The text of this sentence, as printed, seems ungrammatical, though the sense is clear: 'Scimus . . . quod unus . . . frater . . . *qui* melius . . . praedicat . . .' (my italics). It might be a general remark but could conceivably be a reference to Berthold von Regensburg: cf. Roger Bacon's *Opus tertium* in *Opera . . . inedita*, ed. Brewer, p. 310: 'Sed licet vulgus praedicantium sic utatur, tamen aliqui modum alium habentes, infinitam faciunt utilitatem, ut est Frater Bertholdus Alemannus, qui solus plus facit de utilitate magnifica in praedicatione, quam fere omnes alii fratres ordinis utriusque.'

[2] Roger Bacon, *Compendium*, pp. 427–8.

model of scholastic influence we must not go too far in the opposite direction.

It is significant that in Bonaventura's *Sermones dominicales* —the only mendicant collection of the period whose sources have been systematically pursued—there are at least 150 echoes of his Sentence commentary in the fifty sermons which make up the cycle.[1] The editor's brief analyses of a selection of these parallels would provide a basis for a more extended comparison between the ways in which the same idea of the same author functioned in different genres with different forms of thought. A caveat is that Bonaventura's sermons may prove to be more 'intellectual' than those of most sermon cycles of the day. The extent to which the ideas of scholastic theology were translated into the forms of thought of preaching is hard to estimate without more critical editions like that of Bonaventura's *Sermones dominicales*. Possibly there was more of this kind of influence than meets the eye, though the notion that theological teaching provided the content while the preacher provided the form is unlikely to prove correct. Forms of thought affect the very structure of the content, and in tracing the movement of ideas from *quaestio* to *praedicatio* we should look for what changed as well as stayed the same in the process.

Scholastic theology may have helped preachers in a less straightforward but perhaps more important way than by lending ideas: namely, by warning them which topics to avoid. Doctrine was a potential minefield for the popular preacher.[2] There were questions about the ideal of poverty which were especially explosive in the religious atmosphere of the thirteenth century, and subjects like the Trinity, the

---

[1] *Sermones dominicales*, ed. Bougerol, p. 82. The next-largest collection of parallel texts found by Bougerol is fifty-six (in twenty-five sermons) from the commentary *In Lucam*. Bougerol does not give a figure for the number of parallels he has found with sermons by Bonaventura which do not form part of the Sunday cycle.

[2] Cf. the fascinating passage quoted by Jean Leclercq, 'Le Magistère de prédicateur au XIIIᵉ siècle', *Archives d'histoire doctrinale et littéraire du Moyen Âge*, 21 (1946), 105–47, at p. 143 n. 4.

Incarnation, the Eucharist, and the problem of evil which have repeatedly become focal points of religious division in the history of Christianity. A preacher without much academic theology might overstep the bounds of orthodoxy without even knowing he was doing it. The scholastic method, proceeding by problem-solving, tended to bring difficulties into the open in a safely academic atmosphere. A side-effect may have been to give preachers a clearly drawn guide to the minefield.

There is another roundabout way in which scholasticism would have made friars more effective as preachers. It will be remembered that it was normal for preaching to be followed by the hearing of confessions: the two pastoral offices were intimately associated (I. iii). *Quaestiones* in the field of moral theology would give a sureness of touch in hearing confessions. It is significant that the enormously successful *Summa confessorum* of John of Freiburg draws very heavily on Aquinas (above all on the *Secunda secundae* of the *Summa theologica*).[1] The practice in solving moral problems in theory which a friar would acquire through disputations, lectures, and study at Paris would help him judge cases of conscience after he had preached. Confession links preaching and scholastic theology.

Scholastic theology would also have helped form the preacher's self-image. It would have clarified his idea of his mission—notably by exploring its relation to theology.[2] Again, *quaestiones* could deal with questions of conscience that might face preachers: whether it was a (further) mortal sin to preach in a state of mortal sin,[3] for instance, or whether popular preachers sinned mortally if they did not

---

[1] L. E. Boyle, 'The *Summa confessorum* of John of Freiburg and the Popularization of the Moral Teaching of St. Thomas and of Some of his Contemporaries', in A. A. Maurer *et al.* (edd.), *St. Thomas Aquinas, 1274-1974. Commemmorative Studies*, ii (Toronto, 1974), 245–68.

[2] Leclercq, 'Le Magistère', especially pp. 145–6.

[3] '2. Quaeritur utrum peccet praedicator qui praedicat existens in mortali habens conscientiam mortalis...' (ibid. 117); '16. *Question anonyme*. Utrum praedicare in mortali peccato sit peccatum mortale....' (ibid. 129).

induce the people to pay tithes.[1] In general, *quaestiones* on preaching would tend to form a sense both of its high importance in the life of the Church and of the high standards of conduct demanded of the preacher both in and outside the pulpit.[2]

The same may be said of biblical exegesis. The following are some examples from the commentary on Isaiah by Alexander of Hales, OM.[3] On Isa. 1: 22 ('Your silver is turned into dross . . .') he comments that 'Spiritually silver, which is resonant, signifies preaching. . . . *Silver* etc. That silver is turned into dross when the preaching is done for some temporal advantage or for empty glory . . .'[4] Or again, interpreting *spiritualiter* a passage from Isa. 7, 'It is to be noted, however, that the devil principally aims at taking force (*fortitudinem*) of deed away from preachers, since from many he cannot take away force of speech, and then it may be said to them that he shaves off half their beard, which is signified in 2 Kgs. 10, where it is said that Hanon king of the sons of Amon shaved off half of the beards of the servants of David.'[5] Further on he applies the passage beginning 'Behold I will stir up the Medes against them . . .' (Isa. 13: 17–18) to preachers:

---

[1] Ibid. 128–9 (from an anonymous *Quodlibet*, c.1310).

[2] e.g. *Quodlibet I*, q. 3 (c.1263–6), of Eustace d'Arras, OFM, quoted ibid. 119; and see ibid. 115–38, *passim*.

[3] On the question of whether this was written before or after Alexander became a Franciscan see B. Smalley, 'The Gospels in the Paris Schools in the late 12th and early 13th centuries. Peter the Chanter, Hugh of St-Cher, Alexander of Hales, John of La Rochelle', *Franciscan Studies*, 39, An. xvii (1979), 230–54, at pp. 252–3 (the article is continued ibid. 40, An. xviii (1980), 298–369.)

[4] 'Spiritualiter argentum, quod sonorum est, predicationem significat. . . . *Argentum* et cetera. Istud argentum vertitur in scoriam quando fit predicatio pro aliquo commodo temporali vel inani gloria . . .' (and other Scriptural texts are cited in support) (MS BN lat. 15580, fo. 7ra). For Alexander's commentary on Isaiah see I. Brady, 'Sacred Scripture in the Early Franciscan School', in *La Sacra Scrittura e i Francescani* [no editor] (Pontificium Athenaeum Antonianum and Studium Biblicum Franciscanum, Rome and Jerusalem, 1973), 65–82, at pp. 72–3.

[5] 'Notandum tamen est quod principaliter intendit dyabolus a predicatoribus removere fortitudinem operis, quia a multis non potest removere fortitudinem sermonis, et tunc potest dici quod eis radit dimidiam (*ms adds* bar) barbam, quod significatum (sig[m] *ms*) est ii. Reg. x., ubi dicitur quod Hanon (Amon *ms*) rex filiorum Amon rasit dimidiam barbam servorum David' (MS BN lat. 15580, fo. 26va).

Spiritualiter potest hoc legi de predicatoribus vel de demoni-bus. . . . De predicatoribus vero sic exponitur. Per Medos significan-tur ipsi predicatores qui secundum capacitatem audientium debent mensurare verbum dei, et tales non debent predicare propter questum temporalem set tantum modo propter deum. Ultimo Phil. Non quero datum set requiro fructum; et ii Cor. ultimo: Non quero vestra set vos; et iii. Act. dicit Petrus: Argentum et aurum non est mecum. . . .[1]

Spiritually this may be read as referring to preachers, or to demons. . . . When applied to preachers, however, it is explained as follows. By the Medes are signified preachers themselves, who ought to measure the word of God according to the capacity of their hearers, and these ought not to preach for temporal profit, but only for God. In the last chapter of Philippians: 'Not that I seek the gift, but I seek the fruit . . .'; and in the last chapter of 2 Corinthians:[2] 'I do not seek the things that are yours, but you', and in Acts 3 Peter says: 'Silver and gold have I none.'

Or, to take an example from the Dominican Hugues de Saint-Cher:

. . . vel servi Salo(monis) sunt predicatores qui toti (quitoti *ms*) ecclesie serviunt. Hii sunt pincerne qui propinant sponso et sponse vinum sacre doctrine, de quibus dicitur iii° Reg. x. quod unius vestis ornamento erant induti, quos videns regina Saba non ultra habuit spiritum, quia ecclesia de gentibus videns apostolos et sequaces eorum idem predicantes et idem operantes non habuit ultra fiduciam in doctrina philosophorum suorum. Ancille sunt minores predicatores . . .[3]

. . . or the servants of Solomon are the preachers who serve the whole Church. These are the cupbearers who set before the

---

[1] MS BN lat. 15580, fo. 46[va].

[2] An error: the passage is 2 Cor. 12: 14.

[3] MS BL Harley 3254, fo. 99[ra]. Cf. the Venice edition (1703) of Hugues' postils on the whole Bible, vol. iii, 'page' 76, cols. 2 and 3. Hugues is commenting on Eccles. 2: 7: 'Possedi servos et ancillas . . .'. Note that the phrase I have translated 'adornment of a uniform garment' is not in the standard Vulgate text of 1 Kgs. 10: 5, which merely has 'ordines ministrantium vestesque eorum'. Cf. now Smalley, 'The Gospels' (1980), 308–10.

bridegroom and bride the wine of sacred doctrine. It is said of them in 3 Kgs. [= 1 Kgs.] 10 that they were clothed with the adornment of a uniform garment, and seeing them the queen of Sheba no longer had any spirit: because the Church of the gentiles (*ecclesia de gentibus*), seeing the apostles and their followers preaching the same thing and doing the same thing, no longer had any confidence in the doctrine of its own philosophers. The serving-maids are lesser preachers . . .

It may in fact be proposed as an almost certainly fertile research hypothesis that a major function of thirteenth-century exegesis was the inculation of what one might call an ideology of preaching.[1] My random soundings are no substitute for a systematic investigation, but they leave the impression that the value of preaching and the responsibilities of the preacher were advertised with great persistence in the biblical teaching of Alexander of Hales and Hugues de Saint-Cher. It could have helped create a big market for the preaching aids in which the university stationers dealt, and since there is not much evidence for Dominican or Franciscan scriptoria the friars were probably important on the demand as well as on the supply side. The propaganda for preaching in the biblical teaching of Paris masters must also have helped prevent the attractions of pure thought from eclipsing the sense of pastoral vocation among friars studying at Paris.

Passages like those just quoted could also have helped more directly, by providing material for prothemes or the technique for making them easily. The protheme was an important part of the method of sermon-making taught by the *artes praedicandi*, but in many model sermons it was omitted. I image that the protheme was by no means indispensable in 'live' preaching, but no doubt a preacher often wanted to add one to a particular model sermon which lacked one. From the prothemes which are transmitted to us on parchment we

---

[1] Here I should acknowledge a fiche which Beryl Smalley sent me before this line of enquiry occurred to me, quoting Hugues's remarks on preaching when commenting on several passages from the Gospels.

know that a common, in fact probably the most common, subject of the protheme was preaching itself.[1] Whether or not old notes from Bible lectures were pressed into service on such occasions,[2] the repeated application of all sorts of texts to the subject of preaching in Biblical exegesis—assuming the hypothesis just proposed is correct—would have amounted to instruction by example in the art of making prothemes.[3]

Preachers probably learned much else from the Biblical teaching at Paris. At present the best accounts in print—both by Beryl Smalley—of the connections between biblical lectures and preaching deal with the period just before the coming of the friars, and with the period just after the one which concerns us.[4] It has been shown how Stephen Langton taught his pupils how to 'grind the corn of Scripture into the bread of tropology',[5] teaching them a trade they would constantly use when preaching. For instance, he takes the text 'Ephraim hath given gifts to her lovers' (Hos. 8: 9), makes *Ephraim* signify sinners, asks rhetorically 'But how do sinners give gifts to their lovers? Wait and see!', and makes the following moral point: 'Some prostitutes take hire, others offer themselves freely, and so it is with sinners. Some find the opportunity to sin ready waiting them and these *take* hire; others seek out the opportunity; these *give* hire and offer themselves.'[6] Furthermore, manuscripts of Stephen Langton's

---

[1] J. B. Schneyer, *Die Unterweisung der Gemeinde über die Predigt bei scholastischen Predigern. Eine Homiletik aus scholastischen Prothemen* (Munich, Paderborn, and Vienna, 1968), 10 and *passim*.

[2] A difficulty may have been that the 'thema' of the protheme was supposed to be connected verbally or in meaning with the main 'thema' of the sermon, so not any piece of exegesis dealing with preaching would do if this rule were followed.

[3] There were also collections of prothemes available—see Schneyer, *Die Unterweisung*, p. 10—but to judge by the list he gives they were much less common than model sermons.

[4] For the earlier period see her *The Study of the Bible in the Middle Ages* (2nd edn., Oxford, 1952), 253 ff. (In her chapter on 'The Friars' the emphasis is more on new developments, which she was putting on the map.) For the later period, see *English Friars*, ch. II, on 'Teaching and Preaching'.

[5] *Study*, p. 257.

[6] Ibid. 258.

glosses 'are sprinkled over with notes, pointing out the suitability of certain themes for particular kinds of sermons'.[1] Whether or not the notes are by Langton himself, they show how exegesis could help preachers. Thus, for instance, the gloss on the fall of Holofernes is noted as 'an excellent theme on the death of some powerful worldling by whose fate others may be instructed'.[2] Langton and his contemporaries also made use of a related technique, the *distinctio*, which was increasingly prominent in sermons.[3] For example: the raven is black, he feeds on carrion, he cries 'cras cras'; hence he signifies the wicked, blackened with sin, who feed on vanity, who procrastinate...[4] There are even *exempla* in Langton's glosses.[5] The same scholar has shown for the early fourteenth century how indexes to Bible commentaries could be compiled to guide the user to the part which dealt with the Gospel or Epistle of the day, or to help him find material bearing on a given topic.[6] It was even possible to take a commentary to pieces, as it were, and rearrange it as matter for sermons according to the liturgical year.[7]

The history of the relation between exegesis and preaching in the thirteenth century has been less fully explored,[8] but Beryl Smalley's work on the links between preaching and exegesis in the preceding and succeeding periods give us a good idea of what to look for. Commentaries should be

---

[1] Ibid. 254, especially n. 4.

[2] Ibid. 255.

[3] Ibid. 246–9 and 259.

[4] From Langton's gloss on Gen. 8: 6, quoted by Smalley, ibid. 247.

[5] Ibid. 256–7. Smalley suggests that Pierre le Chantre may have been the first master systematically to introduce the *exemplum* into his commentaries on Scripture.

[6] *English Friars*, p. 35.

[7] Ibid. 36 Smalley observes that 'only expositions of the four Gospels or of the whole book of Pauline Epistles would lend themselves to such reorganisation'; but note too her remarks on Lathbury's Lamentations commentary, parts of which ended up as sermons.

[8] A seminal paper on the subject was given by L.-J. Bataillon to a colloquium held at the Sorbonne on 23 January 1982. On the Gospel commentaries of Hugues de Saint-Cher, Alexander of Hales, and Jean de la Rochelle, see Smalley, 'The Gospels', (1979), 249 ff., and especially (1980), 308–10. The link between exegesis and preaching has to take its place with many other themes in these rich articles.

scanned for *distinctiones*[1] and for passages in which the spiritual sense is employed to turn a text into moral teaching.[2] One should look for notes suggesting preaching material in the margins of commentaries,[3] and for indexes which may guide the modern scholar, as well as medieval users, to the preachable material buried in the collection.[4] Attention should also be concentrated wherever the genres of Scriptural commentary and sermon cease to be distinct: commentaries incorporating model sermons, and sermons deriving from commentaries, or vice versa.[5] Evidently there are also other things to look for, but any future on the Bible and mendicant preaching before 1300 should include these lines of inquiry.

It may be safely predicted that the connections between

---

[1] e.g. a distinction on the word *arcus* in the commentary on the Psalms of Nicolas de Gorran: 'Nota arcus malus multiplex est: heretice pravitatis . . . terrene cupiditatis . . . concupiscentie carnalis . . . presumptuose elationis . . . maligne detractionis . . . false adulationis . . . occulte proditionis . . . eterne dampnationis . . . (MS BL Royal 2 C. v, fo. 19[va]). Each 'member' of the distinction is supported by a Scriptural authority, the first being a reference to the text which is the springboard of the *distinctio*.

[2] See, for instance, the way in which the words 'vulnus, et livor, et plaga tumens . . .' (Isa. 1: 6) are turned into an analysis of sin in Alexander of Hales's Isaiah commentary: '*Wlnus ad litteram patens est* et significat peccatum manifestum et apertum. *Livor* plaga absque ruptione cutis et occulta intus, tamen habet putredinem et corruptionem, et significat peccatum occultum. Nichilominus tamen in ipsa anima est corruptio. *Plaga autem tumens* significat peccatum consuetudinis. Sic ergo hic est triplex (*supply* genus) peccati, cui adhibendum fuisset triplex genus medicamenti quod non adhibuerunt. . . . [*col. b*] . . . Notandum ergo quod vulnus est peccatum apertum quod non circumligatur quando non deseretur. Aperitur autem peccatum multipliciter: sibi per cognitionem, proximo per actionem, deo per ipsam essentiam. *Livor* peccatum absconditum quod absconditur tripliciter . . .' (MS BN lat. 15580, fo. 4[ra]).

[3] e.g. in MS BL Harley 3254, in the margin of Hugues de Saint-Cher's postil on Ecclesiastes: 'De ebrietate et cibo', fo. 98[r], left-hand margin; 'Thema in ascentione', fo. 94[v] left-hand margin.

[4] I do not know if such indexes were common in the thirteenth century, but there is an interesting one (incomplete and in bad condition) at the beginning of MS BL Harley 3254 which is the kind of thing to look for.

[5] Note the interesting commentary on Luke of Costantino da Orvieto, OP (even though he is not known to have taught at Paris): see C. Cenci, 'Il commento al Vangelo di S. Luca di Fr. Costantino da Orvieto, O.P. Fonte di S. Bernardino da Siena', *Archivum Franciscanum Historicum*, 74 (1981), 103–45, at p. 130 ff., and the 'Appendice', pp. 143–5, reporting and building on an important discovery of L.-J. Bataillon.

exegesis and preaching in this period will be found to be as close as in the periods on either side.[1] It may not have escaped notice, however, that the relation between all this and the diffusion of prefabricated preaching aids is not quite direct. To show that lectures on the Bible furnished preachers with material, it may be objected, is not to establish anything about the history of *model* sermon collections. But there is a connection, no less real for being oblique. Model sermon collections can be very dry, and sometimes, as we have seen, they consist of little more than divisions or distinctions and Scriptural authorities. In lectures on the Bible, it may be suggested, students would have assimilated in a much less 'dehydrated' form the techniques and habits of thought which they would also find on the parchment of model sermon collections, where they might often seem lifeless and rebarbative. A friar who had followed lecture courses ought to have found it easier to turn model sermons into living ones. He ought to have become more adept at expanding upon Scriptural texts which were quoted with little or no comment.

For much the same reasons university preaching would have equipped friars to use model sermon collections more effectively. Preaching too was a university exercise—no less than lectures on the Bible or disputations were.[2] To attend university sermons was obligatory for all.[3] Though university regulations are not always obeyed, friars are less likely

---

[1] The point of such research would be to give content and life to abstract generalization, rather than to establish an unexpected conclusion.

[2] 'La troisème des charges assignées au maître dans l'enseignement universitaire: praedicare, ne le cède en rien aux deux autres: legere et disputare' (P. Glorieux, 'L'Enseignement au Moyen Âge. Techniques et méthodes en usage à la Faculté de Théologie de Paris au XIIIᵉ siècle', *Archives d'histoire doctrinale et littéraire du Moyen Âge*, année 43, t.45 (1968) 65–186, at p. 161. He cites (p. 148) the much-quoted formula from Pierre le Chantre's *Verbum abbreviatum*: 'Lectio . . . fundamentum . . . Disputatio . . . paries . . . praedicatio vero, cui subserviunt priora, quasi tectum . . .' Glorieux conveniently groups regulations bearing on university preaching (pp. 148-9), and gives a list of surviving collections of university sermons (pp. 150-3), though he only faces squarely for one collection the problem of distinguishing between official university sermons and sermons given in the churches around Paris.

[3] Ibid. 149.

than, say, young students in the arts faculty to have ignored this particular duty.

Moreover, there is reason to think that at least some student friars would have the extra training of themselves delivering university sermons and/or 'collations' (evening sermons). The regulations from which this may be inferred date from the fourteenth century, but it is likely that they are to a great extent codifications of existing practice. There are quite detailed rules about the preaching duties of *bacallarii formati*, bachelors who had completed the requirement to lecture on the Sentences.[1] But university preaching was not the responsibility of these senior men only. A particularly interesting regulation lays it down that no one should be allowed to lecture on the Bible 'ordinarily',[2] or even on the Sentences, or to take the oaths, 'unless he first gives two collations in the presence of the university, or a sermon with a collation . . . and in his own person, so that he may be tested in eloquence and the art of preaching'.[3] Whether the only friars who gave university sermons or collations where those who were soon to lecture on the Sentences (and their academic seniors), or whether even friars who were not among this élite (and who only spent the normal three or four years of study at Paris) could also be called upon to preach before the university, is not yet certain. The question should be settled by further study of university sermons surviving from the thirteenth century, rather than by inferences from later ordinances. It may well turn out that a substantial number of sermons are by friars who never went on to lecture on the Sentences. If so, the practical training afforded by actually preaching before the university takes on a greater importance than if it affected only the *crème de la crème*.

However that may be, the essential point is that academic

---

[1] H. Denifle and A. Chatelain, *Chartularium Universitatis Parisiensis* (Paris 1889–97), ii/1 (1891), 701, No. 1189 (48).

[2] 'Ordinary' lectures on the Bible were given by Masters of Theology and should be contrasted with 'cursory' lectures. See Glorieux, 'L'Enseignement', pp. 109–11 and 119–20.

[3] Denifle and Chatelain, *Chartularium*, ii/1 (Paris, 1891), 699.

preaching provided living models of the same kind of preaching that was embodied in model sermon collections, so that friars who attended university sermons were given innumerable demonstrations of what the finished product should sound like. They would hear very able men—not necessarily friars—doing their best to reach the high standard that would be expected of them. It cannot have been easy to preach well in the distinctive manner which was normal by the second half of the thirteenth century, even with the help of a model sermon collection. University sermons provided a complementary sort of 'paradigm'.

It might here be objected that university preaching was quite a different thing from the popular preaching for which model sermon collections would mainly be used. So far as sermon form or technique is concerned, this is not the conclusion of recent writers. The Rouses argue that 'the type of sermon evolved at the University of Paris through the course of the thirteenth century was an admirable instrument for routine preaching to laymen',[1] and according to Jean Leclercq the language of the sermons is 'à la fois artificiel et populaire'.[2] Rhymed and rhythmical divisions or distinctions, and Scriptural *auctoritates*, are as characteristic of model collections as of university sermons. We have already noted how Guibert de Tournai's sermon to citizens living in communes (printed on pp. 260–71 as an illustrative text) is cemented together by these techniques. In this it is not untypical of model sermons of the period (and it has the added advantage, for us, of being explicitly directed towards preaching to the laity).

It can be and has been argued that these techniques had their functions in popular as in academic preaching. A schematic framework of rhythmic divisions and subdivisions

---

[1] Rouse and Rouse, *Preachers*, p. 84. Cf. their comparison of sermons to clerical and popular audiences by Bonaventura, ibid. 76–7.

[2] *L'Idée de la royauté du Christ au Moyen Âge* (Unam Sanctam, 32; Paris, 1959), 125. Leclercq makes it clear, pp. 127–8, that his analysis applies to sermons delivered to the laity in the vernacular (though written down in Latin) as well as to sermons meant for clerical audiences.

would be easy to fix in the mind.[1] Guibert de Tournai, discussing the *originale principium* of division (in his huge work called *Erudimentum doctrine*), states that its purpose is to avoid confusion and help the memory (*ut cesset confusio et adiuvetur memoria*).[2] This could have been true for popular as well as for learned preaching.

Scriptural *auctoritates* too could have served the needs of popular preachers. Presumably they were a way of establishing the preacher's authority and authenticating the main points of his sermon.[3] A Scriptural text was a quick and economical way of proving a point and impressing an audience. Richard of Thetford recommended in his *ars praedicandi* that the preacher should confirm every member of a division with an authority 'lest it should appear that in dividing he has invented the members'.[4] It is true that there is some uncertainty about the extent to which Scriptural *auctoritates* were used in 'live' sermons to unlearned audiences. *Reportationes* of sermons to the laity are rare, and only a limited amount of work has been done on those we do have. Two studies of particular preachers suggest that *auctoritates* may have been used much more sparingly in some popular preaching.[5] Nevertheless, there seems no dramatic difference between the role of the *auctoritates* in academic and model sermon collections. Model sermons normally have at least one *auctoritas* for each member of a division or subdivision. This holds good even for brief and schematic

---

[1] Cf. Rouse and Rouse, *Preachers*, pp. 84–5, and Leclercq, *L'Idée*, pp. 124–5.

[2] MS BN lat. 15451, fo. 225ʳᵇ. adiuvetur] aduivetur *ms?*

[3] Rouse and Rouse, *Preachers*, p. 86.

[4] 'Facta autem divisione conveniens est de unoquoque membro auctoritatem afferre, ne dividens videatur membra finxisse' (MS Bodleian, Bodley 848, fo. 6ᵛᵃ).

[5] N. Bériou, 'Sermons aux clercs et sermons aux "simples gens": la prédication de Ranulphe de la Houblonnière à Paris au XIIIᵉᵐᵉ siècle', unpublished doctoral thesis (Université de Paris-Sorbonne (Paris-IV), 1980), i. 132*–133*, would seem to imply that one criterion for distinguishing sermons to a public of 'savants' and sermons to 'simples gens' (including Cistercian nuns, etc.) is that the tissue of Scriptural citations is denser in sermons to the former. However this may be in the case of Ranulphe—and Mlle Bériou is properly cautious—I doubt whether this could be shown to be a general and decisive criterion. Delcorno, *Giordano*, p. 183 (and cf. p. 96), says that Giordano da Pisa 'scarta il primo modo di *dilatatio*', i.e. *auctoritates*. But again, it would be rash to generalize from this case.

models. These bear a close resemblance to the schematic abridgements of Paris University sermons by Bonaventura transmitted in MS Milan, Ambrosiana A. 11 and printed in vol. ix of the Quaracchi *Opera omnia* (1901). In the latter (which have the unusual advantage of full and explicit rubrics, so that we can be quite sure of their original audience) it is perfectly usual to find only one *auctoritas* for each 'member'.[1] On the other hand, it is possible to find model sermons which do not confine themselves to one *auctoritas* for each member.[2] Preachers learning from either the written or the live sort of model would in any case have been capable of making adjustments to the technique when giving popular sermons, and of drastically cutting down the number of *auctoritates* if they thought fit.

The essential point is that the live university models would reinforce the lessons in technique to be acquired from studying books of sermons. It may be that the example of university preaching lent prestige to the highly distinctive sermon form characteristic of the thirteenth century and the later Middle Ages. This could have helped to ensure its victory over the older and simpler homiletic technique used by, say, Maurice de Sully. It is true that the fully fledged technique of building a unified structure out of divisions and authorities can be found quite early on in model sermons. It is already the rule in the collection called *Legifer*, which dates from around the middle of the century.[3] It has not yet been established that the fully developed form regularly occurs in university sermons earlier than in model sermons. But the question of chronological priority may be beside the point. If it is the overwhelming success of the form once it had been developed that we are seeking to explain, then the influence

---

[1] e.g. *Opera omnia* (Quaracchi, 1901), ix. 155–6, and contrast the extended version of the same sermon printed ibid. 151–5.

[2] Cf. the Illustrative Text, *passim*.

[3] One manuscript at least of this work—Clm. 7932—looks very early. If one were to estimate the date on palaeographical grounds alone, one could easily mistake it for a manuscript from the first quarter of the thirteenth century.

of university preaching on the élite of the friars cannot be left out of account.

Whether this similarity between university and model sermons extends to content (in so far as content is separable from a form which conditioned the whole pattern of thought) cannot yet be determined with certainty. More comparisons between matched sermons of each type are required.[1] My impression from limited soundings is that there is no general difference, at least before *c*.1300.[2] That the manner and level of religious teaching in the two genres of preaching were broadly similar seems to me to deserve the status of the hypothesis that holds the field; nor do I think we should find it a surprising one. Jean de Verdi said that 'Lectures (*Lectio*) are

---

[1] It will be important not to confuse official sermons *coram universitate* with others which may simply travel with them in a manuscript, or with sermons to non-university audiences in Paris churches. Cf. Bataillon, 'Approaches', pp. 24–5.

[2] In my unpublished thesis on 'The Transformation of the Medieval Sermon' pp. 191–209 (with illustrative transcriptions pp. 271–308) I tried to show that the difference between the content of university and model sermons was not necessarily great. The first comparison, between a sermon from the model collection by Jean Halgrin d'Abbeville and a sermon on the same text edited by M. M. Davy in her *Les Sermons universitaires parisiens de 1230–1231* . . . (Études de Philosophie Médiévale, 15; Paris, 1931), is not strictly relevant, since Jean Halgrin was not a friar. The second comparison is between a model sermon by Guy d'Évreux and a sermon by Jean de Verdi (Verdy) from MS Bodleian, Ashmole 757, fos. 265ra–268rb. (By a stupid oversight I did not use the same set of transcription conventions for this as for the other illustrative texts.) Jean de Verdi is called 'brother' so he was probably a religious, but there is no evidence that he was a friar: cf. P. Glorieux, 'Sermons universitaires parisiens de 1267–1268', *Recherches de théologie ancienne et médiévale*, 16 (1949), 40–71, at p. 63. Glorieux's assumption that the cluster of collections to which Ashmole 757 belongs, and which he discusses loc. cit., can be combined to give a coherent cycle of sermons preached in the years 1267–8, appears to be unfounded. See Bataillon, 'Sur quelques sermons', p. 503 n. 37. Bataillon points out that two of the manuscripts in the cluster, MSS Turin, Naz. D. VI. 1, and Worcester Cathedral Chapter Library F. 5, mix university sermons with sermons to monks. That the sermons in Ashmole 757 really are university sermons appears not to have been questioned, but I do not know whether it is quite certain. The sermon by Jean de Verdi which I compared with a model sermon includes the following remark: 'Lectio principaliter est ad instruendum intellectum, sed predicatio est ad informandum affectum.' (fo. 265vb). This rather suggests a university sermon, as does the fact that the sermon is followed by a *collatio*. However, the ideal evidence that a sermon was preached *coram universitate* is a rubric to that effect. It is lacking here but quite a number of the schemata of Bonaventura's sermons printed in vol. ix of the Quaracchi *Opera omnia* do have rubrics of this sort. In content, as in form, these do not strike me as very different, generally speaking, from schematic model sermons in general circulation.

to instruct the intellect, but preaching is to educate the heart (*ad informandum affectum*).'[1] A passage from Newman's *Idea of a University* (Oxford, 1976) might well be applied to academic preaching in thirteenth-century Paris. 'Let no one suppose that any thing recondite is essential to the idea of a University sermon. The most obvious truths are often the most profitable. Seldom does an opportunity occur for a subject there which might not under circumstances be treated before any other auditory whatever. . . . an academical auditory might be well content if it never heard any subject treated at all but what would be suitable to any general congregation.'[2] Moreover, we have already seen (II. iv) that the audience of model sermons can seem relatively indeterminate, and that they sometimes appear to incorporate sermons that could originally have been preached to academic audiences. In sum, the theory that university preaching provided a similar but complementary formation to that which a friar might get from using written models looks fairly plausible even where content is concerned.

So far we have examined the three principal types of intellectual exercise which made up the official curriculum of Paris University: *disputatio, lectio*, and *praedicatio*. But there is more to any university than its official curriculum, and some of the things that fell outside that of thirteenth-century Paris are also relevant to the preaching of the friars. To begin with, we should not ignore the series of *collationes* given by Bonaventura in the heart of the period that concerns us. His *collationes* on John fall half-way between the genres of sermon and Bible commentary: indeed they seem to have been in some sense complementary to his official lectures on John.[3] Bonaventura also gave series of *collationes* on the Ten

---

[1] Cited above, p. 196, n. 2.

[2] p. 336.

[3] Beryl Smalley reminded me of their importance. Cf. J. G. Bougerol, *Introduction à l'étude de Saint Bonaventure* (Tournai, 1961), 146–7. Note Bougerol's remark that 'Saint Bonaventure . . . fait appel souvent au sens tropologique, afin d'apporter au prédicateur pour lequel il travail, un instrument apostolique immédiatement utilisable' (ibid. 147). Cf. here Balduinus ab Amsterdam, 'The

Commandments (March–April 1267), on the seven gifts of the Holy Spirit (February–April 1268), and on the Hexaemeron, or six days of Creation (April–May 1273).[1] There is some reason to think that one of the friars who heard the last series was the Italian Franciscan who told the story about the fox who had studied at Paris. The anonymous Franciscan includes in his own unfinished collection of sermons (which are also described as *collationes*) an interpretation of the ages of history which he almost certainly got from one of Bonaventura's *collationes* on the six days. On textual grounds it seems more likely that he actually heard Bonaventura's talk than that he read it once it had been 'published'.[2]

The university milieu may also have helped train preachers in a still more informal way, by acting as an entrepôt for stories and anecdotes which could be turned into *exempla* and inserted into model sermons at the point when the latter were turned into living speech. By its nature, the oral aspect of an academic culture does not leave as many traces as the historian could wish, but one can catch glimpses of it via *exempla* that were written down. To illustrate this side of Paris life, it may be permitted to end this part of the book as it began, with a story by the anonymous Italian Franciscan. At least, one version of the story is told by him. It runs as follows:

Tertio dyabolus super huiusmodi (h[us] *ms*), scilicet super divinantes, et super illos qui divinis credunt, accipit potestatem. . . . Cum enim essem Parisius narraverunt michi fratres per omnia fidedigni quod in Boemia civitate que dicitur Praga fuit quidam iuvenis filius cuiusdam baronis qui quandam iuvenculam diligebat. Cum autem nec prece nec pretio eam posset habere, convertit se ad quemdam

---

Commentary on St. John's Gospel, edited in 1589 under the name of St. Bonaventura, an authentic work of John of Wales, O.M. (†ca.1300)', *Collectanea Franciscana*, 40 (1970), 71–96.

[1] Cf. Bougerol, 'Les Sermons dans les "Studia" des Mendiants', in *Le scuole*, pp. 251–80, at pp. 273–4. Cf. above, n. 52.

[2] See D. L. d'Avray, 'A Franciscan and History', *Archivum Franciscanum Historicum*, 74 (1981), 456–82: note especially the italicized passages in Appendix I and the argument on p. 481, which is not sufficiently emphasized in the main text of the article.

(quandam *ms*) qui noverat demones invocare, qui iu|ravit [*fo. xii^(va)*] ei quod per incantationem demonum et per ipsorum auxilium cor illius puelle ad consensum iuvenis inclinaret. In nocte igitur vigilie assumpsionis virginis gloriose intraverunt ambo cameram ubi magus demones (decens *ms*) invocaret. Dixit autem magus iuveni quod dormiret in quodam circulo quem nullo modo exiret, nullo pavore perterritus (perterritu^(us) *ms*), nulla concupiscentia inflamatus. Magus igitur cepit demones invocare iuvene dormiente; accurrunt demones emittentes voces horribiles (*corr. in ms from* terribiles) et strepitum mirabilem facientes, atque unus alteri taliter loquebatur: Percutio ego eum; et alius respondebat: Non ita cito, sed expecta modicum et sic poterimus eum suffocare (sufforare *ms*). Ad ipsorum autem eiulatum expergefactus est iuvenis, totus libidine inflamatus, et ecce apparuit illi quedam puella pulcherrima cum ornatu muliebri et meretricio adornata (*corr. in ms from* adornanata), eius omnino [*col. b*] habens effigiem (efficiem *ms*) quam amabat. Hec ad iuvenem appropinquans sic aiebat: O amor et vita, non poteras me habere aliter quam isto modo; vituperasti enim me et me et [*sic*] male fecisti. Et hiis dictis quasi indignata videbatur quod vellet exire de camera. Iuvenis autem cum vellet sequi eam, magus ad eum clamavit: O Gaufride, caveas ne exeas circulum donec dixero tibi. Sed iuvenis ductus (dictus *ms?*) amore ceco, volens eam apprehendere, cucurrit post ipsam, et statim demon unus apprehendit eum, et torsit collum eius, sic homo torquet collum galine quando vult eam suffocare, et mortuus est. Cumque iaceret in pavimento mortuus, demon os ipsius proprio stercore implevit, quod egerat (egererat *ms*) pre doloris amaritudine. Recesserunt autem (que *or corr. from* que *ms?*) demones portantes eius animam in infernum. Ad hos strepitus intravit mater cameram et invenit suum filium iam defunctum. Plorat et vestes laniat, sed propter in|tollerabilem [*fo. xiii^(ra)*] fetorem compulsa est exire. Cum autem pater ipsius et mater totum supradictum negotium a suo socio didicissent, fecerunt filium suum per quosdam ribaldos sepeliri in quodam campo, tanquam stercus inmundum. Quarto divinantes mentiuntur ...[1]

Thirdly, the devil acquires power over this sort, that is, over diviners and those who believe in them.... For when I was at Paris some completely trustworthy brothers told me that in the city of Bohemia which is called Prague there was a certain young man, son of a

---

[1] MS Birmingham University 6/iii/19, fos. xii^(rb)–xiii^(ra).

certain baron, who loved a particular young woman. Since he was not able to have her for prayer or for price, he turned to a certain person[1] who knew how to invoke demons, who swore to him that, by conjuring up demons, and through their help, he would incline the heart of that girl to consent to the young man. Therefore, on the night of the vigil of the Assumption of the Blessed Virgin they both entered a room where the magician might summon up demons. However, the magician told the young man that he should sleep in a certain circle, and should in no circumstances leave it, however terrified he might be by fear or however inflamed with lust. Therefore, the magician began to summon up the demons while the young man was asleep; the demons rush up letting out terrible cries and making a stupendous noise, and one was speaking thus to the other: 'I'll pound him', and the other was replying: 'Not so fast, but wait a little and so we will be able to strangle him.' The youth was awakened by their howling all inflamed with lust,[2] and behold, there appeared to him a certain very lovely girl made up to look enticing with the adornment used by women and prostitutes, and identical in appearance to the girl he loved. She came up to the young man and said to him: 'O love and life, you weren't able to have me any other way than this, for you have insulted (*vituperasti*) me and done me wrong (*or* done wrong).' And having said this as if she were annoyed, it seemed that she wanted to go out of the room. But when the young man wished to follow her, the magician shouted to him: 'O Geoffrey, beware that you don't leave the circle until I tell you.' But the young man, drawn by blind love and wanting to take hold of her, ran after her, and immediately one demon got him, and twisted his neck as a man twists the neck of a hen when he wishes to suffocate it, and he died. And while he was lying dead on the floor, the demon filled his mouth with his own excrement, which he had produced because of the bitterness of his pain. But the demons went away carrying his soul to hell. At these noises the mother entered the room and found her son already dead. She weeps and tears her clothes, but because of the unbearable stench she was compelled to go out. But when his father and mother

---

[1] The manuscript has *quandam*, making the magician feminine, but the rest of the passage suggests that this is a mistake.

[2] There seems to be a certain discontinuity of thought here. John Waś plausibly suggested to me that the youth was wakened in the middle of an erotic dream. It is possible, however, that the passage is corrupt.

learned the whole aforesaid business from his companion, they had their son buried by some menials (*ribaldos*) in some field, like unclean excrement. Fourthly, diviners tell lies...

The other version of the story which I have found is also circumstantial, but by no means all the circumstances are the same. For instance, the account of why the youth leaves his circle and how he is killed is significantly different:

Then the cleric made two circles on the ground with his sword, and entered one and ordered the young man to enter the other. 'Now,' he said, 'be a man of courage and above all do not leave the circle. But be unmoved by whatever you see and stay steadfastly within the circle. For I tell you beforehand that you would be going to your death, in body and soul, if you go outside the circle.' He promised to keep out of danger, though in truth, as his sins demanded, he was not able to do so, and the cleric opened an evil book and began to read those diabolical words. And behold, suddenly there was a horrible crash and a stupendous noise, as if the house were about to collapse by the power of thunder. Then there entered a certain man, enormously tall, like a giant, black like an Ethiopian, horrible beyond measure in his appearance, and standing next to the young man's circle and giving him a savage look, he seemed to want to smash him to death with an enormous club which he held in his hands. On seeing him the young man was shaken with a very great fear, and began to flee. And when the cleric, who did not dare to leave his own circle, held him by the end of his garment, he [i.e. the young man] suddenly tore away his garment (*excussa veste*) and began to go out. And—what is horrible and astounding to tell—the devil immediately grabbed him and pounded him so much, that there was scarcely a bone remaining that was not broken in two or three parts, and he flung him, thus rolled up and crushed to pieces, into a corner. And, so that by the just judgement of God's permissive will,[1] the punishment might correspond to the crime, and so that he who had been totally defiled by the filfth of lust might give off a filthy smell, the devil bent back his head and his mouth behind his back, squatted, as it were, above the corpse—flung down and pounded up as it was—and excreted into his mouth filth that stank so much that human nostrils could hardly bear it, and leaving

---

[1] 'iusto Dei permittentis iudicio'.

him thus filthy with excrement, said to the cleric: 'What did you call me for?' . . .[1]

It will have been noted that, although the story is unmistakably the same, important details are different: the young man leaves the circle because of terror, for instance, and not because he is lured out by the girl or her image.

It is not surprising that the story got passed around among Franciscans. It appears to have reached the *exemplum* collection in which this second version is found via three friars: a brother So., who had been lector of the local Franciscan convent and who had played some part in the end of the affair,[2] and a brother Conrad and brother Nicholaus of the same province, who would appear to have told the story together on the same occasion to the compiler of the collection or his source.[3] We have already seen that the anonymous Franciscan who gives the version first quoted had learned it from friars when he was at Paris, and it is likely enough that the second version too passed through Paris, which seems to have been the point at which many stories in the *exemplum* collection were gathered.[4] At the convents of the friars at Paris potential *exempla* were available, as it were, in solution. They might be crystallized on to parchment, but one imagines that they often simply stuck in the memory of a friar, to be used in a sermon when occasion arose.

[1] P. Livario Oliger, 'Liber exemplorum fratrum minorum saeculi xiii (excerpta e cod. Ottob. Lat. 522)', *Antonianum*, 2 (1927), 203–76, at pp. 234–5.

[2] '. . . Tunc miserunt ad locum fratrum et rogabant lectorem, qui tibi hec narravit, quod ad domum illius civis veniret, quia eius presentia necessaria esset. Lectore autem occupato, misit Guardianus unum discretum sacerdotem cum socio . . . Clericus vero infirmatus ad mortem . . . confessus fratri nostro, seriem facti narravit per ordinem et tradens libellum illum dyabolicum in manu fratris, rogavit quod lectori daret, qui statim ipsum flammis exureret. Lector accipiens librum, portavit ad ignem et non aperiens statim combus[s]it. . . . Hec narravit tibi frater So., qui tunc ibi lector erat et vocatus a patre fuerat et qui manibus propriis librum in ignem misit. Cui pater iuvenis notus erat et iuvenis ipse, ut dicebat. . . .' (ibid. 235).

[3] This seems to be implied by the words 'Hoc idem narraverunt te audiente, fr. Conradus et fr. Nicholaus eiusdem Provincie. . . .' (ibid.). On the way in which the compilation was put together see Oliger's introduction, ibid. 208–10.

[4] See Oliger's remarks, beginning 'In collectione duo centra narrationum clare indicantur: Parisius et Assisium. . . .' (ibid. 208–9).

In the first part of the book it was argued that the preaching revival of the friars was more successful than the Carolingian one because they succeeded in closing the gap between preaching aids and their users. In this context the role of Paris is prominent. On the one hand, a large number of purpose-built preaching aids were available; and I have attempted to make precise the degree to which Paris outstripped other European centres from this point of view. On the other hand, the influential and fairly numerous minority of friars who were selected to study at Paris were particularly well equipped to handle these preaching aids confidently and effectively. This conclusion appears more predictable than the reasons for it are. The best-known component of intellectual life in thirteenth-century Paris, scholasticism, would only have helped preachers in certain rather round-about ways. The important connections between Paris as university and Paris as centre for mass communication are not obvious, the most interesting being the development of an ideology of the preacher's role, the exposure of young friars to living paradigms in the form of university sermons, whose forms of thought were closer to those of popular preaching than of scholastic exercises, and finally the oral culture of student friars. Together these things must have made up an academic environment in which the stereotyped model sermon collections could take on an extra value.

IV.

Social and other Interpretations

i. *Echoes of the Market Economy*

THE scholastic works of the friars are harder to understand than their sermons, but their sermons are harder to interpret. A historian of technical scholastic thought may often perform a sufficient service if he or she translates the ideas of great writers into modern categories, capturing what is creative and original—*sub specie eternitatis*, as it were—in one age and presenting it to another. This is an intellectually rewarding approach to genres such as disputed questions and Sentence commentaries, because they were a vehicle for some of the more creative ideas in the history of thought, and because the ideas are often abstract and difficult and in need of clear straightforward exposition; rather as twentieth-century science would need exposition by historians of thought if the direct tradition were ever broken.

If we approach thirteenth-century sermons in the same way as the real scholastic genres, the result is disappointing. As we have argued, in this period the sermons of the friars do not normally attempt to propose and solve problems, to apply logic to authority, in the way that the same preachers did when they had their scholastic hats on. In the fourteenth and fifteenth centuries the situation is somewhat different, but that is another matter. In the thirteenth century the contrast is sharp. In scholastic genres one can see knowledge and understanding, brought out by reason from the deposit of Scripture and patristic tradition, advancing with a cumulative certainty and increasing technical virtuosity to which the nearest analogy is twentieth-century natural science. The edifice could not survive without its underlying principles—

belief in revelation and trust in human reason—but while they were accepted scholasticism had the characteristics of a cumulative science, a discipline making objective progress. Sermons, on the other hand, were not normally the medium through which new ideas were expressed. A straightforward representation of them, along the lines that have worked well for a whole series of studies of scholastic philosophy and theology, would be a wearisome thing.

Nor do they have the immediate appeal that makes interpretation and explanation almost superfluous where some sermons from some other periods are concerned. As, for instance, with the sermon which woke the colourful anti-clerical medievalist G. G. Coulton:

Next morning was very hot, and I began to doze very early in the sermon: it was Trinity Sunday and the discourse seemed painfully commonplace. But, later on, I gradually began to feel a quite different atmosphere; the change in the preacher's tone had roused me from sleep. For he was concluding with that passage from Newman's Trinity sermon which haunted Matthew Arnold for all his life: 'After the fever of life, after wearinesses and sicknesses, fightings and despondings, languor and fretfulness, struggling and failing, struggling and succeeding; after all the changes and chances of this troubled, unhealthy state,—at length comes death, at length the White Throne of God, at length the Beatific Vision.'[1]

Occasional passages from thirteenth-century mendicant sermons might have this instant charm for a modern listener or reader, but it would hardly be the rule:

Series of biblical, theological, philosophical, canonical texts, broken up by developments whose relation to the texts is often anything but evident; these developments themselves, divided and constructed according to a plan whose logic escapes us, nourished by associations of ideas which seem to us neither natural, nor, above all, necessary; is it possible that French minds were instructed,

[1] G. G. Coulton, *Fourscore Years. An Autobiography* (Cambridge, 1943), p. 210–11, citing Newman's *Parochial and Plain Sermons*, vi, Sermon xxv.

interested and moved by works of this genre, and that, for centuries, the people of Bossuet, Bourdaloue and Massillon were filled with enthusiasm for this manner of preaching?[1]

Gilson's remarks about Michel Menot's sermons are also a fair description of what a thirteenth-century mendicant sermon looks like at first sight.[2] Gilson went on to argue that we can make sense of such sermons by studying the *artes praedicandi*. This vein of research has proved fruitful, though by now it has been quite fully exploited: a jog-trot through the standard doctrines of the *artes praedicandi* has become rather a commonplace of works on medieval preaching. Furthermore, the *ars praedicandi* has its limitations as a means of capturing that 'logic which escapes us'.

There are, however, other ways of interpreting thirteenth-century sermons. Any approach which penetrates the difficult outer defences they present to the modern student is to be welcomed. One approach which has only just begun to be explored is to interpret mendicant sermons in terms of their social meaning. This is not the same enterprise as studying sermons to find nuggets of evidence for social history, which is by no means a new approach. Lecoy de la Marche's section on 'La Société d'après les sermons', written in the nineteenth century,[3] is a fine example of it, so good that it seems most useful to refer the reader to him and to turn to another sort of 'social' interpretation. The distinction between the two sorts is that historians of 'la société d'après les sermons'[4] are using sermon evidence to answer the question 'What was society like?', whereas historians are now asking whether the social context conditioned the mentality of the sermons.

---

[1] Gilson, 'Michel Menot', p. 95 (my translation).

[2] Except that canonical and philosophical texts are not so very common in sermons of this period.

[3] It forms the third part of his *La Chaire*. Lecoy de la Marche includes chapters on 'L'Église et le monde religieux', 'La Royauté et le monde féodal', 'La Bourgeoisie, le commerce, le peuple', 'Les Femmes et le luxe', etc.

[4] Note especially, apart from Lecoy de la Marche, C. H. Haskins, 'The University of Paris in the Sermons of the Thirteenth Century', in *Studies in Medieval Culture* (Oxford, 1929), 36–71, and L. Bourgain, *La Chaire française au XIIᵉ siècle, d'après les manuscrits* (Paris, 1879), Part III, 'La Société d'après les sermons', pp. 271ff.

'Did the urban soil in which the mendicant orders grew up
have an influence on the type of piety and spirituality which
they proposed?'[1] The question was posed in the *Annales*
programme of research on the friars and the towns. A recent
study which set out to answer more or less the same question
concluded that the preaching of the mendicants was one of a
number of related responses to urban money-making.[2]

Here we are dealing with an intelligently framed hypothesis rather than a solved problem, for the theory has not yet
been tested against the sermons, apart from one or two
isolated soundings in this sea of evidence.[3] As a hypothesis it
is of considerable value because it is the sort which advances
our understanding whatever the answer to the question we
put to the evidence. Whether verified or falsified, it helps. In
the case of mendicant preaching we are lucky enough to have
a wealth of evidence against which to test the theory.

I have found that the hypothesis does not fit all the
evidence and that its explanatory power has definite limits, on

---

[1] 'L'Implantation urbaine des ordres mendiants a-t-elle eu une influence sur le
type de piété et de spiritualité qu'ils proposaient?' (Le Goff, 'Apostolat mendiant et
fait urbain dans la France médiévale: L'implantation des ordres mendiants.
Programme-questionnaire pour une enquête', *Annales: Économies, sociétés, civilisations*, xxiii/2 (1968), 335–52, at p. 344.

[2] B. H. Rosenwein and L. K. Little, 'Social Meaning in Monastic and Mendicant
Spiritualities', *Past and Present*, 63 (1974), 4–32, at p. 5. Lest there be any
misunderstanding, I would like to emphasize that I rate this article highly, and am
very indebted to it. Little seems more cautious in his valuable book *Religious Poverty
and the Profit Economy in Medieval Europe* (London, 1978).

[3] On Guibert de Tournai: D. L. d'Avray, 'Sermons to the Upper Bourgeoisie by a
Thirteenth-Century Franciscan', in D. Baker (ed.), *The Church in Town and
Countryside*, (Studies in Church History, 16; Oxford, 1979), 187–99. On Giordano da
Pisa: D. R. Lesnick, 'Popular Dominican Preaching in Early Fourteenth-Century
Florence', unpublished Ph.D. thesis (Rochester, 1976 [University Microfilm Interna-
tional Cat. No. 76,24013]), especially chs. IV and V, parts of which are perceptive. I
have not seen the same author's 'Dominican Preaching and the Creation of Capitalist
Theology in Late-Medieval Florence', *Memorie domenicane*, NS 8–9 (1977–8),
199–247, cited by C. Delcorno, 'Rassegna di studi sulla predicazione medievale e
umanistica (1970–80)', *Lettere italiane* (1981), 235–76, at p. 273 n. 123. On San
Bernardino: R. Rusconi, *Predicazione e vita religiosa nella società italiana da Carlo
Magno alla Controriforma* (Documenti della storia, 30; Turin, 1981), 119. 178
('... nell'esempio della "fiera di Nostro Signore" emerge con lampante chiarezza
come vi fosse ormai completa assimilazione tra la mentalità mercantile e la
"spiritualità" del tempo'), and 182.

which more below; within these limits, on the other hand, it works quite well. Thus, it is not difficult to find passages which, taken in isolation, confirm the theory that the language of the friars was 'heavily impregnated with a market-place vocabulary'.[1] In a sermon of Guibert de Tournai there is a quite powerful passage in which the Devil is compared to a usurer:

... But that usurer makes his loans without risk, since he has a good security (*vadium*), that is, the sinner's soul; and a good pledge (*plegium*), the justice of God; and a good chirograph, which we gave to him, written in the blood from our souls, when we sinned; with these things the Devil is certain that unless the sinner should buy back his pledge before his death, that is, before the fair breaks up (*divisio nundinarum fiat*) and the shout of *Hale! Hale!* goes up, according to the custom of the French, his security will be [forfeited] in perpetuity. Finally, when he [the Devil] has stripped his debtor of everything and left him naked, and he sees that he is unable to pay, then a gibbet or gallows is erected—just as in the fairs of this world—and there the sinner is hanged. Then he weeps in vain, because he has lost everything, and because he will not be able to go back to the city in which he could do business again.[2]

The passage is from one of two sermons (to merchants) which are governed by a single allegory of trade. Guibert gives the gist of it at the beginning of the first one: 'the good merchant is Christ and just men; the bad mechant is the Devil and unjust men.'[3] The first of these sermons is mainly concerned with Christ and the just, leaving the Devil and the 'Devil's merchants' to the second.

Guibert de Tournai's sermons to merchants are not the only instance. In the sermon for the fourth Sunday of Advent in the *Sermones attrebatenses de ordine praedicatorum* we meet much the same comparison between Christ and a merchant:

---

[1] Rosenwein and Little, 'Social Meaning', p. 23.
[2] D'Avray, 'Sermons to the Upper Bourgeoisie', pp. 197–8.
[3] Ibid. 197.

Item venit sicut mercator ad negotiandum. Ysa. lxii. (xlii *ms*). Dicite
filie Syon: Ecce rex tuus venit, et cetera. Ipse enim ad modum
mercatoris sive mercennarii attulit pretiosas merces in vilibus
pannis, scilicet regnum (regum *ms?*) in paupertate, consolationem in
luctu, saturitatem in esurie. De hiis tribus Mt. v.: Beati pauperes
spiritu, et cetera. Beati qui lugent, et cetera. Beati qui esuriunt, et
cetera. Item quas merces attulerit dominus dicitur (*ms adds and
deletes* Osee) Eze. xxvii (xxviii *ms*): Iuda, id est Christus, et terra
Israel, id est sancti apostoli, ipsi institores tui in frumento primo, id
est in fide, (*ms adds and deletes* baptismum) balsamum, id est spem,
et mel, id est caritatem, oleum sacre scripture et resinam penitentie
apposuerunt in nundinis tuis. Augustinus: Venit celestis negotiator
accipere contumelias et dare honorem, haurire dolorem, et dare
salutem, subire mortem et dare vitam.'[1]

Again, he comes like a merchant to do business. Isa. 62: 'Tell the
daughter of Zion: Behold your king comes, etc.' For in the manner
of a merchant or one working for money (*mercennarii*) he brought
precious goods in worthless cloths, that is, a kingdom in poverty,
consolation in grief, plenty in hunger. On these three things, Matt.
5: 'Blessed are the poor in spirit, etc. Blessed are those who mourn,
etc. Blessed are those who hunger etc.' Again, Eze. 27 says what
goods the Lord brought (*attulerit*): 'Iuda', that is, Christ, 'and the
land of Israel', that is, the holy apostles, 'they were your traffickers
in fresh wheat', that is, in faith, 'balsam', that is, hope, 'and honey',
that is, charity, 'the oil' of sacred Scripture 'and the resin' of
penitence 'they put on the table in your fair'. Augustine: 'The
heavenly businessman came to accept insults and to give honour, to
draw out grief and to give salvation, to undergo death and to give
life.

But the most sustained example from this period I have
found, apart from Guibert de Tournai's sermons to merchants, is in a sermon from the cycle on the Sunday Epistles
by Guillaume Peyraut. The commercial imagery is the more
interesting in that the sermon belongs to an ordinary

---

[1] MS Troyes 1536, fo. 7[ra], from a sermon beginning '*Ipse est qui post me venturus
est . . .* Io.i. Hec verba dixit beatus Iohannes Baptista predicans in heremo. . . .'
(fo. 6[va]).

liturgical collection and is not explicitly addressed to merchants. The sermon is on the text 'Behold now is the
acceptable time'.[1] Peyraut says that Lent is a more acceptable
time to make a profit (*ad lucrandum*) than other times. Firstly,
because money-changers (*cambitores*) are in their places.
Peyraut makes these signify confessors (*penitentiarii*) ready to
hear confessions (and he indicates that confessors are not so
easily available at other times). The exchange which takes
place in confession is a happy one, for the money which the
sinner brings is very base, and that which he brings back is
very precious: he leaves his sins there and acquires the grace
of God.[2] Some people are childish: they wish to take away the
grace of God but do not wish to part from their sins, as if
they did not know the law of exchange. Such people do not
realize what kind of money sin is and what kind of money
grace is.[3]

The second reason why Lent is a good time for making a
profit, continues Peyraut, is that in Lent, in the fair of God, so
to speak, goods for sale are displayed more abundantly, so
that what does not please one may please another. Preaching
is a display of goods for sale, and there is more preaching
during this period than at other times.[4] The third reason why
Lent should be profitable is that while it lasts it is easier to
find the money (vigils, prayers, fasts) with which the kingdom

---

[1] 'Ecce nunc tempus acceptabile' (2 Cor. 6: 2), Schneyer, *Repertorium*, ii. 545, No. 161.

[2] 'Potest etiam intelligi quod dicatur *nunc esse tempus acceptabile* ad differentiam temporis quod est extra quadragesimam. Quadragesimale enim tempus acceptabilius est ad lucrandum quam (*ms adds and expunges* in) alia tempora *triplici* ratione. *Primo* quia cambitores in locis suis inveniuntur tunc: penitentiarii enim inve|niuntur [*fo. 57ra*] parati ad audiendas confessiones, quod non accidit ita aliis temporibus. Et attende quam felix commutatio fiat in foro penitentiali. Vilissima enim est moneta quam asportat peccator, et pretiosissima est illa quam reportat: peccata sua ibi dimittit et gratiam dei acquirit. . . .' (MS BN lat. 16472, fos. 56vb–57ra).

[3] '. . . attendenda est puerilitas quorumdam qui gratiam dei vellent inde reportare, et tamen peccata sua nollent inde dimittere, ac si nescirent legem cambientium. Non agnoscunt tales qualis moneta sit peccatum. . . . Non agnoscunt tales qualis moneta sit gratia dei, qua regnum celorum potest haberi. . . .' (ibid., fo. 57ra).

[4] '*Secundo* quia in quadragesima quasi in nundinis dei venalia habundantius exponuntur, ut cui non placet unum, placeat aliud. Predicatio est expositio venalium, et habundantius predicatur in hoc tempore quam in alio. . . .' (ibid., fo. 57ra).

of heaven is bought.[1] Peyraut observes rather sarcastically that people's fervour seems to fall off after the end of Lent,[2] and then goes on further to develop his image of the fair of God.[3] As with Guibert, this sort of imagery has as its symmetrical counterpart the image of the Devil as businessman. 'And note that the Devil has his business (*negotiationem*) just like God. But there are many differences. . . .'[4] It is not necessary to follow Peyraut through all the differences.[5] It will already be clear that one can find support in the sermons themselves for the theory that the language of the friars was permeated with a market-place vocabulary; and there is, of course, further evidence, from Thomas Lebreton[6] and Nicolas de

[1] '*Tertio* quia in quadragesima facilius invenitur illa moneta qua regnum ce(lorum) emitur, ut sint vigilie, orationes et ieiunia' (ibid., fo. 57[rb]).

[2] 'Aliquis facilius sex diebus ieiunat in quadragesima quam post pascha feria vi[a] (*added in margin*) in septimana, ac si paschale tempus eos impotentes reddiderit; aliquis etiam qui una die in quadragesima dicit psalterium, vix post pascha potest dicere vii psalmos; et qui surgebat ad matutinas in quadragesima vix post pascha potest surgere ad missam' (ibid.). quadragesima] x̃l *ms*.

[3] 'Quid autem precipue emendum sit in nundinis istis ostendit nobis dominus Apo. iii. dicens: Suadeo tibi emere aurum ignitum et probatum ut locuplex fias. Aurum istud est caritas. . . .' (ibid., fo. 57[rb]) and so forth into fo. 57[va].

[4] 'Et nota quod dyabolus habet negotiationem suam sicut et deus suam. Sed sunt in multis dissimiles. . . .' (ibid., fo. 57[va]).

[5] 'Primo in hoc quod dominus illud quod vendit preconsideratur. . .' (ibid.). 'Secundo dissimiles sunt in hoc quod qui emit a dyabolo cum emit letatur, et post sequitur tristitia, ut patet in peccato fornicationis. . . .' (ibid., fo. 57[vb]). 'Tertio sunt dissimiles in hoc quod (*corr., from* que?) cum dyabolo nunquam purum facimus lucrum. Perdit ibi homo primo deum; secundo regnum eternum; tertio. . .' (ibid.). 'Quarto sunt dissimiles in hoc quod deo de suo solvimus, cum nichil boni habeamus quod suum non sit. . . .' (ibid., fo. 58[ra]). 'Quinto in hoc sunt dissimiles quod diabolus melius ostendit et deterius vendit: ostendit enim vinum gaudii presentis, post quod sequitur venenum infernalis tormenti. . . .' (ibid.).

[6] 'Non enim vult dominus [*col. b*] iniquos et dolosos habere in societate sua. Eze. xxviii. In multitudine negotiationis tue repleta sunt interiora tua dolo. Peccasti et eieci te de monte sancto dei. Negotiatores sunt isti usurarii vel peccatores alii qui pro minimo lucro vel etiam pro minima delectatione peccati vendunt animas suas, tota die forum facientes cum diabolo. Nec dico animas suas, immo animas Christi sanguine redemptas, in quo patet eorum dolus et eorum iniquitas. *Dolus*, quoniam vendunt rem alienam. *Iniquitas*, quoniam pro nichilo vel minimo vendunt rem valde pretiosam, vendentes animam et mercantes sibi mortem eternam. Et certe si mercator rem alienam venderet, tanquam fur condempnabilis esset, et si ciphum argenteum daret pro pleno potu vini, fatuus reputari deberet, et quoniam dominus de talibus mercatoribus non curat, ipsos de domo sua tanquam fures et insipientes proicit et flagellat. Quod figuratum est Math. xxi, ubi dicitur quod dominus facto flagello de

Biard[1] (who were more probably friars than not, given their period, though we know nothing of them but their names), from Jean de la Rochelle OM, Guillaume 'de Lavicea', OM[2] from Aldobrandino Cavalcanti, OP,[3] and from Pierre de Reims, OP.[4]

---

funiculis, cepit eicere vendentes et amentes de templo: *Vendentes* animam et *mercantes*, ut dictum est, mortem eternam....' (MS BL Royal 3. A. XIII, fo. 77[ra-b]); from a sermon on the text 'Eice ancillam' (Gal. 4: 30), Schneyer, *Repertorium*, v. 634, s.v. 'Thomas de Lisle' No. 41. Or again: 'Unde tales sunt similes homini lusco, qui semper divertit oculos a sole, vel fraudulento mercatori, qui merces suas pravas sive pravos pannos nunquam expandit ad lucem, sed semper querit tenebram' (ibid., fo. 18[va]); from a sermon on the text 'Ecce rex tuus venit' (Matth. 21: 9), Schneyer, *Repertorium*, v. 632, s.v. 'Thomas de Lisle', No. 2. (I suspect that analogies like this last one were a topos. Cf. Nicolas de Biard: 'Io. iii. Lux venit in mundum et dilexerunt homines magis tenebras quam lucem. Erant enim opera eorum mala. Habens enim pannos dolosos vel merces malas non ponit eas ad lucem....' (MS BN lat. 13579, fo. 17[rb]); from a sermon on the text 'Ecce rex tuus venit' (Matth. 21: 9), Schneyer, *Repertorium*, iv. 229, No. 8.)

[1] Cf. the end of the preceding note, and also the following passage, in which an analogy with profit at a fair is slipped in quite casually: 'Sic Christus misit prophetas qui tormenta male agentibus et gaudia bene agentibus nuntiaverunt. Sed pauci crediderunt. Si enim crederent, peccata non facerent et bona non dimitterent. Credens enim lucrari non postponit, et credens in platea iugulari, vel in taberna, domi remanet' (ibid., fo. 25[va]); from a sermon on the text 'Hic est de quo scriptum est: Ecce ego mitto angelum meum' (Matth. 11: 10), Schneyer, *Repertorium*, iv. 229, No. 12, Hic est] sic est *ms*.

[2] For mercantile imagery in Jean de la Rochelle and Guillaume 'de Lavicea' see below, IV. iii, pp. 226–27, 235.

[3] The image of Christ as the good merchant is the basis of the first half of a sermon (Schneyer, *Repertorium*, i. 174, No. 339) by Aldobrandino on the text 'Simile est regnum caelorum homini negotiatori (*om.* Schneyer) quaerenti bonas margaritas' (Matth. 13: 45): '... Pietas salvatoris apparet in eo quod negotiator factus est et in mundum venit negotiari animas nostras. Unde Simile est regnum celorum et cetera.... Et nota quod in isto negotiatore sunt septem miranda. Unum quod sua pretiosa pro vili pretio tribuit. Augustinus: Venale habeo.—Quid, Domine?—Regnum celorum.—Quo emitur?—Paupertate regnum, dolore gaudium, labore requies, ignominia gloria, morte vita. 2[m] quia nostra vilia care emit. Dedit enim pretiosum sangwinem suum pro nobis. Pe. i. [18]: non corruptibilibus (corrupti[li] *ms*) auro vel argento et cetera. [*fo. 153[va]*] Sed pretioso sangwine (sagwine *ms*). Cor. vi. [20]: Empti enim estis pretio magno. Glorificate et portate deum in corpore vestro. Ymo dedit se totum. Eph. v. [2]: tradidit semetipsum pro nobis. 3[m] est quia nichil habentibus ad solvendum gratis sua bona tradidit, ut patet in pueris. Ps. [105: 24]: pro nichilo habuerunt terram desiderabilem. 4[m] est quia nullum decipit, ymo semper ultra sortem pretii solvit. Ps. [88: 35]: que procedunt de labiis meis non faciam irrita ... 5[m] est quia de datis et acceptis strictam rationem exigit. Luc. xvi [2]: Redde rationem villicationis tue.... 6[m] est quia servos suos super bonis suis negotiari et lucrari voluit. (*ms. adds and deletes a stroke*) Luc. xix. [13]: Negotiamini dum venio. 7[m] est quia servis ad negotiandum bona sua secundum eorum qualitates dividit. Mt. xxv. [15]: uni dedit quinque talenta, et cetera, unicuique secundum propriam virtutem....'

One can also find sermon evidence which fits another part
of the theory we have been examining. It has been argued
that one of the achievements of the friars was in 'helping to
justify wordly commerce in a modified and carefully circum-
scribed form'.[1] Confessional handbooks and scholastic works
are (at least for the thirteenth century) much more important
than sermons as evidence for this theory,[2] but it is interesting
to note that the formula corresponds well enough with what
we find in the *ad status* sermon collection of Guibert de
Tournai. Obvious places to look are his sermons to merchants
and his sermon, about riches, to 'citizens living in communes'
(*cives communiter viventes*). The subject matter and heading
of the latter together imply that its subject is the wealth of
specifically urban élites.

If one reads this sermon about wealth hastily, the overall
impression is of hostility to it. The following passage gives a
good idea of the tone of the greater part of it:

[Riches] leave a man with an insatiable craving. Eccles. 4 [8] 'He is
alone, and has no one else, yet he does not rest from his work, and
his eyes are not satiated with riches.' For the eye of an avaricious
man is insatiable; for there is nothing which can fill the soul except
God. Thus the capacity of the soul is so great that little things do not

---

(MS Bamberg, Msc. Theol. 2, fo. 153[rb-va]. Negotiamini] *otiose abbreviation-stroke
above.*

  [4] 'Fuit etiam hec virgo pretiosa (*omit* pretiosa *or read* virgo margarita pretiosa:)
margarita per virtutis constantiam, pretiosa per martyrii palmam. Hanc emit celestis
negotiator, id est Christus. Emit autem tria a nobis, scilicet: Naturam nostram
nummo sue deitatis. Unde: O admirabile commercium, creator et cetera. Item
temporalia nostra suis celestibus divitiis. Iob. xxii. [24]: Dabit pro terra silicem et
cetera. Mt. xix. [21]: Vende omnia [*sic*] que habes, et da pauperibus, et cetera. Item
spiritualia pro premiis. Mt. v. [1, 3]: cum sedisset, quasi nummos computaturus dixit:
Beati pauperes, quoniam et cetera. Nos etiam emit se ipso. Io. [10, 11]: Bonus pastor
animam dat pro ovibus. i Pe. i. [18]: non corruptibilibus auro et argento et cetera. Nos
sumus enim ille pretiose margarite quas ille sapiens negotiator tam care emit' (MS
BN lat. 15960, fo. 163[ra]) (cf. MS BL Arundel 206, fo. 59[rb] (new foliation), and Ps.-
Anthony of Padua, *Sancti Francisci . . . nec non S. Antonii Paduani . . . opera omnia*,
ed. R. P. Joannis de la Haye (Pediponti 1739), 361; from a sermon with incipit 'Simile
est regnum caelorum thesauro abscondito' (Matt. 13: 44), Schneyer, *Repertorium*, iv.
755, No. 504.
  [1] Rosenwein and Little, 'Social Meaning', p. 31.
  [2] Some of the evidence is collected ibid. 29–31.

fill it. For the soul itself is the image of God, and therefore it is greater than the whole world, and indeed the more it is filled with the transitory things of the world, the less it is filled with God, and so it always stays empty. For material things have in themselves an emptiness (*vanitatem*) and therefore they cannot fill us. For material things are outside us, but the thirst is inside the soul; but it would be stupid for a hungry man to say that he was refreshed simply because he had bread in the cupboard. For these reasons the vice of avarice tends to know no bounds, just as a flame would burn indefinitely if someone were to provide the fuel. Seneca said: if you wish to make a man rich, you should reduce rather than increase his riches. Again, [riches] leave a man with his understanding blinded. For riches cloud the understanding of the rich man so that he cannot tell the difference between his riches and himself, so that if his house is burned, he says that he is burned.[1]

Guibert sounds uncompromising: 'They labour by fair means and foul in order to have, not in order to make restitution, unless they do so at the end, when the bitterness of death is approaching, just as a bloodsucker, when it is full up, vomits out the blood when one puts on salt...'[2] After his diatribe against material riches Guibert implicitly draws the contrast—perhaps inevitable—with the riches that are not of this world: spiritual riches, heavenly riches, and the riches that are above heaven, in God himself. In one passage the contrast is made explicit, and the theme is again the emptiness of earthly riches: '...for temporal riches, like imaginary banquets, deceive those who eat them, and send them empty away.'[3]

Nevertheless, if one reads the small print, so to speak, one finds that in the end Guibert is prepared to justify the wealth of urban élites. A short section at the beginning of the sermon, in which he tries to show that a rich man can be a good man,[4]

---

[1] For the sermon as a whole see the Illustrative Text and for this passage, also d'Avray, 'Sermons to the Upper Bourgeoisie, p. 194 n. 34.

[2] Ibid. 195 n. 35.

[3] Ibid. 195 nn. 36 and 37.

[4] MS BN lat. 15943, fo. cxxvi^{rb–va}.

is perhaps as interesting as the series of criticisms that come after it. It is legitimate to possess temporal riches, he says, when they are acquired without ill-doing, and he cites the example of Abraham, who was rich in gold and silver (Gen. 13: 2). He lists other virtues a rich man must possess before he can regard his wealth as licit. He must remain humble, because wealth nourishes pride. He must use his riches as a pilgrim uses the road, and be like a poor man in the midst of riches; and, of course, he must give alms from his riches: they must be 'distributed with piety'. He continues, using 2 Kgs. 32, 'Berzellai offered food to the king, when he was staying in the camp: for he was a very rich man. For now Christ sojourns (*peregrinatur*) among the poor as if in camp.'[1] He ends the section with a comforting quotation, softening the strictures which follow, to the effect that riches are a hindrance to virtue in bad men, but a help to it in good men.[2]

Nicolas de Biard adopts an attitude to riches very similar to that of Guibert. He thinks that they can be good and useful if used well,[3] though he points out their disadvantages in no uncertain terms.[4] Interestingly enough, poverty also receives a mixed treatment. Nicolas thinks it brings out the worst in many people. It is like wine: good for people who are healthy

[1] D'Avray, 'Sermons to the Upper Bourgeoisie', p. 196 n. 39.

[2] Ibid. 196 n. 40.

[3] 'Notandum autem quod divitie bone sunt et utiles bene utentibus. Ecci. vii (*for* vii *ms has* ii *or* enim; *the text cited in Eccles. 7: 12*). Utilior (*om. ms*) est sapientia cum divitiis. Viator enim si peccuniam [*sic*] habet potest habundanter hospitia necessaria adquirere, a carcere si inclusus fuerit liberari. Sic divites a pauperibus elemosinis hospitum [*sic*] paradisi possunt conducere. Luc. xvi. Facite vobis amicos de mammona iniquitatis, id est divitiis, et cetera. Bona religiosorum comparate sicut ribaldus qui posuit obolum in cambio super acervum peccunie, dicens quod [*fo. 6ra*] particeps; sic divites †per modica elemosina† fiunt socii bonorum religiosorum et particeps. Ps. [18: 63]: Particeps ego sum omnium timentium te, et custodientium mandata tua. Preterea suffragia ecclesie quibus anima a carcere et pena peccati redimitur. Prover. xiii. [8]. Redemptio anime viri proprie divitie' (MS BN lat. 13579, fos. 5vb–6ra); from a sermon on the text 'Divitias et paupertatem ne dederis mihi' (Prov. 30: 8), Schneyer, *Repertorium*, iv, 229, No. 2.

[4] 'Licet ergo sint utiles bene utentibus ut dictum est, tamen propter quinque rationes non petit eas sapientia: et quia viles sunt recte intelligentibus, periculose acquirentibus, nocive habentibus, steriles amantibus, dampnose servantibus...' (ibid., fo. 6ra). These points are then developed forcibly into fo. 6va.

and strong, bad for people with weak heads.[1] (It is true that these ideas of Nicolas de Biard about riches and poverty occur not in an *ad status* sermon but in an ordinary liturgical one. We cannot, therefore, assume—as with Guibert we can—that his remarks are specifically about urban wealth.)

Commerce was not the only source of wealth in towns —property was another, the law a third—but obviously it was important. In the second of Guibert de Tournai's sermons to merchants he shows that he believes the merchants' profits to be in themselves licit. It is true that some kinds of trade are by their very nature immoral. (Guibert gives usury and 'fornication'—by which he presumably means prostitution—as examples of such trades).[2] Again, some are immoral because of the nature of the thing bought and sold, as when people buy or sell things which are not needed for anything except sin.[3] Ordinary buying and selling, however, are only illicit when the disposition of those involved makes them so, that is, when they are motivated by avarice, or over-preoccupied with worldly cares.[4]

ii. Echoes of Different Worlds

The evidence discussed so far supports the theory that 'the preaching of the mendicants ... was one of a number of related responses to urban money-making'.[5] May we then regard the theory as verified? Not necessarily, for a theory is not proved because evidence can be found which fits it. The same evidence may fit incompatible theories, or theories which overlap but do not coincide. When we look for

---

[1] 'Similiter de paupertate; licet sit bona et utilissima patienter et voluntarie (voluntariem *ms?*) sustinentibus, tamen multi faciunt e contrario, et sic faciunt ex ea (*corr. from* exea) suum detrimentum, sicut vinum sanis et fortibus salutiferum est, ita debilibus capite nocivum est. . . .' (ibid., fo. 6ᵛᵃ). (The point is developed at some length.)

[2] D'Avray, 'Sermons to the Upper Bourgeoisie', p. 196 n. 42.

[3] Ibid., n. 43.

[4] Ibid., n. 44.

[5] Rosenwein and Little, 'Social Meaning', p. 5.

evidence *against* this particular hypothesis we find a good deal that does not fit it. It is not wrong, and it is certainly valuable, but it accounts for only one of the 'moods' of the preaching of the friars, and for that in too simple a manner.

What may be said against it? It can be argued—to begin with a secondary objection—that the urban context of most mendicant convents is a redundant way of accounting for their ultimate justification of urban wealth or their use of commercial imagery. Cistercian monasteries were deliberately placed in remote areas, as un-urban as can be imagined, yet St Bernard is fond of the commercial fair motif: 'he compared the monk to a merchant who, while going to the fair, encounters the Lord. After much bartering the merchant-monk gives up his wares to his master and is persuaded to return to his monastery.'[1] The justification of commercial wealth could be regarded as an extension of ideas which are already to be found in patristic works (which would itself be enough to ensure their acceptance in the thirteenth century).[2] It is fair to say, however, that these are points which could be accommodated within a slightly modified version of the theory we are considering. The Cistercians themselves might be regarded as a part of the 'profit economy';[3] Again, it was the mendicants and their immediate academic predecessors, rather than the Fathers, who worked out the detailed guidelines for a commercial morality; and so on.

On a different tack, it is arguable that the theory in question takes too limited a view of thirteenth-century 'society', tending to reduce it to its urban and commercial aspects. Here the objection is not to the explanation of ideas in social terms, but rather to an artificially limited social interpretation. In fact, of course, the friars did not breathe an

[1] J. Leclercq, *Monks and Love in Twelfth-Century France* (Oxford, 1979), 111. Beryl Smalley alerted me to St Bernard's commercial imagery.

[2] See B. Smalley, 'Peter Comestor on the Gospels and His Sources', *Recherches de théologie ancienne et médiévale*, 46 (1979), 84–129, at pp. 88–91, and cf. pp. 102–3 and 124. From this study it appears that the Fathers and twelfth-century exegetes do not specify *urban* wealth but do not exclude it.

[3] As is argued by Little, *Religious Poverty*, Part II, 6.3, especially p. 96.

exclusively urban atmosphere. Though most mendicant convents were in towns, mendicants were not tied to their convents. Indeed, the friars were so mobile, geographically and otherwise, that experience of widely contrasting milieux would have become assimilated into the collective consciousness of the two orders. Friars operated in the countryside as well as the town, as we have seen.[1] Again, it does not seem to have been uncommon for mendicants (especially Dominicans?) to have experience of court life—rather like the Jesuits in the Counter-Reformation period.[2]

Even if the activity of the friars had been confined to the towns, this theory's concentration on the spiritual echoes of the market-place would have been excessive. Commerce would not be the only social fact to impress itself on people in towns. The progressive tightening up of political authority was as much a part of the urban context as the commercial revolution; the political world was a society and one that increasingly conditioned the other social worlds of the thirteenth century.

Thus, it should not surprise us that a fair amount of the imagery in thirteenth-century sermons is taken from this world of political power outside the cities. An image from Pierre de Saint-Benoît reminds us that the idea of the city was associated with royal authority, as well as with commerce. In the kingdom of the conscience, he says, there is a royal city, the heart, whose citizens are the powers of the soul; the land lying around it is the body, and its inhabitants are the body's senses. All these things are put in your charge (says Pierre) as a *bailli* of the heavenly king, so that you may frequently hold assises (*assisias*) there to punish evil deeds and order the execution of the king's edicts. Otherwise you will be held responsible.... What will the king do with treacherous *baillis*

[1] See above, pp. 39–41.
[2] Cf. D. Knowles, *The Religious Orders in England*, i (Cambridge, 1948), 166–8, R. F. Bennett, *The Early Dominicans. Studies in Thirteenth-Century Dominican History* (1937, repr. New York, 1971), 133–6, and W. C. Jordan, *Louis IX and the Challenge of the Crusade* (Princeton University Press, 1979) 55 nn. 108–9.

who gave his kingdom into the hands of his enemies?[1] *Baillivi* must have been a force in people's lives; it is not surprising that we find a reflection in imagery.[2]

One has the feeling that, when these preachers are alluding to the political aspect of social life, they are not too concerned to distinguish between the various categories of kings, 'princes',[3] and feudal lords in general. The common factor seems to be a strong sense of the cohesiveness of political society and the realities of legitimate feudal and governmental power. This awareness of a political society transcending the cities is a dimension of these preachers' consciousness which cannot be dismissed as secondary to the aspect of their thought which can be linked with commercial society.

Nicolas de Biard not only thinks it would be a great wrong if the citizens of a *castrum* refused homage to the count to which it belonged;[4] he implies that it is natural and normal for the *bannus* and statutes of a prince to be observed. (Incidentally, it is interesting that the kind of state he has in

---

[1] 'Primum ergo est regnum conscientie... Ibi enim civitas regia: cor, cuius cives vires anime. Ibi terra circumadiacens: corpus, cuius incole sensus corporis. Que omnia tibi commendata (commendat *ms*) sunt in custodiam ut ballivo regis celestis, ut ibi frequenter teneas assisias ad puniendum malefacta et ad mandandum exequtioni [?] regia edicta, alioquin tibi noveris imputandum. Sap. vi. [4–]: Interrogabit dominus opera vestra, et cogitationes vestras scrutabitur [quoniam—et cetera. Nota totam auctoritatem. Quid (quod *ms*) autem facturus (futurus *ms*) est rex de proditoribus baillivis eius qui regnum eius dederunt in manus hostium regis?...' (MS Venice, Marc. Fondo antico lat. 92 (collocazione 1897, Valentinelli, vi. 36), fo. 65[vb]); from a sermon on the text 'Quaerite primum regnum dei' (Matt. 6: 33), Schneyer, *Repertorium*, iv. 791, No. 125.

[2] Cf. Nicolas de Biard: 'Item veniet ad computandum... Prepara te in occursum eius, amicos in curia per epistolas acquirendo, ut solent facere balivi [*sic*] principum quando sentiunt se non posse de ballivis suis sufficienter reddere rationem....' (MS BN lat. 13579, fo. 5[ra]); from a sermon on the text 'Praeparate corda vestra Domino' (1 Sam. 7: 3), Schneyer, *Repertorium*, iv, 229, No. 1.

[3] It is interesting that in the passage quoted in the previous note we have 'principum' rather than 'regis'.

[4] 'Nota quod dominus venit tripliciter: Ut dominus ad servos per potentiam, ut ei honorem vel homagium magnum faciant, sicut domini terrarum faciunt.... Sed nota quod domino venienti tripliciter [*fo. 16[vb]*] exprobratur. (*Supply* Primo exprobratur?) quia non humiliter recipitur, et sic exprobrant mali christiani. Iniquitas enim magna esset si comes veniret ad castrum proprium et cives ei portas clauderent et homagium denegarent; sic faciunt qui cor et animam peccatis muniunt ne deus ad eos ingrediatur....' (MS BN lat. 13579, fo. 16[va–b]); from a sermon on the text 'Ecce rex tuus venit' (Matt. 21: 5), Schneyer, *Repertorium*, iv. 229, No. 8.

mind in this passage seems thoroughly feudal.[1]) The dreadfulness of being *forbanitus* ('banished' is an inadequate rendering) seems to have impressed itself strongly on Thomas Lebreton. He compares the Lord to a good prince who visits his land, and imprisons, banishes (*forbanizat*), and hangs evil men.[2] Those whom God has banished (*forbannizavit*) in his justice, he recalls in his mercy.[3] When a man does not dare to appear before his lord, because of the crime of *lèse-majesté*, as if he were banished, the son of God is sent to reconcile the banished man.[4] Because of pride the Devil was banished beyond appeal (*forbanitus sine remedio*) from the court of heaven.[5] Pierre de Saint-Benoît's remark that 'All . . . the barons of heaven venerate the person whom they know to be honoured by their king'[6] is just another aspect of the same

---

[1] 'Oportet ergo revereri regia potestas (*supply* et?) maiestas Christi mandata eius observando. . . . Bannus enim et statuta in terra cuiusque principis observantur. Sed non est aliquis qui de terra domini non sit (fit *ms?*) et qui non teneat de ipso quidquid habet. . . . Et nota quod si principes in terra sua statuant (statuat *ms?*) bannum sub pena rerum suarum vel corporis sui, non est qui audeat transgredi edictum. Multo plus non esset bonum domini transgredi (trangredi *ms?*) mandatum, quia . . .' (ibid., fo. 15[va]), Schneyer, *Repertorium*, loc. cit.

[2] 'Est enim dominus sicut bonus princeps qui visitat terram suam, et homines infames incarcerat, forbanizat et suspendit . . .' (MS BL Royal 3. A. XIII, fo. 28[rb]); from a sermon on the text 'Ego vox clamantis' (John 1: 23), Schneyer, *Repertorium*, v. 632, s.v. 'Thomas de Lisle', No. 8.

[3] The wording is slightly odd: 'Dominus enim quos forbannizavit de rigore vel regione iustitie, revocat et reconciliat ad penitentiam ex dispensatione misericordie . . .' (ibid., fo. 28[va]); from same sermon as above. Schneyer, *Repertorium*, loc. cit.

[4] 'Cum enim homo non auderet propter crimen lese maiestatis tanquam forbanitus ante conspectum domini comparere, missus est dei filius qui forbannitum reconciliaret et in locum quem amiserat introduceret. . . .' (ibid., fo. 29[rb]); from a sermon on the text 'At ubi venit plenitudo temporis' (Gal. 4: 4), Schneyer, *Repertorium*, v. 632, s.v. 'Thomas de Lisle', No. 9.

[5] 'Gravissimum enim esset alicui nobili si contingeret eum servire ribaldo vilissimo, de servitio domini sui peccatis suis exigentibus eiecto (electo *ms*). Et certe talis est diabolus. Fuit enim de curia celi per superbiam suam sine remedio forbanitus, et propter hoc abhominabile deberet esse rationali anime tanquam nobilissime creature tali domino deservire. Et proculdubio tales dominus eicit de servitio suo quam cito serviunt tali domino . . .' (ibid., fo. 35[vb]); from a sermon on the text 'Spiritu ferventes' (Rom. 12: 11), Schneyer, *Repertorium*, v. 632, s.v. 'Thomas de Lisle', No. 13.

[6] 'Omnes enim barones celi venerantur quem sciunt amari a rege suo. . . .' (MS Venice, Marc. Fondo antico lat. 92 (collocazione 1897, Valentinelli, vi, 36), fo. 125[vb]); from a sermon on the text 'Vos amici mei estis' (John 15: 14), Schneyer, *Repertorium*, iv. 795, No. 184.

sort of imagery. Another passage from the same collection gives a clear reflection of a feudal world. The Lord has a just *servitium* (feudal service) and a just customary payment (*censum*) in all our lands, because he is the lord. Therefore, we who are his *feodotarii* (feudal tenants) owe him from the manor of our heart the *servitium* of love, which we render to him with good thoughts and desires, and from the land of the body the *servitium* of deed, which we render to him either by doing good, as a *minister* (counsellor?) in the household (*hospitio*), or by suffering ill, as knights (*milites*) in battle . . .[1]

'Just as he who does not wish to do homage loses his fief,' says Nicolas de Biard, 'so too he who does not receive Christ loses paradise; and just as he who does homage keeps his inheritance, so he who maintains fidelity to Christ has paradise. . . .'[2] The assumption is that the feudal law follows its course, controlling the transmission of land by inheritance. The legitimate heir can commit his faith only to his lord; if he does not serve or do in return the *debita servitia*, the inheritance can be taken away; in the same way, if someone does not perform the *debita servitia* which he owes to God he may be deprived of the inheritance of the 'blessed homeland'.[3]

---

[1] 'Secundo habet dominus in omnibus terris nostris iustum servitium, sicut iustum censum, quia dominus est. Nos ergo qui sumus feodotarii eius debemus ei de manerio cordis nostri servitium dilectionis, quod sibi reddimus (reddemus *ms, corr. from* redemus) bonis cogitationibus [*col. b*] et desideriis, de terra corporis servitium operis, quod sibi reddimus sive agendo bonum, ut minister in hospitio, sive patiendo malum, ut milites in bello . . .' (ibid., fo. 68^{va-b}); from a sermon on the text 'Reddite, quae sunt Caesaris Caesari' (Matt. 22: 21), Schneyer, *Repertorium*, iv. 792, No. 141.

[2] 'Sed sicut qui non vult facere homagium feodum perdit, sic qui Christum non recipit paradisum amittit; et sicut qui facit humagia tenet hereditatem, sic qui servat Christo fidelitatem habet paradisum. . . .' (MS BN lat. 13579, fo. 16vb); from a sermon on the text 'Ecce rex tuus venit' (Matt. 21: 5), Schneyer, *Repertorium*, iv. 229, No. 8.

[3] 'Sed nota quod legittimus heres tantum in dominum suum potest committere suam fidem; non servando vel debita servitia non reddendo quod (*omission before/after* quod?) iure hereditario privatur: sic nullus adeo est iustus vel dei filius qui si infideliter se erga eum habeat de bonis a deo sibi commissis, ipsum impugnando, vel si debita servitia non fecerit mandata eius non implendo quin hereditate beate patrie privetur. Mt. xxi. [43]: auferetur a vobis regnum, et dabitur genti fructum suum facienti. Id est, opera facienti et servitia que pro ipso habendo (*ms. adds and deletes* requirendo) requiruntur. . . .' (ibid., fo. 3va); from a sermon on

Inheritance and the transmission of land supply other images. (In thirteenth-century Europe, as perhaps in most pre-industrial societies, the rules and conventions of inheritance were one of the principal social factors in people's lives.) Peyraut says that 'if a kingdom belonged to someone through his father, and the land of some poor knight through his mother, he would be stupid if he clung to his maternal inheritance and neglected his paternal one ... In the same way someone is very stupid who clings to this vale of misery in which our mother Eve placed us, and neglects heavenly things.'[1] We find an echo of a feeling about family land which was probably a common factor between aristocratic peasant and possibly even urban society in a sermon by Nicolas de Biard. He says that it would be wrong (*turpe*) that some land should be put up for sale and not purchased by the kindred (*de cognatione*); in the same way we, as brothers of Christ, ought to purchase the inheritance of the heavenly kingdom.[2]

On the other hand, an *exemplum* in a sermon given by a Franciscan at Paris[3] presents what must have been a fairly common predicament of aristocratic women in the aristocratic imagery of chivalry:

the text 'Praeparate corda vestra Domino' (1 Sam. 7: 3), Schneyer, *Repertorium*, iv. 229, No. 1.

[1] '... Fatuus [*fo. 22va*] esset ad quem pertineret regnum unum ex parte patris et terra alicuius pauperis militis ex parte matris, si adhereret hereditati materne neglecta paterna hereditate, ex quo speraret quod ad hereditatem paternam posset pervenire. Sic valde fatuus est qui huic valli miserie in quam Eva mater posuit nos adheret, celestibus neglectis. ...' (MS BN lat. 16472, fo. 22rb–va); from a sermon on the text 'Dominus prope est' (Phil. 4: 5), Schneyer, *Repertorium*, ii. 544, No. 140.

[2] 'Turpe enim est quod terra aliqua venditioni exponatur quod ab eis qui sunt de cognatione non ematur (amatur *ms*?). Sic est quando [*sic*] fratres Christi sumus hereditatem regni celorum quando venditioni exponit emere debemus. ...' (MS BN lat. 13579, fo. 7va); from a sermon on the text 'Divitias et paupertatem ne dederis mihi' (Prov. 38: 8), Schneyer, *Repertorium*, iv. 229, No. 2. I am not certain how the text should be emended.

[3] From a collection of sermons which, according to Glorieux, 'L'Enseignement', p. 152, were delivered at Paris in the year 1271–2. They are not model sermons, in that they seem not to have been 'published', put into general circulation; though the compilation 'travels' in this manuscript with two model sermon series, the *Sermones de communi sanctorum* of Nicolas de Biard and of Guillaume de Mailly, according to Schneyer, *Repertorium*, vi. 36.

There was a certain girl who was daily under attack from a certain tyrant, and she did not have any man who could defend her against the tyrant, who wished to take away her inheritance for himself. She often cried to the Lord to liberate her from the power of that tyrant. At last there came a certain young knight who offered himself to fight for her. He only (*Tantum*) said to her that he sought nothing from her, except that, if he should conquer the tyrant and live, she should remember him; if, however, he should die, she should keep his tunic for love, in memory. The day of the fight came. That young knight fought with the tyrant from morning to evening, and conquered the tyrant, but he was gravely wounded with five wounds, and the fifth was mortal. Then that girl took his tunic dyed with his blood, as he had asked, and put it in her room in a place such that she saw it whenever she entered the room, and when going in and out she wept for love of him, and quite often she went into the room to see the tunic and remember her friend. Spiritually, that girl was human nature; the tyrant: the Devil; the knight: Christ, who to arm himself against the Devil took a white tunic, that is, flesh in the womb of the Virgin. . . .[1]

The allegory is developed further, but enough has been quoted to show with how much freshness and force a mendicant could deploy imagery impregnated with the pre-occupations and values of feudal and aristocratic society.

The values of gift-exchange and largess survived, as part of the chivalrous ethos, into the age of the commercial revolution, and we find its imagery in sermons together with the imagery of the profit economy. A gift economy has been well described as one in which 'goods and services are exchanged without having specific calculated values assigned to them. Prestige, power, honour, and wealth are all expressed in the spontaneous giving of gifts; and more than just expressed: these attributes are attained and maintained through lar-

---

[1] B. Hauréau, *Notices et extraits de quelques manuscrits latins de la Bibliothèque Nationale* iv (Paris, 1892), 25–6 (MS BN lat. 14952, fos. 70ra–70va); from a sermon 'fratris Auberti minoris', on the text 'Ambulate in dilectione Dei' (Eph. 5: 2), Schneyer, *Repertorium*, vi. 35, No. 25, and also ibid. i. 124, s.v. Albertus de Metz [de metis, Metensis], OM, No. 2; Schneyer also lists here MS BN lat. 14923, fo. 51v, for this sermon).

gess...'¹ Though especially characteristic of the early Middle Ages, this form of political and economic activity had not withered away in the period that concerns us, and we can find echoes of it in sermons. Peyraut, in making a point about the nearness of the Lord at a particular liturgical time, says that 'Princes too are accustomed to give great gifts during great festivals....'²

Both Thomas Lebreton and Nicolas de Biard draw an analogy from the way in which great men, when guests, make displays of generosity to their hosts. Thomas Lebreton says that God denies nothing to those who receive him, in the same way that kings and barons willingly give a hearing to their hosts and frequently confer great privileges and gifts (*donaria*) on them.³ Nicolas de Biard says, 'It is certain that the Lord not only does not oppress his host, but fills him with all good things, just as nobles and those of aristocratic blood (*generosi*) are accustomed to offer courtlinesses and advantages to their hosts.'⁴ It is almost impossible to give an adequate translation of the last phrase, 'curialitates et avantagia...facere', but it belongs to a world of gift-exchange rather than of profit economy.

The two worlds existed side by side, and we should not identify the preaching of the mendicants (or of other popular preachers of the thirteenth century) exclusively with one or

---

¹ Little, *Religious Poverty*, p. 4.

² '*Tertio* prope est dominus quia in proximo secundum representationem ecclesie nasciturus est in mundo isto, et spiritualiter venturus ad eos qui fuerunt preparati; propinquior videtur esse hominibus tali tempore quam multis aliis temporibus, quia multis ecclesie precibus invocatus est. Solent et principes dare magna numera in magnis festis (*corr. from* festibus)....' (MS BN lat. 16472, fo. 22ʳᵇ); from a sermon on the text 'Dominus prope est' (Phil. 4: 5), Schneyer, *Repertorium*, ii. 544, No. 140.

³ '...quasi dicat: Nihil negabit dominus hospitibus suis, sed quicquid petierint, et si non ad votum, tamen (*or* tum?) ad meritum, concedit eis; quemadmodum nos videmus quod isti reges et barones hospites suos libenter exaudiunt et frequenter libertates et donaria magna sibi conferunt....' (MS BL Royal 3. A. XIII, fo. 26ᵛᵃ); from a sermon on the text 'Dominus prope est' (Phil. 4: 5), Schneyer, *Repertorium*, v. 632, s.v. 'Thomas de Lisle', No. 7.

⁴ '...Sed certe dominus non solum non gravat hospitem suum, sed bonis omnibus replet ipsum, sicut nobiles et generosi hospitibus suis curialitates et avantagia solent facere....' (MS BN lat. 13579, fo. 16ᵛᵇ); from a sermon on the text 'Ecce rex tuus venit' (Matt. 21: 5), Schneyer, *Repertorium*, iv. 229, No. 8.

the other of them. The image of Christ as the good merchant
was obviously evocative, but there is no reason to be surprised
to meet him in the guise of the innocent and just son of a good
prince, who lets him be a hostage in order to redeem a
captured and imprisoned army.[1] We should remember the
fascination which the doings of kings and princes seem to
exercise even when the reality of power has left them, let
alone in the thirteenth century when it was becoming far
more real. It is probable enough that people of all kinds,
whether knights, merchants, or peasants, were in the habit of
talking about the court of their local count or of the king of
France. When Peyraut talks about the king of France and his
brother[2] his thought is reflecting his world just as when he
takes his imagery from trade.

iii. Other Interpretations

Commercial imagery is only a subset of social imagery, but
social imagery in its turn is only a subset of a more general
tendency in thirteenth-century preaching to use images,
comparisons, or 'similitudes' more freely than we are accustomed to expect from prose. Aldobrandino Cavalcanti, OP,
devotes the first part of a sermon on St Margaret to the image
of Christ as a good merchant,[3] but the nature of pearls
provides the basis of the imagery of the second half.[4] In the

---

[1] An image from Thomas Lebreton: 'Fecit enim deus pater sicut bonus princeps
qui filium suum innocentem et bonum et iustum ponit in hostagium ut redimat
exercitum (excercitum *ms*) captum et incarceratum' (MS BL Royal 3. A. xiii, fo. 25ʳᵃ);
from a sermon on the text 'Ecce ego mitto angelum meum' (Matt. 11: 10 [but Mal. 3
is cited in the manuscript]), Schneyer, *Repertorium*, v. 632, s.v. 'Thomas de Lisle', No.
6.

[2] '. . . quia non oportet fratrem Christi nimis sollicitum esse de hiis que sunt
necessaria presenti vite tantummodo ad Christum se habeat debito modo, sicut non
oportet fratrem regis Francie nimis sollicitum esse de victu suo et vestitu solummodo
bene se habeat ad fratrem suum. . . .' (MS BN lat. 16472, fo. 22ʳᵇ); from a sermon on
the text 'Dominus prope est' (Phil. 4: 5), Schneyer, *Repertorium*, ii. 544, No. 140.

[3] See above, IV. i, p. 212 n. 3.

[4] Since the sermon is on the text 'Simile est regnum celorum homini negotiatori
querenti bonas margaritas' (Matt. 13: 45), and *margarita* = pearl, the comparison
works not badly from a rhetorical point of view: 'Iste autem negotiator invenit in
mundo isto unam pretiosam margaritam, scilicet virginem˒ istam, et abiit, eam

passage where Christ is compared to a merchant in the Dominican series called *Sermones attrebatenses*[1] he is also compared to a bridegroom,[2] to a traveller in a strange land,[3] and to an abbot giving those under him permission to talk.[4] In Jean de la Rochelle, OM, and Guillaume 'de Lavicea', OM, one meets rather similar groupings of analogies: here too the commercial imagery, which would seem to confirm a social interpretation when taken out of context, is in fact only an also-ran, so to speak, among a number of comparisons and similitudes. In a sermon of Jean de la Rochelle on Matt. 20: 1, God is compared to a traveller (*homini peregrinanti*), to a sower, to a householder, to a man making his servants render their accounts, and to a king providing wedding festivities for his son, in the same breath as he is compared to a merchant.[5]

---

passionibus exponendo et vendidit omnia que habuit ei regnum celorum preparando, et emit eam in eterna patria collocando. Dicitur autem virgo ista Margarita vii[em] de causis. Primo ratione nominis, quia sic vocata est. . . . 2° ratione originis. Generatur enim . . . de rore celi, et ipsa virginitatem servavit ex spirituali dono gratie dei. . . . 3° ratione candoris et pulchritudinis quam habuit in carne et in mente. . . . 4° ratione inventionis, quia in mari invenitur, et ipsa exemplum virginitatis traxit a Maria [*col. b*] que fuit virginitatis primiceria. . . .' (MS Bamberg, Msc. Theol. 2, fol. 153[va-b]); the sermon in Schneyer, *Repertorium*, i. 174, No. 339.

[1] See above, IV. i, pp. 208–9.

[2] '. . . Primus ergo adventus domini fuit in uterum virginis, scilicet per incarnationem. . . . In hoc adventu venit sicut sponsus ad nubendum. . . .' (MS Troyes 1536, fo. 6[vb]).

[3] '. . . Item venit sicut peregrinus. . . .' (ibid., fo. 7[ra]). From the context I am inclined to think that 'traveller' is to be preferred to 'pilgrim'.

[4] '. . . Item venit sicut abbas ad referendum loquelam, quando subditi eius non possunt loqui, et ipse dicit: Benedicite, et tunc locuntur. Ita ante adventum domini homines erant muti ab oratione et confessione et dei laude et bono exemplo, et ita de hiis tenebant silentium. Set dominus adveniens . . .' (ibid., fo. 7[ra]).

[5] Note the confusion—perhaps due to transposition and/or omission—in the passage as transmitted by this manuscript. 'Nota quod deus †paterfamilias in ewangelio comparatur homini secundum vi modos. Comparatur enim homini negotiatori . . . † Comparatur homini peregrinanti. Comparatur homini seminanti. . . . Comparatur homini regi, qui fecit nuptias filio suo. . . . Comparatur homini ponenti rationem cum servis suis. . . . Homini seminanti comparatur ratione creationis. . . . [fo. 18[va]] . . . Item homini negotiatori comparatur ratione redemptionis. . . . Item comparatur homini peregrinanti ratione gratie sive honorum gratuitorum. . . . [fo. 18[vb]] . . . Item homini patrifamilias in presenti ewangelio comparatur, in quantum monet ad meritum voluntatem nostram ad opus bonum, et hoc propter eternum premium . . . Item homini regi ponenti rationem cum servis suis (sui *ms?*) comparatur ratione futuri iudicii, in quo expectat a singulis de singulis rationem. . . . Item homini regi facienti nuptias filio suo ratione beatitudinis et premii que significantur (sig[ur] *ms*)

In his *Dieta salutis*, Guillaume 'de Lavicea'[1] says that the
lustful man is like a stupid merchant who gives a precious
thing for a contemptible price,[2] but this is only one among a
long series of comparisons which he assembles. The lustful
man is also compared to hell (*gehenna*), because in the sin of
lust there is the fire of concupiscence, the worm that is the
biting of conscience, and sulphur, the smoke of ill repute;[3] to a
crow;[4] to a foolish warrior;[5] to a horse;[6] and to a ship.[7] In the
same passage lust is compared to a net,[8] to Greek fire,[9] and to
muck and mud,[10] with an explanation for the comparison and
Scriptural 'confirmation', in each case.

The *Dieta salutis* contains a great number of comparisons
of this kind—the section on lust is not untypical—so many, in
fact, that it is one of the most prominent features of the work.

Although the number of extended comparisons or analogies that Guillaume 'de Lavicea' uses is perhaps rather
exceptional, the technique was well established by the time he
was writing; it is one of the mental habits or customs which
most influenced the directions which the thinking of preachers followed in the thirteenth century and after. In some
preachers, at least, it goes beyond the use of metaphor and
analogies which one finds in prose of all periods.

A few historians have already recognized that this is a

---

per (*ms adds and expunges* festiti) festivitatem nuptialem et inseparabili copula
sponsi et sponse Christi, id est ecclesie....' (MS BN lat. 16477, fo. 18[rb-vb]); from a
sermon on the text 'Simile est regnum caelorum homini patrifamilias' (Matt. 20: 1),
Schneyer, *Repertorium*, iii. 704, No. 11.

[1] The work is printed under the name of Bonaventura, *Opera omnia*, viii (Peltier
edn., Paris, 1866), 248–358. I have checked the passage I discuss against the relevant
folios of MS BL Royal 7. C. I (fos. 38[rb]–39[ra] [new foliation]); there are no variants
radically affecting the sense but one or two worth mentioning: see below, nn. 8–10.

[2] 'Bonaventura', ed. cit. viii. 261.

[3] Ibid. 260.   [4] Ibid. 261.

[5] Ibid.   [6] Ibid.   [7] Ibid.

[8] 'Quinto comparatur luxuria sagenae...' (ibid.). luxuria] luxuriosus *in MS BL
Royal 7. C. I, fo. 38[vb] (new foliation)*. Here, as with the variants given in the next two
notes, the reading of the edition seems preferable.

[9] 'Sexto comparatur luxuria igni graeco...' ('Bonaventura', ed. cit. viii. 261.
luxuria] luxuriosus *in MS BL Royal 7. C. I, fo. 38vb (new foliation)*.

[10] 'Nono comparatur luxuria stercori et luto...' ('Bonaventura', ed. cit. viii. 262.
luxuria] omitted *in MS BL Royal 7. C. I, fo. 39ra (new foliation)*.

phenomenon worth isolating and analyzing. Nicole Bériou has discovered in the sermons of Ranulphe de la Houblonnière 'tout un système d'analogies, appuyé sur le jeu incessant des comparaisons...'.[1] Siegfried Wenzel has studied the similes in the fourteenth-century English Franciscan handbook called *Fasciculus morum*.[2] The imagery which plays such a large part in the sermons of Jean Gerson have been examined in detail by Louis Mourin.[3] Mourin had the impression that the images of Gerson 'forment partie d'un vaste édifice, d'un grand répertoire...'.[4]

If so, the idea was not a creation of Gerson's. In the early thirteenth century Guillaume d'Auvergne tried to construct just that: a vast repertory of comparisons, following on a theoretical exposé.[5] This treatise on the external surfaces of the world, *De faciebus mundi*, is an intriguing attempt to construct a general science of symbolism. Material objects are the *facies mundi*. Contrasted with them are *sententiae*, which are spiritual objects, in so far as they are represented by material objects. To each spiritual object corresponds a number of *facies*, and a number of *sententiae* go with each material object. With this underlying principle as a basis, Guillaume analyses the different ways of drawing comparisons.[6] In its way, his general theory of comparisons is an impressive achievement.

In his second book, the 'applied' part of the work, he gives what Valois called 'des listes interminables de comparaisons

---

[1] Bériou, 'Sermons aux clercs et sermons aux "simples gens"': i. 97, and see pp. 97–100, *passim*. See too her 'L'Art de convaincre dans la prédication de Ranulphe d'Homblières', in *Faire Croire. Modalités de la diffusion et de la réception des messages religieux du XIIᵉ au XVᵉ siècle* (Collection de l'École Française de Rome, 51; Rome, 1981), 39–65, at pp. 55–6. Mlle Bériou tells me that she plans to take her investigation of comparisons further.

[2] S. Wenzel, *Verses in Sermons. Fasciculus morum and its Middle English Poems* (Cambridge, Mass., 1978), 51–4.

[3] L. Mourin, *Jean Gerson, prédicateur français* (Bruges, 1952), 441–96; and also id., *Six Sermons français inédits de Jean Gerson* (Paris, 1946), 529–34.

[4] Ibid. 531.

[5] For an analysis see N. Valois, *Guillaume d'Auvergne, évêque de Paris (1228-1249). Sa vie et ses ouvrages* (Paris, 1880).

[6] My summary is derived from Valois, ibid. 226–9.

et de métaphores'.[1] He compares the human soul to a fiancée, to a temple, and to a cloister, and compares sin to blindness, to leprosy, to dissonance, to stench, to hardness. This is a selective list; and as for the idea of virtue, Guillaume finds no fewer than thirty-four *facies* to represent it.[2] One may or may not think that these lists were worth making;[3] they are certainly interesting to students of thirteenth- and fourteenth-century preaching, in which comparisons of this sort play so large a part. Guillaume almost certainly designed the *De faciebus* to help preachers.[4] It would be interesting to see—without necessarily working on the hypothesis of direct influence—how many of his comparisons turn up in the sermons of specified preachers.

In the mean time, it seems evident that the idea of freely exploiting comparisons and similitudes as a preaching technique was in the air around the turn of the twelfth and thirteenth centuries. We find it in Jacques de Vitry,[5] and it also seems to have been attractive to two interesting Englishmen, Thomas of Chobham and William de Montibus.[6] Both of them had studied at Paris, quite probably under Pierre le Chantre (which would place them in the same

---

[1] Ibid. 229.

[2] See ibid. 229–30.

[3] Noel Valois did not: 'Combien Aristote montrait plus de goût dans ce 21ᵉ chapitre de la *Poétique* où il traçait les règles de la métaphore!...' (ibid. 230), cf. ibid. 231.

[4] It begins with the words: 'Veritas evangelica predicatoribus, quasi quibusdam paranimphis, est commissa, ut ipsam custodiant, ipsam in manifestum producant, ipsam denique humano intellectui matrimonio indissolubili, tanquam sponso, conjugant....' (quoted ibid. 225 n. 1).

[5] Cf. the introduction to his *Sermones in epistolas et evangelia dominicalia totius anni* (Antwerp, 1575): '...ex authoritatibus scripturarum novi et veteris testamenti, ex sanctorum Doctorum & expositorum variis et moralibus sententiis, ex sanctorum Patrum vita et exemplis, ex rationibus et *similitudinibus secundum naturas animalium & proprietates inanimatorum, divinis sententiis propter laicos et simplices adaptis....*' (my italics); from the 'Proemium' (unpaginated).

[6] They both belong to the early stages of that pastoral movement which is one of the great facts of English religious history in the later Middle Ages. The best study of it is the unpublished Oxford D.Phil. thesis of Leonard Boyle—'A Study of the Works Attributed to William of Pagula, with special reference to the *Oculus Sacerdotis* and *Summa Summarum*' (1956). The scope of this thesis is far broader than its title suggests.

'school' as Foulques de Neuilly and Jacques de Vitry himself).[1]

Thomas of Chobham's treatise on preaching[2] includes a section on persuasion through similitudes in which we find an articulate rationale for their use in sermons:

... [E]st ... considerandum quod omnis res que suaderi debet animo auditoris multo melius insinuabitur per similitudines [*fo. 82ʳᵃ*] quam per simplicem et nudam veritatem, ut si velit homo dicere alii quod prava societas vitanda est, quia sepe colligit homo sordes et malitias ex prava societate, efficacius persuadebit ei dicens hoc modo: Qui tangit picem inquinabitur ab ea, sicut legitur in Ecclesiastico, quam si diceret simpliciter: Qui propinqus est pravo socio pravos mores addiscet ab eo.... Intellectus enim humanus naturaliter debilis et inbecillis est per se ad videndum verum, et ideo desiderat adiutorium similitudinum, per quas expressius veritatem possit videre....'[3]

It ... should be considered that everything which ought to be put over successfully (*suaderi*) will be introduced into the mind of the hearer much better through similitudes than through the simple and naked truth; as, if a man were to want to say to another that evil society should be avoided, because a man often picks up dirty characteristics and bad habits from evil society, he will persuade him more easily if he speaks to him in this manner: 'He who touches pitch will get dirty from it', as is read in Ecclesiasticus [13: 1], than if he were to say simply: 'He who is near to an evil companion will learn evil habits of behaviour from him.' ... For the human intellect is naturally weak and feeble at seeing the truth through its own

---

[1] H. MacKinnon, 'William de Montibus, a Medieval Teacher', in T. A. Sandquist and M. R. Powicke (edd.), *Essays in Medieval History presented to Bertie Wilkinson* (Toronto, 1969), 32–45, at pp. 32–3, thinks it is probable that William had been a pupil of Pierre le Chantre. F. Broomfield, *Thomae de Chobham Summa Confessorum* (Analecta Mediaevalia Namurcensia, 25; Louvain and Paris, 1968), p. xxxi, suggests that Pierre le Chantre was probably Chobham's teacher. On Thomas see too Baldwin, *Masters, Princes, and Merchants*, 34–6.

[2] J. J. Murphy deserves the credit for recognizing the exceptional interest of this work, which stands out in the generally rather stereotyped genre of *artes praedicandi* and gives the rationale of procedures which are normally explained with dry technicality. See his *Rhetoric in the Middle Ages. A History of Rhetorical Theory from Saint Augustine to the Renaissance* (Berkeley, Los Angeles, and London, 1974), 317–26.

[3] MS Cambridge, Corpus Christi College 455, fos. 81ᵛᵇ–82ʳᵃ.

strength, and therefore it desires the help of similitudes, through
which it may see the truth more clearly. . . .

A little later he returns to this point: 'It is therefore necessary,
as was said above, that we should explain the truth by natural
similitudes when we have to convince the infirm mind of
something in sermons.'[1] In the remainder of this section of the
treatise[2] he first reinforces his point by arguing that Christ, the
Apostle Paul, etc., had used 'similitudes', and then proceeds
to analyse the 'three types of such similitudes in Holy
Scripture'.[3] This typology is interesting in itself but need not
detain us here.

There is another passage which helps explain the passion
for similitudes near the beginning of Chobham's treatise:
'. . . The third thing is that he should know the natures of
animals and also of other things, because there is nothing
which moves the hearts of an audience more than the
properties of animals and of other things . . . for similitudes of
things, because they seem to be something novel, move the
soul more easily and in a more pleasurable way . . .'[4] It will

---

[1] 'Est igitur necesse, sicut predictum est, cum infirmo animo debemus aliquid
persuadere in predicationibus, per naturales similitudines veritatem explicemus. . . .'
(ibid., fo. 82ra).

[2] Ibid., fo. 82^{ra-va}.

[3] 'Sunt autem tria genera talium similitudinum in sacra scriptura, sicut ostendimus
in principio . . .' (ibid., fo. 82rb). This 'as we showed at the beginning' is probably a
reference back to a passage which starts on fo. 2vb, where we are told that 'Parabola
autem et enigma sunt comunes [*sic*] modi significandi in theologia et in philosophia
. . . Philosophi tamen distingunt iiii^{or} genera similitudinum . . .' (ibid.) —and so on.
The use of the phrase 'modi significandi', with its overtones of speculative grammar,
is another of the interesting things about this treatise.

[4] 'Tertium est ut sciat naturas animalium et etiam aliarum rerum, quia nihil est
quod magis moveat corda auditorum quam proprietates animalium et aliarum rerum
de quibus predicatur bene assignate, quia similitudines rerum quasi quedam
novitates facilius et deletabilius [*sic*] movent animam, ut si dixero: Mus in pera, ignis
in gremio, serpens in sinu magis movet quam si diceretur pravus (pravu^{us} *ms*) homo
in vicinia. Similiter si dixero: Qui tangit picem inquinabitur ab ea, magis moveo
intellectum hominis quam si dicerem: Qui adheret pravo homini depravabitur ab eo'
(ibid., fo. 2vb); 'de quibus predicatur bene assignate' should probably be interpreted
to mean 'which well fit the things which are being preached about', in which case
some such word as 'eis' may have dropped out of the text before the phrase. The two
examples he gives at the end of the passage are used again near the beginning of the
section on persuasion through similitudes.

be noted that properties from the world of nature are treated as similitudes; *proprietates rerum* were, of course, a most important source of comparisons for sermons.

Elsewhere in the treatise Thomas of Chobham devotes a fair amount of space to the use of natural properties—more than can be conveniently quoted or summarized here.[1] He formulates in a helpfully explicit way the idea of the natural world as a 'universal and publick Manuscript'—a distinctive form of thought which is common to both medieval and early modern preaching.[2] Thomas says:

Dominus enim diversas creaturas creavit diversas naturas habentes, non solum ad sustentationem hominum, sed etiam ad doctrinam eorum, ut per ipsas creaturas non solum inspiciamus quid nobis utile sit in corpore, sed etiam quid sit utile in anima . . . Nulla enim creatura est que non predicet deum esse potentem qui eam creavit, et deum esse sapientem qui eam disposuit et informavit, et misericordem qui eam in esse (inesse *ms?*) conservavit. Et ut largius dicamus, non est aliqua creatura in qua non possumus (possunus *ms*) considerare aliquam proprietatem eius que nos trahat ad [*fo. 80ra*] imitandum deum vel aliquam proprietatem que nos moveat ad fugiendum diabolum. Totus enim mundus diversis creaturis plenus est, quasi liber scriptus, variis literis et sententiis plenus, in quo legere possumus quicquid imitari vel fugere debeamus . . .[3]

The Lord . . . created different creatures with different natures not

---

[1] Most of the two sections headed 'De narrationibus rerum necessariarum' (fos. 79va–80ra), and 'De narratione artis inveniendi personas' (fo. 81ra–vb) (which precedes the section on persuasion through similitudes discussed above), is relevant, and there may be others which I have missed. Note that on fo. 81rb, in the middle of the discussion of *proprietates rerum*, there is a passage on interpretation of names. There are structural similarities between the two techniques.

[2] Cf. the chapter on '. . . "Nature, that universal and publick Manuscript"' in Bayley, *French Pulpit Oratory 1598–1650*, pp. 149 ff.

[3] MS Cambridge, Corpus Christi College 455, fos. 79vb–80ra. Cf. the following passage from 'Bonaventura', *Opera omnia*, ix (Quaracchi, 1901), 19: 'Deus enim creaturas fecit propter homines non solum nutriendos, sed etiam instruendos . . .' (The whole section beginning 'Sextus modus est exponendo *metaphoras* secundum proprietatem rei . . .' (ibid.) is interesting for the study of similitudes). The part of the pseudo-Bonaventura *Ars concionandi* from which this comes is either the same as or very close indeed to the treatise on preaching of Richard of Thetford, another English *ars* which comes early in the history of the genre. Cf. Murphy, *Rhetoric in the Middle Ages*, p. 327.

only for the sustenance of men, but also for their instruction, so that through the same creatures we may contemplate not only what may be useful to us in the body, but also what may be useful in the soul ... For there is no creature which may not preach that the God who created it is powerful, and that the God who gave it its order and form is wise, and that the God who conserved it in being is merciful. And—speaking in a wider sense—there is no creature in which we may not contemplate some property belonging to it which may lead us to imitate God, or some property which may move us to flee from the Devil. For the whole world is full of different creatures, like a manuscript (*liber scriptus*) full of different letters and sentences (*or* meanings) in which we can read whatever we ought to imitate or flee from ...

Or again later: '... it is necessary for the preacher to contemplate the natures and properties of things, through which properties the creator himself may be understood, so that the whole world may be like a kind of book, in which we may read God. ...'[1]

Though it is tempting to dwell longer on Chobham's analysis of *proprietates*—on the six 'persons' for whom the preacher must discover properties,[2] for instance, or the (consciously) half-arbitrary nature of the signs in this symbolic language[3]—one must leave it with a plea for

---

[1] '... oportet predicatorem considerare naturas rerum et proprietates, per quas proprietates ipse creator possit intelligi [*fo. 81*[rb]] ut totus mundus sit quasi liber quidam in quo deum (tantum *ms*) legamus. ...' (MS Cambridge, Corpus Christi College 455, fo. 81[ra-b]).

[2] 'Item variatur ars inveniendi circa personas alio modo. Sunt enim vi persone circa quas oportet predicatorem diversas invenire proprietates. Prima persona est deus cum angelis suis. Secunda persona est diabolus cum demonibus suis. Tertia persona est ecclesia militans. Quarta persona est ecclesia triumphans. Quinta persona est anima iusti generaliter considerata, que est sponsa Christi. Sexta potest esse sinagoga diaboli ...' (ibid., fo. 81[ra]).

[3] e.g.: 'Verumtamen in hac assignatione proprietatum (*corr. from* proprietatem) magna cautela opus est. Quamvis enim aliqua proprietas alicuius animalis conveniat deo, tamen potest esse aliud (a[d] *ms*) impedimentum in ipso animali propter quod non potest deo adaptari nomen eius. Verbi gratia lupus rapit oves a pastore; similiter et deus rapit oves a diabolo. Non tamen deus potest dici lupus quia lupus non rapit nisi ut dispergat, et ideo odiosum est nomen lupi, et rapina eius numquam sit (*sic in ms for* fit?) aliquo bono fine. ... Caute ergo providendum est quibus animalibus deus comparetur, et quibus non; licet enim dominus habeat forsitan [*fo. 81*[rb]] aliquas proprietates communes cum vulpe, non tamen dicitur deus vulpes, et hoc ideo

further study. The essential point here is that Thomas of Chobham is sketching an attitude to imagery which differs from our own so much in degree that it is almost a difference in kind. Thomas is helpful to us because (like Guillaume d'Auvergne) he tries to formulate explicitly some of the conventions or forms of thought which create this difference. Here it may be reiterated that the commercial imagery of mendicant sermons should be explained primarily in terms of these conventions; the social and economic changes themselves—the rise of towns and profit economy—being only a secondary and in a sense accidental part of the explanation.

Thus, the *Similitudinarius* of William de Montibus has its similitude based on the market-place,[1] but it is a leaf in a forest of others, most or all of which have nothing particularly to do with trade or towns. The *Similitudinarius* is something like a dictionary of images for sermons,[2] and William is so indefatigable in collecting his similitudes that it would be amazing if commercial imagery had escaped altogether. In short, the approach to imagery and comparisons in these treatises of William de Montibus, Thomas of Chobham, and Guillaume d'Auvergne merely confirms the interpretation that the sermons themselves suggest to the attentive reader.

---

contingit quia quedam animalia habent precipuas et innatas sibi proprietates malas, ut lupus rapidam [*sic*] crudelitatem, et vulpes dolositatem. Unde cum audiuntur nominari ista animalia, statum (*sic in ms for* statim) creduntur significare illas precipuas et innatas proprietates suas malas. Unde et corvus, licet habeat aliquas proprietates communes que forsitan conveniant domino, tamen propter precipuam eius malam proprietatem, scilicet quia non nutrit pullos suos dum albi sunt, sed pascit eos cum nigrescant, potius intelligitur per corvum diabolus quam deus. . . .' (ibid., fo. 81va-b).

[1] 'Item mundus forum est in quo sancti se et sua pro deo vendunt, emunt aurum cum thesauro abscondito. Negotiamini, inquid dominus, dum venio. Hic emit Iacob primogenita [*sic*] Esau guloso, lenticulam tribuens, id est carnalibus carnalia relinquens. Hic: malum est, dicit omnis emptor, set in recessu gloriatur. In hoc foro sunt venditores olei, et qui cuprum vendunt ut aurum' (MS BL Cotton Vespasian B. XIII, fo. 101ra). For the place of this manuscript (which I have chosen because it is convenient) in the tradition of the *Similitudinarius* see H. MacKinnon, 'The Life and Works of William de Montibus', unpublished D.Phil. thesis (Oxford, 1959), 63 and 72. There may be a few other cases of commercial imagery in the *Similitudinarius*, which I have only examined cursorily.

[2] For a description of the work see MacKinnon, ibid. 225–34.

The habit of making similitudes overlaps with another form of thought in mendicant (and not only mendicant) preaching, the almost automatic recourse to Scripture as a means of putting over an idea. Often what the preacher takes from Scripture is an image. The commercial imagery which we have examined could be classified as a manifestation and almost inevitable consequence of the impregnation of preaching with biblical imagery. A familiarity with the Bible would in itself be enough to put allegories and analogies based on trade into a preacher's mind. It is arguable that if such images had been absent from preaching, the historian would be faced with a harder problem than that of their presence. The whole allegory of trade in Guibert de Tournai's sermons to merchants starts from the phrase of Luke 19: 13, 'Trade till I come' (*Negotiamini dum venio*), from the parable of the talents, which would have been familiar to any friar. When Jean de la Rochelle says that God 'is compared to a man of business because of the redemption', he immediately proceeds to quote Matt. 14: 45–6: 'The kingdom of heaven is like a man of business (*homini mercatori*) seeking fine pearls. But having found one precious pearl he went and sold all he had and bought it.'[1] The image of Christ as the good merchant in a sermon by Aldobrandino Cavalcanti on Matt. 13: 45 follows naturally enough from the words 'homini negotiatori' in this text.[2] New Testament texts alone could have been enough to sow the seeds of commercial imagery in the minds of the thirteenth-century preachers (or of St Bernard), whatever had been going on in the society around them. Nor, of course, did they specially pick out commercial imagery from the other kinds in the Bible, for they cast their nets wide.

Biblical imagery permeates their sermons in a way and to a degree which is not common to all sermons of all periods.

---

[1] 'Item homini negotiatori comparatur ratione redemptionis. Unde dicitur Mt. xiii: Simile est regnum celorum homini negotiatori querenti bonas margaritas. Inventa autem una pretiosa margarita abiit et vendidit omnia que habuit et emit eam. . . .' (MS BN lat. 16477, fo. 18ᵛᵃ); from a sermon on the text 'Simile est regnum caelorum homini patrifamilias' (Matt. 20: 1), Schneyer, *Repertorium*, iii. 704, No. 11.

[2] See above, IV. i, p. 212 n. 3.

Their own familiarity with Scripture was such that analogies, parallels, and images from the Bible became a way of thought. Even if the Scriptural language was not figurative in the first place (as it was with New Testament parables) it would frequently become so—turning into a spiritual sense —in the process of being adapted to a different context. For the rules of preaching ensured that texts came thick and fast, confirming the many divisions in the average sermon, and often they could only be relevant in a figurative sense. The obsession with the newly invented concordance would force Scriptural texts on a preacher's attention even if they did not spontaneously come to mind. In a perhaps slightly less artificial way the collections of *distinctiones* would do the same; in fact, one of the functions[1] of *distinctiones* may have been to make readily available to the preacher Scriptural texts which could provide a basis for imagery. Thus, the *distinctio* collection by the Franciscan Maurice (Salimbene's friend) has an entry under *Negotiatio* ('business, trade')[2] which is full of Scriptural texts, including 'Negotiamini dum venio',[3] the text which is the springboard for his confrère Guibert de Tournai's allegory of trade. Shortly before this entry in the manuscript I have used we find entries for *Navicula* ('boat')[4] and *Nebula* ('cloud'),[5] also well provided with Scriptural texts.

It is unnecessary further to labour the point that the language of commerce had a mental context as well as a social context; and if the social context has been given undue emphasis, that may perhaps be explained by the mental context of modern historiography. Allegories of trade and the like reflect an urban social context. That is true but less significant than the two closely related mental habits which

---

[1] In the history of ideas, as in social history, one can distinguish between function and conscious purpose.

[2] MS BN lat. 3270, fo. 226[ra–b].

[3] 'Item [est negotiatio] bone vite, qua emuntur merita: xix Luc.: Negotiamini dum venio. . . .' (ibid., fo. 226[rb]).

[4] Ibid., fos. 224[va]–225[rb].

[5] Ibid., fo. 225[rb–vb].

gave rise to them: namely, the passion for similitudes and for incessantly quoting the Bible.

Apart from the commercial imagery, there is not much to connect the content of preaching with the urban environment or the commercial revolution. Guibert de Tournai discusses the wealth of urban élites and the legitimacy of profit in his *ad status* collection, as we have seen, but this is natural in sermons 'to citizens living in communes' or 'to merchants', and sermons to these categories are natural in a collection catering for so many conditions of men. Social categories which one could class together as 'upper bourgeoisie' are given a respectable place in the collection, but in no sense do they dominate it. And when we turn to the model sermon collections for Sundays and Feast-days which form the bulk of our evidence for mendicant preaching, we do not find that commercial morality is a principal or even a prominent theme.[1] Of course, commercial morality was discussed in other genres—confessional handbooks, scholastic theology, canon law.[2] Moreover, if we move forward to the fifteenth century we can find sophisticated economic thought in sermons by Bernardino da Siena.[3] But if we confine ourselves by genre to model sermons and chronologically to the thirteenth century, the economic world of the urban bourgeoisie seems very far away.

It would be wrong to discount the possibility that there were links between towns and preaching of a subtler kind.

---

[1] By its nature this is not the sort of proposition one can illustrate by examples, and a quantitative 'content analysis' is out of the question when nearly all the evidence is in manuscript; but my assertion can be tested by any scholar able to spend time with one of the model collections discussed in this book; and it is to be hoped that monographs on individual collections will further validate it by attempting to falsify it.

[2] Cf. G. Le Bras, 'Conceptions of Economy and Society', in M. M. Postan *et al.* (edd.), *The Cambridge Economic History of Europe*, iii. *Economic Organization and Policies in the Middle Ages* (Cambridge, 1963), 554–75, at pp. 555–6.

[3] Cf. R. de Roover, *San Bernardino of Siena and Sant'Antonio of Florence. The Two Great Economic Thinkers of the Middle Ages* (Boston, Mass., 1967), and R. Rusconi, *Predicazione e vita religiosa nella società italiana da Carlo Magno alla Contrariforma* (Documenti della Storia, 30; Turin, 1981), 119, 167–70.

The relatively high level of sophistication in model sermons intended mainly for popular preaching—a sophistication which makes it hard to distinguish between them and sermons to clerics or even to academics—may be an indirect reflection of the high cultural level of the merchant class (but of course the cultural attainments of members of the noble and knightly classes were also far from negligible). The numerical symmetry which rules over the divisions and subdivisions of sermons may possibly reflect the merchant class's preoccupation with number. (But one could explain it in other ways: as a device to aid the memory, or simply as a particular manifestation of a general mental habit, of which the patristic obsession with number mysticism may be an ancestor.) Even if there is anything in these very speculative observations, they cannot affect the general conclusion that socio-economic interpretations are of limited value so far as the content of mendicant preaching is concerned. Even if correct, they do not direct our attention in such a way as to help us see what the preaching of the mendicants was really like.

By a kind of principle of natural selection, those sermons, or parts of sermons, which can be related to economic society tend to get more attention than their frequency warrants. The historian in our time is programmed to notice such aspects of other times because he knows that they will be of interest to his peers and his public. This kind of selection is legitimate provided that no one mistakes the part for the whole; but the scene is more interesting if we take a broader view. The first step is to recover the truism that 'society' cannot be reduced to economic society. In the first three chapters of this book an attempt was made to link the content of the sermons not only with the towns but with the other subsocieties which used and transmitted them, and in particular with the academic and religious society of Paris. It has further been argued, in this last chapter of the book, that the tightening of governmental authority was itself a social fact which left its mark on the content of the sermons. Even when 'society' is understood in this more flexible sense, however, it leaves a lot to be desired as an interpretative tool.

There is a fallacious antithesis which may explain why historians tend to be too satisfied with this tool. It is that the things which may be said about medieval preaching fall into two categories: those which may be related to 'society', on the one hand, and, on the other, the stock of doctrines which are not of interest to the historian because they are more or less timeless. There is an instinct—not in itself unhealthy—that it is not the historian's business to redistribute passages of medieval sermons into pigeon-holes of theology *à la longue durée*: God, the Trinity, original sin, incarnation, redemption, sacraments, etc. But the latter approach, which can indeed be far from lively unless the writer has exceptional gifts, is not all that is left to the historian if he wishes to go beyond a social and 'contextual' interpretation of mendicant preaching.

It will have been noticed that we have already gone beyond it in another direction. It has been argued that commercial, feudal, and other kinds of social imagery should be regarded as one manifestation of a mental habit. The passion for similitudes, carried to these lengths, is a distinctive form of thought. It is not timeless (though its time was long). It cannot be ranged under the heading of any particular dogma: rather, it is a manner of representing doctrines to the imagination. On the other hand, this mental phenomenon cannot be explained in socio-economic terms unless we artificially reduce it to one of its constituent parts.

iv. Beyond 'the Context'

It is therefore appropriate to close this study by pointing out what lies beyond its boundaries: those habits of thought whose history seems to have a rhythm often only remotely connected with the way their various social contexts work. The investigation of these habits of thought is not quite the same thing as the history of dogma or the history of ideas *tout court*. It is not directly concerned with the elements of a belief system which remained unchanged over time, nor with those ideas of creative individuals which depart from the beaten tracks. It might be added, however, that in an indirect way the study of habits of thought is intimately linked both with the history of doctrinal continuities and with that of individual creativity. Without grasping what is conventional at a particular time, we cannot see clearly either what is perennial or what is original.

There is nothing particularly new about this sort of investigation. Huizinga's phrase 'modes of thought'[1] means something very similar. So do the twin concepts of *langage* and *mentalité*, moulded by Jean Guitton long before they were made fashionable by semiologists and post-war French historians. For Guitton the word *langage* takes under its umbrella many things, including literary and didactic genres, generally accepted oppositions of concepts, and all the topoi of discourse.[2] *Mentalité* is 'that thought which is anterior to thought, that mental humus in which the most personal idea must necessarily be rooted, that innate table of categories and values, in a word the totality of those implicit assumptions, which are imposed on us by our environment and which rule our judgements . . .'.[3]

The study of the 'language and mentality' of thirteenth-century sermons is therefore concerned with mental facts that belong to a particular period, not with the timeless element in preaching; but these mental facts are often more usefully

---

[1] J. Huizinga, *The Waning of the Middle Ages* (London, 1924), 186, corresponding to 'denkwijzen' in the Haarlem 1919 edition (p. 343). Cf. the phrases 'symbolische denkwijze' (Haarlem 1919 edn., p. 345), 'De symbolische denkorde', (ibid., p. 339), and the word 'Gedachtenvormen' in the subtitle.

[2] 'Et par langage nous n'entendons pas seulement le vocabulaire, mais aussi toute cette matière qui devance la pensée, qui la suscite, l'aide et le prolonge, tout en lui demeurant étrangère: ainsi les genres littéraires ou didactiques, les exemples classiques, les citations, les maximes, les métaphores et les mythes familiers . . . Dans le langage il faudrait encore faire entrer les divisions communes, et tous les "lieux" du discours. Le domaine où le philosophe pénètre n'est pas une terre inconnue qu'il peut décrire et nommer à son gré. Des divisions ont été formées avant lui; des repartitions faites; des oppositions de concepts sont devenues classiques' (Guitton, *Le Temps et l'éternité chez Plotin et Saint Augustin* (Paris, 1933), p. xi.

[3] Ibid., p. xii (my translation).

studied in their own terms than explained by social context. In what remains of this study it may be permitted to suggest a partial framework for investigation. The more developed parts of it arise out of consideration of the sermon collections studied in this book, and so far as these collections are concerned I would hope to test and document them properly in a subsequent work; however, a very similar miscellany of theories could usefully be tested against the mass of mendicant and other thirteenth- and fourteenth-century sermon material which remains virgin territory, and that is a sufficient justification for setting down this skeleton programme here. It may be broken down into questions, hypotheses, and method.

One of the questions which it is most useful to ask when studying mental habits is difficult to formulate adequately. It has been said that between different men

various distinct instruments, keys, or *calculi* of thought obtain, on which their ideas and arguments shape themselves respectively, and which we must use, if we would reach them. The cogitative method, as it may be called, of one man is notoriously very different from that of another; of the lawyer from that of the soldier, of the rich from that of the poor. The territory of thought is portioned out in a hundred different ways. Abstractions, generalizations, definitions, propositions, all are framed on distinct standards . . .[1]

These calculi of thought differ not only between man and man but also between period and period, or genre and genre. Thus, the distinctive calculus of a genre characteristic of the period before the coming of the friars has been sensitively treated by Christopher Holdsworth. He points out that a twelfth-century treatise on the sacrament of the alter

is not built around chapters which divide the matter to be discussed in a logically ordered manner, it is not a thesis which advances point by point, citing the relevant authorities. . . . We are here . . . moving

---

[1] *Newman's University Sermons*, edd. D. M. MacKinnon and J. D. Holmes (London, 1970), 344.

around the question of the nature of the Sacrament not by
arguments derived from the way the Sacrament is celebrated, nor
by accumulation of statements made by earlier writers, but by a
chewing over of the biblical text in a way which seems to us
arbitrary and fanciful.[1]

Or again, on John of Forde's manner of interpreting the Song
of Songs:

For us the track he followed in pursuit of his quarry seems strange,
full of doubling backs, of sudden changes onto a parallel path,
reached by a bewildering jump, but to John and his audience this
was the way one would expect to go on that journey. The whole
wood of Scripture, they believed, could be used to understand any
of its parts ... And this route, too, had a shape they knew (perhaps
mostly before they became monks) in the structure of romance, and
in the way that paintings, whether in books or on walls, and
carvings, too, told their stories.[2]

We must try, in the same way, to find out how the territory of
thought is portioned out in thirteenth-century sermons. Some
scholars have worked on the assumption that treatises on the
art of preaching provide the little key. Of course the *artes
praedicandi* can take us a long way, but they can also be an
inadequate and misleading guide precisely because most men
are very imperfectly aware of their own calculi of thought. (For
instance, the *artes* tend to use scholastic terminology to
describe procedures that have nothing much to do with
scholasticism, defined in any useful sense.) Thomas of
Chobham does much better than is usual, but his is an unusual
ars, much more perceptive than the dry and practical little
handbooks of which the genre is largely made up; and even he
cannot excuse us from doing our own observing and thinking.
So where is the key? It has been argued already that it is not the
'scholastic method', whose forms of thought differ greatly

---

[1] C. J. Holdsworth, *'Another Stage ... a Different World'. Ideas and People around
Exeter in the Twelfth Century* (Exeter, 1979), 18.
[2] Ibid. 20.

from those of preaching. Sermons had their own principles for organizing thought, and we will not find them by looking outside sermons. The problem is elusive but central.

Another question which may be put to mendicant sermons is: 'What were their topoi, and in particular, what were their "generally accepted oppositions of concepts"?' The idea of research on topoi is almost banal now to literary scholars, though historians have not used it much except where historiographical problems are concerned. As a self-conscious scholarly approach, *Toposforschung* seems to go back to Ernst Robert Curtius, who made it the 'methodology', 'heuristisches Prinzip',[1] of his famous work on European Literature and the Latin Middle Ages. He deals with a broad spectrum of topoi, ranging from the topos of the modest beginning ('Unaccustomed as I am to public speaking' would be an English version), through the consolation topos, in which the deaths of great men from the past are instanced to console the mourner, to the topoi of the ideal landscape and the goddess Natura. Curtius has been criticized (but reverently) for sometimes missing individual literary achievements through an over-preoccupation with the history of topoi,[2] but as the critic himself points out,[3] Curtius believed that analysis of topoi was an essential preliminary to the study of individuality. Without *Toposforschung* we will mistake traditional motifs and structures for originality.[4] But topoi are interesting in themselves, aside from the detection of originality. The emergence of a new topos, or a new combination of topoi,

[1] *Europäische Literatur und lateinisches Mittelalter* (2nd edn., Berne, 1954), 92.

[2] P. Dronke, *Poetic Individuality in the Middle Ages* (Oxford, 1970), especially 11–18.

[3] Ibid. 18–19.

[4] The criticisms of Curtius by F. P. Pickering, 'On Coming to Terms with Curtius', in his *Essays on Medieval German Literature and Iconography* (Cambridge University Press, 1980), 177–90, seem to me misconceived (though the essay contains good constructive ideas). On p. 179 Pickering alludes to an intriguing suggestion for which he regrettably gives no reference: 'Curtius suggests that we should read more widely in the Fathers "as literature". We should address to them not the theologian's stock questions (God, Trinity, Christology, Grace, etc.), nor accept his word for what is interesting and important; we should, says Curtius, read the Fathers—for their topoi!'

amounts to a shift in the mentality of the articulate; to discover that a topos is ancient, on the other hand, is to observe the *longue durée* of a mental habit. Because originality counted for relatively little in model sermon collections these make a particularly rich field for *Toposforschung.*

A third question worth putting to mendicant sermons is: 'How are abstract and concrete modes of thought combined in this genre?' The question itself sounds abstract, but in fact it is a fundamental one, worth putting to any kind of source for the history of the imagination. Propositions about general and abstract relations affect the mind in an essentially different manner from propositions about individual and concrete things, which tend to have a far greater impact on the imagination and/or the emotions and which are, therefore, apprehended much more keenly. In different genres these two kinds of thinking are distributed in different patterns. The problem is to discover what regular patterns of distribution, if any, may be discerned in the sermons of the friars.

It goes without saying that historians could approach the mental habits embodied in medieval sermons in many other ways. In principle, the only limit is the fertility of the historian in devising questions. Recent work on *exempla*, for instance, has shown what unfamiliar landscapes can come into view when a genre in which historians have long been interested is approached from new standpoints.[1] Rather than attempting to lengthen the list of possible questions here, it seems useful to suggest possible answers to the three questions suggested above, in the form of hypotheses to be tested.

In answer to the question, 'What were the calculi of thought in model sermon collections', a twofold hypothesis may be proposed, the first part of which is perhaps rather obvious, and the second part of which may seem a little fanciful. Nevertheless, they arise out of observations—some

---

[1] Schmitt, *Le Saint Lévrier*, and C. Brémond, J. Le Goff, and J.-C. Schmitt, *L"Exemplum'* (Typologie des Sources du Moyen Âge Occidental, 40; Brepols, Turnhout, 1982).

of what follows has already been adumbrated in our earlier comparison of preaching with scholasticism—and deserve to be tested by more systematic ones. The more obvious hypothesis is that the order of treatment in a sermon cycle is not logical or systematic but liturgical, in the sense that it is determined by the cycle of Gospel and/or Epistle readings for the Sundays and/or Feast-days of the year. One implication of this is that a cycle of sermons is by its nature repetitive, since the cycle of liturgical readings was not divided according to themes into watertight compartments; much less so at least than a scholastic *summa*. Two qualifications need to be borne in mind, however. The first is that on an ordinary saint's day a preacher does not seem to have had to take his initial text from any specific reading. (At least, no one has yet demonstrated that *de sanctis* sermons followed any fixed cycle of readings; we cannot be sure until someone has properly tried.) The second is that even for a Sunday or major Feast-day the readings only provided a springboard. The preacher, or writer of model sermons, had a good deal of freedom in choosing where to jump. He did not have to comment on the whole reading, and in fact it was unusual to do so in this period. Once he had chosen his initial text from the Gospel or Epistle,[1] he could branch out in all sorts of directions, some or all of which might be unconnected with the special theme of the liturgy of the day.

This brings us to the not so obvious calculus of thought at the level of the individual sermon. It is my impression that there are rules for combining ideas within a sermon which are implicit, so much taken for granted by preachers that they would hardly have been conscious of them, and, therefore, off the beaten track of the *artes praedicandi*. It must be emphasized that they do not hold good for all sermons, by any means, but they are applicable to and helpful for understanding many of them.

---

[1] Occasionally the text was taken from elsewhere in the liturgy of the day, but these exceptions need not concern us here.

One may begin with a negative rule which may be formulated by illustrating its opposite, using the comparative method of which more will be said below. A nineteenth-century discussion of university preaching recommends the preacher

to place a distinct categorical proposition before him, such as he can write down in a form of words, and to guide and limit his preparation by it, and to aim in all he says to bring it out, and nothing else.... nor will a preacher's earnestness show itself in anything more unequivocally than in his rejecting, whatever be the temptation to admit it, every remark, however original... which does not in some way or other tend to bring out this one distinct proposition which he has chosen. Nothing is so fatal to the effect of a sermon as the habit of preaching on three or four subjects at once.[1]

The tendency of mendicant preaching was just the opposite. The sermons of the friars start from a single text, but fan out from it. Although the whole sermon may be based on one sentence or phrase of Scripture, or often on one word or image, we seem, in many cases at least, to be taken far afield and in many directions from this point of departure. The text is in fact not so much an idea as a matrix of ideas.

This does not mean that there is no principle of cohesion in mendicant sermons, though it is elusive when one tries to fix it in words. One could call it a tendency to turn each sermon into an artistically constructed microcosm of Christian doctrine. Not all of it, obviously—but the more themes that could be brought into a sermon the better, so long as they could be arranged in an aesthetically satisfying symmetrical structure. For *aficionados* of Hermann Hesse, there is something reminiscent of the glass bead game about the way they arrange their ideas into patterns. The often numerically symmetrical divisions and distinctions can be a means of achieving, and an outward expression of, an elegant parallel-

[1] J. H. Newman, *The Idea of a University* (Oxford, 1976), 333.

ism of thought. Another analogy—which fits sermons much better than the scholastic genres for which it has sometimes been used—would be with the iconography and layout of a Gothic cathedral, in which theological ideas are expressed in stone within a symmetrical aesthetic scheme. Or again (for the similitude habit is infectious), the preaching of the friars operated rather like a kaleidoscope: the patterns of dogmatic and moral ideas were continually being shaken up, from sermon to sermon, to make new combinations, equally symmetrical. Content and form are almost inextricably linked in this calculus of thought. It would be hard to read any social meaning into it, except by the most far-fetched of analogies. It is not at all like our own pattern of thought, but until we learn to appreciate it, as a form of thought which was also a form of art, the sermons of the friars will continue to seem strange.

There is an affinity between the tendency to turn each sermon into a symmetrical artistic synthesis and the habit of distinguishing different senses of a word or applications of an image. (The 'four senses of Scripture' topos could be regarded as a special case of this habit.) If the Scriptural text at the beginning of a sermon was the matrix of ideas to be symmetrically deployed, the distinguishing habit served as midwife. It could perform the same function with a Scriptural text in a subdivision of the sermon. Indeed, a Scriptural text was not required, for distinctions could open up in different directions a word or image not taken from Scripture. We may suppose that this way of playing different motifs on the same word or image had retained in the age of the friars the aesthetic attraction which Gilbert Foliot exercised when he used the *distinctio* method in a synodal sermon in the late twelfth century: 'The whole sermon was varied with certain *distinctiones*', wrote one of those who heard him, 'adorned with flowers of words and sentences and supported by a copious array of authorities. It ran backwards and forwards on its path from its starting-point back to the same starting point.'[1]

---

[1] Quoted by R. W. Hunt, 'English Learning in the Late Twelfth Century', *Transactions of the Royal Historical Society*, 4th ser., 19 (1936), 19–35, at pp. 33–4.

There were many different sorts of *distinctiones*,[1] but an aesthetic element, not separable from the content, may turn out to be a factor common to most. The tendency to formulate distinctions and divisions in what is not far from being a rhymed verse metre is a more extrinsic manifestation of the aesthetic element in sermons.[2]

When we turn to our second question and try to formulate hypotheses about the topoi of mendicant preaching, the habit of distinguishing and dividing again proves to be important. This becomes clear[3] if we try to make a provisional list of some of the commonest topoi (provisional because the frequency and meanings of these topoi still need to be observed systematically rather than impressionistically). *Intellectus... affectus... effectus; corde... ore... opere; voluptuosi... ambitiosi... cupidi; fides... proles... sacramentum*: these little clusters of concepts (or near equivalents) will, it may be predicted, be prominent in any thorough future study of topoi in mendicant preaching. This is in effect to predict that stereotyped free-floating divisions will be found to be among the most characteristic commonplaces of the genre. Though these topoi are not actually distinctions on a word (at least as I have stated them), there is an evident family resemblance to the distinction mentality.

---

[1] Cf. R. H. and M. A. Rouse, 'Biblical Distinctions in the Thirteenth Century', *Archives d'histoire doctrinale et littéraire du Moyen Âge*, année 49, t. 41, (1975), 27–37, on the changing character of collections of *distinctiones*.

[2] Cf. D. L. d'Avray, 'The Wordlists in the "Ars faciendi sermones" of Geraldus de Piscario', *Franciscan Studies*, 38, An. xvi (1978), 184–93. The word-lists turn out to be a dictionary of rhymes—double rhymes indeed—to be used in forming divisions of sermons. In other *artes praedicandi* we find what amount to rules which in our terms belong to the realm of verse: cf. ibid. 186 n. 8. (Cf. now Wenzel, *Verses in Sermons*, p. 75 ff.) I do not see why we should suppose that these techniques were purely mnemonic in purpose. Thomas Waleys says that such rhymes may be used in sermons to the clergy 'ad tollendum fastidium auditoribus'. Cf. d'Avray, 'Wordlists', p. 185. Waleys says that a 'pulcerrima sententia divisionis' often has to be rejected for want of a word with a suitable rhyme, and goes into details of how to compile word-lists to make it easier to find rhymes (though he does not rise to Gerald's refinement of a system of double rhymes) (ibid. 185–8). It is interesting that he had first criticized preachers who fill whole sermons with '*bilis* et *trilis*, et *osus* et *bosus*' (ibid. 185). This kind of condemnation, inconsistent with practice, may have been a topos.

[3] Nevertheless, it was a remark of L.-J. Bataillon which made the point clear to me.

Formulae like *intellectus-affectus-effectus* and *fides-proles-sacramentum* belong to the history of the association of ideas. In the right context one knows that when one sees the first concept of the cluster the others will almost surely follow. The clusters are like molecules in which the individual concepts are held together by some mutual attraction. Some of these molecules are more interesting than others. The 'in thought, word, and deed' topos (*corde-ore-opere*) seems rather banal, though this is possibly because it is a way of dividing up human activity that we ourselves take for granted. On the other hand, the *fides-proles-sacramentum* topos is definitely interesting, because it could not have been predicted if it had not been invented (by Augustine?),[1] and because of the way in which the connotations vary between different writers and times. The importance of this topos of the 'three goods of marriage' in *ad status* sermon collections of the central Middle Ages is established.[2] In this genre they are found together with certain other topoi of marriage preaching: the essential goodness of marriage, which was founded in paradise and honoured by the Lord's presence at the wedding feast at Cana; the ideas of *officium* (marriage's initial function of peopling the earth), *remedium* (marriage as a remedy for incontinence after the fall), and *debitum* (each partner's duty to have intercourse if the other wants it); the heinousness of adultery and the many crimes it involves; the obligation to abstain from intercourse at certain times, and so on.[3]

This enables us to propose a hypothesis, namely, that the same topoi will be found in sermons for the second Sunday after Epiphany, which form (so far as is known) the largest genre of marriage preaching in the later medieval centuries and after. Of course, one will not expect all these topoi in all sermons for this Sunday, but it is worth testing whether all or most of them are commonly found in a large sample.

---

[1] *De bono coniugali*, ed. Josephus Zycha in *Corpus Scriptorum Ecclesiasticorum Latinorum*, 41 (Prague, Vienna, and Leipzig, 1900), xxviiii/32, p. 227.

[2] D'Avray and Tausche, 'Marriage Sermons', pp. 80, 92–3.

[3] Ibid. 118 and *passim*.

Marriage tended to be discussed in sermons for the second Sunday after Epiphany because it was then that the Gospel of the marriage feast of Chana was read. On an impressionistic survey a common pattern seems to be a treatment of marriage in the literal sense, and then of other levels of 'marriage': the marriage of Christ's divine and human natures, the marriage of Christ and his Church, the marriage of the soul to God. (It remains to be seen how far this pattern was the norm, and how far particular preachers lent an individuality to the scheme.) It will be noted that this is in its way an artistic synthesis, fanning out from the word or image of marriage (*nuptiae*), of the sort which has just been described; perhaps a more than usually inevitable one, granted the use of marriage imagery in the Bible. For the history of associations of ideas it would be interesting if, as seems likely, these clusters of ideas—topoi about marriage proper and the topos of different levels of *nuptiae*—were so closely and regularly associated with each other and with a particular time of year as to be necessarily engraved on the mental calendar of the clergy who used model sermon collections. In that case they would probably also have become engraved on the minds of the lay audience of sermons. If a man or woman heard one of these liturgical marriage sermons in many Januaries of their life, the cumulative effect would presumably be much greater than that of an occasional *ad status* sermon. (It will be interesting to see whether future research in the field of mass communications will show that it is more effective when cumulative, as one would expect;[1] in any case, the tendency of scholars in the 1940s and 1950s to suggest that the effects of mass media are severely limited has been reversed.[2]) As

---

[1] 'Our knowledge of the overall effects of mass communication will remain limited unless research can be directed upon the effects of cumulative exposure to mass communications'. (J. T. Klapper, *International Encyclopedia of the Social Sciences*, iii (1968), 89). I do not know whether much research has been done on this since Klapper wrote.

[2] S. H. Chaffee, 'Mass Media Effects: New Research Perspectives', repr. in *Mass Communication Review Yearbook*, i (Beverley Hills and London, 1980), 77–108, especially pp. 100–1.

more research is done on sermon collections, it seems likely that other clusters of notions will be found to be specially linked with other Sundays and times of year; in this way we may be able gradually to reconstruct the mental calendar of mendicant preaching.

Turning to the third question, about the relative proportion of abstract and concrete thinking in the sermons of the friars, there are two related hypotheses which seem to merit investigation. The first arises out of the observation of Jean-Claude Schmitt that in collections of *distinctiones* the words distinguished are more usually abstract.[1] Since the number of thirteenth-century *distinctiones* collections is not unlimited, it would be possible to measure this quantitatively,[2] but the hypothesis could profitably be extended to and verified for the words which serve as the basis of *distinctiones* in sermons proper. Here, by the nature of the evidence, quantitative figures would almost be impossible to obtain except for restricted samples, but if scholars who take in hand particular sermon collections for editions or monographs were to direct their attention to this problem then significant findings could be expected.

The same may be said of the other related hypothesis, which is that in the sermons of the thirteenth century and after the two kinds of thinking tend to separate themselves

---

[1] 'Dans les *distinctiones* les prédicateurs trouvaient, derrière une liste de mots le plus souvent abstraits, la somme des significations symboliques de ce vocabulaire. Les recueils d'*exempla* offraient de leur côté la matière concrète d'un *corpus* de récits dont le prédicateur pouvait faire usage dans ces circonstances et devant des auditoires particuliers: d'où le choix de mots plus concrets, et parmi ceux-ci d'un grand nombre de termes désignant des catégories sociales' ('Recueils franciscains d' "exempla" et perfectionnement des techniques intellectuelles du XIIIe au XVe siècle', *Bibliothèque de l'École des Chartes*, 135 (1977), 5–21, at p. 18).

[2] At present it should be regarded as a hypothesis rather than a certain conclusion. L.-J. Bataillon points out that in the *distinctiones* of Maurice de Provins 'Le choix des mots bibliques relevé est très vaste: mots abstraits (noms de vertus ou de vices, de mystères), mots d'action, mais aussi noms très concrets: les éléments, les animaux, les instruments', and that 'Bien que moins riche, le vocabulaire retenu par Nicolas de Biard est aussi varié . . .' ('Les Instruments de travail des prédicateurs au XIIIe siècle', in G. Hasenohr and J. Longère (edd.), *Culture et travail intellectuel dans l'Occident médiéval* (Éditions du Centre National de la Recherche Scientifique, Paris, 1981), 197–209, at pp. 202–3). But Schmitt's theory is perceptive and fruitful.

out in such a way that the divisions and subdivisions (which will often take the form of *distinctiones* on a word) are abstract, and the rest of the sermon concrete. The *exempla* which helped fill the framework of divisions and subdivisions evidently represent a concrete manner of thinking. The Scriptural texts which seem to confirm every member of each division with automatic regularity in the sermons as transmitted are a less clear-cut case; one would expect them to be concrete rather than abstract because so much of the Bible consists of narrative or imagery, but this needs to be verified by analyzing the texts cited by particular preachers. Similitudes and comparisons, which are, as we have seen, a characteristic technique of thirteenth-century (and later) preaching, seem to be a deliberate attempt to present ideas in a concrete and, therefore, more vivid way. Thomas de Chobham, it will be remembered, claimed that to say 'He who touches pitch will get dirty from it' was much more effective than to say 'He who is near to an evil companion will learn evil habits of behaviour from him.'[1] Thomas was aware that this sort of language had a special impact on the imagination and emotions, and speaks of moving the hearts of an audience, and of moving the soul more easily and in a more pleasurable way.[2]

Sometimes similitudes or images, instead of serving to fill in the structure of divisions, are themselves the basis of the structure.[3] In such cases the framework of the sermon loses its abstract character. If the structure of divisions and subdivisions is not built around an image or comparison,

---

[1] See above, IV. iii, p. 230.
[2] See above, IV. iii, p. 231.
[3] Cf. Cruel, *Geschichte*, p. 281: 'Ganz anders gestaltet sich aber die thematische Predigt, wenn der Gegenstand nicht unmittelbar in's Auge gefasst und dialektisch behandelt, sondern wenn er mittelbar unter dem Bilde irgend eines sinnlichen Objectes betrachtet wird, wobei nicht die Unterschiede sondern die Aehnlichkeiten aufgesucht werden und die Vergleichungspunkte dann die Theile der Rede ergeben. Hier ist zunächst nicht sowohl der Verstand als die Phantasie thätig, welche die abstracten Lehren gleichsam mit Fleisch und Blut bekleidet und in einer greifbaren Gestalt vor Augen hält, wodurch die Rede besonders eindringlich und leicht behaltbar wird.' L.-J. Bataillon pointed out to me in a personal communication that whole sermons of Pierre de Saint-Benoît are built round comparisons.

however, my impression is that it tends to be highly abstract, though in a different way from scholastic works.

An illustration of how abstract and detached from any concrete context the divisions of a sermon might be is provided by the *Ars faciendi sermones* of the Franciscan Géraud du Pescher.[1] This contains word-lists which can be shown to be a sort of dictionary for making the double rhymes that preachers tried to achieve between the different members of a division.[2] A preacher who used these curious word-lists could have formed the division of his sermon entirely in a vacuum. He would be combining words—usually very abstract—without reference to any concrete context.

An example will make this clear. A preacher might turn to the following passage in the word-list's section:

Inexpressibilis: malorum punitio, miseria, calamitas, incendium, luctus, dolor, jactura. *Optabilis*: Dei dilectio, divina gratia, proximi caritas, Christi amplexus, Dei subsidium, divinus amor, rectitudo; eadem *optanda*. *Odibilis*: culpe transgressio, superbia, iniquitas, defectus, excidium, severitas, mors; eadem *odienda*. . . .[3]

The way in which he would use this becomes obvious if we rearrange the words in columns:

	(1)	(2)	(3)
Inexpressi*bilis*	malorum punit*io*	miser*ia*	calami*tas* . . .
Opta*bilis*	Dei dilect*io*	divina grat*ia*	proximi cari*tas* . . .
Odi*bilis*	Culpe transgress*io*	superb*ia*	iniqui*tas* . . .[4]

From this a rhymed division for a sermon could be extracted, as it were by turning the handle. If we join each of the three adjectives ending in *–bilis* to the noun that immediately follows them we get the following division:

[1] Edited by F. Delorme, 'L'"Ars faciendi sermones" de Géraud du Pescher', *Antonianum*, 19 (1944), 169–98.
[2] Cf. above, p. 248 n. 2.
[3] Cf. d'Avray, 'Wordlists', p. 185.
[4] Ibid. 189.

Inexpressibilis punitio

Optabilis dilectio

Odibilis transgressio.[1]

Or the preacher might join the adjective to the next noun but one, in which case he would get the following division:

Inexpressibilis miseria

Optabilis divina gratia

Odibilis superbia.[2]

And so on.[3] The division can be formed without reference to real and individual things, and without concrete imagery to mitigate the abstractions. This *ars* is, of course, an extreme case, and furthermore the author belongs to the first half of the fourteenth century, but it seems symptomatic of a tendency that is well under way in the period which more immediately concerns us.

Such hypothesis about the structure of abstract and concrete thinking in sermons can only be verified by concentrated study from that particular angle. It may prove especially fruitful where sermons for saints' days are concerned, and enable us to define more precisely why they can fail so signally to leave a sense of the saint's personality— even if it is a saint like St Francis (but 'fail' may be the wrong word, in that it assumes that this is what the sermons were trying to do). The more we can 'mould' the concepts we use to describe concepts, to make them more sensitive instruments of analysis, the more productive this sort of investigation will be. The distinction between 'concrete' and 'abstract' is rather crude and unsatisfactory, though it has the advantage of being in general use.

Moulding terms and concepts to fit them for analysing a

---

[1] Cf. d'Avray, 'Wordlists', p. 189.

[2] Ibid.

[3] The word-lists do not always work quite so slickly as in the example I have given, and the system is not quite the same in every section, but the extract chosen represents the general way in which this bizarre dictionary works.

given subject-matter is a method universally, though often unconsciously, practised by historians. In this sense all historians have to be applied analytical philosophers. A sophisticated set of conceptual instruments will not force the scholar to see facts and relations for which there is no evidence, but a clumsy set will allow him to miss facts and relations for which there *is* evidence, and to confuse phenomena which are essentially distinct (the indiscriminate application of the adjective 'scholastic' to thirteenth-century sermons is a case in point).

A method which is less generally followed and which is particularly appropriate for the history of preaching is systematic comparison between different periods. A study of sermons which confines itself to one period cannot tell us what is distinctive about that period. Only comparisons can bring out the difference between short-term trends and the *longue durée* of Western preaching; the similarities and the differences are equally interesting. The historian of humanist preaching in Renaissance Rome expressed the hope that his study would 'provide a foil against which other styles of preaching can be examined so that new light can be thrown on them',[1] and historians of medieval preaching should take their cue from this.

The least-neglected area of comparative study is the contrast between the early medieval homily, which comments on the whole text of Gospel and Epistle readings in an unstructured manner, and is heavily dependent on patristic writers, and the preaching of the central and later Middle Ages.[2] From the thirteenth to at least the end of the fifteenth century the continuity in the mainstream of preaching is striking, but even in this period there is scope for comparative analysis. The difference between preaching north and south of the Alps deserves fuller investigation: while I think it

---

[1] J. W. O'Malley, *Praise and Blame in Renaissance Rome. Rhetoric, Doctrine, and Reform in the Sacred Orators of the Papal Court* c.1450–1521 (Duke University Press, 1979), 4.

[2] Cf., for example, Cruel, *Geschichte*, pp. 1–4 and 279–90.

unlikely that many striking differences will be found in, say, Aldobrandino Cavalcanti, OP, there are other Italians (notably Remigio de' Girolami, OP and Ambrogio Sansedoni, OP) who do seem to belong to another world. Again, there are some significant contrasts between the thirteenth and the fourteenth centuries. Beryl Smalley has drawn attention to the 'politicization' of sermons in the fourteenth century, when it became customary to give addresses on political occasions and to use them to make propaganda for the political programme of a ruler or a party.[1] In the sermons of Gerson we find that *quaestiones* play a significant part,[2] and this, if typical, may represent the sort of scholastic influence which is not characteristic of the previous century. Then there is a much more strikingly different fourteenth-century development, the mystical preaching of Meister Eckhart and his disciples.[3] Moving forward to the fifteenth century, we find that the mainstream tradition of preaching in the manner which goes back to the thirteenth century may be contrasted with at least two different sorts of preaching: not only the humanist genre,[4] but also another and simpler sort, which has affinities with the early medieval homily. It is an English development, though continental analogues cannot be ruled out.[5] In an English context, a comparison between the mainstream tradition and Wycliffite sermons would also be of great interest.[6] The distinctive features of thirteenth-century

[1] See Miss Smalley's précis of her paper in the report on the Medieval Sermon Studies Symposium held at Oxford in 1979, pp. 2–3; the report is a supplement to the *Medieval Sermon Studies Newsletter.*

[2] Mourin, *Jean Gerson*, pp. 341–2.

[3] The bibliography on German mystical preaching is enormous. See K. Morvay and D. Grube ['unter Leitung von Kurt Ruh'], *Bibliographie der deutschen Predigt des Mittelalters. Veröffentlichte Predigten* (Münchener Texte und Untersuchungen zur deutschen Literatur des Mittelalters, 47; Munich, 1974), iv. 69ff. For an evocation of Eckhart's sermons and personality see R. W. Southern, 'Meister Eckhart', in his *Medieval Humanism and other Studies* (Oxford, 1970), 19–26.

[4] See above, p. 255.

[5] H. Spencer, 'English Vernacular Sunday Preaching in the Late Fourteenth and Fifteenth Century, with Illustrative Texts', unpublished D.Phil. thesis (Oxford, 1982), includes a discussion of late medieval vernacular homilies.

[6] Lollard sermons can—though did not necessarily—take the homily form, so these two late medieval English developments cannot be separated. Cf. Spencer,

sermons will stand out more clearly if we compare them with these other sorts of medieval preaching. An especially fruitful approach is to compare the ways in which they treat the same Sunday Gospel and Epistle reading.

There is no reason why the comparative method should be kept within the confines of the Middle Ages. In post-medieval Catholic Europe, at least, sermons do not necessarily become so different that they are not worth comparing with those of the thirteenth century, for the Gospel and Epistle readings of the liturgical year continue to be the framework of many sermon collections. I have carried out the experiment of comparing thirteenth-century and (French) seventeenth-century sermons for the second Sunday after Epiphany— those that start from the Gospel of the marriage feast at Cana. There are prominent common features, notably an emphasis on the goodness of marriage and on love in marriage. There are also major changes. To begin with, it is more normal in the seventeenth century for a sermon to deal with human marriage alone: in the thirteenth, because of the habit of fanning out from a word or image to distinct levels of meaning, the marriage of man and woman is nearly always discussed together with other 'marriages', such as the marriage of God with the soul, or of the divine and human natures of Christ. Again, as a rule there are fewer quotations from Scripture in seventeenth-century sermons. Neither of these changes is peculiar to marriage preaching: they represent general developments in preaching. There are also innovations more specific to marriage preaching. In the seventeenth century the ideas of grace and vocation are to the fore in marriage preaching: the couple must be in a state of grace for the wedding; the sacrament of marriage will increase their sanctifying grace and give them special graces to cope with the duties, troubles, and dangers of married life;

---

ibid., ch. 4, pp. 189–257. A definitive edition of the principal Wycliffite sermon cycle is being prepared by Anne Hudson and Pamela Gradon. (See now Hudson, *English Wycliffite Sermons*, i, (Oxford, 1983).)

but before getting married a person must have a special grace of vocation for that state of life and for the partner he has chosen. This idea of a personal vocation to the married state may be a spin-off from the idea of the personal priestly vocation which was in the air in the seventeenth century. That thirteenth-century marriage sermons say almost nothing on the subject of grace and vocation is an important 'negative fact' of which we would hardly be aware without the comparative method. If the historical sense is a feeling for what could *not* have happened in a period then this method is a way of refining it.

The kind of history which these various methods could be used to write would not be to everybody's taste. Many good historians do not, in any case, find the history of ideas and attitudes interesting, but even those who do often tend to assume that it should take one or more of three forms. One is the study of the great men and near-great men in the history of thought: the attempt to salvage the lost originality and creativity of the past. When this entirely legitimate approach is adopted the historian wastes little time with writers who had no original ideas. Thirteenth-century sermons, however, are not the best place to look for original ideas. Another is the attempt to link ideological with social development. This approach has much to offer, and class explanations are only one form of it.[1] Nevertheless, it has already been argued that a social explanation of mendicant preaching has its limitations. The third approach is to try to answer the question 'What did ordinary people believe?' What indeed: it is a question our sources rarely answer. Sermons, perhaps, come nearer than most kinds of evidence to telling us. Mark Pattison argued that the preachers of any period 'are as necessarily bound to the preconceived notions, as to the language, of those whom they have to exhort. The pulpit does

---

[1] Alexander Murray's *Reason and Society in the Middle Ages* (Oxford, 1978) attempts to explain the emergence of a rationalizing mentality in terms of the increased rate of social mobility in the central Middle Ages, if one may so simplify a book of many ideas.

not mould the forms into which religious thought in any age runs, it simply accommodates itself to those that exist. For this very reason, because they must follow and cannot lead, sermons are the surest index of the pevailing religious feeling of their age.'[1] The fact remains that we never know how much the audience of popular preachers assimilated, or how far preachers were really bound by the preconceptions of their hearers. So far as the history of mass religion is concerned, sermons take us to water but do not let us drink.

Nevertheless, there is a place for a history of the ideas of the articulate, somewhere between the histories of creative thinkers and of popular beliefs. Neither quantitative nor qualitive criteria have to apply to the history of attitudes. In any period the set of those who have left written traces of their thoughts behind them forms only a tiny proportion of society *tout court*, and much of what they have written is mediocre and unoriginal. Such articulate subsets of society are none the less valid and interesting units to study. The history of their attitudes has its own coherence and rhythms, which may often be affected only rather remotely by the society around them; though when projected, as by sermons, their attitudes influence this wider society to an extent which cannot be ignored even though it cannot be precisely known. It is for this kind of history that the methods outlined above are appropriate, and the sermons of the friars are a rich and scarcely exploited source for it.

---

[1] From his essay 'Tendencies of Religious Thought in England' 1688–1750', in *Essays and Reviews* (2nd edn., London, 1860), 267. Professor Christopher Cheney gave me the reference.

Illustrative Text

A Sermon for the Upper Class of the Cities

From MS BN lat. 15943, fos. cxxvi^{ra}–cxxx^{ra}

AD CIVES COMMUNITER VIVENTES SERMO

QUI amat divitias fructum non capiet ex eis. Ecces .v. Ostendit nobis Salomon divitiarum periculum; ligant enim per amorem affectum, et post laborem non relinqunt fructum; que duo notantur*a* in [*col. b*] verbo proposito. ¶ Sunt autem temporales. Sunt spirituales. Sunt celestes. Sunt et supercelestes. ¶ De temporalibus. Iob. xxxi.: Si letatus sum super divitiis meis multis, et quia plurima reperit manus mea. Sequitur: Oriatur michi tribulus et pro ordeo spina. Non enim confidebat Iob in divitiis suis nec delectabatur*b* in specie auri vel in cantitate acervi. Hoc enim curandum est ne quis temporalia diligat et in eis fiduciam ponat. Ps. Speravit in multitudine divitiarum suarum, et prevaluit in vanitate sua. ¶ Divitie autem temporales licite habentur quando acquiruntur sine pravitate. Gn. xiii. Erat Abraham dives valde in possessione auri et argenti. Ps. Nolite sperare in iniquitate et rapinas nolite concupiscere. Divitie si af(fluant), no(lite) cor app(onere). Aurum enim et argentum nec bonos nec malos faciunt, sed usus eorum bonus est, abusio mala. Sollicitudo*c* peior. Questus turpior. Ut dicit Bernardus: Avarus enim terrena esurit ut mendicus, fidelis condempnit ut dominus. Ille possidendo mendicat. Iste contempnendo servat. ¶ Custodiuntur cum humilitate .i. Thi. vi. Divitibus huius seculi precipe non sublime sapere, nec sperare in incerto*d* divitiarum, sed in deo vivo. Non sublime sapere, quia sicut

---

a notantur] no^{ur} *ms.* *b* delectabatur] delectabitur (delc̄abī) *ms.* *c* Sollicitudo] Sollicito *ms.* *d* incerto] incirco *ms.*

paupertas nutrit humilitatem, ita divitie superbiam, quia incrassati recalcitrant. ¶ Exo. ix. De cinere creantur vesice. In incerto divitiarum, quia incerte sunt et mutabunde, sed in deo vivo, quia divitie sunt deus mortuus. Non enim [*fo. cxxvi*^{va}] possunt iuvare cultores suos sicut nec ydola. ¶ Sumuntur cum frugalitate et mediocritate. Prover. xiii. Est quasi pauper, cum in multis divitiis sit. Sapientes enim sic utuntur temporali subsidio sicut peregrinus via, et viator fatigatus umbra: corpore pausans, sed mente ad aliud tendendo, recedere festinat. Seneca: magnum est non corrumpi divitiarum conturbernio. Magnus ille est qui in divitiis pauper est. Ecci. xviii. Memento paupertatis in tempore habundantie, et necessitatem paupertatis in die divitiarum. ¶ Distribuuntur cum pietate ii. Reg. xix. Berzellai prebuit alimenta regi cum moraretur in castris. Fuit enim vir dives nimis. Nunc enim Christus peregrinatur in pauperibus velud in castris. Prover. xvii. Substantia divitis urbs roboris eius, et quasi murus validus circumdans eum. Custodiunt enim divitie divitem sicut murus domum vel fortitudo urbem. Eze. xxxii. Convertam flumina eorum in oleum, quod fit quando divitie convertuntur in opera misericordie. Gregorius: Divitie sicut impedimenta sunt improbis^e ita in bonis sunt adiumenta virtutis. ¶ Divitie etiam temporales periculose possidentur quia sunt breves et transitorie. Quantumcumque enim valeant et magni pretii constent, durare non possunt. Sap. v. Quid vobis^f profuit superbia? aut divitiarum iactantia quid contulit vobis?^{g} Transierunt omnia tanquam umbra, et tanquam nuntius precurrens, et tanquam navis que pertransiit fluctuantem aquam; aut avis que transvo|lat [*col. b*] in aere cuius nullum invenitur argumentum itineris illius; aut tanquam sagitta emissa in locum destinatum. Temporales divitias comparat umbre quia frigida est et obscura, et sequitur fugientes et fugit sequentes, quia temporalia ignem caritatis extingunt, lucem veritatis obnubilant, et fugiunt

---

^{e} improb' *ms* (*I have failed to trace the quotation, so do not know which case Gregory used*). ^{f} vobis] *probably* nobis *in ms.* ^{g} vobis] *probably* nobis *in ms.*

appetentes honores, et fugientes insecuntur; et qui huiusmodi
desiderant non eas assequantur. Ecci. xi. Si sequtus fueris,
non apprehendes; et non effugies, si precurreris; et in[h] .xxxiiii.
Quasi qui apprehendit umbram et sequitur ventum, sic qui
attendit ad visa mendacia. Umbram crescit contra noctem, et
affectus divitiarum contra mortem. Lu. xii. Anima mea multa
bona habes et cetera. Stulte hac nocte et cetera. Sic est omnis
qui thesaurizat et non est in deum dives. Comparantur etiam
divitie nuntio precurrenti, quia divitie male acquisite sunt
eterne pene prenuntie; et navi transeunti aquam fluctuantem,
quia mentem quasi ventis et procellis expositam relinqunt
inquietam; et avi transvolanti, quia nichil est mobilius ave,
nichil mutabilius prosperitate.[i] Comparantur etiam sagitte
emisse ad locum destinatum, id est ad infernum. Sagitta enim
in altum emissa, quia veras pennas non habet, cito labitur, et
amantes temporalia, licet ad modicum erigantur, cito tamen
ad infernum labuntur. ¶ Fallaces et deceptorie: Mt. xiii.
Sollicitudo istius seculi et fallacia divitiarum suffocat verbum,
et sine fructu efficitur. Fallacia divitiarum est, quia promit-
tunt sufficientiam, et relin|qunt [*fo. cxxvii[ra]*] deficientiam et
vanitatem. Apoc. iii. Dicis quia dives sum, et nullius egeo, et
nescis quia tu es miser et miserabilis et pauper et cecus et
nudus. Miser es in te ipso, miserabilis coram proximo.
Pauper, cui multa deficiunt. Cecus, quia ante te non vides.
Immo apposito obolo ex una parte et marcha[j] ex alia,
marcham reicis, obolum accipis, quia relicta possessione
eterna accipis temporalem. Sicut enim speculum decipit
tigridem que alludit primitus umbre, deinde[k] fracto speculo
comperit nichil esse, ita divitie decipiunt divitem. Ps. Dormi-
erunt et nichil invenerunt omnes viri divitiarum in manibus
suis. Et nudus cuius turpitudo apparet. ¶ Penales et obligatorie. Obligatur enim dives ut cognoscat eum a quo date sunt
ei divitie, sicut obligatur per feodum ille qui tenetur
recognoscere dominum suum. Iere. ix. Non glorietur dives in

---

[h] in] ī (sic) *ms, perhaps for* in eiusdem (*the passage is Ecclus. 34: 2*). [i] prosperitate]
prospertate *ms.* [j] marcha] marcham *ms.* [k] deinde] demum *ms?*

divitiis suis, sed in hoc glorietur, scire et nosse[j] me; et ideo sicut digni sunt amittere feodum, qui non de illo serviunt domino suo in necessitate, ita digni sunt amittere temporales divitias qui non distribuunt eas ad honorem domini sui membris suis in necessitate positis. Naum. Diripite argentum diripite aurum, et non est finis divitiarum ex omnibus vasis desiderabilibus. Iere. xv. Divitias tuas et thesauros dabo in direptionem. Sunt etiam penales. Ecci. xxxi. Laboravit dives in congregatione substantie. ¶ Culpabiles et noxie. Ecci. xi. Si dives fueris non eris immunis a delicto.—Non quia in rebus sit vitium, sed in ipso animo; sicut nichil differt utrum egrum in lecto ligneo aut in aureo colloces—quocumque illum transtuleris [*col. b*] morbum suum transfert—sic nichil refert utrum eger animus in divitiis an in paupertate ponatur. Malum enim suum illum sequitur.[1] Eccl. xiii. Bona est substantia cui non est peccatum in conscientia, et Gregorius: Non est census in crimine sed affectus. ¶ Sunt autem breves et transitorie, quia in momento deficiunt. Apoc. xviii. Ve Ve civitas illa magna, que amicta erat bysso, et purpura, et cocco; una hora destitute sunt tante divitie. Nam momentaneum est quod delectat, eternum quod cruciat. ¶ Quia deficientes ad modum sompnii cor afficiunt. Iob. Dives cum dormierit nichil secum auferet. Aperiet oculos suos nichil inveniet. Sic enim dormit esuriens et dormiendo afficitur, et tamen non reficitur, immo magis exinanitur, ita divitie non satiant, sed magis sitim avaritie provocant. Iob .xviii. Exardescit contra eum sitis. Lu. vi.[m] Comedes et non saturaberis; quia quo plus sunt pote plus sitiuntur aque. Quanto enim plura ligna in igne ponuntur tanto maior ignis generatur. Crescit amor nummi quantum ipsa pecunia crescit. ¶ Quia resoluti post sompnium nichil inveniunt. Ps. Ne timueris cum dives factus fuerit homo, et cum mul(tiplicata) fu(erit) gl(oria) do(mus) eius, quoniam, cum interierit, non su(met) omnia. Propter hoc stultum est in eis confidere que non possunt permanere. Prover. xi. Qui

---

[j] nosse] nosce *ms.* [m] Lu. vi.] sic; *but see Micah 6: 14.*

---

[1] The scribe appears to have thought that *sequitur* went with the next sentence.

confidit in divitiis suis corruet. Valde enim demens est qui in unda volvitur et planta figere conatur. Ideo anima sancta cui nichil extra deum sufficit, nichil extra deum querit, et sua habundantia fit ei onerosa, et hoc ipsum graviter tolerat quia festinans ad patriam in itinere [*fo. cxxvii*[*va*]] multa portat. ¶ Quia sicut flos sine[*n*] fructu preveniunt. Lu. ii.° Divites dimisit inanes. Unde sicut flos in hyeme ad quamdam[*o*] temperiem prosilit, et non proficit nec fructum facit, ita est de divitiis in statu presentis temporis. Unde .v. Sapientie significantur[*p*] per umbram, spuman, fumum, et sompnum. Umbra nichil habet solliditatis[*q*] et cito preterit. Spuma inflat. Fumus excecat. Sompnus oculos spirituales ligat; et sicut narcisus umbram variam et superficialiter decoram captat in aquis, ita stultus falsam gloriam querit in temporalibus et transitoriis divitiis. Divitie enim sunt sicut flos cardui similis lanugini. Carduus enim aculeos pungitivos habet inferius, florem vero superius qui cito evanescit quam impetus venti sicut tenuissimam plumam cito abicit,[*r*] ita pecunia cito deficit. Unde vani sunt qui hanc multo labore acquirunt sicut pueri qui papiliones capiunt et avolante papilione apertis manibus nichil inveniunt et frequenter in foveam cadunt. ¶ Sunt etiam fallaces et deceptorie, quia relinqunt vanitatem in cogitatu. Lu. xii. Hominis cuiusdam divitis uberes fructus ager attulit et cogitabat intra se: Quid faciam. Non habeo quo congregem fructus meos. Destruam horrea mea et cetera, et sequitur: Stulte, et cetera. Ecce cogitatio sine effectu: deluduntur enim in cogitationibus suis sicut homines melancolici, aut dormientes famelici et sitibundi. ¶ Relinqunt etiam insatiabilitatem in appetitu. Ecces. [*col. b*] iiii. Unus est et secundum non habet, et tamen laborare non cessat, nec satiantur oculi eius divitiis. Insatiabilis enim est oculus cupidi; nichil enim potest animam replere nisi deus. Unde tanta est anime capacitas quod non repletur modicis. Ipsa autem anima ymago est dei, et ideo maior est toto mundo, immo quanto magis repletur

---

[*n*] sine] sive *ms?* [*o*] quamdam] quemdam *ms.* [*p*] significantur] *or* signantur (Signtur *ms*). [*q*] solliditatis] sic. [*r*] qui cito evanescit . . . cito abicit] sic. *in ms, perhaps for* qui cito evanescit, quoniam impetus venti (illum) sicut tenuissimam pluman cito abicit.

temporalibus,[s] minus repletur deo, et ita semper remanet vacua. Res enim in se vanitatem habent, et ideo non replent. Res etiam sunt extra. Sitis autem est in anima. Fatuus autem esset esuriens qui se refectum diceret eo quod panem in archa tantum haberet. ¶ Propterea[t] aviditatis vitium semper tendit in infinitum, sicut ignis semper adureret si quis ei materiam apponeret. Seneca: Si vis divitem facere, non divitiis addendum, sed divitiis detrahendum. ¶ Relinqunt etiam cecitatem in intellectu. Obnubilant enim divitie intellectum divitis ita ut inter se et divitias non distinguit,[u] ita ut si domus eius comburitur, dicit se combustum. Hee sunt divitie egyptiorum qui interpretantur 'tenebrosi'. He[br]. xi. Fide[v] Moyses grandis * * * eligebat magis affligi cum populo dei quam temporalis peccati habere iocunditatem, maiores divitias estimans thesauro egyptiorum improperium Christi. Sicut enim ursus excecatur ad fervorem pelvis oculis suis obiectum, ita dives ex appetitu ardenti divitiarum, et sicut ursus ligatus circa stipitem, et sicut equs educens molam in circuitu execatur, sic avarus est circa immobilia alligatus; [*fo. cxxviii[ra]*] nunquam in Christo figitur, sed cum creaturis volubilibus volvitur, donec post vertiginem et cecitatem in infernum labatur. Lu. xvi. Mortuus est dives et sepultus in inferno. Apoc. vi. Omnes divites absconderunt se in speluncis. ¶ Quia etiam relinqunt sterilitatem in fructu. Ecces. v. Quid prodest possessori, nisi quod divitias oculis suis cernit? Sic etiam asinus cernit eas. Unde de quodam dicit Oracius: quidam memoratur Athenis sordidus et dives, populi contempnere voces sic solitus: 'populus me sibilat. At michi plaudo ipse domi simul ac nummos contemplor in archa.'[1] Lu. ii[w] Esurientes implevit bo(nis), et di(vites) di(misit) ina(nes). ¶ Sunt etiam penales et obligatorie, quia obligant possessorem ad dandum elemosinam. Prover. xi. Alii dividunt propria et ditiores fiunt; ab eo enim qui nichil portat nichil petitur.

---

[s] *supply* tanto. [t] Propterea] Þ *ms.* [u] distinguit] distingunt *ms.* [v] *erasure after* Fide *in ms.* [w] Lu. ii] sic *in ms, but see Luke 1: 53.*

---

[1] Hor. *Sat.* i. 1, 64–7.

¶ Obligant etiam ad dei notitiam, quia .i. Reg. ii. Dominus pauperem facit et ditat; licet aliqui quanto magis sunt ditati[x] tanto magis domino sunt ingrati. Iere. xv.[y] Magnificati sunt et ditati, et preterierunt sermones meos pessime. ¶ Obligant etiam ad restitutionis iustitiam. Lu. xix. Ecce vir nomine Zacheus, princeps publicanorum et ipse dives. Sequitur: Domine, ecce dimidium bonorum meorum do pauperibus; si quem defraudavi, reddo quadruplum: hoc est: capitale quod habui, et quod inde lucratus fui, pono in consilio ecclesie; et quod inde lucrari potuit, quamvis non lucratus fuerit, de hoc conteror; et nutrimentum carnis quod [*col. b*] inde acquisivi expono contritioni et penitentie. Hii sunt .iiii. denarii sive quadruplum usurariorum. ¶ Obligant etiam ad precavendam dyaboli astutiam, quia .i. ad Thy. vi. Qui volunt divites fieri incidunt in temptationem, et laqueum dyaboli, et desideria multa que mergunt hominem in interitum et perditionem. Laqueus enim dyaboli sunt divitie, licet paucos inveniamus qui ab hoc laqueo velint liberari, sed magis irretiri; que mergunt, inquit, hominem: quando aliquis submergitur, quicquid tenet secum submergit; unde cum avari ita fortiter teneant divitias quod eas dimittere nolunt, nec restituere, nec dare pauperibus, signum est quod submergantur. Unde Crates philosophus thebanus, demersis[z] in mare divitiis: Abite, inquid, pessimi pessime divitie; submergam vos ne submergar a vobis. ¶ Non sunt autem tantum obligatorie sed penales, quoniam ardor est in ambiendo, labor in acquirendo, timor in possidendo, dolor in perdendo. ¶ De ardore Ecci. v. Noli anxius esse in divitiis iniustis. Est enim dives sicut apis que dicitur burdo, que pinguescit de labore aliarum apum. Ardent enim pre cupiditate respectu sui, et pre invidia respectu proximi. Prover. xxviii. Vir qui festinat ditari, et aliis invidet, ignorat quod egestas[a] superveniet ei. De labore. Ecci. xxxi. Laborabit dives in congregatione substantie. Laborant enim per fas et nefas ut habeant, non ut

---

[x] sunt ditati] ditati sunt *ms, with transposition signs.* [y] Iere. xv] *sic in ms, but see Jer. 5: 27-8.* [z] *or* de mersis. [a] egestas] egestat *ms.*

restituant, nisi in fine, adveniente mortis amaritudine, sicut sangui|suga [*fo. cxxviii*^{va}] repleta evomit sanguinem superposito sale. Iob. xx. Divitias quas devoravit evomet, et de ventre eius extrahet eas deus. Ideo Prover. xxiii. Noli laborare ut diteris. Et nota quod ita est de divite sicut de balena; devorat enim alios pisces, sed post mortem eius, plures participant de bonis eius. Ecci. xiii. Venatio leonis onager in heremo; sic pascua divitum pauperes. Leo participat rapinam aliis bestiis, sed postquam participata fuerit, devorat bestiam sibi proximam; sic quidam divites videntur esse curiales sed deficiente substantia nec proximo nec alii amico parcunt. ¶ De timore Ecces. v. Dulcis est sompnus operanti, sive parum sive multum comedat. Saturitas autem divitis non sinit^b eum dormire; si enim videt pauperem, estimat eum furem. Si divitem, estimat eum raptorem; semper enim tabefit in se ipso sicut lignum viride quod est decisum in decremento lune. Tabescit interiori putredine. Hii sunt divites sine luce gratie, sed in indefectu positi sapientie. Hii dormire non possunt pre sollicitudine. ¶ De dolore. Ecci. xli. O mors quam amara est me(moria) t(ua) homini iniusto habenti pa(cem) in s(ubstantiis) s(uis); et Apo. xviii. Qui divites facti sunt longe stabunt propter timorem tormentorum flentes et lugentes; unde visi sunt multi divites in fine proferre loculos suos et abscondere sub stramentis lectorum suorum. Recitat autem magister Iacobus de Vitriaco^c de quodam paupere qui cantabat cotidie in mane, sed invento thesauro, sine [*col. b*] proposito ob industriam perdidit cantum et letitiam. Sic cum divites tales letitiam habent ipsa est presagium tristitie. Sic enim magni^d pisces, dum in tranquillo tempore ludunt in maris superficie, signum est tempestatis future. Unde tempestate emergente descendunt magni pisces ad profundum maris, parvi vero elevantur ad superficiem, quia mali divites in tempestate iudicii descendent in profundum inferni. Pauperes autem et humiles elevabuntur ad regnum et eternitatem. ¶ Sunt etiam culpabiles et noxie, quia auferunt a rationali libertatem, a

---

^{b} sinit] sinis *ms*. ^{c} Vitriaco] vit^i *ms*, *i.e.* Vitri, (= *Vitry*). ^{d} magni] magis *ms?*

concupiscibili iocunditatem, ab irascibili securitatem, ab
omni vi communiter felicitatem. ¶ De libertate: patet ratio
est virtus libera secundum se, sed cum est alligata materie non
est libera, propter quod, Mr. x.: Facilius est camelum intrare
per foramen acus, quam divitem in reg(num) ce(lorum).[1] Ita
enim onerant divitie amatores suos quod raro possunt cor
levare in celum per devotionem. Unde Bernardus: bone Petre,
Christum sequi non poteras oneratus, super illud: ecce nos
relinquimus omnia, Mt. xix, et Seneca: Nemo cum sarcinis[e]
enatat. Sunt enim divitie sicut quedam mola asinaria alligata
collo divitum,[f] que submergunt eos in profundum cupiditatis
in presenti, et in futuro in puteum eterne dampnationis; immo
deplumant eos sicut virgule viscate deplumant aves se illis
affricantes; spine enim sunt, et ideo anima sanctis affectioni-
bus et cogitationibus deplumatur; circa terram volvitur;
sursum volare non potest, quia libera non est. Immo sicut
muscipule et laquei capiunt aves et feras, sic divitie avaros;
[*fo. cxxix*[ra]] ut enim dicit Augustinus: iusto dei iudicio fit ut
divites a divitiis quas iniuste acquirunt volunt capi; iustissime
teneantur. Sic enim avis credit capere escam et capitur. Immo
divitie sunt quasi compedes quibus avarorum pedes scilicet
affectus constricti miserabiliter alligantur. ¶ De iocunditate
Ecces. v. Divitie conservate in malum domini sui. Pereunt
enim in afflictione pessima. Auferunt enim letitiam mentis et
inducunt tristitiam. Unde affligunt possessorem ita quod[g]
bibere nec comedere potest ad satietatem, nec vestiri ad
necessitatem. Contra illud in eodem: omni homini cui dedit
deus divitias atque substantiam, potestatemque tribuit ut
comedat ex eis, et fruatur parte sua, et letetur de labore suo.
Hoc donum dei est. Iste autem cunctis diebus vite sue comedit
in tenebris et in curiis multis, et in erumpna atque tristitia. In
tenebris, quia comedit disferendo tempus propter hospites
quos timet, ideo comedit de nocte; et in curiis multis, ut sit

---

[e] sarcinis] bicinis *ms?* [f] divitum] divitium *ms.* [g] *supply* nec.

[1] For *regnum dei*. The scribe (or author) probably made the substitution under the
influence of the parallel passage in Matt. 19: 24.

animus eius semper in sollicitudine, et in erumpna, hoc est, in omnimoda indigentia subtrahendo sibi necessaria, et in tristitia videndo quod alii suum superflue expendunt, et videns cor suum singulis morsellis a familia sua devorari. ¶ De securitate. Seneca: Vicinus dives irritat cupiditatem. Unde sicut cadaver non potest esse securum in medio canum aut avium, ita nec divites in medio cupidorum,[h] quia divitie sunt eis sicut cibus et potus in medio esurientium. Iob. v. Cuius messem famelicus comedet, et ipsum rapiet armatus, et bibent sitientes divitias eius. ¶ De amissione fe|licitatis [*col. b*]. Ia. v.: Agite nunc divites, plorate ululantes. Divitie v(estre) putrefacte[i] sunt et cetera. Sicut enim videmus de ceco mortuo quod devoravit alios pisces, sed cum mortuus fuerit omnes participant de bonis eius, ita est de divite devorante substantiam pauperis; sed ulterius, sicut falcones, quando moriuntur, licet in vita sua ceperint gallinas et honorifice parati fuerint, tunc mortui sepeliuntur in fimo, galline autem, que viles erant et in fimo pascebantur, mortue tamen portantur ad mensam regiam: ita de divitibus, qui sepeliuntur in inferno, et de pauperibus, qui elevantur ad regnum. ¶ Sunt etiam divitie spirituales. Prover. x. Manus fortium divitias parat; quia in fortitudine et fervore istas oportet acquirere. Iste autem sunt .iiii. divitie conscientie de quibus in Ps. Gloria et divitie in domo eius. Hoc est in anima que est domus divina, ubi est pura conscientia. Non est enim census super censum corporis, nec oblectamentum super cordis gaudium. ¶ Sunt etiam divitie sapientie. Ysa. vi.[1] Divitie salutis sapientia et scientia: Timor domini ipse est thesaurus[j] eius. Timor in resilitione a malo per effectum; scientia in distributione boni per intellectum; sapientia in sapore per effectum. ¶ Sunt etiam divitie bone vite quo ad se ipsum. Ecci. xiiii.[2] Homines divites in virtute pulcritudinis; et Prover. ult. Multe filie congregaverunt

---

[h] cupidorum] cupidiorum *ms.* [i] putrefacte] pii *ms.* [j] est thesaurus] thesaurus est *ms, with transposition signs.*

---

[1] In fact from Isa. 33: 6.
[2] In fact from Ecclus. 44. The scribe omitted the *l* of *xliiii.*

divitias; Tu supergressa es universas. ¶ Sunt etiam divitie
bone fame quo ad proximum. Prover. xxii. Melius est nomen
bonum quam divitie multe. Ecci. xliiii. Laudemus viros
gloriosos; et sequitur: Homines [*fo. cxxix*^{va}] magni virtute
prediti divitiis^k et cetera. ¶ Sunt etiam divitie celestes que
competunt animabus beatis que possunt dicere in bono illud
Zach. xi. Benedictus dominus! divites facti sumus. Non sunt
autem hee divitie quales mundane, que sunt transitorie et
breves. Iste vero perpetue sine defectione. Non deceptorie et
fallaces, sed sunt vere sine imperfectione. Non obligatorie et
penales, sed melliflue sine afflictione. Non noxie et culpabiles,
sed sincere sine infectione. ¶ Sunt ergo sine defectione. Ios.
xxii. In multa substantia atque divitiis revertimini ad sedes
vestras. Substantia est res perseverans sicut accidens deficiens,
quia iste temporales divitie deficiunt, celestes vero perpetue
sunt. Prover. iii. Longitudo dierum in dextera eius et in
sinistra illius divitie et gloria. ¶ Sunt sine imperfectione;
temporales enim sicut fantastice epule comedentes fallunt et
inanes dimittunt. ¶ Iste vero perfecte reficiunt. Nee. ix.
Comederunt et saturati sunt, et habundaverunt divitiis;^l
omnia enim eis succedunt ad votum. ¶ Sunt enim sine
afflictione; temporales enim possessorem affligunt. ¶ Iste
iocunde sunt. Prover. x. Benedictio domini divites facit, nec
sociabitur eis afflictio. ¶ Sunt etiam sine infectione. In illis
temporalibus, quia est materia corruptibilis, locum habet
infectio. In hiis vero non, ubi perfecta erit nature purgatio.
Phil. ult. Deus meus impleat omne desiderium nostrum
secundum divitias suas in gloria in Christo Iesu, id est meritis
Christi Iesu, qui sine peccato fuit in via, et nunc sine pena in
gloria. Unde et per ipsum purga|bitur [*col. b*] natura nostra et
tunc erunt perfecta desideria. ¶ Hee sunt plene divitie quia ibi
erunt vera plena cognitio, sincera dilectio, perfecta fruitio,
continua laudatio. ¶ De primo Prover. xiiii Corona sapien-
tium divitie eorum. ¶ De secundo Iob. xxi. Iste moritur^m

---

^k Homines . . . prediti divitiis] sic *in ms, but cf. Ecclus. 44: 3.* ^l habundaverunt
divitiis] sic *in ms, but cf. Neh. 9: 25.* ^m moritur] moritus *ms.*

robustus, sanus, et dives et felix; viscera eius plena sunt adipe, et medullis ossa illius irrigantur; boni enim moriuntur in bonis gratuitis et ideo impinguantur adipe caritatis. ¶ De tertio Ps. Spera in domino, et fac bonitatem; et pasceris in divitiis eius. ¶ De quarto Ps. Filie Tyri in muneribus vultum tuum deprecabuntur; omnes divites plebis. Ista munera sunt laudis munia. Ista deprecatio est timor reverentialis, per quem est in se ipsum resilitio. ¶ Sunt etiam divitie supercelestes et ille sunt in deo. iii. Reg. x. Magnificatus est Salomon super omnes reges terre divitiis et sapientia. Iste vero sunt in magnificentia potentie, in sapientia providentie, in affluentia misericordie, et magnificentia glorie. ¶ De primo Ro. x. Idem dominus omnium, dives in omnes qui invocant illum. Dominus nomen est potentie. i. Paral. xxix. Tue sunt divitie, domine, et tua est gloria. Tu dominaris omnium. ¶ De secundo Ro.[1] xi. O altitudo divitiarum sapientie et scientie dei et cetera. ¶ De tertio Eph. ii. Deus, qui dives est in misericordia, propter nimiam caritatem suam, qua dilexit nos, cum essemus mortui peccatis vivificavit nos in Christo. Ro. ii. An divitias bonitatis, et patientie, et longanimitatis eius contempnis? ¶ De quarto Hester. i. Assuerus fecit grande convivium cunctis prin|cipibus [*fo. cxxx^{ra}*] et pueris suis ut ostenderet divitias glorie regni sui.

---

[1] There is an indication that the scribe began to write the abbreviation for *Regum*, then changed his mind.

Appendix

Preaching and the *Pecia* System of the Paris University Stationers

PARIS has a central place in the history of thirteenth-century mendicant preaching, not only because of the sermon collections written by Paris friars, but also because of the university stationers, who played an important role in diffusing model sermons and other preaching aids. This appendix groups together some of the details and technicalities of *pecia* transmission which are too rebarbative for the main text but too relevant to the theme of the book to be omitted. Section (i) is a preliminary working list of the mendicant preaching aids which were made available by the *pecia* system. Section (ii) is a case-study, dealing with the *pecia* transmission of the Franciscan *Collationes fratrum*.

In both parts the results are provisional. Despite the excellent work that has been done on the *pecia* system,[1] the ground has never been systematically cleared.[2] The task is important for the history of culture and for textual criticism.

It is true that a *pecia* manuscript tradition can by no means be presumed to be textually more reliable than manuscripts belonging

---

[1] The foundations were laid by J. Destrez, *La Pecia dans les manuscrits universitaires du XIIIᵉ et du XIVᵉ siècle* (Paris, 1935). The study of the system has been carried much further by the work of the Leonine Commission of Editors of Aquinas. For a summary of their progress see P. M. J. Gils, 'Codicologie et critique textuelle. Pour une étude du MS. Pamplona, Catédral 51', *Scriptorium*, 32 (1978), 221–30, at p. 225 n. 13. See too A. Brounts, 'Nouvelles Précisions sur la "pecia". A propos de l'édition léonine du commentaire de Thomas d'Aquin sur l'*Éthique* d'Aristote', *Scriptorium*, 24 (1970), 342–59, and J. P. Reilly, 'A Preliminary Study of a Pecia', *Revue d'histoire des textes*, 2 (1972), 239–50. Rouse and Rouse, *Preachers*, is among other things a model study of the *pecia* transmission of a preaching aid. I am indebted to Richard Rouse for constructive criticisms, and I have been helped at every turn by the advice of L.-J. Bataillon.

[2] Destrez did not live to complete his *opus magnum* on the subject. His *Nachlass*, now kept at the Couvent St-Jacques/Le Saulchoir in Paris, deserves to be edited at least in part. So far all that has appeared is J. Destrez and M. D. Chenu, '*Exemplaria* universitaires des XIIIᵉ et XIVᵉ siècles', *Scriptorium*, 7 (1953), 68–80. I abandoned an initial intention of presenting what I have learned from Destrez's *Nachlass* because of the difficulty of giving adequate references.

to a tradition independent of the university 'stationers' (or even equally reliable).[1] For all that, it may be that in a critical edition of a sermon collection the *pecia* tradition should be given a privileged position. A sermon collection by an obscure or anonymous author or compiler is important mainly because of its influence. An edition of one of these collections would not have the same purpose as an edition of a classical author or a great scholastic theologian, where the clear priority is to get as close to the author's text as possible. Unless the preacher is a great man, using sermons as a vehicle for original thought, it is arguable that we should concentrate on the most influential part of the tradition, which may often be a 'bad' *pecia* text.[2]

The textual criticism of *pecia* traditions has its own special problems. Sometimes there were two interchangeable sets of exemplar pieces; sometimes an exemplar piece got worn out and had to be remade; sometimes more than one consecutive exemplar piece was remade, and the divisions between the pieces within this block ended up in different places after the remaking. All this can make the edition of an entire text a formidably complicated undertaking. The edition of an individual sermon, from manuscripts all descended from one exemplar piece, would be much simpler than an assault on an entire collection. Piecemeal editions of this kind might also be a more intelligent way of tackling the problem of what the friars and their contemporaries preached. Editions of a number of sermons on the same texts and themes from different collections would probably be more economical of effort and productive of results than editions of entire collections by second-and third-rank preachers.

At present little editorial work of any kind has been done on *pecia* sermon collections. The field is wide open for scholars with the right textual gifts.[3] The catalogue of works which follows, dry as it is, should indicate at the same time the range of choice open to a friar

---

[1] Cf. A. Dondaine, 'Apparat critique de l'édition d'un texte universitaire', in '*L'Homme et son destin d'après les penseurs du Moyen Âge* (Actes du 1er Congrès International de Philosophie Médiévale [Louvain, 1958]; Louvain and Paris, 1960), 211–20, at pp. 211–12.

[2] Of course, one needs a readable text, and the editor will naturally make (not silently!) the emendations that an intelligent contemporary user would have made mentally.

[3] Use of the Destrez *Nachlass* would make the task easier. See above, p. 273 n. 2.

who wanted a preaching aid, and the range of opportunity open to modern researchers.

i. *Works for Preachers with a* Pecia *Transmission*

We have two lists of works made available by the *pecia* system at Paris, one for 1275 or shortly after,[1] the other for 1304.[2] I do not know whether they are both from the same 'stationers'. It is in any case a reasonable assumption, until proof to the contrary is forthcoming, that there were other stationers performing just the same function for whom lists have not survived. Nevertheless, these two lists make a natural starting-point.

The first sermon collection on the first of the two lists is entitled 'Sermones fratris Guillermi Lugdunensis de dominicis, super epistolis . . .'.[3] The author is Guillaume Peyraut (whose *Summa* of virtues and vices the béguine bought in Paris). These sermons on the Sunday Epistle seem to have been written after the 'vices' part of the *Summa* but before the 'virtues' part, and before Peyraut's sermons on the Sunday Gospels.[4] The next item on the *pecia* list is Peyraut's collection of 'Sermones . . . de sanctis'.[5] This collection (which includes sermons for great feasts like Epiphany as well as saints' sermons) survives in fewer manuscripts than the series on the Sunday Epistles and the Sunday Gospels,[6] which were in turn less widely copied than the immensely popular *Summa*.[7]

The next three names on the list are Thomas Lebreton,[8] Guillaume de Mailly,[9] and Pierre de Saint-Benoît.[10] They are an

---

[1] On the dating see Destrez, *La Pecia*, p. 32 n. 1.

[2] H. Denifle and A. Chatelain, *Chartularium*, ii/1 (Paris, 1891), 107–12, No. 642.

[3] Ibid. i (Paris, 1889), 647, No. 530.

[4] Dondaine, 'Guillaume Peyraut', p. 204.

[5] Denifle and Chatelain, *Chartularium*, i (Paris, 1889), 647, No. 530.

[6] Dondaine, 'Guillaume Peyraut', p. 205.

[7] For lists of manuscripts see Kaeppelli, *Scriptores*, ii. 133–47.

[8] 'Sermones fratris Thome Britonis de dominicis, tam de epistolis quam de evangeliis, lxj pecias, scilicet *Abiciamus* . . . Item, Sermones ejusdem *Precinxisti*, scilicet Commune Sanctorum, xlvij pecias . . .' (Denifle and Chatelain, *Chartularium*, i (Paris, 1889), 647).

[9] 'Item, Sermones *Abiciamus* de Mali de dominicis . . . Item, Sermones ejusdem de festis . . .' (ibid. 648).

[10] 'Item, Sermones fratris Petri de Sancto Benedicto, scilicet *Desideratus* de dominicis . . . Item, Sermones ejusdem de festis, scilicet *Suspendium* . . . Item, Commune Sanctorum, scilicet *Nimis honorati sunt* . . .' (ibid.).

obscure trio. It is at least fairly clear that Pierre de Saint-Benoît was a Franciscan.[1] It is also clear that he knew both Paris and Orleans[2] and that he was familiar with academic arrangements.[3] The two series by Thomas, which the list describes as 'de dominicis...' and '*Precinxisti*, scilicet Commune sanctorum' respectively, have only recently been identified.[4] Since he is called 'brother' he was not a secular priest; no firm evidence that he was a friar has yet been found, though it is likely enough at this particular period. Guillaume de Mailly is another shadowy figure. In his sermon on St Benedict he has quite a lot to say about monks,[5] but it would be rash to draw any firm inferences from this.

For the next two collections on the first *pecia* list no author is named, but on the other hand we can be a little more confident about the orders within which they were produced. The 'Sermones Alleabatenses'[6] would seem to be Dominican, if they may be identified with the 'Sermones attrebatenses (attrabetenses?) de ordine predicatorum' in a Troyes manuscript.[7] The next item on the list is a collection of 'sermons called *Legifer*',[8] which is certainly Franciscan.[9]

The *Legifer* collection has been called the 'most important of the *Collectiones fratrum*'[10]—this last phrase being used to designate the important body of anonymous Franciscan sermon collections.[11]

---

[1] This is attested by a Venice manuscript which has both an attribution and *pecia* indications: see Bataillon, 'Sur quelques sermons', p. 497 n. 10; pp. 496–502 of this article put Pierre on the map.

[2] See above, III. i, p. 161.

[3] See above, II. iv, pp. 114–15.

[4] By Bataillon, 'Approaches', pp. 26–7, and especially p. 34 n. 46, where he shows that they may be found under the name of Thomas de Lisle in Schneyer's *Repertorium*, v. 631–9 (*de tempore*), and 663–70 (*de communi sanctorum*).

[5] MS BN lat. 16475, fos. 302rb–307ra; sermon on the text 'Ingredere benedicte' (Gen. 24: 31), Schneyer, *Repertorium*, ii. 491, No. 104.

[6] 'Item Sermones Alleabatenses de dominicis...' (Denifle and Chatelain, *Chartularium*, i (Paris, 1889), 648).

[7] The words go with the beginning of a series of 'Omelie dominicales' in MS Troyes 1536, fo. 3^r (bottom). L.-J. Bataillon first drew my attention to this.

[8] 'Item, Sermones dicti *Legifer* tam de dominicis quam de festis pecias xxxv...' (Denifle and Chatelain, *Chartularium*, i (Paris, 1889), 648).

[9] D'Avray, '"Collectiones Fratrum" and "Collationes Fratrum"', p. 153.

[10] Schneyer, *Geschichte*, p. 159, and id., 'Die Erforschung der scholastischen Sermones', p. 8.

[11] Cf. J. B. Schneyer, 'Die überraschende Fülle der lateinischen Sermonesliteratur im frühen Franziskanerorden', *Franziskanische Studien*, 58 (1976), 122–8, at pp. 124–7.

The phrase *collectiones fratrum* would also seem to have a more specific, and contemporary, meaning. It is found in a Paris manuscript of the *Legifer* collection,[1] where it is probably a corruption or variant form of 'collationes fratrum'. The evidence for this is an Admont manuscript,[2] where the *festivale* part of the collection has the rubric 'Here begin the Feast-day sermons, from collations at the houses of the friars (*apud fratres*)'.[3] This would fit the system of *collationes* at Paris, but decisive evidence has yet to be found. There is not much colour in the *Legifer* collection, but it is a particularly good representative of some forms of thought characteristic of thirteenth-century preaching. It helps save one from the process of natural selection by which historians are attracted away from the more essential parts of a sermon by the patches which are entertaining or which tell him about social habits and customs. A detailed account of the problems which its *pecia* transmission poses is given in the second part of this appendix.

After *Legifer* in the *pecia* list comes a collection described as '... Sermones provinciales de Tussia, qui incipiunt *Sapientia Sanctorum* ...'. This description can only fit Aldobrandino Cavalcanti, whose Florentine context explains the 'Tuscia', and who did indeed write a sermon series beginning 'Sapientiam sanctorum narrant populi' (Ecclus. 44: 15).[4] Whether the Paris *pecia* system in fact played much part in the diffusion of this sermon collection is uncertain, for no manuscript of it with *pecia* indications is known; but it should become clear in the second part of this appendix that a shortage of surviving *pecia* manuscripts does not prove much. Aldobrandino is followed in the list by the entry '... Nova legenda omnium Sanctorum ...'. It seems likely that this is the *Golden Legend* of Jacopo da Varazze. There is nothing incongruous about this item: saints' *Lives* had their place in the spectrum of preaching aids.

There are three more relevant items in this first list. Two of them are sermon cycles of Nicolas de Biard: the 'Sermones Biardi, de dominicis ...' and the '... Sermones ejusdem de festis ...'. It has been argued that he was a Franciscan, but the arguments are taken

[1] D'Avray, '"Collectiones Fratrum" and "Collationes Fratrum"', p. 154 n. 1.

[2] Once again it was L.-J. Bataillon who told me of its existence.

[3] D'Avray, '"Collectiones Fratrum" and "Collationes Fratrum"', pp. 154–5.

[4] Schneyer, *Repertorium*, i. 169 ff. For his life see *Dizionario biografico degli Italiani*, xxii (Rome, 1979), 601–3.

from sermons which are not by him.[1] The last collection on the list, the 'Distinctiones Mauricii', must be those which Salimbene was asked to help compile by their Franciscan author.[2]

At the beginning of the fourteenth century several of the same collections were still on hire, as the *pecia* list for 1304 shows. On it we find the 'de dominicis et festis' sermons of Nicolas de Biard and Guillaume de Mailly,[3] and the 'Sermons of Lebreton' also reappear.[4] This must be the 'de dominicis' collection mentioned on the first list, for on both lists the number of pieces is sixty-one. Further down the later list there is a collection described as the 'Precinxisti' sermons,[5] which is presumably the same as the 'Commune sanctorum' series of the same name which is attributed to Thomas Lebreton on the first list, for the number of pieces is forty-seven in both cases.[6]

There are also some collections of sermons on the 1304 list which do not appear on the earlier one. An important addition is the *ad status* collection of Guibert de Tournai.[7] It was probably the most popular of the medieval collections of sermons *ad status*.[8] It is followed on this second list by the mysterious item 'In Sermonibus "Compendii" . . .'.[9] It does not appear on the first list and has not been identified. A less enigmatic newcomer is Guido d'Évreux: the entry 'In Sermonibus Guidonis . . .'[10] must refer to the elaborate preaching *Summa* described above (II. i). There is another set of sermons which finds a place in the 1304 list but not the earlier one, the summary sermons or 'themata' of Nicolas de Gorran.[11] They are listed together with his own works, not with the other sermon collections and preaching aids.

For the works which could have been useful to preachers seem

---

[1] See Bataillon, 'Approaches', p. 33 n. 42, correcting Hauréau and Schneyer.

[2] See above, p. 13.

[3] Denifle and Chatelain, *Chartularium*, ii/1 (Paris, 1891), 109.

[4] 'In Sermonibus Britonis, lxj pecias . . .' (ibid.).

[5] 'In Sermonibus "Precinxisti", xlvij pecias . . .' (ibid.).

[6] I cannot explain why the two series by Thomas Lebreton are separated on the second list.

[7] 'In Sermonibus Gilberti "Ad status" . . .' (Denifle and Chatelain, *Chartularium*, ii/1 (Paris, 1891), 109).

[8] Cf. d'Avray and Tausche, 'Marriage sermons', p. 85 and n. 62. I am not counting the *Communiloquium* of John of Wales as a sermon collection.

[9] Denifle and Chatelain, *Chartularium*, ii/1 (Paris, 1891), 109.

[10] Ibid. 110.

[11] 'Item, in Thematibus de diebus dominicis et sanctis, lxviij pecias. xxxij den.', included in the list of 'Opera fratris Nicolai de Gorham', ibid. 108.

to be grouped together. Only informally, for the group does not form a watertight compartment and it is not clearly marked off from what has gone before. One might conceivably take it to begin with the entry 'In Concordanciis Biblie',[1] for a concordance to the Bible must have been a great help in constructing a sermon in the form then fashionable. The next two entries are a treatise 'On the Properties of Things' and a 'Legend of the Saints'—presumably the well-known works by Bartholomew of England and Jacopo da Varazze respectively.[2] The latter work and just possibly the former could have been put in this part of the list because they were thought to be useful for preachers.

Nearly all the works on the list from this point to the beginning of the canon law section could have been useful to preachers—not only the sermon collections, but most of the others as well. The clearest exception is the *De ortu scientiarum*[3] of Robert Kilwardby. The *De oculo morali* of Pierre de Limoges is an ambiguous case. Is it a preaching aid or a scientific treatise? Probably the former, but the question may be badly posed: we assume that either the moralizing or the science must be the whole point, but this could reflect an anachronistic attitude to genre on our part.[4] The *De tribus dietis* of Robert de Sorbon,[5] whatever the purpose for which it was intended,[6] contains a great deal of material which would have been usable in a sermon or sermons on penitence. The *Lives of the Fathers*,[7] whose influence has not received the attention from historians that it deserves,[8] were a rich mine for *exempla*.

---

[1] Ibid. 109.

[2] 'De Proprietatibus rerum . . . In Legenda sanctorum . . .' (ibid.).

[3] Ibid. Now edited critically: Robert Kilwardby *De ortu scientiarum*, ed. Albert G. Judy, (Auctores Britannici Medii Aevi, 4; London, 1976).

[4] My examination of this work (listed in Denifle and Chatelain, *Chartularium*, ii/1 (Paris, 1891), 109) has been very cursory, but it deserves detailed study in the context of the general question of ambiguous genre in the period, and from this point of view it could usefully be compared with a work like the *Liber de moribus hominum et de officiis nobilium super ludo scaccorum* of Jacopo da Cessole.

[5] 'In Tribus dietis, xlj pecias . . .' (Denifle and Chatelain, *Chartularium*, ii/1 (Paris, 1891), 110.

[6] P. Glorieux, *Aux origines de la Sorbonne*, i. *Robert de Sorbon*, (Études de Philosophie Médiévale, 53; Paris, 1966), 56, describes it as a 'Traité de la pénitence à l'usage des fidèles . . .'—but were they meant to read it in Latin?

[7] 'De Vitis patrum, xliiij pecias . . .' (Denifle and Chatelain, *Chartularium*, ii/1 (Paris, 1891), 110).

[8] Cf. G. Philippart, 'Vitae Patrum. Trois travaux récents sur d'anciennes traductions latines', *Analecta Bollandiana*, 92 (1974), 353–65, especially p. 364.

Two works actually described as *exemplum* collections are listed:
the *Liber de exemplis sacre scripture* of Nicolaus de Hanapis, OP,[1]
and the 'De habundancia exemplorum'[2]—probably the work of that
title by Humbert de Romans.[3] Alphabetical books of material are
well represented. The list includes two (presumably) alphabetical
treatises listed as 'De abstinentia' and 'In accidia'.[4] The latter has
not to my knowledge been identified. It is likely that the former is
by Nicolas de Biard,[5] who also wrote a *distinctio* collection which is
listed under his name in this same *pecia* list.[6] The *distinctiones* of
Salimbene's friend Maurice de Provins, which were, as we have
seen, included in the earlier *pecia* list, reappear here.[7] There is,
finally, the *Pharetra*, an anthology of writings from the Fathers
arranged not in alphabetical but in systematic order.[8]

By no means all of the works 'published' by the stationers at Paris
appear on the two surviving *pecia* lists. We have, for instance, a
surviving *pecia* exemplar of Pierre de Reims's *Sermones de tempore
et de sanctis*,[9] and two of the vices sections of Peyraut's *Summa*;[10]
there is at least one *pecia* copy of sermons by Jean de la Rochelle;[11]
and, as those who have worked on Jean Destrez's papers will know,
the list of preaching aids with a *pecia* transmission could be
extended considerably further.[12] The range of works available from

---

[1] 'In Exemplis Sacre Scripture...' (Denifle and Chatelain, *Chartularium*, ii/1
(Paris, 1891), 109. Cf. Bloomfield, Guyot, Howard, and Kabealo, *Incipits*, p. 99, No.
1006, and Welter, *L'"Exemplum"*, pp. 230–3.
[2] Denifle and Chatelain, *Chartularium*, ii/1 (Paris, 1891), 109.
[3] Kaeppeli, *Scriptores*, ii. 285–7, No. 2012, and Welter, *L'"Exemplum"*, pp. 224–8.
Note, however, that there is also a work with the incipit 'Accidia. Homo accidiosus
est sicut canis famelicus', one of the titles of which is *Tractatus exemplorum de
habundancia adopcionum ad omnem materiam in sermonibus secundum ordinem
alphabeti*, which is possibly by John of Wales. See Bloomfield, Guyot, Howard, and
Kabealo, *Incipits*, p. 29, No. 0172.
[4] Denifle and Chatelain, *Chartularium*, ii/1 (Paris, 1891), 109.
[5] Cf. Bloomfield, Guyot, Howard, and Kabealo, *Incipits*, pp. 168–9, No. 1841.
There are other attributions.
[6] 'In Distinctionibus Byardi...' Denifle and Chatelain, *Chartularium*, ii/1 (Paris,
1891), 109. Cf. Bloomfield, Guyot, Howard, and Kabealo, *Incipits*, p. 23, Nos. 0103
and 0104.
[7] 'In Distinctionibus Mauritii, lxxxiiij pecias...' Denifle and Chatelain, *Chartularium*, ii/1 (Paris, 1891), 109.
[8] See above, II. i, especially p. 77.
[9] MS Assisi 452, according to Destrez and Chenu, *'Exemplaria'*, pp. 72 and 75.
[10] Ibid. 75.
[11] Duval-Arnould, 'Trois Sermons synodaux' (1976), 351, 353, 389.
[12] Attention may here be drawn to the material in Destrez's *Nachlass* on: Philippe
le Chancelier, Jean Halgrin d'Abbeville (and cf. *Catalogue* vi. 136), Évrard de Val

the stationers is thus impressive. This production of works for preachers within the penumbra of the university, taken together with activity of Paris friars in composing preaching aids, gives Paris a good claim to be regarded as a centre of mass communication as well as of scholastic thought.

ii. A Case of Pecia Transmission: the Collationes fratrum

The problems which can arise when we study a work with a *pecia* transmission, and the inferences which can sometimes be drawn about popularity and diffusion, may be illustrated from the case of the Franciscan *Collationes fratrum*. In the earlier Paris *pecia* list the work is described, as we have seen, as the 'Sermones dicti *Legifer* tam de dominicis quam de festis, pecias xxxv . . .' (above, n. 23). It has long been believed that MS Troyes 1215 is the *pecia* exemplar.[1] Only one obvious *pecia* copy of the whole work has come to light so far: MS Zurich, Zentralbibliothek Rh. 181. From this one might infer that the *pecia* 'edition' of the *Legifer* sermons was a commercial failure: one exemplar, one surviving copy of it, *ergo* little demand for it at Paris.

When the two manuscripts are compared in detail the picture becomes less clear-cut. It begins to appear that the Zurich manuscript cannot be a straightforward copy from the Troyes exemplar. In attempting to account for the odd relationship between the two manuscripts one is led to think that the *pecia* edition cannot after all have lain almost unused at the Paris stationers' shop. The data which the historian has to explain are set out below. By a 'physical' *pecia* I mean the quire or booklet which a scribe would hire out. In an exemplar the *pecia* mark ought to come

---

des Écoliers (=Eberhardus de Valle Scholarum) and, among the friars: Guillaume Peyraut, OP (especially for his *Summa* and his sermons on the Sunday Gospels); Guibert de Tournai, OM (especially for his liturgical sermon series); Jacques de Lausanne, OP; Bertrand de la Tour, OM; Guillaume 'de Lavicea', OM (for his *Dieta salutis*); and Arnould de Liège, OP, for his *Alphabetum narrationum*. Destrez discovered a *pecia* exemplar of the *Alphabetum*: see Destrez and Chenu, '*Exemplaria*', pp. 72 and 74. (When this book was going through the press L.-J. Bataillon informed me of another sermon collection, by Costantino da Orvieto, which has a *pecia* transmission. MS Arras 549 (formerly 840) is a copy with *pecia* marks. Apparently Destrez noticed the manuscript, but confused the modern and former call numbers.)

[1] Destrez and Chenu, '*Exemplaria*', pp. 74 and 75.

at the beginning of a physical *pecia*. In the *pecia* copy the mark can come anywhere in a quire, but should match the beginning of a physical *pecia* in the exemplar. If the marks are numbers it should be the same number. In the case of the Zurich and Troyes manuscripts everything is as it should be up to and including the start of the eighteenth *pecia* (except for the tenth). From the twenty-third to the start of the twenty-fifth *pecia* (inclusive) relations between the two manuscripts are again apparently normal. After that their relationship becomes very peculiar, as will be apparent.

MSS Zurich, Zentralbibliothek Rh. 181 (= Z), and Troyes, Bibliothèque Municipale 1215 (= T)

Pecia No.

3 *Pecia* mark in Z, fo. 265^v, corresponds to incipit of physical *pecia* in T, fo. 9^r.

4 *Pecia* mark in Z, fo. 268^r, corresponds to incipit of physical *pecia* in T, fo. 13^r.

5 *Pecia* mark in Z, fo. 270^v, corresponds to incipit of physical *pecia* in T, fo. 17^r.

6 *Pecia* mark in Z, fo. 273^v, corresponds to incipit of physical *pecia* in T, fo. 21^r.

7 Probable *pecia* mark in Z, fo. 276^r, corresponds to incipit of physical *pecia* in T, fo. 25^r.

8 *Pecia* mark in Z, fo. 278^v, corresponds to incipit of physical *pecia* in T, fo. 29^r.

9 *Pecia* mark in Z, fo. 280^v, corresponds to incipit of physical *pecia* in T, fo. 33^r.

10 Probable *pecia* mark in Z, fo. 282^v, does not match incipit of physical *pecia* in T, fo. 37^r. (In Z, fo. 282^v, there is an 'x' in inner margin beside the incipit of a sermon on the text 'Derelinquat impius viam suam . . .'. In T, fo. 37^r, a new physical *pecia* begins with the words 'peccatum; ipsi enim patri atribuitur potentia . . .'. These words occur in Z, fo. 283ra, but I can detect no *pecia* marks in the margin.)

11 *Pecia* mark in Z, fo. 285^r, corresponds to incipit of physical *pecia* in T, fo. 41^r.

12 *Pecia* mark in Z, fo. 287^v, corresponds to incipit of physical *pecia* in T, fo. 45^r.

13 *Pecia* mark in Z, fo. 290^r, corresponds to incipit of physical *pecia* in T, fo. 49^r.

14 *Pecia* mark in Z, fo. 292^v, corresponds to incipit of physical *pecia* in T, fo. 53^r.

15 *Pecia* mark in Z, fo. 295^r, corresponds to incipit of physical *pecia* in T, fo. 57^r.

16 *Pecia* mark in Z, fo. 297^v, corresponds to incipit of physical *pecia* in T, fo. 61^r.

17 *Pecia* mark in Z, fo. 300^r, corresponds to incipit of physical *pecia* in T, fo. 65^r.

18 *Pecia* mark in Z, fo. 303^r, corresponds to incipit of physical *pecia* in T, fo. 69^r.

19 Probable *pecia* mark in Z, fo. 306^v, inner margin, does *not* correspond to incipit of physical *pecia* in T, fo. 73^r.

20 Possible *pecia* mark in Z, fo. 309^v, outer margin, does *not* correspond to incipit of physical *pecia* in T, fo. 77^r. (The 'possible *pecia* mark in Z' might conceivably be a Scriptural reference.)

21 Probable *pecia* mark in Z, fo. 312^r, inner margin, does *not* correspond to incipit of physical *pecia* in T, fo. 85^r. (It is conceivable, but highly unlikely, that the 'xxi' in T is not a *pecia* indication, but refers instead to the 'Dominica xxi^a', the first sermon for which is on that page.)

22 Probable *pecia* mark in Z, fo. 314^v, inner margin, does not correspond to any division in T. (Again, the 'probable *pecia* mark in Z' might conceivably be a Scriptural reference.)

23 Beginning of the *de sanctis* series in both Z and T. *Pecia* marks at head of Z, fo. 319^r, and T, fo. 90^r.

24 *Pecia* mark in Z, fo. 322^r, corresponds to incipit of physical *pecia* in T, fo. 94^r.

25 *Pecia* mark in Z, fo. 324^v, corresponds to incipit of physical *pecia* in T, fo. 98^r.

26 *Pecia* mark in Z, fo. 327^v, inner margin (probably to be read 'xxvi'), corresponds to *pecia* mark ('xxvi^a') in T, fo. 102^v. (This is *not* the beginning of a physical *pecia*: the *pecia* number in the T occurs half-way down the outer margin of a verso folio!)

27 *Pecia* mark ('xxvii') in Z, fo. 330ᵛ, does *not* match *pecia* mark ('xxviiª') in T, fo. 107ʳ, but *does* correspond to incipit of page in T on which *pecia* mark occurs.

28 *Pecia* mark in Z, fo. 333ᵛ, inner margin, corresponds to *pecia* mark—*not* to a physical *pecia*—in T, fo. 111ᵛ, lower half of outer margin [much as in *pecia* 26, above, and also *pecia* 30, below].

? [In Z, fo. 336ᵛ, binder has amputated what may be a *pecia* mark.]

30 Probable *pecia* mark (partly amputated by binder) in Z, fo. 339ʳ, corresponds to *pecia* mark ('xxxª')—*not* to a physical *pecia*—in T, fo. 120ᵛ, outer margin; the *pecia* marks in the two manuscripts are roughly beside the beginning of a sermon.

31 *Pecia* mark in Z, fo. 342ʳ, corresponds to incipit of physical *pecia* in T, fo. 125ʳ.

32 In Z, fo. 346ʳ, *pecia* mark beside the words 'Can. iii ubi scriptum est per vicos et plateas queram', but no corresponding *pecia* mark beside these words in T.

33 *Pecia* mark (with the first 'x' concealed by the binding) in Z, fo. 349ʳ, corresponding to *pecia* mark ('xxxiiª'—*sic* for 'xxxiiiª') in T, fo. 134ʳ. In T the mark comes about half-way down the left-hand margin, so this is not a physical *pecia*.

34 Probable *pecia* mark (partly hidden by the binding) in Z, fo. 351ᵛ. Apparently no *pecia* mark in T.

35 Possible *pecia* mark (mostly amputated by binder) in Z, fo. 353ᵛ. Apparently no *pecia* mark in T.

A personal communication from L.-J. Bataillon lifted this complex problem on to a new plane with the suggestion that the Zurich manuscript is not after all a copy of the Troyes manuscript and that the Troyes manuscript is not the original true exemplar but an 'exemplar fallito',[1] that is to say, an abortive second exemplar. He pointed out that there are errors in the Troyes manuscript that

[1] A concept developed by Dr Concetta Luna, in connection with the transmission of Egidio da Roma's commentary on the Sentences.

have not been transmitted to the Zurich manuscript,[1] and that some of the physical signs associated with *pecia* exemplars seem to be significantly absent in the Troyes manuscript. He also observed that the scribe sometimes seemed to be trying to fill up space at the end of the quire, as though he were trying to make a facsimile of an existing *pecia* exemplar.

This theory has the ring of truth, and the added advantage of making some of the peculiarities we have observed a little easier to understand. It provides an explanation for the cases where the Troyes *pecia* mark comes *within* a quire (as if in a *pecia* copy rather than a *pecia* exemplar). What could have happened is that the scribe gave up his effort to make a facsimile *pecia*, but continued, for some reason, to note the *pecia* divisions in the exemplar he was copying. On this hypothesis he would have given up the effort to do a facsimile towards the end of the Sunday series, resumed it at the beginning of the Feast-day series, and then abandoned it again. The theory makes reasonable psychological sense of the behaviour of the Troyes scribe.

Two problems remain: the tenth *pecia* and the twenty-seventh *pecia*. A possible solution is that the original (lost) exemplar was being well used and that some pieces had to be remade. Suppose that the ninth and tenth *peciae* were remade together and that the break between the ninth and the tenth *peciae* was made at a new point (we know that this could happen[2]). The Zurich manuscript might have been copied from the lost true exemplar before these two *peciae* were remade, and the Troyes manuscript after.[3] The Zurich manuscript would reflect the original tenth *pecia*, and the Troyes manuscript the remade one.

The hardest problem is the twenty-seventh *pecia*. Why should the Zurich *pecia* mark fit, not the Troyes *pecia* mark, but the incipit of the page on which the Troyes *pecia* mark is found? The following explanation is offered only tentatively.

The twenty-sixth and twenty-seventh *peciae* were remade in the

---

[1] e.g. Z, fo. 373va: 'Excusatio in peccatis. Prov. xxii: Dicit piger: Leo est foris in medio platearum, occidendus sum. Item Prov. xx. Dicit piger: Leo est in via, leena in itineribus.' T, fo. 21ra, omits the words 'Prov. xxii: Dicit . . . sum. Item', through homoeoteleuton.

[2] Gils, 'Codicologie', p. 228.

[3] Alternatively, but less probably, the Troyes 'exemplar fallito' could have been copied before the remaking of these two pieces, and the Zürich manuscript after.

lost exemplar, not necessarily (indeed, probably not) at the time when the ninth and tenth *peciae* were remade. In the process the twenty-seventh *pecia* was begun at a slightly earlier point in the text than before. Nevertheless, the old *pecia* division was marked, some way down the first page of the new quire. (It would not be beyond the wit of man to guess reasons for this.) This was before either the Troyes or the Zurich manuscript was copied. When the scribe of the Troyes manuscript came to this point he tried to do a facsimile, beginning his quire at the new *pecia* division, but copying the mark, a little further on, which marked the original beginning (before the remaking) of the twenty-seventh *pecia*. The scribe of the Zurich manuscript ignored this mark in the lost exemplar, and simply indicated in his manuscript the passage which began the remade twenty-seventh *pecia* in the lost true exemplar. This is a very complicated hypothesis, but why should we expect a simple one?

However that may be, the existence of an 'exemplar fallito' (coupled with the possibility that some *peciae* had to be remade) suggests that the original lost exemplar must, despite appearances, have been sought after in Paris. If it had been left on the shelf all these complications might have been avoided. As it is, they are evidence that the *Legifer* was, after all, thought attractive in the circles which patronized the university stationers.

Bibliography

There is an excellent survey of recent work on medieval preaching which makes a systematic bibliography unnecessary: C. Delcorno, 'Rassegna di studi sulla predicazione medievale e umanistica (1970–80)', *Lettere italiane* (1981), 235–76. The most recent developments in the field can be followed in the valuable *Medieval Sermon Studies Newsletter*, published from the English Department of the University of Warwick, edited first by Gloria Cigman, and now by Pat Odber. J. Longère's *La Prédication médiévale* (Études Augustiniennes; Paris, 1983) is the most up-to-date general guide to the subject. One essay which I saw too late to make use of it in this book is important and relevant enough to deserve special mention: Zelina Zafarana, 'La Predicazione Francescana', in Società Internazionale di Studi Francescani, *Francescanesimo e vita religiosa dei Laici nel '200. Atti dell'VIII Convegno Internazionale, Assisi, 16-18 ottobre 1980* (Università degli Studi di Perugia; Assisi, 1981), 203–50. A subject which I have neglected, because I am not competent to deal with it, is the relation between preaching and architecture, on which see G. Meersseman, 'L'Architecture dominicaine au XIIIe siècle. Législation et pratique', *Archivum Fratrum Praedicatorum*, 16 (1946).

The following list includes only works to which reference has been made in the footnotes; nearly all the works cited have been included. To make it easier to find the full reference to works which are cited in an abbreviated form in the notes, I have not separated printed primary sources from modern secondary works and unpublished theses.

ALBERTANO DA BRESCIA, *Albertanus Brixiensis. Sermones Quatuor*, ed. M. Ferrari (Fondazione Ugo da Como; Lonato, n.d.).

ALESSANDRI, L., *Inventario dell'antica biblioteca del S. Convento di S. Francesco in Assisi compilato nel 1381* (Assisi, 1906).

ANTHONY OF PADUA, *Sermones dominicales et festivi*, three vols., edd. B. Costa *et al.* (Padua, 1979). [Ps.-] ANTHONY OF PADUA, in *Sancti Francisci... nec non S. Antonii Paduani... opera omnia*, ed. R. P. Joannis de la Haye (Regensburg, 1739).

AUGUSTINE, *De bono coniugali*, ed. J. Zycha, in *Corpus Scriptorum Ecclesiasticorum Latinorum*, 41 (Prague, Vienna, and Leipzig, 1900), xxviiii, 32.

BALDUINUS AB AMSTERDAM, 'The Commentary on St. John's Gospel, edited in 1589 under the name of St. Bonaventura, an authentic work of John of Wales, O.M. († ca.1300)', *Collectanea Franciscana*, 40 (1970), 71–96.

—— 'Tres sermones inediti Joannis de Rupella in honorem S. Antonii Patavini', *Collectanea Franciscana*, 28 (1958), 33–58.

BALDWIN, J. W., *Masters, Princes, and Merchants: The Social Views of Peter the Chanter and his Circle*, two vols. (Princeton, 1970).

BARRÉ, H., *Les Homéliaires Carolingiens de l'école d'Auxerre* (Studi e Testi, 225; Vatican City, 1962).

BARZILLAY-ROBERTS, P., *Stephanus de Lingua Tonante. Studies in the Sermons of Stephen Langton* (Toronto, 1968).

BATAILLON, L.-J., 'Approaches to the Study of Medieval Sermons', *Leeds Studies in English*, NS 11 (1980), 19–35.

—— 'Bulletin d'histoire des doctrines médiévales. Le treizième siècle (suite)', *Revue de sciences philosophiques et théologiques*, 64 (1980), 101–31.

—— 'Iacopo da Varazze e Tommaso d'Aquino', *Sapienza*, 32/1 (1979), 22–9.

—— 'La predicazione dei religiosi mendicanti del secolo xiii nell'Italia Centrale', *Mélanges de l'École Français de Rome. Moyen Âge—Temps Modernes*, 89/2 (1977), 691–4.

—— 'L'Emploi du langage philosophique dans les sermons du treizième siècle', in A. Zimmermann (ed.), *Sprache und Erkenntnis im Mittelalter* (Miscellanea Mediaevalia, Veröffentlichungen des Thomas-Instituts der Universität zu Köln, 13/2; Berlin and New York, 1981), 983–91.

—— 'Les Crises de l'Université de Paris d'après les sermons universitaires', in A. Zimmermann (ed.), *Die Auseinandersetzungen an der Pariser Universität im xiii. Jahrhundert* (Miscellanea Mediaevalia, Veröffentlichungen des Thomas-Instituts der Universität zu Köln, 10; Berlin and New York, 1976), 155–69.

—— 'Les Instruments de travail des prédicateurs au XIIIᵉ siècle', in G. Hasenohr and J. Longère (edd.), *Culture et travail intellectuel dans l'Occident médiéval* (Éditions du Centre National de la Recherche Scientifique; Paris, 1981), 197–209.

—— 'Sur quelques sermons de Saint Bonaventure', in *S. Bonaventura 1274–1974*, ii. *Studia de vita, mente, fontibus et operibus Sancti Bonaventurae* (Grottaferrata, 1973), 495–515.

BAYLEY, P., *French Pulpit Oratory 1598–1650. A Study in Themes and Styles, with a Descriptive Catalogue of Printed Texts* (Cambridge, 1980).

BEATRIJS VAN TIENEN, *Vita Beatricis. De Autobiografie van de Z. Beatrijs van Tienen O. Cist. 1200–1268*, ed. L. Reypens (Antwerp, 1964).

BEAUMONT-MAILLET, L., *Le Grand Couvent des Cordeliers de Paris.*

Étude historique et archéologique du XIIIᵉ siècle à nos jours
(Bibliothèque de l'École des Hautes Études, IVᵉ Section, 325;
Paris, 1975).

BENNETT, R. F., *The Early Dominicans. Studies in Thirteenth
Century Dominican History* (1937; reissued New York 1971).

BERG, D., *Armut und Wissenschaft. Beiträge zur Geschichte des
Studienwesens der Bettelorden im 13. Jahrhundert* (Geschichte und
Gesellschaft, 15; Düsseldorf, 1977).

BÉRIOU, N., 'La Prédication au béguinage de Paris pendant l'année
liturgique 1272–1273', *Recherches Augustiniennes*, 13 (1978),
105–229.

—— 'L'Art de convaincre dans la prédication de Ranulphe
d'Homblières', in *Faire Croire. Modalités de la diffusion et de la
réception des messages religieux du XIIᵉ au XVᵉ siècle* (Collection de
l'École Française de Rome, 51; Rome, 1981), 39–65.

—— 'Sermons aux clercs et sermons aux "simples gens": la
prédication de Ranulphe de la Houblonnière à Paris au XIIIᵉᵐᵉ
siècle', unpublished doctoral thesis ('troisième cycle') (Université
de Paris-Sorbonne (Paris-IV), 1980).

BERTHIER, J. J.: see Humbert de Romans.

BERTHOLD VON REGENSBURG, *Vollständige Ausgabe seiner Predigten*, edd. F. Pfeiffer and J. Strobl (Vienna, 1862 and 1880) [1965
reprint with 'Vorwort' and 'Anhang' by Kurt Ruh].

BIBLIOTHÈQUE NATIONALE: see *Catalogue générale* ...

BLOOMFIELD, M. W., GUYOT, B.-G., HOWARD, D. R., AND KA-
BEALO, T. B., *Incipits of Latin Works on the Virtues and Vices
1100–1500 A.D., including a Section of Incipits on the Pater Noster*
(Medieval Academy of America, 88; Cambridge, Mass., 1979).

BONAVENTURA, *Opera Omnia* (Quaracchi, 1882–1902).

—— *Sermones dominicales*, ed. J. G. Bougerol (Bibliotheca
Franciscana Scholastica Medii Aevi, cura PP. Collegii S. Bonaventurae, 27; Grottaferrata, 1977).

BONIFACIO, E.: see Guibert de Tournai.

BOUGEROL, J. G., *Introduction à l'étude de Saint Bonaventure*
(Tournai, 1961).

—— 'Les Sermons dans les "Studia" des Mendiants' in *Le
scuole* ... (q.v.), pp. 251–80.

—— (ed.).: see Bonaventura.

BOURGAIN, L., *La Chaire française au XIIᵉ siècle, d'après les
manuscrits* (Paris, 1879).

BOYLE, LEONARD, A Study of the Works Attributed to William of Pagula, with special reference to the *Oculus Sacerdotis* and *Summa Summarum*, unpublished D.Phil. thesis (Oxford, 1956).

—— 'The *Summa confessorum* of John of Freiburg and the Popularization of the Moral Teaching of St. Thomas and of Some of his Contemporaries', in Armand A. Maurer *et al.* (edd.), *St. Thomas Aquinas, 1274–1974. Commemorative Studies*, ii (Toronto, 1974), 245–68.

BRADY, I., 'Sacred Scripture in the Early Franciscan School', in *La Sacra Scrittura e i Francescani* [no editor] (Pontificium Athenaeum Antonianum and Studium Biblicum Franciscanum; Rome and Jerusalem, 1973), 65–82.

BRÉMOND, C., LE GOFF, J., AND SCHMITT, J.-C., *L''Exemplum'* (Typologie des Sources du Moyen Âge Occidental, 40; Brepols, Turnhout, 1982).

BROOMFIELD, F.: see Thomas of Chobham.

BROUNTS, A., 'Nouvelles Précisions sur la "pecia". A propos de l'édition léonine du commentaire de Thomas d'Aquin sur l'*Éthique* d'Aristote', *Scriptorium*, 24 (1970), 343–59.

BÜHLER, C. F., 'A Lollard Tract: On Translating the Bible into English', *Medium Aevum*, 7 (1938), 167–83.

CAPLAN, H., 'Classical Rhetoric and the Medieval Theory of Preaching', *Classical Philology*, 28 (1933), 73–96.

CASUTT, L., *Die Handschriften mit lateinischen Predigten Bertholds von Regensburg, O. Min.* ca.*1210–1272* (Fribourg, 1961).

Catalogue général des manuscrits latins, vi (Bibliothèque Nationale; Paris, 1975).

CENCI, C., *Bibliotheca manuscripta ad Sacrum Conventum Assisiensem* (Il miracolo di Assisi. Collana storico-artistica della basilica e del sacro convento di S. Francesco-Assisi, 4; Casa editrice Francescana: Assisi, Regione dell'Umbria, Sacro Convento di Assisi, 1981).

—— 'Il commento al Vangelo di S. Luca di Fr. Costantino da Orvieto, O.P. Fonte di S. Bernardino da Siena', *Archivum Franciscanum Historicum*, 74 (1981), 103–45.

CHAFFEE, S. H., 'Mass Media Effects: New Research Perspectives', in D. Lerner and L. M. Nelson (edd.), *Communication Research —A Half Century Appraisal* (Honolulu, 1977), 210–41; repr. in

Mass Communication Review Yearbook, (Beverley Hills and London, 1980), 77–108.

CHARLAND, TH.-M., *Artes praedicandi. Contribution à l'histoire de la rhétorique au Moyen Âge* (Publications de l'Institut d'Études Médiévales d'Ottawa, 7; Paris and Ottawa, 1936).

CHENU, M. D., *Introduction a l'étude de Saint Thomas d'Aquin* (Université de Montréal, Publications de l'Institut d'Études Médiévales, 11; Montreal and Paris, 1950).

—— *La Théologie comme science au XIIIᵉ siècle* (Paris, 1957).

—— 'Monks, Canons and Laymen in search of the Apostolic Life', in his *Man, Nature and Society in the Twelfth Century. Essays on New Theological Perspectives in the Latin West*, selected, edited, and trans. by J. Taylor and L. K. Little (Chicago University Press, 1968; Phoenix edn., 1979), 202–38.

—— see also Destrez and Chenu.

CLANCHY, M. T., *From Memory to Written Record. England 1066–1307* (London, 1979).

COSTA, B., et al.: see Anthony of Padua.

CRUEL, R., *Geschichte der deutschen Predigt im Mittelalter* (Detmold, 1879).

CURTIUS, E. R., *Europäische Literatur und lateinisches Mittelalter* (2nd edn., Berne, 1954).

DAVIS, C. T., 'An Early Florentine Political Theorist: Fra Remigio de'Girolami', *Proceedings of the American Philosophical Society*, 104/6 (1960), 662–76.

—— 'Education in Dante's Florence', *Speculum*, 40 (1965), 415–35.

D'AVRAY, D. L., 'A Franciscan and History', *Archivum Franciscanum Historicum*, 74 (1981), 456–82.

—— 'Another Friar and Antiquity', in K. Robbins (ed.), *Religion and Humanism* (Studies in Church History, 17; Oxford, 1981), 49–58.

—— '"Collectiones Fratrum" and "Collationes Fratrum"', *Archivum Franciscanum Historicum*, 70 (1977), 152–6.

—— 'Portable *Vademecum* books containing Franciscan and Dominican Texts', in A. C. de la Mare and B. C. Barker-Benfield, *Manuscripts at Oxford. An Exhibition in Memory of Richard William Hunt ... on Themes selected and described by some of his Friends* (Exhibition catalogue, Bodleian Library; Oxford, 1980), 60–4.

D'AVRAY, D. L., 'Sermons to the Upper Bourgeoisie by a Thirteenth-Century Franciscan', in D. Baker (ed.), *The Church in Town and Countryside,* (Studies in Church History, 16; Oxford, 1979), 187–99.

—— 'The Transformation of the Medieval Sermon', unpublished D.Phil. thesis (Oxford, 1976).

—— 'The Wordlists in the "Ars faciendi sermones" of Geraldus de Piscario', *Franciscan Studies,* 38, An. xvi (1978), 184–93.

—— AND M. TAUSCHE, 'Marriage Sermons in *Ad Status* Collections of the Central Middle Ages', *Archives d'histoire doctrinale et littéraire du Moyen Âge,* année 55, t. 47 (1980), 71–119.

DAVY, M. M., *Les Sermons universitaires parisiens de 1230–1231* . . . (Études de Philosophie Médiévale, 15; Paris, 1931).

DELCORNO, C., *Giordano da Pisa e l'antica predicazione volgare* (Biblioteca delle *Lettere Italiane,* 14; Florence, 1975).

—— 'Il racconto agiografico nella predicazione dei secoli xiii–xv', in *Atti dei convegni lincei,* 48. Covegno Internazionale, *Agiografia nell'occidente cristiano secoli xiii–xv* (Accademia Nazionale dei Lincei; Rome, 1980), 79–114.

—— *La predicazione nell'età comunale* (Florence, 1974).

—— 'Rassegna di studi sulla predicazione medievale e umanistica (1970–80)', *Lettere Italiane* (1981), 235–76.

DELISLE, L., *Le Cabinet des Manuscrits de la Bibliothèque Nationale,* ii (Paris, 1874).

—— 'Le Clergé normand au xiiiᵉ siècle', *Bibliothèque de l'École des Chartes,* 2. Série, 3 (1846), 479–99.

DELORME, F., 'L'"Ars faciendi sermones" de Géraud du Pescher', *Antonianum,* 19 (1944), 169–98.

DE MATTEIS, M. C., *La 'teologia politica comunale' di Remigio de' Girolami* (Bologna, 1977).

DENIFLE, H., AND CHATELAIN, A., *Chartularium Universitatis Parisiensis* (Paris, 1889–97).

DE ROOVER, R., *San Bernardino of Siena and Sant'Antonio of Florence. The Two Great Economic Thinkers of the Middle Ages* (Boston, Mass., 1967).

DESTREZ, J., *La Pecia dans les manuscrits universitaires du XIIIᵉ et du XIVᵉ siècle* (Paris, 1935).

—— AND CHENU, M. D., 'Exemplaria universitaires des XIIIᵉ et XIVᵉ siècles', *Scriptorium,* 7 (1953), 68–80.

DE TROEYER, B., *Bio-Bibliographia Franciscana Neerlandica ante*

Saeculum XVI, I. Pars Biographica: Auctores editionum qui scripserunt ante saeculum XVI (Nieuwkoop, 1974).

DEVAILLY, C., 'La Pastorale en Gaule au IXᵉ siècle', *Revue d'histoire de l'église de la France*, 59 (1973), 23–54.

DOBIACHE-ROJDESTVENSKY, O., *La Vie paroissiale en France au XIIIᵉ siècle d'après les actes épiscopaux* (Paris, 1911).

DONDAINE, A., 'Apparat critique de l'édition d'un texte universitaire', in *L'Homme et son destin d'après les penseurs du Moyen Âge* (Actes du 1ᵉʳ Congrès International de Philosophie Médiévale [Louvain, 1958]; Louvain and Paris, 1960), 211–20.

—— 'Documents pour servir à l'histoire de la province de France. L'Appel au Concil (1303)', *Archivum Fratrum Praedicatorum*, 22 (1952), 381–439.

—— 'Guillaume Peyraut. Vie et œuvres', *Archivum Fratrum Praedicatorum*, 18 (1948), 162–236.

DOUAIS, C., *Essai sur l'organisation des études dans l'ordre des Frères Prêcheurs au treizième et au quatorzième siècle 1216–1342* (Paris and Toulouse, 1884).

DOUIE, D. L., *Archbishop Pecham* (Oxford, 1952).

—— 'Archbishop Pecham's Sermons and Collations', in R. W. Hunt, W. A. Pantin, and R. W. Southern, (edd.), *Studies in Medieval History Presented to F. M. Powicke* (Oxford, 1948), 269–82.

DRONKE, P., *Poetic Individuality in the Middle Ages* (Oxford, 1970).

DUFEIL, M. M., *Guillaume de Saint-Amour et la polémique universitaire parisienne 1250–1259* (Paris, 1972).

DUVAL-ARNOULD, L., 'Trois Sermons synodaux de la collection attribuée à Jean de la Rochelle', *Archivum Franciscanum Historicum*, 69 (1976), 336–400; ibid. 70 (1977), 35–71.

ELM, K. (ed.), *Stellung und Wirksamkeit der Bettelorden in der städtischen Gesellschaft* (Berlin, 1981).

ÉTIENNE DE BOURBON, in A. Lecoy de la Marche (ed.), *Anécdotes historiques, légendes et apologues tirés du recueil inédit d'Étienne de Bourbon, Dominicain du XIIIᵉ siècle* (Société de l'Histoire de France; Paris, 1877).

Faire Croire. Modalités de la diffusion et de la réception des messages religieux du XIIᵉ au XVᵉ siècle (Collection de l'École Française de Rome, 51; Rome, 1981).

Felder, H., *Geschichte der wissenschaftlichen Studien im Franziskanerorden bis um die Mitte des 13. Jahrhunderts* (Freiburg im Breisgau, 1904).

Fidelis a Fanna, *Ratio novae collectionis... S. Bonaventurae* (Turin, 1874).

Forni, A., 'Kerygma e adattamento. Aspetti della predicazione cattolica nei secoli XII e XIV', *Bulletino dell'Istituto Storico Italiano per il Medio Evo e Archivio Muratoriano*, 89 (1980–1), 261–348.

—— 'La "Nouvelle Prédication" des disciples de Foulques de Neuilly: intentions, techniques et réactions', in *Faire Croire* (q.v.), pp. 19–37.

Franz, A., *Drei deutsche Minoritenprediger aus dem xiii. und xiv. Jahrhundert* (Freiburg im Breisgau, 1907).

Freed, J. B., *The Friars and German Society in the Thirteenth Century* (Cambridge, Mass., 1977).

Friend, A. C., 'Life and Works of Odo of Cheriton', in University of Oxford Committee for Advanced Studies, *Abstracts of Dissertations for the Degree of Doctor of Philosophy*, ix [dissertations accepted during 1936] (Oxford, 1937), 43–8.

—— 'Master Odo of Cheriton', *Speculum*, 23 (1948), 641–58.

Gatch, M. McG., *Preaching and Theology in Anglo-Saxon England: Ælfric and Wulfstan* (University of Toronto Press: Toronto and Buffalo, 1977).

Gils, P.-M. J., 'Codicologie et critique textuelle. Pour une étude du MS. Pamplona, Catedral 51', *Scriptorium*, 32 (1978), 221–30.

Gilson, E., 'Michel Menot et la technique du sermon médiéval', repr. in his *Les Idées et les lettres* (Paris, 1932), 93–154.

Girotto, S., *Corrado di Saxonia, predicatore e mariologo del sec. xiii* (Biblioteca di Studi Francescani, 3; Florence, 1952).

Glorieux, P., *Aux origines de la Sorbonne, i. Robert de Sorbon* (Études de Philosophie Médiévale, 53; Paris, 1966).

—— 'L'Enseignement au Moyen Âge. Techniques et méthodes en usage à la Faculté de Théologie de Paris au XIIIᵉ siècle', *Archives d'histoire doctrinale et littéraire du Moyen Âge*, année 43, t. 35 (1968), 65–186.

—— *Répertoire des maîtres en théologie de Paris au XIIIᵉ siècle*, two vols. (Études de Philosophie Médiévale, 17, 18; Paris, 1933).

—— 'Sermons universitaires parisiens de 1267–1268', *Recherches de théologie ancienne et médiévale*, 16 (1949), 40–71.

GRABMANN, M., *Die Geschichte der scholastischen Methode*, i (Freiburg im Breisgau, 1909).

GRUNDMANN, H., *Religiöse Bewegungen im Mittelalter* (Berlin, 1935) [the later edition (Darmstadt, 1970) includes 'Neue Beiträge'].

GUERRINI, P., 'Gli statuti di un'antica Congregazione Franciscana di Brescia', *Archivum Franciscanum Historicum*, 1 (1908), 544–68.

GUIBERT DE TOURNAI, *De modo addiscendi*, ed. E. Bonifacio (Turin, 1953).

—— *Tractatus de pace*, ed. E. Longpré (Quaracchi, 1925).

GUITTON, J., *Le Temps et l'éternité chez Plotin et Saint Augustin* (Paris, 1933).

HASKINS, C. H., 'The University of Paris in the Sermons of the Thirteenth Century', in *Studies in Medieval Culture* (Oxford, 1929), 36–71.

HASKINS, G. L., AND KANTOROWICZ, E. H., 'A Diplomatic Mission of Francis Accursius and his Oration before Pope Nicholas III', *English Historical Review*, 58 (1943), 424–47.

HAURÉAU, B., *Notices et extraits de quelques manuscrits latins de la Bibliothèque Nationale*, six vols. (Paris, 1890–3).

HINNEBUSCH, J. F.: see Jacques de Vitry.

HINNEBUSCH, W. A., *The Early English Friars Preachers* (Rome, 1951).

—— *The History of the Dominican Order*, i (New York, 1966), ii (New York, 1973).

Historia Occidentalis: see Jacques de Vitry.

HOLDER-EGGER, O.: see Salimbene.

HOLDSWORTH, C. J., *'Another Stage... a Different World'. Ideas and People around Exeter in the Twelfth Century* (Exeter, 1979).

HOLMES, G., 'The Emergence of an Urban Ideology at Florence c.1250–1450', *Transactions of the Royal Historical Society*, 5th ser., 23 (1973), 111–34.

HUDSON, A., *English Wycliffite Sermons*, i (Oxford, 1983).

HUIZINGA, J., *The Waning of the Middle Ages* (London, 1924).

HUMBERT DE ROMANS, *De eruditione praedicatorum*, in *Maxima Biblioteca Veterum Patrum*, xxv, (Lyons, 1677).

HUNT, R. W., 'English Learning in the Late Twelfth Century',

Transactions of the Royal Historical Society, 4th ser., 19 (1936), 19–35.

JACOPO DA VARAZZE, *Legenda Aurea vulgo Historia Lombardica dicta*, ed. Th. Graesse (Dresden and Leipzig, 1846).

JACQUES DE VITRY, *The Historia Occidentalis of Jacques de Vitry. A critical edition*, ed. J. F. Hinnebusch, OP (Spicilegium Friburgense, 17; Fribourg, 1972).

—— *Sermones in Epistolas et Evangelia dominicalia* (Antwerp, 1575).

JEAN DE LA ROCHELLE, *Eleven Marian Sermons*, ed. K. F. Lynch (Franciscan Institute Publications, Text Series, No. 12; The Franciscan Institute, St-Bonaventure; New York, Louvain, and Paderborn, 1961).

—— '*Tractatus de divisione multiplici potentiarum animae*, ed. P. Michaud-Quantin (Paris, 1964).

—— 'Tres sermones inediti . . . in honorem S. Antonii Patavini': see Balduinus ab Amsterdam.

JORDAN, W. C., *Louis IX and the Challenge of the Crusade* (Princeton University Press, 1979).

KAEPPELI, T., 'Der literarische Nachlass des sel. Bartholomaeus von Vicenza O.P. (†1270)', in *Mélanges Auguste Pelzer* (Université de Louvain, Recueil de Travaux d'Histoire et de Philologie, 3ᵐᵉ Série, 26ᵐᵉ Fascicule; Louvain, 1947), 275–301.

—— *Scriptores Ordinis Praedicatorum Medii Aevi* (Rome, 1970–).

KEPPLER, D., 'Beiträge zur Entwicklungsgeschichte der Predigtanlage', *Theologische Quartalschrift* (Tübingen), 74 (1892), 52–120, 179–212.

KER, N. R., *Catalogue of Manuscripts Containing Anglo-Saxon* (Oxford, 1957).

KNOWLES, D., *The Religious Orders in England*, i (Cambridge, 1948).

—— AND HADCOCK, R. N., *Medieval Religious Houses: England and Wales* (London, 1971).

LANGLOIS, CH.-V., 'L'Éloquence sacrée au Moyen Âge', *Revue des deux mondes*, 115 (1893), 170–201.

LAZZERINI, L., '"Per Latinos Grossos . . ." Studio sui sermoni mescidati', *Studi di Filologia Italiana*, 29 (1971), 219–339.

LE BRAS, G., 'Conceptions of Economy and Society', in M. M. Postan *et al.* (edd.), *The Cambridge History of Europe*, iii. *Economic Organization and Policies in the Middle Ages* (Cambridge, 1963), 554–75.

LECLERCQ, J., 'Le Florilège d'Abbon de Saint-Germain', *Revue du Moyen Âge latin*, 3 (1947), 113–40.

—— *L'Idée de la royauté du Christ au Moyen Âge* (Unam Sanctam, 32; Paris, 1959).

—— 'Le Magistère du prédicateur au XIIIᵉ siècle', *Archives d'histoire doctrinale et littéraire du Moyen Âge*, 21 (1946), 105–47.

—— *Monks and Love in Twelfth-Century France* (Oxford, 1979).

—— *Recueil des études sur St Bernard et ses écrits*, iii (Rome, 1969).

LECOY DE LA MARCHE, A., *La Chaire française au Moyen Âge*... (2nd edn., Paris, 1886).

—— (ed.): see Étienne de Bourbon.

LE GOFF, J., 'Apostolat mendiant et fait urbain dans la France médiévale: L'implantation des ordres mendiants. Programme-questionnaire pour une enquête', *Annales Économies, sociétés, civilisations*, 23/2 (1968), 335–52.

—— *et al.*, 'Enquête du Centre de Recherches Historiques: Ordres Mendiants et urbanisation dans la France médiévale', *Annales: Économies, sociétés, civilisations*, 25/4 (1970), 924–65.

Le scuole degli Ordini Mendicanti (secoli xiii–xiv) (Convegni del Centro di Studi sulla Spiritualità Medievale, 17 [1976]; Academia Tudertina: Todi, 1978).

LESNICK, D. R., 'Dominican Preaching and the Creation of Capitalist Theology in Late-Medieval Florence', *Memorie domenicane*, NS 8–9 (1977–8), 199–247 [not seen].

—— 'Popular Dominican Preaching in Early Fourteenth-Century Florence', unpublished Ph.D. thesis (Rochester, 1976) [University Microfilm International Cat. No. 76,24013].

LINSENMAYER, A., *Geschichte der Predigt in Deutschland von Karl dem Grossen bis zum Ausgange des vierzehnten Jahrhunderts* (Munich, 1886).

LITTLE, A. G. (ed.), *Liber exemplorum ad usum praedicantium saeculo xiii* (British Society of Franciscan Studies, 1; Aberdeen, 1908).

—— *Studies in English Franciscan History* (Publications of the University of Manchester, Historical Series, 29; Manchester University Press and London, 1917).

LITTLE, A. G., AND PELSTER, F., *Oxford Theology and Theologians* c.*a.d.* *1282-1302* (Oxford Historical Society, 96; Oxford, 1934).

LITTLE, L. K., *Religious Poverty and the Profit Economy in Medieval Europe* (London, 1978).

LONGÈRE, J., *La Prédication médiévale* (Études Augustiniennes; Paris, 1983).

—— *Œuvres oratoires de maîtres parisiens au XIIe siècle. Étude historique et doctrinale*, two vols. (Études Augustiniennes; Paris, 1975).

LONGPRÉ, E., 'Bonaventure (Saint)', in *Dictionnaire d'histoire et de géographie ecclésiastique*, ix (Paris, 1937), cols. 741–88.

—— (ed.): see Guibert de Tournai.

LYNCH, K. F., (ed.): see Jean de la Rochelle.

MACKINNON, H., 'The Life and Works of William de Montibus', unpublished D.Phil. thesis (Oxford, 1959).

—— 'William de Montibus, a Medieval Teacher', in T. A. Sandquist and M. R. Powicke (edd.), *Essays in Medieval History presented to Bertie Wilkinson* (Toronto, 1969), 32–45.

MCKITTERICK, R., *The Frankish Church and the Carolingian Reforms, 789-895* (London, 1977).

MANSI, *Sacrorum conciliorum nova et amplissima collectio* . . ., xxii (Venice, 1778).

MEERSSEMAN, G., 'La Prédication dominicaine dans les congrégations Mariales en Italie au XIIIe siècle', *Archivum Fratrum Praedicatorum*, 18 (1948), 131–61.

—— 'Notice bio-bibliographique sur deux frères prêcheurs silésiens du xiv s. nommés Peregrinus', *Archivum Fratrum Praedicatorum*, 19 (1949), 266–74.

MERCIER, P., *XIV homélies du IXe siècle* (Sources Chrétiennes, 161, Paris, 1970).

MICHAUD-QUANTIN, P., 'Guy d'Évreux O.P., technicien du sermonnaire médiéval', *Archivum Fratrum Praedicatorum*, 20 (1950), 213–33.

—— (ed.): see Jean de la Rochelle.

—— *Sommes de casuistique et manuels de confession au Moyen Âge* (Analecta Mediaevalia Namurcensia, 13; Louvain, Lille, and Montreal, 1962).

MOORMAN, J. R. H., *A History of the Franciscan Order from its Origins to the year 1517* (Oxford, 1968).

MORVAY, K., AND GRUBE, D., ['unter Leitung von Kurt Ruh'], *Bibliographie der deutschen Predigt des Mittelalters. Veröffentlichte Predigten* (Münchener Texte und Untersuchungen zur deutschen Literatur des Mittelalters, 47; Munich, 1974).

MOURIN, L., *Jean Gerson, prédicateur français* (Bruges, 1952).

—— *Six Sermons français inédits de Jean Gerson* (Paris, 1946).

MURPHY, J. J., *Rhetoric in the Middle Ages. A History of Rhetorical Theory from Saint Augustine to the Renaissance* (Berkeley, Los Angeles, and London, 1974).

MURRAY, A., 'Piety and Impiety in Thirteenth-Century Italy', in C. J. Cuming and D. Baker (edd.), *Popular Belief and Practice* (Studies in Church History, 8; Cambridge, 1972), 83–106.

—— *Reason and Society in the Middle Ages* (Oxford, 1978).

—— 'Religion among the Poor in Thirteenth-Century France: The Testimony of Humbert de Romans', *Traditio*, 30 (1974), 285–324.

O'CARROLL, M., 'The Educational Organisation of the Dominicans in England and Wales 1221–1248: a Multidisciplinary Approach', *Archivum Fratrum Praedicatorum*, 50 (1980), 23–62.

—— 'The Lectionary for the Proper of the Year in the Dominican and Franciscan rites of the thirteenth century', *Archivum Fratrum Praedicatorum*, 49 (1979), 79–103.

OLIGER, P. L., 'Liber exemplorum fratrum minorum saeculi xiii (excerpta e cod. Ottob. Lat. 522)', *Antonianum*, 2 (1927), 203–76.

—— 'Servasanto da Faenza O.F.M. e il suo "Liber de Virtutibus et Vitiis"', in *Miscellanea Francesco Ehrle*, i. *Per la storia della teologia e della filosofia* (Studi e Testi, 37; Rome, 1924), 148–89.

O'MALLEY, J. W., *Praise and Blame in Renaissance Rome. Rhetoric, Doctrine, and Reform, in the Sacred Orators of the Papal Court, c.1450–1521* (Duke University Press, 1979).

OMONT, H. A., *Concordances des numéros anciens et des numéros actuels des manuscrits latins de la Bibliothèque Nationale...* (Paris, 1903).

ORLANDI, S., *'Necrologio' di S. Maria Novella*, i (Florence, 1955).

OWST, J. R., *Literature and Pulpit in Medieval England* (2nd edn., Oxford, 1961).

—— *Preaching in Medieval England* (Cambridge University Press, 1926).

PANTIN, W. A., 'John of Wales and Medieval Humanism', in J. A. Watt *et al.* (edd.), *Medieval Studies Presented to Aubrey Gwynn S.J.* (Dublin, 1961).

PARKES, M. B., 'The Literacy of the Laity', in D. Daiches and A. Thorlby (edd.), *Literature and Western Civilization. The Medieval World* (London, 1973).

PATTISON, M., 'Tendencies of Religious Thought in England, 1688–1750', in *Essays and Reviews* (2nd edn., London, 1860).

PERUZZI, S. L., *Storia del commercio e dei banchieri di Firenze in tutto il mondo conosciuto dal 1200 al 1345* (Florence, 1868).

PFANDER, H. G., *The Popular Sermon of the Medieval Friar in England* (New York, 1937).

PFEIFFER, F., AND STROBL, J. (edd.): see Berthold von Regensburg.

PHILIPPART, G., 'Vitae Patrum. Trois travaux récents sur d'anciennes traductions latines', *Analecta Bollandiana*, 92 (1974), 353–65.

PICKERING, F. P., 'On Coming to Terms with Curtius', in his *Essays on Medieval German Literature and Iconography* (Cambridge University Press, 1980).

PIRENNE, H., 'L'Instruction des marchands au Moyen Âge', *Annales d'histoire économique et sociale*, 1 (1929), 13–28.

POWICKE, F. M., *The Thirteenth Century 1216-1307* (Oxford, 1962).

—— AND CHENEY, C. R., *Councils and Synods with other Documents relating to the English Church*, ii, two parts (Oxford, 1964).

Rashdall's Medieval Universities, edd. F. M. Powicke and A. B. Emden (Oxford, 1936).

REILLY, J. P., 'A Preliminary Study of a Pecia', *Revue d'histoire des textes*, 2 (1972), 239–50.

REMIGIO DE' GIROLAMI, OP, *Contra falsos ecclesie professores*, ed. F. Tamburini [with a preface by C. T. Davis] ('Utrumque Ius', Collectio Pontificiae Universitatis Lateranensis, 6; Rome, 1981).

RENARD, J.-P., *La Formation et la désignation des prédicateurs au début de l'Ordre des Prêcheurs (1215-1237)* (Fribourg, 1977).

REYPENS, L., (ed.): see Beatrijs van Tienen.

RHODES, W. E., 'The Italian Bankers in England and their Loans to Edward I and Edward II', in T. F. Tout and J. Tait (edd.), *Historical Essays, first published in 1902 in commemoration of the Jubilee of the Owens College, Manchester* (Publications of the

University of Manchester, Historical Series, No. 6; Manchester, 1907).

RICHTER, D., *Die deutsche Überlieferung der Predigten Bertholds von Regensburg* (Münchener Texte und Untersuchungen zur deutschen Literatur des Mittelalters, 21; Munich, 1969).

ROBERTSON, D. W., 'Frequency of Preaching in Thirteenth-Century England', *Speculum*, 24 (1949), 376–88.

ROBSON, C. A., *Maurice of Sully and the Medieval Vernacular Homily* . . . (Oxford, 1952).

ROGER BACON, Fr. *Rogeri Bacon opera quaedam hactenus inedita* ed. J. S. Brewer (Rolls Series, London, 1859).

ROSENWEIN, B. H., AND LITTLE, L. K., 'Social Meaning in Monastic and Mendicant Spiritualities', *Past and Present*, 63 (1974), 4–32.

ROUSE, R. H., AND ROUSE, M. A., 'Biblical Distinctions in the Thirteenth Century', *Archives d'histoire doctrinale et littéraire du Moyen Âge*, année 49, t. 41 (1975), 27–37.

—— and —— *Preachers, Florilegia and Sermons: Studies on the Manipulus florum of Thomas of Ireland* (Toronto, 1979).

—— 'The Verbal Concordance to the Scriptures', *Archivum Fratrum Praedicatorum*, 44 (1974), 5–30.

RUSCONI, R., 'Predicatori e predicazione (secoli IX–XVIII)', in the Einaudi *Storia d'Italia, Annali 4*, pp. 951–1035.

—— *Predicazione e vita religiosa nella società italiana da Carlo Magno alla Contrariforma* (Documenti della Storia, 30; Turin, 1981).

SALIMBENE, *Cronica Fratris Salimbene de Adam*, ed. O. Holder-Egger, in Monumenta Germaniae Historica, Scriptores, vol. xxxii (1905–13).

S. Bonaventura 1274–1974, five vols. (Collegio S. Bonaventura; Grottaferrata, 1973–4).

SCHMITT, J.-C., *Le Saint Lévrier. Guinefort, guérisseur d'enfants depuis le XIIIᵉ siècle* (Paris, 1979).

—— 'Recueils franciscains d'"exempla" et perfectionnement des techniques intellectuels du XIIIᵉ au XVᵉ siècle', *Bibliothèque de l'École des Chartes*, 135 (1977), 5–21.

SCHNEYER, J. B., *Beobachtungen zu lateinischen Sermoneshandschriften der Staatsbibliothek München* (Bayerische Akademie der Wissenschaft, philosophisch-historische Klasse, Sitzungsberichte, Jahrgang 1958, Heft 8; Munich, 1958).

SCHNEYER, J. B., 'Die Erforschung der scholastischen Sermones und ihre Bedeutung für die Homiletik', *Scholastik*, 39 (1964), 1–26.

—— 'Die überraschende Fülle der lateinischen Sermonesliteratur im frühen Franziskanerorden', *Franziskanische Studien*, 58 (1976), 122–8.

—— *Die Unterweisung der Gemeinde über die Predigt bei scholastischen Predigern. Eine Homiletik aus scholastischen Prothemen* (Munich, Paderborn, and Vienna, 1968).

—— *Geschichte der katholischen Predigt* (Freiburg im Breisgau, 1969).

—— 'Predigten Alberts des Grossen in der Hs. Leipzig, Univ. Bibl. 683', *Archivum Fratrum Praedicatorum*, 34 (1964), 45–106.

—— *Repertorium der lateinischen Sermones des Mittelalters für die Zeit von 1150–1350*, 9 vols. to date (Münster, 1969–80).

—— 'Winke für die Sichtung und Zuordnung spätmittelalterlicher lateinischen Predigtreihen', *Scriptorium*, 32/2 (1978), 231–48.

SCHÖNBACH, A., 'Studien zur Geschichte der altdeutschen Predigt. Fünftes Stück: Die Überlieferung der Werke Bertholds von Regensburg, II', *Sitzungsberichte der philosophisch-historischen Klasse der kaiserlichen Akademie der Wissenschaft* [Vienna], 152 (1906), 1–112.

SMALLEY, B., *English Friars and Antiquity in the Early Fourteenth Century* (Oxford, 1960).

—— 'L'Uso della Scrittura nei "Sermones" di Sant'Antonio', in *Il Santo*, 21, ser. II, fasc. 1 (1981), 3–16.

—— 'Oxford University Sermons 1290–1293', in J. J. G. Alexander and M. T. Gibson (edd.), *Medieval Learning and Literature. Essays presented to Richard William Hunt* (Oxford, 1976), 307–27.

—— 'Peter Comestor on the Gospels and His Sources', *Recherches de théologie ancienne et médiévale*, 46 (1979), 84–129.

—— 'Robert Bacon and the early Dominican School at Oxford', *Transactions of the Royal Historical Society*, 30 (1948), 1–19.

—— 'The Bible in the Medieval Schools', in *The Cambridge History of the Bible*, ii. *The West from the Fathers to the Reformation*, ed. G. W. H. Lampe (Cambridge, 1969), 197–220.

—— 'The Gospels in the Paris Schools in the late 12th and early 13th Centuries. Peter the Chanter, Hugh of St-Cher, Alexander of Hales, John of La Rochelle', *Franciscan Studies*, 39, An. xvii (1979), 230–54; ibid. 40, An. xviii (1980), 298–369.

—— *The Study of the Bible in the Middle Ages* (2nd edn., Oxford, 1952).

SMETANA, C. L., 'Ælfric and the Early Medieval Homiliary', *Traditio*, 15 (1959), 163–204.

—— 'Ælfric and the Homiliary of Haymo of Halberstadt', *Traditio*, 17 (1961), 457–69.

SOUTHERN, R. W., 'Meister Eckhart', in his *Medieval Humanism and other Studies* (Oxford, 1970), 19–26.

SPENCER, H., 'English Vernacular Sunday Preaching in the Late Fourteenth and Fifteenth Century, with Illustrative Texts', unpublished D.Phil. thesis (Oxford, 1982).

SPICQ, C., *Esquisse d'une histoire de l'exégèse latine au Moyen Âge* (Bibliothèque Thomiste, 26; Paris, 1944).

STAMM, G., *Predigten des 'Schwarzwälder Predigers'*, (Kleine deutsche Prosadenkmäler des Mittelalters, 12; Munich, 1973).

—— *Studien zum 'Schwarzwälder Prediger'* (Medium Aevum, 18; Munich, 1969).

Storia d'Italia, Einaudi, vol. ii/1 (Turin, 1974).

SWEET, J., 'English Preaching 1221–1293', unpublished B.Litt. thesis, (Oxford, n.d.).

—— 'Some Thirteenth-Century Sermons and their Authors', *Journal of Ecclesiastical History*, 4 (1953), 27–36.

TAMBURINI, F. (ed.): see Remigio de' Girolami.

THOMAS OF CHOBHAM, *Summa confessorum*, ed. F. Broomfield (Analecta Mediaevalia Namurcensia, 25: Louvain and Paris, 1968).

THOMSON, W. R., 'The Image of the Mendicants in the Chronicles of Matthew Paris', *Archivum Franciscanum Historicum*, 70 (1977), 3–34.

TIBBER, P., 'The Origins of the Scholastic Sermon, *c.*1130–*c.*1210', unpublished D.Phil. thesis (Oxford, 1983).

UNGUREANU, M., *La Bourgeoisie naissante. Société et littérature bourgeoises d'Arras au XIIe et XIIIe siècles* (Mémoires de la Commission des monuments historiques du Pas de Calais, 8; Arras, 1955).

VALOIS, N., *Guillaume d'Auvergne, évêque de Paris (1228–1249)*. *Sa vie et ses ouvrages* (Paris, 1880).

VAN DER WALT, A., 'Bede's Homiliary and Early Medieval Preaching, unpublished Ph.D. thesis (London, 1980).

Vita Beatricis: see Beatrijs von Tienen.

VÖLKER, P.-G., 'Die Überlieferungsformen mittelalterlicher deutscher Predigten', *Zeitschrift für deutsches Altertum und deutsche Literatur*, 92 (1963), 212–27.

VON NAGY, M., AND DE NAGY, N. C., *Die Legenda aurea und ihr Verfasser Jacobus de Voragine* (Berne and Munich, 1971).

WEISHEIPL, J. A., *Friar Thomas d'Aquino. His Life, Thought, and Work* (New York, 1974; 2nd edn., Oxford, 1975).

WELTER, J.-TH., *L'"Exemplum" dans la littérature religieuse et didactique du Moyen Âge* (Paris and Toulouse, 1927).

WENZEL, S., *Verses in Sermons. Fasciculus morum and its Middle English Poems* (Cambridge, Mass., 1978).

WILLIAMS-KRAPP, W., 'Das Gesamtwerk des sog. "Schwarzwälder Predigers"', *Zeitschrift für deutsches Altertum*, 107 (1978), 50–80.

ZERFASS, R., *Der Streit um die Laienpredigt. Eine pastoralgeschichtliche Untersuchung zum Verständnis des Predigtamtes und zu seiner Entwicklung im 12. und 13. Jahrhundert* (Freiburg im Breisgau, Basle, and Vienna, 1974).

ZIEGLER, J. G., *Die Ehelehre der Pönitentialsummen von 1200–1350* (Regensburg, 1956).

ZINK, M., *La Prédication en langue romane avant 1300* (Nouvelle Bibliothèque du Moyen Âge, 4; Paris, 1976).

ZUMKELLER, A., *Manuskripte von Werken der Autoren des Augustiner-Eremitenordens in mitteleuropäischen Bibliotheken* (Cassiciacum, 20; Würzburg, 1966).

INDEX OF MANUSCRIPTS

I exclude manuscripts which are mentioned in the book but which I have not worked on. Chapter and section references are supplied, as well page numbers, to indicate the contexts in which each manuscript is used.

General Index

Names of modern scholars are not included